Everycountry

© 2022 Flavio Ferrari Zumbini – all rights reserved
First edition in English - © 2023, all rights reserved

Translated by Sharon E Hudson
Cover by Daniele Zizzi – the cover uses pictures from Freepik.com
Illustrations, graphics, and flipbook by Daniele Zizzi
Map of Phileas Fogg's journey by Roke on Wikipedia

Thank you to Harry Mitsidis for the Foreward
and to Silvia Ongaro and Sonia Lombardo for their invaluable help

Flavio Ferrari Zumbini

EVERYCOUNTRY

A Journey to ALL 193 NATIONS of the World,
from Afghanistan to Zimbabwe

Would you like to travel with me?
Find me at www.everycountry.travel

or on any of the main social media platforms

CONTENTS

FOREWORD

YEAR 1   pg.9

YEAR 2   pg.55

YEAR 3   pg.95

YEAR 4   pg.119

YEAR 5   pg.169

YEAR 6   pg.223

YEAR 7   pg.287

YEAR 8   pg.323

YEAR 9   pg.415

FOREWORD

"If I had wanted a normal relationship, I would have chosen her. But I wanted nothing more than adventure, fun and of course, the school of travel".

Indeed, this intangible 'school of travel', whose curriculum is neverending and whose unwritten exams one is sometimes destined to fail, fuels many of the great travellers of the world. Ideas blossom during the journey, life-changing choices are made, and problems come into focus. And when opportunities are missed, and relationships end, new paths immediately appear on the horizon.

Flavio Ferrari Zumbini is one of the few people to have visited every country in the world. People ask how many countries there are and the answer is itself subject to debate. Most of us within this community of people agree to accept 193, the current number of Permanent Members of the United Nations, as a clear standard. The website that I have founded, NomadMania, is the global authority in terms of who has visited every country. Based on our meticulous research, as of the end of September 2023 there are around 300 people to have legitimately achieved this.

What does 'legitimately' mean? That is also subject to debate. Does merely crossing a border count? Those who are serious about travel, like the many members of Nomad-Mania, myself and Flavio, will surely answer no. You must explore. You must experience. You must understand what the essence of a country is.

In the pages of this book, Flavio manages to convey,

often humorously, what he has learned with such commitment. Through an intimate chronicle of his years on the road and the way he slowly visits every sovereign state, he weaves together his own circumstances, emotions, highs and lows, with what makes each country what it is. He explains that Liberia's Monrovia was where NASA planned to land shuttles in case of emergency. He explores whether giving away sweets to children at a school in Laos is what he, in fact, should be doing. He experiences the world, from Nauru to El Salvador, one country at a time, discovering all the petals of an intricate flower opening itself up in all its colourful glory.

It is precisely the series of unique vignettes that make this book not only extremely personal, but also an exercise in humanity. Flavio is not the traveller to tick off places to boast about his achievements. He is the thinking traveller, totally addicted like many others, but always conscious of the sacrifices he makes, aware that there should be an inherent code in travelling which makes him reflect on his actions and others' reactions. It is this interplay that makes this book an excellent read, quite different to many others of their kind.

With 'EVERYCOUNTRY', you will explore, experience and, hopefully, understand for yourself the essence of these countries.

Harry Mitsidis,
The Biggest World Traveler,
Founder of NomadMania

YEAR 1

'I love to travel' is a statement that almost everyone has uttered at some point in their lives, often with sincerity, but sometimes purely to avoid appearing boring. It's a phrase that can work well when you meet someone new and don't know what to say. It never fails to appear on your CV, right there in the line below the declaration that you're 'an avid reader of books', despite so far having finished only a few. Too many people consider travelling purely as entertainment. To them, it's simply the reward for a whole year's hard work and consequently, this love results only in a brief embrace.

In reality, travel requires a lasting relationship since it is part of an ongoing and essential path of education. It's a school for adults, where you once more become awestruck children, learning without an immediate purpose, studying all the subjects, and getting to know many new people, just as you did when you were young. The beauty of it is that you are simultaneously both student and teacher. I too had the love of travel on my CV and had repeatedly made a solemn proclamation that I wanted to travel, only to never actually set off.

Imagine for a moment that you've just lost your job and have neither a home nor a partner, let alone any children or

EVERY COUNTRY

pets. For me though, this wasn't a sad picture at all, quite the opposite in fact. I was 36 years old, in good physical condition, with a newly renewed passport, savings and a desire to gain experience. In short, what I'm describing was not just my life, but the perfect opportunity to leave.

For a few months, I mulled over the idea seriously and decided I wanted to make up for the trips I had never taken in the past. My work was declining rapidly, and it was clear that it would soon disappear altogether, so I would have to start again from scratch. At my age, resuming work either immediately or in a year's time would have little effect on my future career, whilst a year dedicated to travel and study could change my life for the better. Finally, my CV would be able to shout, 'I love to travel' instead of whispering it.

By the time the work ended, the idea had already fully developed, and I rushed to get on a plane. I was so determined that I made an ambitious pact with myself: no half-measures. I would be away for a whole year and would spare no expense to make this work.

I was ready to spend a huge amount: up to €100,000 to be precise, having set this money aside over time with the distant idea of studying for a very expensive master's degree. But during the months that I was evaluating what to do with my future, all I could do was dream about possible trips and I hadn't consulted any university websites at all. Perhaps after having already studied so much, I was bored with the idea of taking a new course, or maybe I simply wouldn't know which master's to aspire to.

What job would I want to do when I got back? I didn't know and neither did I want to think about it. My whole mind was consumed by wanting to know the world. I wasn't running away from a problem; I had a goal. My travels were not motivated by a reaction to my loss of work, an attempt to run away from a difficult situation, or self-pity. I just wanted to understand more, a desire nurtured and matured over many years but never yet expressed. I had found my ideal master's degree.

Understanding the world better is quite a vague goal. Initially, for me, it signified visiting the nation of India, which is in fact like a whole continent in terms of population and diversity of religion and culture. Then I wanted to add China, an African country, and perhaps a few more nations outside of Europe to the list, so as to get an idea of the other 95% of the world, or rather of those people who don't live in the big Western cities, which was the only reality I could say I knew.

As a child, I used to be excited when I found a parked car with a foreign number plate, but this only lasted until my parents started to send me to Germany for the summer to study the language. After the umpteenth unfamiliar plate, the effect had faded. This true enthusiasm soon came to be directed at an inflatable globe that I had kept on my desk for years, on the Pacific Ocean side, where all there seems to be is water.

While at university, I'd had the opportunity to study in Australia for a few months and had consequently deluded

EVERY COUNTRY

myself that I'd completed that part of the map because, after all, I'd been close to it. At the time, it hadn't disappointed me at all that Australia had turned out to be a kind of Europe thousands of kilometers away. In addition, I'd studied in Berlin with the Erasmus program (a student exchange initiative between European universities), and whilst still little more than a boy had visited some major European cities during the holidays.

My first employment had been in Luxembourg. Then my passion for poker had turned the game into a successful job, allowing me to visit the United States. I may have looked like someone who had already travelled enough, but these experiences were all concentrated in cities of the so-called West. I had seen some diversity within this 5% of the planet, yet I only knew one petal of this colourful flower we call the world, and with a whole year at my disposal, it would be possible to go further and finally discover more.

I primarily wanted to explore Asia because two-thirds of the world's population lives there. Indeed, China and India alone are home to almost a third of the entire human race. If a billion Chinese and a billion Indians decided to go and live on Mars tomorrow, those two nations would still remain the most populous on Earth. In a nutshell, the curiosity that pushed me towards India was driven by the numbers.

Usually, those who leave for such long periods have many other motivations in play alongside their curiosity. It could be fund-raising, finding themselves, or even demonstrating how peaceful and beautiful the world is. I didn't think about any of this. I left for a year, without a very precise plan, with money in my pocket, many books under my arm, and a great desire to discover. I never would have dreamed that in later years my simple adventure would become such a comprehensive challenge!

While frantically trying to arrange as complete a trip as possible to India, I found myself in **Nepal (1)**. There was a group leaving on just the right day, I didn't need a visa in advance, and I was in a crazy hurry to get started. This small, mountainous country is what separates the two great Indian and Chinese civilisations, which made it a more than satisfactory choice, even more so since at this point, I had no experience in how to organise such an adventure. A group trip was ideal, and in the end, I only had to press a button to sign up, pay and pack my bags.

Consequently, my arrival in this new world was so cushioned that I received mixed impressions from it. I definitely knew that life in the West was better, but coming into contact with the poverty here somehow didn't strengthen this conviction. Indeed, the novelty, the charm of the mountains, and the spiritual atmosphere that you could almost breathe, all served to sweeten my perception of poverty during those early encounters. I was enthralled by those who showed me that the Nepalese have almost nothing and yet have everything they need, that they endure deprivation with pride and with the freedom of those who have no attachment to material possessions. I listened in wonder as they explained that they had sufficient dignity and therefore didn't need to hide their poverty but instead could display it.

I think that deep down I had also left to get away from life in the centre of Rome, intending to observe how one might be happy thanks to social bonds rather than status and

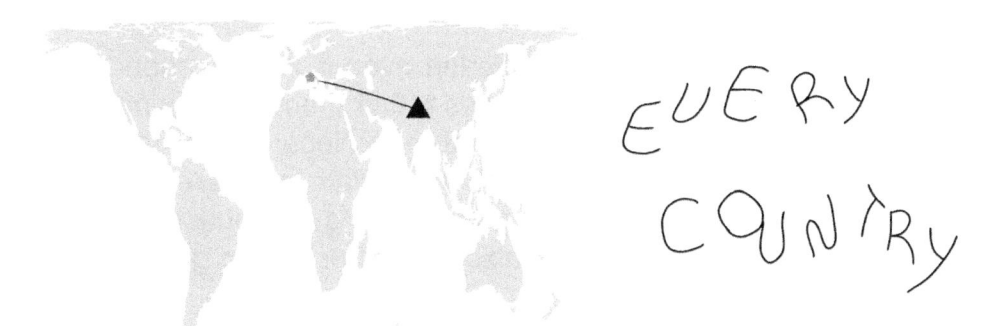

EVERY COUNTRY

material goods. I was ready to let myself be more convinced by those beautiful, elegant words than by what my own eyes saw. Perhaps I was eager to change a few opinions, to say that I had discovered a new world and to feel the beneficial effects of travelling. But I was getting it all wrong, leaning towards this ridiculous idea of 'romantic poverty' that can only be conceived by a rich man on a short visit.

A poor person, even if they live in beautiful countryside, surrounded by family, knows only too well that this is a difficult condition. Just like that of the wretch who lives miserably in a shack on the outskirts of a megalopolis, surrounded by chimney stacks, rubbish and nearby factories. Even a superficial tourist has no difficulty seeing these latter conditions as harsh and troubling.

But if, as was my experience in Nepal at that time, there is good weather and you can breathe in the magic of the mountains, all combined with the personal joy of finally leaving, then the smile of a local person is enough to make that poverty seem acceptable. A cow wandering slowly past, or the laughter of some children, can make you think that these people lead a frugal but serene life as if the renunciations of certain material things had been voluntary. And then, if the children let themselves be photographed and the adults make the tourist feel like a guest instead of a customer, you will inevitably return home with stories of what a genuinely happy life they live there. A few images captured on your phone will be presented as more reliable evidence than any statistics showing how bad things are in the country.

Poverty brings great suffering even if you experience it wearing beautiful, exotic clothes rather than a scruffy pair of very western jeans. I would return to Nepal a second time to go trekking, and certain scenes remain impressed on my memory. At the end of the day, anything the tourists hadn't eaten was collected and mixed together in one giant dish, as if to form a huge meatball. Then everyone ate their fill from this concoction. Even people with decent employment by local standards, such as a job in the tourism industry, were happy to take advantage of the leftovers and nothing disgusted them or was refused.

When I was in Kenya, a man who worked at the car wash secretly ate what was left of my lunch basket from a previous safari. He had found it underneath the seat of the Jeep when he was cleaning it. Inside there had only been a fruit juice and a miserable chicken leg that I had already bitten into the day before, but he finished it off. The man also had another, proper job in the city, and yet he was clearly hungry. These were the first awakenings from the naive stupor enfolding those who, like me, were identifying poverty only by certain images, clothing, and behaviours. But there would be many more such rude awakenings in store for me…

One thing I had understood straight away was that if you wait for other people you'll never leave. In those first few weeks, I texted my friends to urge them to join me at some stage and I would continue to do so for the entire nine years of travel that I then undertook, thinking that it would be enjoyable to travel together. As always, there were many solemn promises when considering future trips, but then when it came down to it, apart from during the first year, it was rare for anyone to come, despite me being able to communicate my every movement well in advance.

Which is why it was better just to get on the road. I certainly couldn't expect, nor did I want, to have someone in tow all the time, and I ended up finding new friends on the way. Becoming friends whilst travelling is easy and is part of this new educational path, this school for adults. The relationship starts without embarrassment, as it would between students, or when you go out with a girl for dinner. If you don't know what to say, there's a menu to look at, a waiter breaking the silence or a polite request for something to be passed that revives the conversation. Then, if everything has gone well, you can move onto more personal things. It's so easy to talk endlessly whilst travelling, there's always some pressing question to ask or information to exchange. You can invite someone to join you on the road for a while without seeming intrusive. If something comes up, you find yourself confiding in your fellow travellers. And there's no question of how to pay the dinner bill as it's obvious that everyone pays for themselves.

Having had a glimpse of them in Nepal, I had begun to read books on castes to prepare for the trip to India, never thinking that I would find them in **Japan (2)**. Here it's the locals who see me as wrapped in a kind of poverty. I'm the one who is ill-equipped and a little uncivilised, although also perhaps somewhat 'romantic' in their eyes because I appear free.

My poker background led me to look into the world of gambling. The most popular game is *pachinko*, a type of slot machine, which combines animation and music with an impressive series of metallic noises generated by the many falling metal balls. The noise is deafening and everything is aimed at allowing the brain to shut down for a few hours. The more noise there is, the more the players seem to relax. The balls offer the same feeling that you have under a waterfall as the din generated by all that water on your head somehow empties the mind.

This business is managed by the *Burakamin* that is, the Japanese untouchables. They are the often-tattooed local criminal element who run the brothels and indeed the gambling. Officially the metal balls that have been won cannot be converted into money, but the untouchables offer this service in plain sight.

The Japanese love to frequent these places where the ball bearings are continually falling as they feel at ease there. But those same Japanese who mix with the outcasts in the gambling halls would never bathe with one of them for fear of losing their purity, and this is the main reason for a strange ban. Public bathhouses cannot be frequented by people with tattoos. Traditionally, this excludes the *Burakamin*, who stand out because of their body art but nowadays also ink-loving tourists are forbidden to enter. In reality, for many Japanese, even non-tattooed tourists could be considered to contaminate the water. After all, I began by saying that they saw me as not very civilised in general, imagine if I was also sporting tattoos.

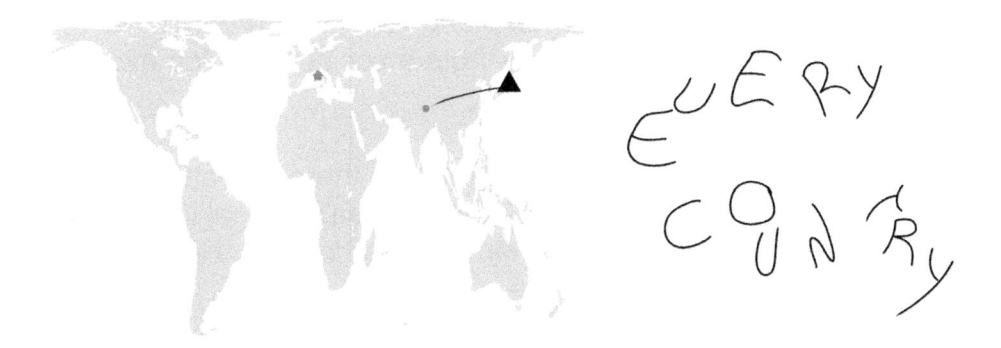

I had started playing poker quite by chance. Lonely evenings whilst working abroad had prompted me to try the online version, and I had won. I played with discipline, trying to understand the mathematics behind it, regularly winning money. After doing this for a few months, I decided to dedicate myself to the game full-time. A few years later, Italy was among the first countries in the world to regulate online poker, categorising it among games of skill and therefore officially making legal an as yet unregulated sector. It was a crazy boom, and I was the expert on this novelty.

From that point, as well as playing, I began to work for those who offered poker in Italy. But soon other games of chance were also legalised, and this made online poker become less important. Just as quickly as it had exploded, it was going out of fashion. All my expertise was now worth almost nothing. Along with the loss of my job, my skills were now no longer particularly unique and that's why I had to reinvent myself. Fortunately, while practising poker in Italy, I had never felt like an outcast!

The contempt of people in high social positions towards those at the bottom is still deep in the rest of the world, much more so than in the West, and the Japanese have their own form of 'racism' towards foreigners. They don't consider them inferior but deem their own race to be superior. It's a nuance that you can feel. It's not that you are rubbish, as in our standard prejudice, but that I am better. All these thoughts are of course masked by excessive motions of respect and kindness, even whilst rapidly exiting the bath into which a foreigner has just stepped. The best example of such behaviour is a bow that only inclines to 15°, which seems respectful unless you grasp the contempt behind it.

In addition to *pachinko*, the Japanese have an entertainment market that is unique in the world, which provides them with the most extravagant things. These belongings, clothes and amusements can seem crazy from the perspective of someone who doesn't understand how great a desire there is to differentiate themselves from a society in which everyone seems to be the same.

Since costs are rarely a problem, there are also many erotic antics. It's a country where a man's sexual life takes place largely outside the marriage relationship. He spends very little time with his wife, while an exclusive and lasting relationship is only ever established with the workplace. It's there that you make every effort to appear perfect in the eyes of others and you always make sure to avoid any discussion.

The Japanese waste time because they refuse to say 'No' openly. A direct 'No' is tantamount to an accusation of dishonesty, as if they are suggesting that your proposal is a scam. Being able to say a clear, succinct 'No' would shorten every procedure, and a meeting lasting hours, (to which no one would dream of being late), could be reduced to a few minutes. The most experienced protagonists learn to interpret non-verbal signals, but there remains an element of uncertainty, and the business always seems to end with an agreement. The results of the work are proverbial, but the effort is such that I wonder if, among the group of industrialised countries, Japan paradoxically is actually one of the least efficient. But observations of this kind, as well as being superficial, are futile, since this obsessive search for perfectionism is basically a religion, a philosophy of life.

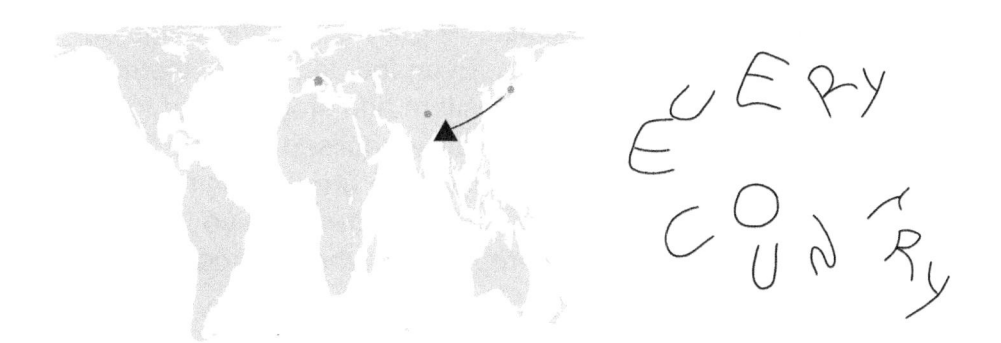

My trip to India was similarly elusive. I wanted it to be so especially perfect that I was still not content with what I had organised, so, in the meantime, I went to **Myanmar (3)** or Burma as it was previously known. The entry visa was complicated to obtain, but an agency had taken care of everything and made the procedure simple. The spirituality of Nepal had entered me gently, imperceptibly, without disturbance. I hadn't even found the corpses cremated in public troubling. I'd found Japanese religiosity impenetrable but relaxing. Those temples deep in nature transmitted peace in their frenetic world. Indeed, nature is so well cultivated there that it becomes a magical place of itself, whereas we in the West tend to enclose the sacred within four walls, which I think is one of our limitations. But now in Myanmar, the incredible superstitions that surrounded the religious sector troubled me. Everything was based on astrology, and I didn't feel able to cope with it.

I was ferociously judging all this when the beauty of the Shwedagon Pagoda in the capital Yangon relieved my disapproval somewhat. The sound of the straw brooms of the volunteers who come at sunset to clean fascinated me more than a prayer. The pale light gave the place a mystical quality, and the thought that without a favourable horoscope, you can't marry the love of your life became less intolerable.

With that out of my system, I could now direct my outpouring of annoyance towards the military junta, in this case with full justification. Their control of the country was total, with soldiers everywhere and iron censorship. Dictatorships invest such energy to wear down and obstruct every last one of their opponents, but in nations with an underworld where illegal activities are going on, they don't always put such intense effort into suppressing these pursuits since they aren't a direct threat to their power.

In Myanmar itself, for example, entire areas of the so-called golden triangle existed, illegally producing drugs despite being under the regime. Even the Japanese, the most honest people in the world, hesitate and stop short of totally opposing gambling because they've realised that the cost of fighting these last die-hards would be greater than that the harm they cause. Indeed, some small relief valve is a necessary thing and society progresses when space is made for some diversity experiments, albeit with limitations. Dictatorships like the junta in Myanmar, however, are too afraid for their own survival and are ready to pay an insane cost to eradicate the slightest political resistance.

Speaking of high prices, a balloon ride over the magnificent temples of Bagan turned out to be expensive and consequently, the group I had left with decided against taking it. Now I had already had to push a little in Nepal to have the experience of flying over Everest, and here I couldn't convince anyone, so at the last minute I tried to go alone but found that everything was fully booked. I completely understand saving money, but had I really travelled as far as Myanmar only to miss participating in the most beautiful activity despite its cost being only about 5% of the total expenditure? I would have to be a little more resourceful and take matters into my own hands.

I don't understand this way of travelling where you go to a beautiful and faraway place and then are tight over every expense. We'd spent hours going around currency exchangers to find a better conversion rate, meaning that I lost a good part of the afternoon just to save a few euros.

Maybe the time had come for me to break away from the group. It turned out to be easier than expected. Having explained the reasons, there were no hard feelings, and I could complete the trip with total freedom. I was able to return twice more to the Shwedagon Pagoda at sunset to enjoy the evening cleaning spectacle. Despite my aversion to horoscopes, I participated firstly in the rituals for those born like me, on a Monday, and then a second time I said that I had come into the world on a Sunday to change things up a little. This time I went with a different guide, who explained what was happening and so instead of judging ignorantly, I now found myself listening.

This paring down of my expenses to the bone was allowing me to spend a lot less than I had budgeted, but I never thought I would go on a free trip! I briefly returned to **Italy (4)** to take advantage of a few small benefits that were still left over from my old employment contract. I had a poker tournament already paid for and went to participate. I jokingly made a bet with a friend of mine, also a player, that if one of us placed in the first three, he would buy the other an entire holiday. Where? After many ideas and some slightly malicious suggestions from friends who wanted to make it fun for themselves as well, the final decision was to go to the Arctic Circle together to feed reindeer whilst wearing the kimonos bought in Japan…

After all this, I was eliminated straight away from the tournament. I'd only returned for this, since my personal quest was to travel full-time, so I said goodbye to everyone and, having nothing already organised, I flew to **Portugal (5)** where a girl I had dated lived. After a few days, my friend phoned to tell me that he was in the final and there were nine of them left. I was rooting for him regardless, but of course, it was mostly the top three places that interested me. By the end of the evening, I had a paid holiday in my pocket. My friend had triumphed, and I was overjoyed.

I'd got a free trip, but on the other hand, my plan to understand the world a little better seemed to have stalled all too soon. After only three countries and having not yet set foot in India I was back in Europe, intent on having fun, after participating in one of the usual poker tournaments.

The trip from the bet was easily organised, and departure was scheduled for a couple of weeks later. We would go to Helsinki in Finland and from there then move further on into the Arctic Circle. We planned to visit Santa's house where there were reindeer farms open to tourists, and where eccentric visitors were probably commonplace, so two more fools who wanted to feed the animals whilst dying of cold in kimonos would pass unnoticed. Or almost!

I took a tour of **Switzerland (6)**, went into **Belgium (7)** and then I stayed a few days in the **Netherlands (8)**, guided more by flight prices than by any logical order. It was foreign travel, but still in my European environment and the magical atmosphere that I had slowly created around myself by going to distant and diverse places had already dissipated. The departure for Finland was put off for two weeks and so I continued to **Ireland (9)** and the **Czech Republic (10)**. Then I returned briefly to Rome as I had to get the kimono.

The journey as I had originally conceived it had already been severely interrupted, but even worse, I was now actually at home. One thing however was to my advantage. Those first few months had made it clear to me that I had a lot to learn about packing. All the travel books emphasise the importance of carrying very little with you. Big luggage means a small traveller and vice versa. They are right of course, but I would go further. The superfluous is not only useless, but it also becomes an obstacle as it's all stuff you must carry with you every time you move. I was so anxious to get the journey back on course, that I was imagining having to fast track to make up for lost time, effectively changing hotels almost every night and to do this, I had to travel light.

In Rome, I was able to do some effective baggage trials. I watched various advice videos, did a few experiments and came to the conclusion that I would have to go to the Arctic Circle with just hand baggage. If I could manage it there, it would be easy anywhere else. I left and returned via my parents' house, packed only what I needed, changed clothes, leaving the kimono of course, and resumed the adventure.

Also, this exuberant Japanese attire made me think. As absurd as the example was, I was finally packing exactly what I needed on the road, not what I liked or considered important here at home. That blue suit may certainly be your favourite for a dinner in Rome, but on the road, you'll be another person. Those clothes won't work for you anymore, in fact, they won't seem at all attractive in the place you now find yourself. Finally, I was visualising myself immersed in the journey instead of seeing the same old me, just in different places.

We went to feed the reindeer in Rovaniemi, in **Finland (11)**, in temperatures of -20°C, wearing kimonos and little else. It was an amusing escapade, and I'd had my first experience with extreme cold and had successfully managed to travel with only hand luggage. I would never carry a large case again.

It was time to pick up where I had left off, so still undecided about the trip to India that I wanted to be so wonderfully flawless, I chose to go to **Thailand (12)** on my own, in an attempt to deepen the flow of Buddhism that had both frightened and intrigued me in Myanmar. Now, a man in his forties who goes to Thailand alone saying he wants to study Buddhism, usually tries to be funny and imply that he is actually going to visit prostitutes, but I avoided the classic centres of sex tourism. I was genuinely curious about a religion I knew nothing about, and I wanted to remedy a huge error of perception that I'd had. I'd thought that Buddhism was the majority religion in Southeast Asia, which was completely incorrect. Islam is dominant in that region, and without that information, my comprehension had been limited. In Myanmar, I hadn't understood how they had felt threatened, why there was this ferocity and inhumane treatment of the Muslim ethnic group, and this continuous talk of a nation that feels oppressed and surrounded. Visiting the Islamic areas of Thailand soon brought me back to my 'trip of a lifetime' atmosphere, my new school.

I moved around the country like a whirlwind, content to be constantly on the move. Now that I had almost nothing with me, even packing in the evening was fun, like a small household activity that offers a certain satisfaction and involves little effort.

Subsequently however, I decided to spend a couple of weeks in the same place as I wanted to have calm to plan as much as possible for the next stage of my journey and make a decision on India. In doing so, I also had my first opportunity to assess what I was experiencing. It was a dream, the best choice I had ever made in my life. I didn't feel any hardship or sense of remoteness. I lacked nothing. After all, until now, the biggest discomforts had been not having hot water or a bedside table next to the bed. I had recently even briefly been home. It was all so straightforward that I should have taken some of the bets that my friends had proposed before my departure when they were certain that I would not last on the road for a year. Right now, it would have seemed like taking candy from a baby, things were going so well for me.

I calmly found time to write down my initial thoughts on the trip. I had started out convinced that the West was the best place in the world to live and I hadn't changed my mind, but at that moment, dilapidated Nepal seemed not nearly as bad as I had imagined. Whereas super-technological Japan, which I had thought to be comparable to the West, had seemed to me to be a slightly less appealing place to live than expected.

According to some surveys, I had just visited the happiest country in the world, Finland, about which I had held no preconceptions. I had expected the weather to be pretty lousy, but it wasn't the cold that was the problem, you just had to wrap up for that. It was the darkness that put me in a bad mood. An entire winter in those conditions didn't appeal to me and even the locals were well aware of that. Amusingly, a huge, self-deprecating billboard had greeted me at the airport, proclaiming that, 'Nobody in their right mind would come to Helsinki in winter. Except you, you badass. Welcome!'

Being free to explore, I was happy in every country. I was embracing other people's beauty and I would leave their problems there as soon as I moved on. In short, I was a very selfish tourist. I was, however, reading up on how I should behave. For example, I was struck by the suggestion not to visit places where they exploit elephants, but the reasoning – that animals are not meant to entertain us – did not convince me much. Humans are not born to toil, plough fields and carry bricks, but in the end, everyone earns a living by doing thankless activities and this also applied to the Thai elephant. I will change my mind when I have a better reason for it, such as the course of training to which the elephant is subjected being truly cruel.

I left Thailand as soon as I realised that staying in the same place had made me spend too much time on the internet and it would be good to get back on the road. And that despite perusing all that online cesspit of information, the only pages I had not consulted were those on travel to India.

After uninstalling the few games I had on my phone, I continued to neighbouring **Laos (13)** where I stayed for two weeks with another group trip. The reality was that I had not yet found the courage to set off completely alone to countries where I was not sure what to expect. Thailand is very touristy and safe, whereas in Laos I didn't yet feel equipped to anticipate all the difficulties and dangers I could face, and 15 days is a long stay without a good guide to make everything that you don't understand on your own more interesting.

This was the first time I had entered a school carrying sweets and pens, to be greeted by hordes of children who jumped all over me. The expense was minimal and with a trifling sum you could give something to everyone. But is it right to behave in this way? What would you think of a man bursting into a school in Rome, interrupting lessons and starting to give out gifts? Our children don't need pens and sweets but imagine that this man starts handing out €20 notes. I may not know the correct ratios, but the weirdness is unmistakable. Perhaps I would have been better off giving money to someone who knew how to administer it wisely, although then of course, I would have missed out on that direct, intoxicating gratification. All the children were smiling for me, I was Santa Claus. And in a country like Laos, you can walk into a place of work, curious about what is going on, and people will interact with you and explain! Imagine if a tourist in Italy were to wander into a public office wanting to observe the Italian employees as they work...

But my encounter with these bizarre privileges was only just beginning. From Asia, I flew to Africa, where three of my friends had arranged to spend time in the Kenyan home one of them owned. They had known that I had been travelling continuously and for the first time someone had sought me out. Africa was not at the centre of my plans, but I gladly accepted.

I spent 40 days with them travelling between **Kenya (14)**, Zambia and Tanzania. The encounter with Africa was even more gentle than the one that I'd experienced in Nepal. Poverty surrounded me, but I was spending all my time planning safaris from the luxury of a swimming pool in Malindi, so I was untroubled and very happy. In no time at all, thanks to our enthusiasm and the four of us challenging each other to come up with the biggest suggestion, we went a little overboard and booked more or less all the safaris we could. The next week a huge Maasai man showed up, with his beautiful Jeep, ready to take us on an adventure. He was ready, but was I?

I didn't quite know what to expect from a single day in a Jeep, let alone 22 days on safari – yes, we had booked that many! It was total madness. I only had hand luggage with very few things, what was I supposed to buy?

After investigating everything from special underwear to tents, all my preparation for the adventure culminated in the purchase of a classic khaki shirt like the ones the 'professionals' wear in the photos – I wanted one of those too. Entering a national park was exciting at first then increasingly less so, much, much less in fact. The first zebra we encountered was met with a flurry of photos, all of them out of focus as the large Maasai, as gruff as he was competent, continued to keep going despite our obvious interest. And after an hour I found myself agreeing with him. Who cares about a zebra, I've now seen hundreds of them. After 20 days, I didn't even turn around for a giraffe or an elephant. I've been on about 50 safaris to date, so when a cheeky guide smirks and asks me what I'd like to see, I bring him down to size by replying, 'An elephant giving birth', and I too break into a sly grin. Now let's see if you can satisfy me!

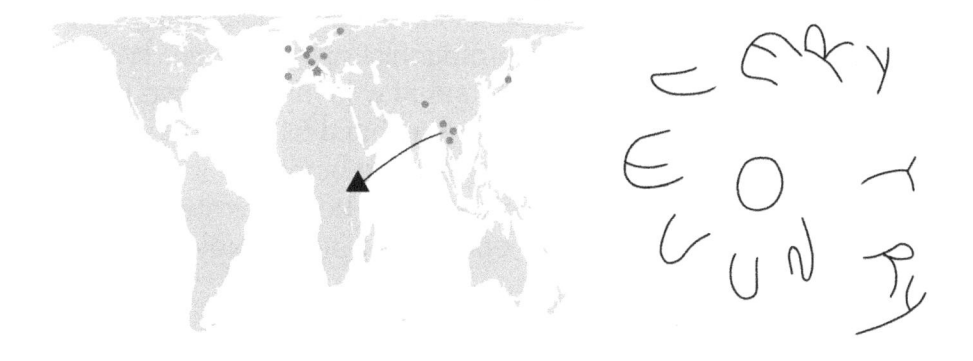

You have to be most alert at dawn and dusk on safari because it's cooler and therefore some animals are more active. In the hottest hours, their feet become blistered, or rather the paws do. After all, animals walk barefoot. It's trivial when you think about it, but certain self-evident facts can only be proven first-hand. This also highlights the suffering of adults and children who are so poor that they don't have shoes and have to avoid the asphalt road because it's scorching, even for their heavily calloused feet.

After several days surrounded by animals, I had come to two conclusions. Firstly, that I really had gone over the top. Perhaps I was compensating for some of the missed experiences on my group trips, and now that I was approaching the halfway point of the year, I wanted to do as much as possible, but I had to be more rational. I was wasting money and having little fun doing the same experience over and over again. I had seen all the big animals on the first day. One more week on safari, with an untrained eye like mine, would result in every animal seeming like a cheetah, that is, a species where the individual animals are identical. Secondly, the TV depiction of the savannah is excellent. From my couch, I had already watched so much, but those were only the highlights. Now I was experiencing and understanding the passage of time in that environment better. It was boring, just like this long journey of mine, about which I select intense thoughts and moments, while in reality it's mainly made up of very long downtimes, endless waiting, and slow travel.

On the tenth day, a wonderful novelty interrupted my 'boredom'. We were going to watch the animals from the high vantage point of a hot-air balloon, so it was possible to follow the course of the river where they all went to drink without disturbing them with the noise of the Jeep. I would finally feel a bit like Phileas Fogg, the protagonist of *Around the World in 80 Days*. An hour of balloon safari was more intense than whole days by car. The giraffes may have blue tongues, but it is seeing them run from that vantage point that is the real spectacle. The leaping gazelles finally demonstrated to me why they are the absolute epitome of agility. Never would

I have imagined that they could move like that despite the many documentaries I have seen.

For the first time, I felt that the journey was changing me and being at the scene of the action, my emotions were not the same as usual. Back at home, I had hoped that I would see a big hunt with lions mauling a zebra while I watched, but instead, I now enjoyed seeing herds defending their young from a predator. This happens, but in the old documentaries I had grown up with, this was never shown as they had preferred to film blood flowing.

In Nairobi, I visited my first slum, Kibera, a cluster of several settlements that housed over a million people. My friends wanted to show off and we went in with a kind of small van full of presents for the children. We had put in $100 apiece, so we had bought a mountain of stuff. We were allowed to interrupt every lesson or activity, and everyone was chasing after us. Queues of people followed us and, better than Santa Claus, we were like fairy-tale kings, tossing coins to their subjects.

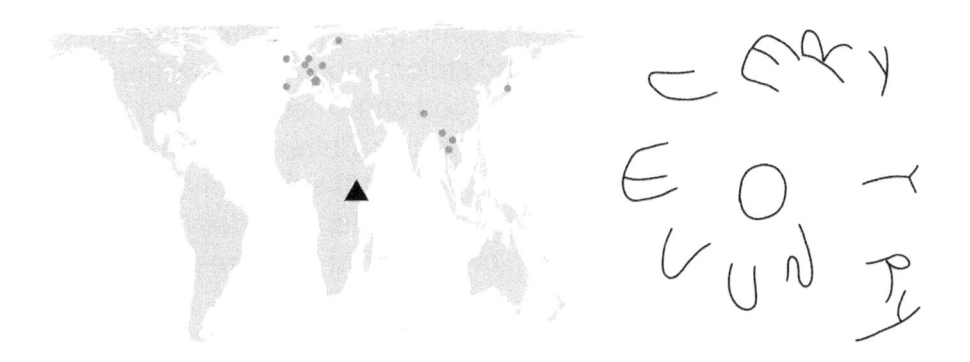

But the true understanding of how widespread the poverty is around you came from seeing the girls in every place you went. So many young people would appear next to you and it was easy to invite whoever you wanted to dinner, the answer invariably being 'Yes, I'll gladly come.' Now it's obvious that poverty prompts, even forces, the search for any solution. But I would never have thought that so many girls, with regular jobs and normal homes, would behave in this way. On the surface, they didn't appear to be people who were hungry or in need of anything in particular. They were young and therefore usually without children to support, yet they were invariably in difficulty, struggling to find the money to cover basic necessities. These societies where you work hard, are broadly average, don't expect to support six children on one salary, and yet don't manage to achieve a respectable life, are frightening.

I took a girl with me on one of the safaris and for her, it was the first time. Just like me only a few days earlier, she had never seen a wild animal or even set foot in a national park, despite being Kenyan. But I had now progressed to the position of the experienced one, and like everyone who has just learned something, I took great pleasure in excitedly explaining my recent discoveries to those around me, despite not yet understanding their every nuance.

The overland crossing of the border with **Tanzania (15)** was complete chaos and confusion, with people shouting, and all manner of offers, along with demands for money. And I had to pay a tax to go through all that! I thought about the working environment I'd come from, where some casinos would require you to buy an expensive ticket to get in and probably lose your money. All that was missing in Tanzania was a red carpet and a welcome glass of champagne.

Borders are often breeding grounds for shady activities, the preserve of the marginalised, where the authorities turn a blind eye. With currency exchangers, smugglers, an underworld of illegal trading, and stolen goods that now merely have to cross one final barrier, you can smell the corruption. If you arrive by plane, you miss this fraternity of outcasts and are met instead by the ever-present stacks of duty-free Toblerone that lie in wait for you. At the land borders of some countries, they invent their own form of duty-free, and on balance, I understand these improvised and illegal businesses better than an official welcome which always consists only of shelves full of cigarettes and alcohol.

Amidst some jostling, Tanzania began with yet another safari. I took one inside the caldera of a volcano where a unique ecosystem had been established, so that I could observe some slightly different animals. The pilot of our tiny scheduled flight to Dar es Salam was also a little different, since he wanted to do everything his own way, without even checking our boarding passes. Completely convinced that he knew what he was doing, he flew to Zanzibar only to discover his huge mistake. He was then obliged to make a further, impromptu flight to take us to our destination. Then off we went to **Zambia (16)** a country created by the British to prevent the Portuguese from uniting Angola with Mozambique.

I arrived at Victoria Falls where the mist produced by the water is visible from kilometres away. The spectacle is breathtaking, the noise is deafening and, just as a Japanese person might meditate under a strong stream of water, I was able to sleep with great pleasure listening to that incredible roaring sound. It's remarkable that a tap that leaks a few drips at intervals makes for a restless night, whilst a waterfall can grant you the best sleep of your life. It's almost impossible to look away from the cascading water, in fact, only a volcano with its bubbling lava is more magnetic. I did a punishing raft ride in the Zambezi and even bathed, safely, on the edge of the waterfall's sheer drop.

I've been amazed at the differences I've experienced surrounding the handling of money. In Myanmar, the banknotes had to be scrupulously clean, with no creases. In Japan, anything made of paper holds religious significance. We in Italy have wallets that allow you to hold banknotes flat, but here in Zambia, they purposely mistreat them. Crumpling money is customary, arguably to emphasise contempt, whilst elsewhere it has to be treated with respect, reinforcing the value and effort that is behind it.

For some people, polite upbringing dictates that it should be given with both hands or with the free hand touching the elbow of the outstretched arm. The moment of payment is all important and in addition to the money there is the gratitude for having received something, so all my attention, demonstrated by both my arms, is focused on the person receiving the money. It's normal for us to put money in front of other people without touching their hands, indeed we have saucers in front of the tills for this reason. There are rules about passing it into someone's hand keeping it as hidden as possible, whereas we would only do this if it was charity, a tip or a bribe. In some traditions, you make eye contact when paying, which wouldn't come naturally to me.

Regardless of how the money is treated, from an economic point of view, I had to come back down to earth. You go to the falls on your honeymoon. Everything was so luxurious for western tourists, and so expensive that my previous habit of issuing generous dinner invitations had dwindled into eating sandwiches.

Finally, the time came to set foot in the long dreamed of **India (17)**. It had been intended to be the first and main stage, but I kept on postponing it. Perhaps because by visiting India I was afraid of feeling that the aim of the journey had been fulfilled with the year only half over. In the end, I found a compromise of sorts to reassure myself that entering India did not equate with having reached the final stage.

I had organised an initial tour of the north of the country and booked a tour that would take me from there to tiny **Bhutan (18)**, which is described in tourist guidebooks as a forgotten mountain paradise. An inaccessible place until a few decades ago, it has a unique style with perfectly reconstructed fortress-monasteries. It has invented its own Gross National Happiness index that has resonated with many, the concept being to aim for well-being that goes beyond the production of commodities. And in this index, of course, Bhutan places at the top of the world rankings, basically just behind the usual leader, Finland, and other Northern European countries. In reality though, to give an idea of Bhutan's extreme underdevelopment, life expectancy is low, half of the female population is illiterate, television was only permitted in 1999, superstition is at ridiculous levels, but above all, young people dream of nothing else but emigrating to the United States. In short, I doubt they are among the happiest people in the world.

In the other index that seeks to go beyond economic aspects alone, namely the United Nations Human

Development Index, Bhutan ranks 127th but is constantly improving. They boast of maintaining certain traditions and preserving the homogeneous nature of the population. Indeed, since the 1980s about 100,000 *Lhotshampa*, a Bhutanese ethnic group with foreign origins, have been expelled because they are Nepalese in customs and beliefs, and perhaps also politically too Maoist. That's about 15% of the total population. In other countries, this would rightly be called ethnic cleansing.

Yet tourists, as a rule, are content to be deceived because they want to believe that paradise exists somewhere. And to be so, it must remain untouched and difficult to reach. In Bhutan, that is in this pseudo-paradise, they oblige you to buy an all-inclusive package to visit, setting the cost at a premium. The kingdom wants to generate a good income from the small number of tourists it manages to accommodate and to leave this impression of being a little-travelled destination. Of course, with these constraints, the guide becomes a sort of guardian who shows the beauty, hiding the deprivation and despair, images that don't fit in well with the general concept. But I didn't fall for it as I had done with the romantic poverty of Nepal, and I put what little experience I'd already had to good use. When there is a requirement to be chaperoned anywhere in the world, whatever the particular reason, that place verges on hell.

On my return to India, I was ready for a long train journey and was intent on visiting still more countries. Amongst the e-books and paperbacks, I still had Chikamatsu's texts unopened, half of Orwell's *Burmese Days* to finish, and I'd read a few pages of Maraini's and Tucci's books. I was lost in the study of Buddhism, Kenya's colonial history, and castes. I knew nothing about Hinduism, I had never heard of the *Bhagavad Gita*, I had no idea who Arjuna was, and I was not familiar with Layla and Majnun. *Shantaram* accompanied me on the long nights on the train because I was also searching for some action in my own small way. Instead, I found mostly noise and confusion, but I didn't give up.

They were hectic weeks. I was racing around like a madman, intent on seeing as much as I could, because this country really is like an entire continent, just as I had imagined. I kept discovering names of states within it that have more inhabitants than Italy and cities more populous than Rome. Now, I think I know all the cities of a million people in Europe at least by name, maybe because of their proximity or perhaps due to the European football cups I used to follow. Whereas I had never heard of some with ten million people in India. And despite two degrees from a good university in Italy, I was still used to stereotyping: the snake charmer, the heat, the monstrous traffic, a few half-naked holy men, and cows on the tracks.

I had read in the books that there were more computer engineers in Bangalore than in the whole of Italy, and this information had made an impression on me. However, I had only become acquainted with a semi-literate person who spoke a little English and pointed out to me the Indians who were sporting a pen in their breast pocket to show off to everyone that they knew how to write. This person took care of some of the street children. They weren't orphans, on the contrary, they were running away from their families because they had been abused and mistreated. Sleeping outside at that age, in the company of desperate men, adds horror to an already tragic situation. The children are constantly robbed of the money they have earned begging. They are introduced to alcohol and drugs and some of them are recruited to go to the tourists to ask for a pen or a book as a gift from the shop they are standing in front of, which they would then return to the accomplice trader later. It was a world that I couldn't have ever imagined.

I had been trying to explore the many lives unfolding alongside the tracks of the trains, but also when I left the crowded trains, every street seemed to me to be the one that led back to the station, a swarm of constantly moving people, often carrying something. Accustomed to the confusion and the litter, I had learnt to appreciate the change in the smell of the street immediately after rain, indeed, I pretended it smelt like freshly cut grass, although in reality, it was just a stench. And I had discovered with my own eyes that despite the rules I had read about in the books, in the end, the whiter you are, the higher caste you are and vice versa. There was never slavery as we usually understand it, but some of the dynamics were similar.

This was one of the factors that had made it possible for a handful of Englishmen to assert themselves so easily over such a huge and diverse continent-nation. Previous to that, it had been the Islamic minorities or, if you will, a small number of Brahmins who ruled, so it's hardly surprising that the few ruled over the many and that the many were so diverse. Even when Europeans arrived in China, it was foreigners who were dominant over the Han ethnic group, which today makes up more than 90% of the population. China, though rich in diversity, is more homogeneous than India. So, saying that you know a significant part of China is more convincing than the same claim about India, where the discovery of new things never ends.

If anything, in China there is a real divide between the cities and the countryside, which is still home to about

40% of the population, because regardless of their ethnic group, their lives are truly different. In Japan, the uniformity is almost total. Large scale urbanisation has amplified the homogeneity, since 95% of the people inhabit cities in fairly similar conditions, whereas in India, the majority remain in villages and there are huge disparities in living conditions between them and the city dwellers.

So, despite the many landmarks, and the guides hired to help me explore, I carried with me the knowledge that I hadn't truly seen very much. I had spent more time talking to other Westerners than to Indians, especially on the trains. Would I really be giving it all up after a few more months and a handful of other countries? To revitalise myself, I booked a trip to Iran to take a little more risk and hopefully see fewer Westerners. A country with close ties to India, now a theocracy, it had been one of the villains in my classical studies. We had all been supposed to cheer for democratic, enlightened Greece as it triumphed over these barbaric Persians.

The fear of being in the **Islamic Republic of Iran (19)**, namely in an enemy country, disappeared immediately. As a tourist, there was little to be afraid of as there was no hatred for foreigners. Even an uninformed person or someone who believes that Bhutan is a paradise or that the €5 North Face T-shirts in the Kathmandu market in Nepal are original would immediately realise that the country was less scary from the inside than from outside. Although it may be the case that Iran threatens the West, wants to destroy Israel, and continuously rages against the free world, on the other hand, it treats tourists as guests to whom all attention should be paid.

I finally had a well-trained guide who made the visit to Isfahan a memorable day. Religious oppression, which also has political power, falls on all Iranians, particularly on women, who are badly mistreated and considered inferior. The obligatory veil irritated me, but this was minor compared to the hatred I would feel in the future.

It was time to conclude this year by heading to the other enormous country, that is, China, but I wanted to be sure to find more adventure on the way. After a lengthy investigation and constant second thoughts, I finally plucked up courage, deciding that, along with China, I would also visit the inhospitable terrain of Mongolia and, pushing my boundaries even further, I would go to North Korea.

I really wanted to poke my nose out of my comfort zone because the experience in Iran had not been at all impactful. In Burma I had slept untroubled on a bench in the bus station, surrounded by rubbish, whilst waiting for my bus that was hours late. I'd been in the slums in Africa, in India I had slept in third class on a train, surrounded by strangers for days on end. I had booked the cheapest planes I could find, regardless of inconvenient schedules or long connections, though until the previous year I had made fun of a friend of mine who had flown overnight with Ryanair to save money. I had just a small bag with me. In short, I had gained some new experiences but fewer than I had hoped. I had changed but I was not a different person. Now I just wanted to level up, to the point where I was willing to go to the middle of nowhere in Mongolia and, even more audaciously, to the most mysterious nation in the world, the most closed, the most threatening with its nuclear experiments. What had been triggered in me? Perhaps I just wanted a grand finale.

While an agency was arranging the visa for North Korea, I went to the **United States (20)** to the familiar Las Vegas to briefly catch up with my friends and former colleagues. I was happy to see some people once more but went reluctantly because I didn't want to interrupt the adventure again. I had some money that had been left on deposit at the casino thinking at the time that I would play some tournaments in the future. Now I wanted to withdraw it to use it very differently. I was dreaming of a new kind of gamble, the delight in taking risks on the Mongolian plateau, not at the green table. So, I stayed for the bare minimum time and from there chose the first flight that would take me to Ulan Bator, the capital of **Mongolia (21)**. At 44 hours in total, it was one of the longest I had done, but this type of hardship to save money was beginning to make sense, whereas having given up the balloon flight to save $80 still stung.

I was looking for action in Mongolia and this time I found it. Four days on the back of a camel in the Gobi Desert in a supposed search for dinosaur bones, followed by ten days in those Soviet vans that are as hideous as they are indestructible. The drivers are capable of repairing almost anything themselves. They find their way in places without real roads or signs. Rather, there are some direction markers called *ovoo*, which are piles of stones, placed one on top of the other so that those who pass by can keep adding to them as a kind of prayer. Superstition, which I so despise, played a useful role in this case, acting as a warning. If a lot of people add a stone to a spot, it indicates that it's dangerous.

On the rare occasions that you meet another car, you stop for a moment to see if you can be of mutual assistance. If someone was in need, it would be inconceivable to drive on as it's a matter of life and death. If a code of conduct has been developed to help each other between truck drivers on European motorways, imagine how much more necessary this is in the middle of the desert. I would discover years later that this behaviour, called the bystander effect, has been methodically studied. That is, if many people could help, as in the centre of Rome for instance, paradoxically there is a risk that no one will. While on the other hand, it is obvious that in places like Mongolia it is up to you to help because you are the only one there, you have no backup.

Useful information when travelling in dangerous places goes like this: if you want to do your own thing, follow your instincts, in other words, don't look at anyone in particular and keep your head down as it's hard for someone to take the initiative and that's what you want. If, on the other hand, you need help, don't talk to the crowd, single out one person and address them directly.

On arrival each evening, the reward for these intrepid drivers was a bottle of vodka, with which they would destroy themselves indiscriminately, and yet be ready to leave the next morning in perfect condition. In that atmosphere of total freedom, it is difficult to control oneself and everyone drinks too much. If you are drunk your tent becomes a castle. The vodka had to be handed over strictly on arrival therefore, and never before. The bottles were under lock and key in a trunk managed by my guide.

During the day, the sky is truly bluer than anywhere else in the world. As in all deserts, there are hardly any clouds, and so, in the endlessly long hours in the van, your eyes reveal to you an understanding of why the Mongols took that sky as their God. The wilderness is unique with few traces of humans and practically no visible wildlife except for the birds that circle continuously. It had been forecast to be relatively warm, but instead of gentle rays of sun warming my face, I was welcomed to the desert by being snowed upon for days. For the night, there were only Mongolian tents called *ger*, and sometimes not even those were available, and it was necessary to resort to more commercial tents bought in the capital. One night I slept inside the minivan because I was afraid that everything was going to collapse on my head under the weight of the snow and the force of the wind. But there were other more traumatic experiences.

I didn't wash for a fortnight. Upon returning to the capital, my first hot shower in a hotel room made me scream with joy. Possibly when people sing as they stand beneath the water, they think that no one will hear, but my shout was audible in the lobby three floors below. When you are dirty there's a rising crescendo of discomfort until about the fourth or fifth day, when, having reached a plateau of filthiness, I'd say you then remain in equilibrium there. Or rather, it can take a very long time to get worse. These days I know how to take a full shower, including my hair, with a 1½ litre bottle of water. But in Mongolia, it was too cold and windy to attempt to wash.

The second event which was traumatic in the more literal sense occurred on one of the usual snowy nights. My tent was a long way from the place designated for the bathroom so, despite the rule that one had to go to the kind of improvised toilet, namely a screen in front of a hole that had been dug earlier, I unzipped the tent, undid my various pyjama outfits and urinated without feeling at all guilty. Suddenly, a huge, unfamiliar man ran towards me out of nowhere, and jumped on me, punching my chin with tremendous force, then ran away. It was the first real punch I'd ever taken in my life. For those few moments, before he ran off, I was scared because I had been completely unable to defend myself. If he had continued beating me, I wouldn't have stood a chance. I didn't even scream, no one noticed anything.

More dazed than in pain, I quickly fell asleep without brooding over what had just happened. All day I had been delighted to be lost in nature far from civilisation, but now I was paying a price and I no longer liked this free and wild world. One single bad episode had completely changed my perception of the place. In travel books, the author always writes that the next morning they believe it all to have been a dream, but that possibility didn't even cross my mind for a moment. I remembered the incident well and still had a face like a balloon. There was no trace of the attacker but luckily all my teeth were still visible.

I left the country without ever having a valid explanation of what had happened and now had a 48-hour train ride across the desert in front of me, providing ample time to ponder the idea that freedom is stimulated by unlimited space. I had managed not to think about tomorrow as I drank vodka with Mongolians in the snow, I had even forgotten that I would soon be going to North Korea. I had experienced this absence of future thoughts involuntarily; it was not what I was looking for. I wasn't running away from a boring job, deadlines, or car payments. Thanks to poker I had already experienced this privilege of being a totally free 'citizen'. I used to get up at five in the afternoon, I had turned a room into a sort of office where I would play in my underwear with my feet on the table. I had felt that I was living without rules even within 15 m². What struck me most was the location. I was immersed in a nature I knew nothing about, where alone I would only have survived a few hours. Such an environment allows you to savour untamed freedom but at a price. In my case, it had only cost a punch, but what about for others? How many poor wives, daughters and sisters spent those nights with a completely drunk man? When there are no laws, the strongest makes the law.

The train took me to Beijing in **China (22)**. My physical body had been put to the test and had done a great job. It was perhaps the first time I had ever contemplated my body in amazement at its capabilities. I had considered myself strong, yet I had suffered from the cold more than anyone else and I had been powerless against the large man who had beaten me. But the fear had lasted only a few seconds, I no longer thought about the punch and the trauma had now become an experience because whilst travelling you live the best and worst adventures of your life, and on the whole, the worst ones become stories to tell.

My entry into China was truly uneventful. I had managed to get a fairly accurate idea of the place without ever having set foot in it, like Salgari or Karl May who accurately portrayed the places in which their books were set, despite never having seen them. There was a time when it was difficult to form an impression of a place and even a traveller of the calibre of Marco Polo filled his tales with fantasies and make-believe characters, making it difficult to distinguish between the real and the imaginary. We would have to wait for James Cook before we had realism in our notes and maps or, to get an actual glimpse of something, for the paintings of Thomas Ender which allowed us to get an idea of what a glacier looks like or catch a peek at a scene in Brazil. These days it's easy to find a YouTuber who has already filmed each and every corner, which is a fantastic service for those who can never go in person.

After a fortnight's journey, in Chongqing, I broke my personal record of ignorance set earlier with the Indian cities. This one had almost 30 million inhabitants, being among the most populous in the world, and yet I had never heard of it.

In Beijing, it was time for an important meeting, the compulsory briefing before travelling to North Korea, during which it was explained to us what the rules were and how the trip would be conducted. It was a memorable day. Since I had decided to go, I had alternated between excitement and fear. Now I was in the relaxed phase. The person conducting the briefing was very well prepared and professional and had already been to North Korea over 150 times accompanying tourists. Overall, it seems that about 6,000 foreigners enter each year for short visits. Unofficial statistics, however, suggest that more than 150,000 Chinese make the trip. So, I wasn't really doing anything unique and yet I still felt a little special.

The Italian Foreign Ministry's website which provides

information to travellers tends to advise against travel to many countries outside Europe. It doesn't offer varying degrees of risk, making it a truly badly designed site that sounds like a mother screaming at her child, always with the same intensity whether he's leaving his shoes in a mess or about to throw himself off the balcony. But with North Korea, it was easy to see that you were really taking a risk. My travel insurance clearly specified that this nation was excluded. No embassy would have been in a position to help me. Your passport is retained on arrival, your mobile phone doesn't work, there is hardly any internet, and you have no access to local currency. You are completely in the hands of a nation that dreams of having nuclear weapons and, at least according to the gossip, is prepared to use them to destroy the part of the world to which I belong and with which I identify. As such, the alarm of the various sites and the apprehension of friends and family were understandable.

You arrive in **North Korea (23)**, at the beautiful, modern airport of Pyongyang, but there is no-one there. At customs, everything is checked, and woe betide anyone who has anything related to religion or politically inappropriate in their possession. From then on you are followed by three government officials who act as tour guides and full-time guards. In comparison, in Bhutan one is as free as a bird. One guide is in front of the group, and another secures it to make sure no one escapes the supervision. The final guide is the one who usually answers questions and gives explanations. Every evening you are locked up in a hotel, where you can go to the bar, walk around the lobby or play pool in a dedicated room, but you are absolutely forbidden to go outside. You cannot have any contact with a North Korean who is not working for you. The whole tour is organised, and nothing is left to chance.

You travel to see reality with your own eyes, without the filters of a documentary or a report, but this whole trip is merely a photo with filters that the dictatorship creates for the tourist. In essence, the tourist is only allowed to see what the government wants them to. However, I consider the experience equally interesting because the adventure is surreal. You drive around in a city that seems empty because very few North Koreans own cars and the roads are gigantic, sometimes even four lanes wide. You visit a large number of locations in a very short time, it feels like teleportation. Wherever you arrive everything is already organised, there's never a queue. Basically, these days are conducted at the same pace as that of the President of the Republic on an official visit.

North Korea, besides being a communist country in its own unique way, is one big eugenics experiment, because it's perhaps the last nation where the population is completely homogeneous. The roots of North Korea are to be found in hatred of foreigners and of Japan in particular. Everyone must be pure Korean, so locals are rarely sexually attracted to Westerners. This is also partly true for the Japanese, who are similarly very homogeneous, but it is certainly not forbidden. You may have heard that there are areas in Tokyo where Japanese people are known to go in search of contact with foreigners.

Among North Koreans, the differences are profound and affect their entire existence. Their system of classification of people is called *Songbun*. Essentially, people are divided into three major classes and many subclasses (apparently over 50), the 'regime faithful', the 'uncertain' and the 'enemies'. Current estimates put about 25% of the population in the upper class, that is, the loyalists. In Pyongyang, all citizens are in the upper class. Citizens considered 'enemies' are not allowed to enter the capital. Being there is a privilege, even if you clean the bathrooms. You still live in the city, with electricity for many hours a day, schools, and medical care. And above all, you eat since there is a constant supply of groceries. Loyalty is largely measured by genetics. Those who are descended from early communists, or from those who served the regime, are at the top. In particular, it is the descendants of those who fought against the Japanese who are in the upper class.

This North Korean class designation is an almost closed system. You enter it in your late teens via an examination administered by the party. Based on scrutiny of you and especially your family, you are assigned a class. This exam will shape your whole life, not just your graduation. If you are assigned a low class, you will not go to university even if you are at the top of the school. The party will always decide which university you will go to and which job you will do, and from that point on your life will consist of serving the regime to climb a few sub-classes and to be fed.

In certain regions, the 'enemies' of the regime (the last macro-class of the system) are grouped together in desolate areas where survival is hard. But there are those who are even worse off, those who end up in actual concentration camps called *Kwalliso*. These camps are intended for anyone who opposes the regime and for political prisoners.

Directly and openly confronting the regime, as we understand it, carries the death penalty. But in North Korea, as in so many totalitarian countries, opposing does not necessarily require direct confrontation. It is considered rebellion even just to let a sentence or thought slip out. It is subversion maybe to listen to something forbidden or to be in contact with undesirable people. A whisper or a suspicion may be enough for a conviction and spies are everywhere. In addition, quite simply, some of the crimes we consider common are instead classified as political offences. Theft can be seen as a revolutionary act.

All those who end up in concentration camps confess to the crime they are accused of. Torture is practised on a large scale. For minor offences, there are 'ordinary' camps, where you usually work for the regime and stay for short periods of imprisonment. Apparently, about 200,000 people live in concentration camps in North Korea today.

North Korea is a nation that holds its citizens captive and makes its people live in an unprecedented personality cult. Kim Il-Sung, the invader of the South, died in 1994 but is still the eternal leader. He is buried in a mausoleum where one must be elegant to enter. Within the crypt, it is forbidden to put your hands in your pockets, cross your arms or bring any objects, banknotes or even medicine with you. Inside there is the only moving walkway in the world that doesn't make you walk faster, but slower, so you can admire the propaganda pictures on the walls, listen to music and put yourself in the right frame of mind to enjoy this para-divine vision, a mummy. You access the body after rotating brushes clean your shoes and jets of air purify you. It is forbidden to take pictures, but foreigners are welcome because then the North Koreans there on pilgrimage have the impression that such worship goes far beyond their borders. Pilgrimage is the right term since for a North Korean this is not a simple visit, it's sacred. In groups of four, you proceed to pay your respects, bowing from each of the compass points from which the mummy is observed and having completed the tour around the near-divine body, you can exit this immense, dark and austere mausoleum that was deliberately built without windows.

If pictures of the leader appear on television, you must applaud, and his face is everywhere in the newspaper, so it is forbidden to fold or tear it. Statues are only to be photographed in their entirety, and you have to bow in front of them and get off your bike if you pass nearby. Imagine that there is the same picture in every room of your house, in every public place, omnipresent on TV, on every billboard, and on every building. The Kims then, the current as well as the previous ones, also have the gift of relative omniscience, not absolute. Kim Jong-Un doesn't know everything about nature. He does, however, know everything that is possible for a man to know, in every field. That's why when he speaks, about any subject, he cannot be wrong. He is suggesting what is currently, the ultimate possible human knowledge, and indeed, one must always take notes on what he says. No word can be forgotten or ignored, which explains why the regime broadcasts pictures of senior generals beside him with notepads and pens, avidly recording his every utterance.

But when it comes down to visiting, it is simpler and more straightforward for the tourist than it seems. The real problem is the moral issue. When I went to Myanmar with its terrifying military, or Iran with its supreme leader who thinks he is some kind of interpreter of God's will on earth, only a fraction of my money went to the bad guys. The rest supports the locals. In North Korea, 100% of my money goes into the pockets of Kim and the regime. With that they will try to develop their nuclear arsenal further, maintain concentration camp facilities for heroic political prisoners, and buy yet another Mercedes, which they somehow manage to get despite the sanctions. Not a penny escapes scrutiny, even the tip to my guards goes to people who are loyal, and therefore, at least in part, complicit with the regime. Am I also complicit?

Upon leaving the country, it was relaxing to find myself in narrow-minded, restrictive China. The infamous Tiananmen Square, with its lampposts full of cameras, its microphones eavesdropping on you, and the absence of any place to eat or sit down to avoid gatherings that could escalate into protests, seemed a pleasant place.

The return ticket was to Italy. A year had passed, and the time for taking stock was approaching. I had left to study, and I had made some progress. But I was more intrigued by a personal change that I felt was beginning to take place, firstly because anyone who travels a lot is already wanting to change and therefore you just have to go with what you feel, but I was also changing because such a journey had finally taken me out of my routine and comfort zone. As a result, I had gained in courage, which then manifested itself in very different ways, like going to North Korea or keeping the same socks on my feet for 15 days in Mongolia.

On the other hand, however, I still felt that I had achieved and experienced less than I had hoped for. If I hadn't been forced into a tent, I would have continued to use hotels, so that once I was there, I could say 'goodbye' and close the door. That way I would never have met anyone, as practically, from the evening until the next morning it was as if I was no longer travelling because a comfortable, modern hotel room is a 'non-place'. I had been consciously making a mistake in spending money on beautiful accommodation instead of, say, hiring the best guide, and yet I had claimed that I wanted to know the world. I had been studying all the time, but I was always falling behind. I had been reading books constantly, but I should have organised myself better and arrived prepared. Only then would I have been able to fully enjoy the country I was visiting, to recognise and observe, and to ask intelligent questions without wasting time on information that could be found anywhere.

The discomfort of the trip to Mongolia and the absurdity of being in North Korea had crowded my thoughts and so I had postponed the final decision, but the idea of continuing and improving was already developing within me. On the flight back I was wondering more 'how' to say that I was going on, rather than 'if'. My immediate thoughts jumped to the fact that the budget for this incredible school for adults had been €100,000 and I had spent less than half of that. I was searching for an acceptable justification for other people that would make the decision to continue seem reasonable, but in reality, who was I accountable to? If even I, who prided myself on being unfettered and free, had such qualms, then perhaps I still had a lot to learn from the school of travel about freedom.

YEAR 1

NEPAL	JAPAN	MYANMAR
ITALY	PORTUGAL	SWITZERLAND
BELGIUM	NETHERLANDS	IRELAND
CZECH REPUBLIC	FINLAND	THAILAND
LAOS	KENYA	TANZANIA
ZAMBIA	INDIA	BHUTAN
IRAN	UNITED STATES	MONGOLIA
CHINA	NORTH KOREA	

23/193

YEAR 2

Possibly I'm very good at explaining myself to people, or perhaps they had already been expecting me to continue travelling, but in the end, no one was surprised by my announcement. Those who had initially been unconvinced that I would stay on the road for a whole year were now telling me that they didn't believe I would ever return! And this time they were right.

I stayed in Rome just long enough to book everything in advance for a whole year. I hadn't suffered at all with loneliness and knew that I would stay on the road without a second thought, so I felt confident in this course of action. Planning and paying up front can save a lot of money if you're prepared to take the risk. I chose non-refundable flights at bargain prices, not wasting a single one. Many would see the absence of planning as part of the freedom offered by travel, but it wasn't like that for me. My freedom was total because I was now choosing whatever I wanted. With the internet and so much information available, wandering around aimlessly no longer makes as much sense as it probably once did, and. I had left a generous margin of free days between adventures, which would give me more than enough flexibility.

I had spent much less than budgeted in the first year, but not because of any good financial management on my part. Quite the reverse, I'd simply miscalculated, using my past trips as a benchmark and then multiplying this by the total period. In other words, I'd based my estimates on the costs incurred when travelling in peak season, staying in a good hotel, taking taxis everywhere, and so on. In contrast, I now had a whole year to choose my travel dates from and plenty of time to wait for a bus.

Also, some of the countries visited last year were cheaper than those I'd travelled to in the past. In short, although travelling is expensive, it can become affordable for many people given time, flexibility, and few pretensions. I admire those who set off with little money throwing themselves wholeheartedly into every opportunity. It's right that this school should be available to as many people as possible, indeed, it would be wonderful if at least some travel experiences were accessible to all who want them, in the same way as a basic education is paid for by society through the state.

On the other hand, I genuinely don't understand those who travel to other countries and want to get things for nothing or almost free. When you leave home in your own country, do you hitchhike? Do you eat for free? Do you not want to pay for accommodation? Being a visitor doesn't justify such parasitic behaviour, besides which, you must be invited to consider yourself a true guest, not merely thrust unasked upon the host. The mere fact of travelling does not in any way authorise taking advantage of others.

Having made a game plan, I needed to use my stay in

Rome to obtain a visa for Uzbekistan, which was rather complicated. The embassy was within walking distance of my house and since they never answered the phone, I decided to go in person. It was my first encounter with a way of behaving that I had not even imagined possible. The embassy employees, who I imagine are adequately remunerated for their work, made it explicitly clear to me that in order to get a visa I had to go to a specialised agency, which would deliver back to them the documents that I had practically ready in my hand at that precise moment! I'm not exactly naive, so I had grasped what was going on behind the scenes, but I was so happy about the start of my new adventure that I just laughed the episode off. Unperturbed, I booked the trip with the agency, biting the bullet in the hope of getting it done quickly because I was going to apply for a visa to Russia soon afterwards. But even with the agency's intercession, my passport was retained for several days. Since I couldn't go far, I decided to tackle the final leg of the famous Camino de Santiago in **Spain (24)** to pass the time.

The full route involves leaving France and arriving in Galicia almost 800 km later. I walked the last 100 km and then the 90 that lead to the sea. One hundred is enough to have officially completed the pilgrimage and receive forgiveness for some sin. At one time, when the route was really dangerous, and there was no distinction between sin and crime, pardon at the end of the route could mean that you wouldn't have to go to jail. Today, there are still those who walk for various reasons that would fall into a 'spiritual' category, such as devotion or to make a small sacrifice. I went with exactly the same mentality I'd had doing yoga in India, pure curiosity. I enjoyed the practice itself, without giving any weight to the religious implications.

I displayed my beautiful conch shell symbolising the pilgrim the whole time, but I never prayed along the way. It was not faith that gave me strength, nor did I feel I had to repent for anything in particular. Although I usually had headphones with me as my inseparable friends during long journeys, I didn't use them this time. I kept my own company during the day, and the nights in dormitories full of strangers were entertaining. Unlike in a hotel, everyone would constantly strike up conversations with each other, chatting as passionately and easily about foot blisters as about how you could turn your life around, jumping from topic to topic just as you would in a good marriage.

It's true that a journey can't be solely a reward but should also involve education. I would suggest to those who are thinking of getting married that they embark together on a great adventure such as the Camino de Santiago, a honeymoon minus the honey, experiencing real life, a common path and mutual support. The school of travel gratifies you and fills you with satisfaction where you least expect it. For me, who certainly hadn't any notion of marrying, this experience in Spain, so close to home, emerged from something that had been merely a stopgap whilst waiting for a document.

Having obtained the Uzbek visa, it was now the turn of the Russian one, which also required leaving my passport in the agency's custody for a few days. In the intervening time,

I flew to **Turkey (25)** where my identity card was sufficient for entry. As a Roman, I was impressed by Istanbul on account of its beauty and, for once, also because I had studied and understood a little history at school. What I hadn't been at all aware of was the origin of the Turks in the very Mongolia that I'd recently visited, 5,000 km away. Nor did I know that the Uzbeks too were so close to the Turks. I was beginning to realise, however, that while it's understood in all cultures of the world that a promise must always be kept, the same is not true for a time commitment. My new Turkish friends were never punctual and totally unapologetic.

I returned to Rome to collect my passport and unsurprisingly given its proximity to the Uzbeks, took a plane back to Istanbul, from where I continued on to Tashkent, the capital of my next destination. I had some wonderful moments in **Uzbekistan (26)**, but also my first confrontation with that great enemy of the traveller, diarrhoea. I knew never to drink if there was ice in the glass because it could have been made with tap water. I avoided raw food and always looked for peeled, boiled or cooked dishes. I knew to be wary of eating seafood and wouldn't touch ice cream that might have gone off and become contaminated before re-freezing. And now I had discovered that buffets were also dangerous. Despite only cooked foods being selected, keeping them warm under a lamp for a long time, at about 40°C, provided the perfect conditions for bacteria to breed and contamination to occur. I spent days locked in my room, or more precisely in the bathroom. I tipped the hotel guy heavily to bring me rice, boiled potatoes and litres of tea and luckily, was able to leave the country just in time as the famous Uzbek visa was only valid for a fortnight.

Whilst in the Ferghana Valley I had wanted to meet the only Uzbek I knew, a boy who had studied with me in Germany. At the time I'd helped him fill some large gaps in his knowledge. We had somehow found each other again on Facebook and I was pleased that he wanted to meet me, as this indicated that he had been successful, but what held me back was not the diarrhoea, but the impossibility of communicating. At the time we had conversed in good German but now I could hardly remember anything of the language, and he didn't know a word of English. For months we had readily discussed complex topics, yet now we found that we were no longer even able to exchange simple sentences without the help of an online translator.

Back to Istanbul and from there to Moscow, in **Russia (27)** was another beautiful historical combination, made unintentionally, as I flew from the so-called second Rome to the third. The arrival was actually another departure as I was about to travel the entire Trans-Siberian Railway, 9,288 km of track leading all the way to the Pacific Ocean, practically next to Japan. Despite my good intentions to get to know as many locals as possible, the language barrier meant that during those long days on the train, I spoke mainly to Westerners. None of the Russians or Asians really understood English, not even the lady in charge of the dining car. Every day I would try something random from the incomprehensible menu and then, just to be safe, order an omelette on the side, this being the only word I could read well in Cyrillic. In the evenings, that same restaurant carriage would come alive as alcohol levels rose exponentially. There would be the biggest laughs and demonstrations of friendship, as well as dirty looks at the slightest misunderstanding. The restaurateur may have spoken no English, but she did have the admirable gift of being able to single-handedly keep a dozen completely drunk Russian men at bay.

I was starting to talk about my journey on social media to an audience that used to follow me for poker. In turn, I would also follow other travellers, for inspiration, and to understand how they viewed their trips and what they were looking for.

Everyone agreed that the slow flow of the landscape past the window is fascinating and stimulates the mind almost as much as walking for hours every day on a route like the Camino de Santiago. It's true that on the Trans-Siberian Railway it's the journey itself that is the destination as you savour the passage of time, but for me the speed of flying was still indispensable. I had been on the move for more than a year and as such, didn't need downtime or distinct transitions to feel out of my old world and routine. I changed seasons, schedules, tastes and cultures all the time, and consequently, in my situation, I believed the plane, so despised by those who profess to be true travellers, to be a powerful tool at my disposal and certainly not an obstacle.

Land routes can indeed sometimes become monotonous, with all motorways often looking similar. Even this latest 55-hour train journey through Russia continually showed the same single image of an ocean of trees from the window. *Around the World in 80 Days* was published in 1872 when the aeroplane did not yet exist, but the book's great success was partly due to its glorification of technological innovations. The world has changed profoundly. We contend with environmental issues that were once unimaginable, we are in a hurry in real life and therefore some people seek slowness by contrast.

Perhaps as in the novel, variety adds spice to the adventure, but the choice between plane, train, carriage or submarine for me remains secondary. The length of the journey is not fundamental either, as long as you give yourself time to break the routine, forget for a while what awaits you on your return and spend at least one whole day without thinking about home. When you do, you are in the right place at the right time, because the school of travel requires your full, undistracted attention if it's to be able to teach you.

From Vladivostok, the last stop on the world's longest railway, I had a flight to Vietnam. For a few months it had been possible for Italians to enter without a visa, provided they stayed less than a fortnight, but the visa requirement still appeared on the terminals of the Russian airport. I attempted in vain to show the notices of the rule change but even the official websites, written in English, were not convincing. I had learned to consult *Timatic*, the software that manages airport terminals in most parts of the world, but evidently not these here in Vladivostok.

Provided the terminals are as up to date as the online version, I know what the operator will see on the screen during check-in and can prepare accordingly. But on that occasion, I was forced to buy an alternative flight and chose to go to Japan where I didn't need a visa and then from there to **Vietnam (28)**. It was clearly written on the terminals in Tokyo that the rule had changed, and I left without any problems.

I was upset by the episode and the waste of money; however, I decided that there was no point in getting angry about such things and so, like a prudent administrator, I created an entry for 'Contingencies' on my expense sheet and allocated €5,000, (5% of the total budget) giving it up in my mind as wasted once and for all. For future incidents like this, I would mentally take the money from there so that I could move on with a smile. Those were the best years of my life and as much as it lay in my own hands, I didn't have to ruin my days with regret.

I had found a tour guide who offered me the original experience of working as a farmer for a few days, whilst staying with his family. Of course, it's a tourist experience where you pay as if you were in a hotel yet live like a poor farmer, but as inconvenient as it may sound when put like that, I wanted to do it. I would experience the same living conditions, eat together with them, try to communicate with the locals, and maybe even learn to do a little work in the garden.

By each evening I was physically exhausted, which I really liked. Many say it frees your mind, but mine was already quite free. I wanted to see the results of my work with my own eyes and feel satisfaction. I was disappointed, however, by the minimal communication at the table. We really didn't understand each other at all. I felt more involved when we were working, and the instructions were communicated to me by example. The farmer took my hands as they held the hoe and made me perform the necessary movement. I can still remember the feeling of his hands touching mine. They were nothing but callouses, thick and hard, yellowed and deformed, and marked by years of toil.

On the final day, I was entrusted with taking care of the grave that was right in the middle of the property. Ancestor worship may be romantic, but when mortal remains are placed in the house or in a field, they can become a condemnation. The family feels imprisoned, compelled to stay even if the land becomes barren.

I decided that I would try another physical labour experience in a place where I could communicate. It surprised me that some travellers kept showing pictures of people they couldn't speak with, but to whom they had made great proclamations of eternal friendship. Perhaps when we travel, we let our feelings go and this combines with the tendency that people have to share over-amplified emotions on social media, lying to others, and I wonder if maybe also to themselves. In any case, I was interested in a different reality as I wanted to communicate in earnest, to ask questions, to answer theirs, to understand. I found the solution by offering myself a few months later as a bricklayer in the Philippines.

I went to **Cambodia (29)** and felt content that I had largely stopped using hotels. The more I travelled, the more these generic buildings took me away from the atmosphere of the place I was in, much like an airport does, and deposited me into the world of privilege every night.

More and more often I was alone, in the sense that I was not in the company of a group of Italians like myself, but could this be considered a 'solo' trip, as so many like to say? Personally, I have never used the expression. Messner in the mountains, or someone who crosses a desert or Antarctica accompanied only by their thoughts could be described as journeying 'solo', but I was only alone in the sense that I was not in the company of people I already knew. In reality, I was surrounded by people, I had a working mobile phone, credit cards in my pocket, a hospital a few minutes away, an insurance policy and so on. In fact, there was often a tourist guide who was working for me staying in the room next door. Nothing could be less like solo travel than this…

I found the courage to go to the Khmer Rouge death camps and the genocide museum. I had already learned of the existence of the *Ujamaa* in Tanzania, a rural community where work and its fruits were shared equally. It was essentially a kind of rural communism that had dragged millions of people into the countryside with disastrous results, but here in Cambodia they had gone much further. Moving the population of entire cities into rural areas, they had abolished all rights and worst of all, exterminated a huge percentage of the population. I had truly known very little about this.

I still had three weeks to go before my visit to the United Arab Emirates, so I decided to return to Thailand, to the same place where I had already stayed because it was cheap and pleasant. I took the opportunity to re-read *Around the World in 80 Days*, which I could now claim to have experienced first-hand. In the novel, a man travels to win a £20,000 bet, whereas I was travelling thanks to the money I had previously won by betting the smart way! I more or less remembered the plot and it was gripping. Verne manages to tell of mysterious customs and distant peoples, and he does so through the thoughts of the various characters, because the protagonist, the famous Phileas Fogg, is too focused on the enterprise and is described as follows, *"[...] as for seeing the city, he did not even think about it, because he belonged to that category of Englishmen who make their servants visit the countries they pass through."* It was wrong 150 years ago, but today how many people still have the arrogance to think that their own way of life already has the best of everything?

I left Thailand much earlier than planned, having found a discounted plane ticket to **Taiwan (/)**. It was clear from my books that what little was left of ancient China could be found right there because it had been liberated, (or stolen, depending on one's point of view), by the nationalists who, having lost the civil war, had fled to this formerly Japanese island. It's an interesting place, with incredible mountains and an aboriginal population that is rarely talked about but provokes great interest among scholars. The geopolitical situation is complicated, and so I do not include Taiwan in the count, simply because it is not a permanent member of the United Nations and that's the parameter I'm following. I've travelled far and wide and for the first time in my adult life, here in this place, I had the pleasure of wasting time, without feeling any guilt.

The famous Dubai in the **United Arab Emirates (30)** awaited me next. I had dinner on the highest publicly accessible floor of the *Burj Khalifa*, the world's tallest skyscraper. I was with someone who had worked there for ten years and was, therefore, able to explain to me in detail the modern forms of exploitation of labour that are helping to make this city so rich in buildings and attractions. Making moral assessments is everyone's responsibility, but a tourist like me who had been to North Korea, what was he supposed to feel? Walking around London I never think of past exploitation, or about poverty in Indonesia while in Amsterdam. I admire St Petersburg and certainly do not mourn the thousands of workers enslaved to build it. Here in Dubai though, I feel discomfort, because it's happening now and right before my eyes. I had even felt grief in the Cambodian concentration camps where I had just been and that tragedy happened in the late 1970s, while I felt no sorrow for the tales of Mongolian barbarities, or the piles of skulls made by Tamerlane in Uzbekistan. When is the exact moment when a horror story becomes just a story?

However, I realise that if I were extraordinarily rich, apart from not charging income tax, Dubai could offer services that are unique in the world. Here there is always a fast track for those with money, a first-class option. If I were part of the so-called middle class, maybe the US would be the best place for me, while I have no doubt that for a lower-class person, based on local standards, the place to live would be Europe. For now, I don't think too much about money, but at the end of this trip, when I have spent a large portion of my savings, will I be in the middle like I used to be or maybe high up like the last few years before my travels? Or will I be right at the bottom since I will be starting from scratch at almost 40?

Following on, mysterious **Turkmenistan (31)** was the destination. The personality cult surrounding the leader is ridiculous. You see him on YouTube singing and driving cars, always giving orders, and showing off athletic or military skills that he obviously does not possess. The previous president had filled the capital with golden statues of himself, including one that actually rotated to follow the movement of the sun.

The book he had written was to be revered like the Koran, learnt by heart and is the subject of questioning in every examination, including the driving test! Elections are a farce where the opponents go on TV and say they will vote for the dictator who is elected with percentages you wouldn't get even if you asked what water tastes like! But for me, having been in North Korea, I felt I'd seen it all before, and it was actually not as bad here because Turkmenistan is a neutral country that tortures its own citizens but does not threaten others.

On arrival the corruption was perceptible at every juncture, in fact, I had already been asked for money at the airport, some sort of visa surcharge fabricated on the spot, an extra $27, which I mentally took from my contingency money. Paradoxically, this was actually a good sign when comparing it to the situation in North Korea where the corruption of the individual is unimaginable as it would never escape the total control exercised by the regime.

I had organised my visit to the so-called 'Gates of Hell', accompanied, obviously, both because it's in the middle of the desert and it's obligatory to have someone to watch over the tourist outside the capital. This huge gas-filled hole has been burning continuously for at least 50 years and offers a fantastic spectacle, especially at sunset, when the light changes, enhancing the stark contrast between darkness and flames. It also suddenly gets cold because it's still a desert and without sunshine the temperature plummets despite being so close to such a furnace.

There's only one thing to do at night by the crater, namely drink, both for fun and to keep warm. My guide definitely overdid it, to the point that in the morning I couldn't wake him up. He was so drunk that he had fallen asleep where we had bivouacked, unable to reach his tent. I tried to revive him with coffee, then with some forceful tugging, but to no avail, however at least he was breathing. My mobile had no signal and his was switched off, so I had almost decided to dismantle the camp and load the tent, blankets and guide into the car. However, the thought of having to get behind the wheel, even if only as far as where the mobile phone would regain reception, was quite distressing. There were constant checkpoints, and I would have to give explanations in Turkmen about a situation that resembled a comedy film. Even in Italian I might not have been able to adequately explain what I was doing in the middle of the desert, without a licence, in a car that wasn't mine, in the company of a man whose name I couldn't remember, who was alive but unable to speak or open his eyes for more than a second. I was sure to get into trouble and they were going to ask me for who knows how much money not to throw me in jail.

I decided to wait, passing the time by piecing together what he had consumed, namely a bottle of vodka and 14 cans of beer. He was lucky he hadn't ended up in the crater. Eventually, he recovered, we got into the car and drove back to the capital, Ashgabat. At least the road in the middle of the desert was straight. Once again, although I had been in a 'hellish' place, it was a man rather than nature that had scared me.

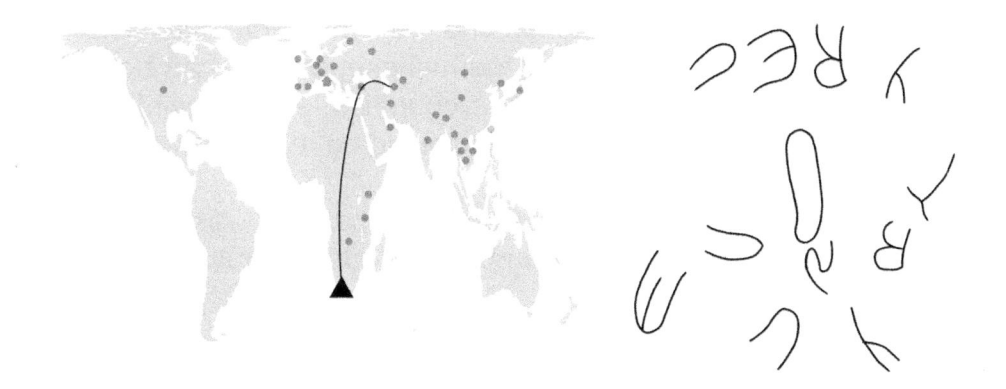

I had booked my Istanbul-Cape Town ticket long ago at a reduced price and was excited at the thought of flying over the entire African continent. It's a great exercise that helps you realise how huge it is. Our traditional maps don't do the size justice. Travelling continually showed me how naive I was and what huge misjudgements you can make about places you don't yet know, like the time a genuinely concerned American friend called me to ask if I was alright in Rome when there had been a flood in Germany, over 1,000 km away from me.

I arrived in Cape Town in **South Africa (32)** and found it to be one of the most beautiful cities in the world from a natural point of view. Until then I had been impressed by Dar es-Salam, but now first place was not in question. It would take Rio to make me doubt it. In this relatively small region, there is great biodiversity. The richness of the flora is impressive, although reading guides and books about the different countries talking about such things always makes me smile. The individual figures never add up if you look at them all together, and the total if you look at percentages is much more than 100%. Italy is perhaps the worst offender here since so many Italians consider our country to be on par with Brazil.

The same phenomenon was evident with the large, fast-expanding cities. According to my guidebooks, Dubai, Shanghai and Mecca together had already recorded having more than 100% of the cranes in the world. However, the most common falsehoods that still persisted concerned the number of languages spoken and the number of hours slept at night by the many great men whose exploits had been recounted to me in the various countries, all impossible to verify, and therefore completely safe to be repeated.

According to percentages and statistics, this was my first encounter with a truly violent nation. Some statistics can perhaps be open to interpretation, for instance, how many of the deaths counted occurred in fights between illegal miners? It's known that many people will be prepared to steal and kill as they go into the tunnels abandoned by the mining companies, hoping that there is something left. Are there fights between different ethnic groups? Do rapes occur mainly in slums? Nevertheless, those numbers, even when stripped of circumstances in which I could not find myself and considering that I could choose to only go out during the day and keep to safe areas, showed that South Africa has a very high rate of robberies, thefts and violence.

I travelled around with a wonderful guide until I met a Greek girl, who had been roaming about like me, with whom I went on to **Namibia (33)**. Across the border was another world entirely. The country was safe, the nightmare of violence was gone, and all I had to concentrate on was guarding my shoes, which were constantly in danger of being adopted as a home by scorpions or being stolen by jackals! We camped for a few days on the property of a family whose first question for us was whether or not we were vegetarians. The man was pleased when we said we weren't. 'Good,' he said, 'because in my house chicken is a vegetable. Have you noticed that the lion sleeps peacefully during the day because he eats meat while the zebra has to chew grass continually to survive?' And he put these notions into practice each evening as he offered us a barbecue where for every 100 g of meat there was perhaps a small leaf of salad, more to garnish the dish than to be eaten.

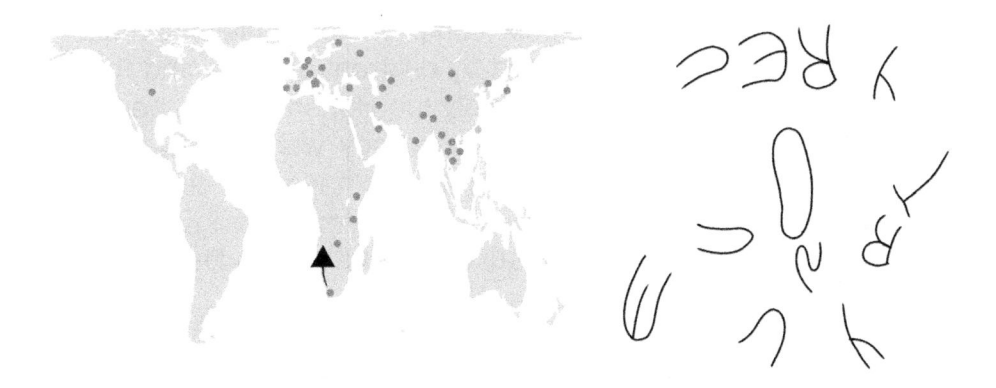

Next, in the company of a large group, I took a cultural tour that visited some beautiful towns that are still German and discovered subjects I had never previously been aware of. The first genocide, in the sense of the attempted total elimination of a people, was perhaps perpetrated by the German occupation forces against the Herero people right where I was now. Today there is great tension over the scale of that event (although it is historically known to have happened), and the complicity of other tribes because of the billions in reparations that have yet to be decided. I used to think that such issues were matters of principle and respect for those who paid with their lives, whereas in fact there are definite economic interests associated with all this. But what struck me most was the controversial argument of the Germans, or their descendants, here in Namibia who claim that the first genocide was perpetrated by the British against the Boers in South Africa a few years before the extermination of the Hereros. That is, whites against other whites who insisted on remaining slave owners. Their lands were burnt, and concentration camps set up to exterminate these peasant farmers, most of whom were originally from the Netherlands. I had heard with my own ears the hatred that some South African whites harboured against the British, without realising it came from a war fought in the early 1900s, perhaps because current focus is understandably on more recent history where whites were united against blacks until the fall of Apartheid.

My attention was captivated as I learned about the *San*, also known as Hottentots or Bushmen, among other things. It's difficult to untangle this complicated jungle of names because they were assigned by different peoples and then adopted by Europeans. Possibly the Hottentots can be distinguished from the *San* because they were familiar with agriculture. In any case, these names have one characteristic in common: they are derogatory terms referring to people who have managed to survive in the Namib Desert, the oldest and among the driest and least hospitable in the world.

They have distinctive clicking tongues, are nomadic hunter-gatherers, and have never domesticated any animals. They are excellent trackers and able to store water inside ostrich eggs to cope with drought. They never wash which certainly has disadvantaged them in encounters with others, but this is the desert where every drop of water is precious. They are described as very short but have additional physical characteristics that were not mentioned in any of my books. Women have steatopygia, which is basically a large accumulation of fat in the buttocks and macronympha, or elongated labia of the vulva, whilst men are thin, but their bellies can expand. In the past, similar physical characteristics were made a mockery of, and some *San* were even exhibited in human zoos.

In Walvis Bay, people told me of the importance of their town, which has the only deep-water harbour along this coast, possibly explaining why the British and Germans fought over it. However, there are also traces of agreements between the two colonisers in the geography of Namibia, the most obvious being the 'Caprivi Strip', a tract of land stretching eastwards for over 400 km before reaching the Zambezi River. Germany was under the illusion that, thanks to this salient, it could access Tanzania, another of its colonies on the other side of Africa, whilst remaining within its own territory or waters but, actually not all of the route is navigable. I had experienced difficulties in the water in my own small way whilst rafting on the Zambezi. Here I instead tried sandboarding, an expensive and not very enjoyable activity that exists mainly to put a spectacular photo of oneself on social media.

The Namibian desert is perfection, being exactly the image that comes unconsciously to any child when drawing a sand dune. I was persuaded by the group to go on safari, which I hadn't really had any desire to do again, but in fact it turned out to be both beautiful and convenient. In Etosha they had created artificial watering holes, so there was no need to chase the animals, you could just wait for them to come and drink. In Kruger Park in South Africa (named after a very racist, Christian Boer), they also have effective methods to simplify the search. They send the Jeeps in different directions on asphalted roads and as soon as someone finds something they alert the others, who can then quickly cover the intervening distances on the good roads. I was discovering the world and was growing in my conviction that you have to actually go to a place to really understand it.

From South Africa I had to return to Thailand again to save money on the flight, and then entered **Malaysia (34)** where I had found a luxury hotel at a rock-bottom price thanks to booking so ridiculously far in advance. I've said that these establishments all have identical rooms, but the pool here was unique, located as it was in the inner courtyard, so it was in the shade. I still hadn't understood the extent to which the women wanted to avoid the sun. The completely white skin of some Asians is indeed beautiful and without exposure to the sun aging is delayed, but it takes a tremendous effort to protect themselves in those conditions and requires continual renunciation of a number of activities.

When I used to go jogging in the fields, I imagined that the women farmers must have been regarding me as I would have thought of a pig who rolls around in a pigsty, tiring himself out with seemingly no purpose. Running causes me to tan, sweat, and smell bad. I voluntarily expend physical effort in a way that is incomprehensible to those whose daily life already involves quite enough hard toil. In any event, the urge to run was about to temporarily pass even from me, not due to the sun, but because my experience as a bricklayer in the **Philippines (35)** was about to begin.

I had wanted to experience physical labour as a way of life, looking for interaction with locals to get to know the reality of their different existences, but I was well aware that for people like me who don't have any practical skills, volunteering is usually a joke. Worse, it can even become counterproductive. The proliferation of orphanages artfully created for Western volunteers who pay to take care of children who have parents that are just exploiting them is well known, which is why I intended my volunteering to be quite different.

I would contribute financially to the project, as well as work in person to build a classroom. A typhoon had destroyed the school building and taken many lives with it and now it was a question of constructing a more resilient structure. I slept in a small room with a woman with three children who had been abandoned by her husband. In the morning, I would eat rice for breakfast and go to work with my lunchbox, full of rice. When I returned in the evening, I would eat more rice, the same that had been cooked all at once in the morning.

But I was not here for the good food, what I wanted was a month as a real builder in the company of Filipino professionals where I could finally talk to everyone because the use of English is widespread. I would learn more about the reality of life for them, we could exchange ideas and indeed, I could share my own perspective on the world. After all, even when you feel like you're learning nothing on your travels, you may perhaps be teaching something to someone else.

My contribution to work by carrying bricks soon became even more limited because the walls had been erected and now it was a question of doing something else, but I was unable to perform most of the new tasks. I was a disaster as a carpenter, and despite having spoken well of my body in Mongolia, I was now disappointed as I barely knew how to do anything. Eventually, I was given the job of painting and there I did my best. I wasn't afraid of getting hurt, and the worst that I could do was drop some paint in my eyes while working on the ceilings. Standing on the ladder didn't faze me, and the fatigue was just what I wanted.

Everyone in the neighbouring classrooms knew me and came to watch while I pretended to take orders. One of the qualities of our society is the shift in roles according to circumstances. The director of a large company leaves the office and is confronted by a 20-year-old trainer at the gym who scolds him, telling him to get off his backside and jump faster, and that's how I'd wanted it to be during the construction. I was financing the work, but during the day I was a painter at the foreman's command. But the idea of exchanging roles is non-existent in hierarchical societies, and the situation is even worse in tribes, where an elder is always an elder and a warrior always a warrior whatever the circumstance.

Aside from the work, talking to these people was instructive. One man had been living in a Red Cross container with his family for years. He asked me ten times for the shoes I would come to work in before putting on the protective ones, and in the end, I gave them to him when I left, even though they were my only pair. After travelling such distances, I had learnt the importance of good shoes, something I hadn't fully appreciated when living in the city with its well-paved streets.

Besides being able to make someone happy with a small gift, I had realised that I was not harming anyone with my volunteering as an unskilled person, however, if the purpose was really to help students, it would have been more profitable to hire other professionals with the money I was spending to support myself for a month in the Philippines. They each earned $10 a day and were obviously worth at least twice as much as me on the job. I was spending $50 a day just to be there, so I could have hired five workers, who would have contributed ten times as much as I did for the construction. This reasoning is mathematically correct, but in reality, I was there for myself, not for others.

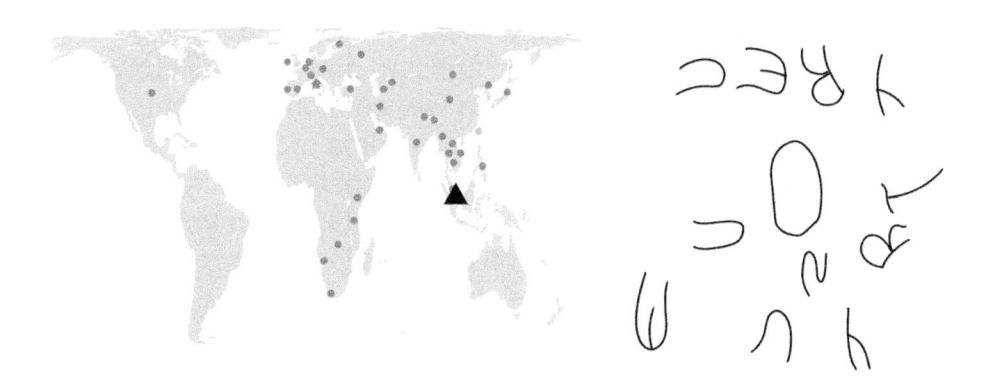

Being a labourer in the Philippines certainly qualifies as being 'outside' the comfort zone for a city boy who knows how to use a pen but not a paintbrush. Wanting to get out of that protective confinement is a valid reason in itself to find the self-confidence and prove to yourself that you can do it. There is no need to be excessively afraid of change and difficulties. As far back as Mongolia I had begun to have more confidence in my body and now as a labourer, through highs and lows, I had managed to do hard work every day. After such a change in life's direction for a few years, it was possible that any future job would be far less comfortable than my past employment had been, but I would immediately be able to put what I had learnt into practice and not be frightened if the new reality seemed harder. Stepping out of my comfort zone had enabled me to worry less about the future.

In the evenings I would go out with a local girl. Dinner in the most luxurious restaurant cost about $10 and I could finally avoid the plain rice. However, what made the girl happy when she went to a place like that for the first time was unquestionably the service. No one had ever treated her in such an attentive and considerate manner. In comparison, on leaving the restaurant, all I had noted as worthy of mention was the food. The only other entertainment was karaoke, where one by one, each person, including the most tone-deaf, sings for the others. At home in Italy, those who volunteer to sing tend to be at least reasonably good, whilst it is acceptable for everyone, even the most ungainly to dance, whereas in the Philippines moving to the music whilst others watched required a certain amount of skill.

The month ended and I left before they had put the glass in the windows, but they did a mock inauguration for me, in the way that some politicians do, to make it look like the date had been honoured. I had reached **Singapore (36)** when the real inauguration with all the glass completed had taken place, where I had wanted to sleep in a hotel. After a month in a tiny room, with almost no furniture and roosters crowing from 3 am, I wanted to enjoy a few comfortable nights. It's important on a long journey to have some of these moments when both mind and body are at their best. Of course, it only lasts a short time, but the memory remains with you during the moments of discomfort on the road.

I bought a new pair of shoes because I didn't like wearing flip-flops when I was out and about. In general, I like to be in a state where I can run away, carry my case for kilometres, shoo a dog, or in extreme circumstances, try to defend myself if I have to. The only things that flip-flops are exceptional at is killing mosquitoes, and mine, complete with an image of the King of Hearts wielding a sword behind his head, have claimed victims in dozens and dozens of countries. I have flapped them around so much that the king's image has now faded, more from the pounding than from their frequent contact with shower, rain and sea water.

This tiny island of Singapore has global importance because enormous quantities of goods are transported from here. Once a British colony, it belongs geographically to Malaysia, but the majority of the population is Chinese, which is what led to it becoming an independent nation. When colonialism came to an end, Singapore was ready to take its place as part of Malaysia but was not accepted because this fledgling nation risked having a population too skewed towards ethnic Chinese. Today Malaysia is probably kicking itself as Singapore is even richer, per capita, than Great Britain itself!

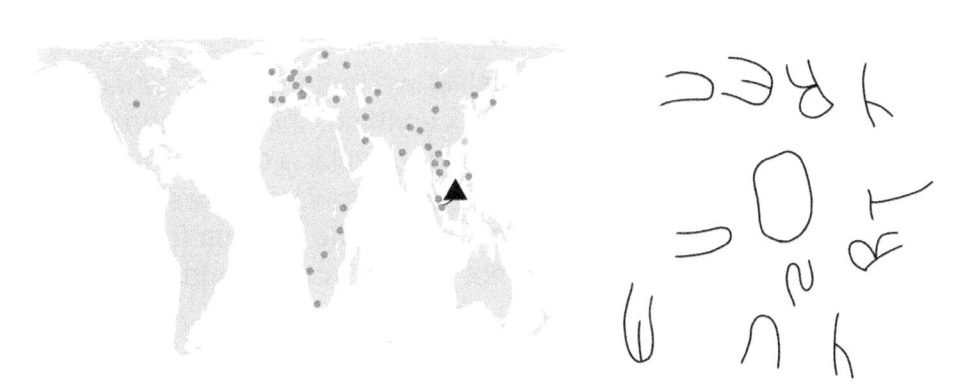

The architect of this economic miracle was an enlightened man, who made the country the best place in the world to do business, albeit with some huge limitations in that he tolerated no opposition, and wanted no adversaries, essentially, he was a dictator. Economically enlightened, not at all interested in a personality cult and sometimes pliable, yet it remains a dictatorship that exercises censorship and applies very severe penalties. Some have called the city-state a kind of Disneyland with the death penalty. Anyone who wants to can leave the country without asking permission and without explanation, but no one ever leaves.

I proceeded to **Brunei (37)**, another small, rich nation, in this case, where wealth is concentrated in the hands of a few. The Sultan owns the largest palace in the world with 1,788 rooms, and if you need to pee, don't panic because there are 257 bathrooms. The garage houses the world's largest collection of luxury cars. Everything is taken to excess. It's obligatory to show gratitude for every service received since they are still in an era of gifts and not rights. His subjects consider everything to be his, so if he shares something it's generosity. Do they not see how that enormous fortune, accumulated mainly through oil, belongs to everyone and it is unfair for him to spend it so lavishly on himself?

People pray for the Sultan in the mosque, and they hail him, but at least they don't go as far as the extreme personality cults of North Korea and Turkmenistan. On the other hand, as in those two countries, the leader is seen as infallible and perfect, so the possibility of criticism is eliminated at the root. In addition, here they have a huge playground, completely out of proportion to their needs, donated by the royal family that loves its subjects so much, exactly like North Korea or Turkmenistan. Perhaps it serves to provide a bit of fun and create the impression that this too is thanks to the leader.

In such countries, carnival as we understand it, where it is permissible to joke about everything, including those in power, albeit without threatening to replace them, is not tolerated. Brunei is the dullest nation I have ever visited, yet one member of the ruling family became famous for throwing some of the most opulent parties in the world. Women from his *harem* attended, he flew in prostitutes from all over the world for the occasion, and he imported luxury items to impress. Apparently, he spent over 10 billion dollars in this way!

I fled at full pelt to **Indonesia (38)** where another experience booked in some moment of euphoria awaited me: fasting. Many religions, including the major ones, have rules about it and billions of people still fast by choice at certain times of the year. It's a disciplinary experience that I wanted to try, but as often happens to me, I had gone too far. The exercise consisted of eating free quantities of only two types of fruit for one day, then just one type. From there I would fast completely for three days. The first day of complete fasting was hard and I may have had a bit of a fever in the evening. But then it got gradually easier, and I also went for walks and did some yoga. I was participating in the fast together with other people, all women. The experience was entitled something like 'proceed to an inner cleansing'. My companions paid more attention to the motivational talk than I did, but I remain of the opinion that they were just looking for a crash diet.

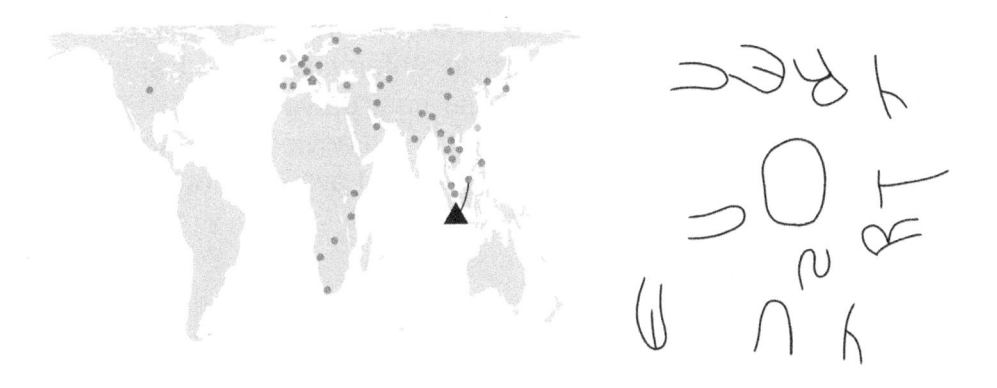

At the end of this crazy week, I ordered two portions of Balinese suckling pig in a characteristic restaurant and thought back to my clumsy attempts at yoga in a school that had called itself authentic and traditional. They may be authentic local realities, but is it possible that there was never a single Indonesian in either the restaurant or the yoga school? In Ubud, a tourist town in Bali, every building contains a wellness centre, be it with herbs, minerals, plants or whatever else. There's always a Westerner who runs the place and shows up dressed as an Indian holy man claiming to know some secret, that somehow has been revealed to him but not to the rest of the world.

A mere handful of pages have passed in this book, but the second, and theoretically final, year of the trip was already coming to an end. At the time, I honestly thought I would be finishing it up and wanted to do so by visiting South America for a few months, with half an idea in mind to try and get to Antarctica.

I arrived in Buenos Aires, **Argentina (39)** and discovered that it was a kind of Italy. My reading was in full swing. Between learning about the Dutch explorations in Indonesia and taking in stories of a woman brought to Brunei from the United States to please the party spendthrift, I was trying to gain a good understanding of the immigration figures for South America, but I hadn't realised the extent to which Italians had influenced their society and culture. I felt pretty much at home, albeit whilst surrounded by a different language. I enrolled in a two-week full-immersion Spanish course with the aim of learning a few hundred words so that at least I would be able to exchange a few thoughts during the long South American trip. In the meantime, I researched and documented how to get to Antarctica without spending a fortune, because the trips cost upwards of $10,000. Once the short course was over, I still envied those Italians who say they understand Spanish right away without having studied it and get away with speaking it.

The desire for nature and the dream of Antarctica compelled me to go to Patagonia, more than three hours by plane from the capital. I was no longer surprised by the great distances which are badly represented on maps of the Southern Hemisphere since an error is inevitable because you can't portray the world using only two dimensions. It's reasonable to neglect the South at the expense of the North because about 90% of the population lives above the equator. Conversely, in this book it makes more sense to use the Gall-Peters projection as a map, which better renders the proportions between the continents, albeit at the cost of distorting the distances, especially the vertical ones. Interestingly, although I was studying Spanish with little luck, the most widely spoken language South of the equator is Portuguese thanks to Brazil, Angola, Mozambique and East Timor.

I adopted a strategy of going in person to the agencies selling the famous Antarctic trip, with the aim of making myself available for a last-minute package. Such adventures are often booked a year or even two in advance, and consequently some people end up not being able to travel, sometimes close to the date. The companies then resell that place, as an extra passenger on board costs them almost nothing, so they are happy to lower the price in order to fill their seats. The people working in those agencies are often Filipinos, so it was easy for me to gain favour with them. I had built a classroom for their students and now I felt I deserved a fast track if a seat became available.

Anxiously awaiting the call, I started trekking. Even in Rome, my speciality is to get lost on foot, but the paths in this part of the world are really easy to follow, so I went by myself. I was accustomed to a tent, but I didn't feel like sleeping alone outdoors as there was constantly a strong wind. It wasn't tough and dangerous like Mongolia had been, but every night I was happy to go back to the comfort of the hostel and pretend to understand what the others were saying in Spanish.

Dead tired, I slept very well at night, and yet I missed the partying and the noise that there had been in the dormitories during the Camino de Santiago. The walkers in both Spain and Patagonia, however, paid just as much attention to others' sleep in the mornings. There was great concentration when they started to get dressed, somersaulting to put on their trousers soundlessly, and then at the end, the zip of the anorak always came with a loud snap. They all fasten noisily. Finally, there's the tricky exercise of stepping softly with boots on and closing the door. Along with annoyance, there is always a slight feeling of guilt that someone has already started.

One morning I was awakened by a very special phone call saying that there was a vacancy for Antarctica with departure in two days! I zipped up my anorak so quickly that I woke up the few who had withstood the sound of the phone call and having hurriedly paid online so as not to lose the place, I rushed to catch a domestic flight to Ushuaia, the southernmost city in the world, from where I would soon embark for Antarctica. The price? $3,000.

Amid my euphoria I found a few moments to think about

the poor person who had booked, paid a hefty sum, and then had not travelled. Who knows what trouble had befallen them, maybe a bereavement or an illness. But I was happy for myself. The worst, cheapest cabin on the ship was waiting to welcome me, but having just come from the bunkhouse, it seemed downright luxurious to me. Besides, there was a bottle of wine and a slice of cake on my bed with a thank you for the classroom construction! Little things bring joy.

The ship is reinforced to withstand the ice and if you are imagining some sort of cruise, think again. This is an expedition. It costs an arm and a leg but there is little organised entertainment and definitely no gala dinners. Instead, there are lectures on board about the importance of ice for the study of climate, penguins and birds.

The passage from Ushuaia to the Antarctic Peninsula is through the stormiest sea in the world. The discomfort is constant, accompanying you for 40 hours, and when you finally arrive in **Antarctica (/)** you realise that it is no ice lolly, but actually a desert full of mountains. Whereas at the North Pole, there is really only ice, there is earth underneath at the South Pole, and the average elevation is close to 3,000 m. The Arctic is an ocean surrounded by continents, while Antarctica is a continent surrounded by oceans. It is about 14 million km^2 in size, larger than Europe and only slightly smaller than Russia. It was only recently 'discovered', indeed, man became acquainted with distant planets before this lost continent. Its existence, however, had already been imagined, albeit for the wrong reason, for if in fact the earth is round, the thought was that it needed a counterweight down there to remain balanced!

The view in the summer is enchanting, with a tranquillity that makes me think of an all-white death, not frightening but serene. I had the book on Shackleton's incredible adventure in this part of the world with me, along with the great classic *Moby Dick*, so seeing the whales was fascinating. I was on a metal monster that could withstand great impacts and overcome incredible limitations, but at one time the whale was more capable of travelling the sea than man. It's as if today an animal were able to go to Mars and back every year. And it is by chasing them that man has made great geographical discoveries.

During the disembarkation, I got to know the modern equivalent of whalers, those who really reveal the world to us, the scientists. Some would spend the whole winter there in the dark. They lived and worked with iron discipline, obliged to shave, exercise, communicate with family members, wear a suit and tie on Sundays and have lunch together to prevent themselves from becoming dehumanised. I was able to send a postcard to my nephew from one of these scientific bases, but I didn't have a tie to wear myself to prevent my own degradation. In North Korea, the only other time that I'd needed one, I'd used the ribbon that had tied the hotel pillows to simulate wearing one and to show respect for the mausoleum where Kim Il-Sung's mummy is locked up. I had brought only hand luggage, even to Antarctica, because a big jacket and boots were provided on board. There's no space for a tie when you are enrolled in the school of travel.

I returned to Argentina where I attended a barbecue at which they cut the meat with a spoon because of how tender it was. I sent a photo to my host in Namibia who was a fan of charcoal with a few smiley faces, but he never replied. I wonder if he thought I was teasing him when in fact I was looking for his expert opinion.

From Buenos Aires, I took a 20-minute flight to Montevideo in **Uruguay (40)**. If it were possible, I felt even more at home here. Everything reminded me of Italy and as I strolled down Garibaldi Street, named for an Italian national hero, I thought of how many immigrants had walked here, owning nothing, just hoping for a new life. Communication with Italy used to be difficult. Imagine the excitement of receiving a letter or a phone call, combined with the anxiety over the news you were about to receive. Some people truly were brave.

On my postcard from Antarctica, which would be in transit for over a year like the letters of yesteryear, I had written a pitiful 'Hello from Uncle Penguin'. Nowadays all communication is faster than the postcard and we are constantly updated, but I have met people who are still isolated from their families. Obviously, this applies to the scientists in Antarctica, but likewise, the Filipinos on board the ship, won't see anyone for months and have little internet or telephone to rely on. They can just send and receive a few photos for free on close family birthdays. Millions of men and women sacrifice themselves to offer a better future to others. Remittances from migrants are the first item in the budget of some nations and create tremendous envy in those who don't receive them. The money that is sent is eagerly awaited, way, way more than mere postcards! Every time I land and see those big welcoming committees at the airport for the returning loved one, and I feel happy. A journey is still a big event, and the homecoming, for those who manage to return, is a celebration. In India, I had been moved by the gravestones of the British who died on the return journey. They were so close, they had probably finally felt safe to be returning home, only to drown at sea, their bodies never found.

There is never anyone waiting for me, but as usual, I am the privileged one: I travel by choice and return home when I want to.

I entered **Paraguay (41)**, a country unknown to most, including me. There are few books that open the doors to this part of the world. In the end, it's a huge, under-explored swamp. The bravest and most intrepid are the birdwatchers who go into the interior with cameras costing thousands of euros and endure uncomfortable conditions for days, all to spot a bird. The allure of a flying creature is obvious, but there are more than 10,000 species, and some of them actually quite ugly, so why would you want to see so many? Good question, isn't it? You might be forgiven for asking me the same thing about visiting so many countries, but at least there are only 193 of these to date…

Peru (42) is certainly worth a visit. I had booked the Inca Trail, which is some 40 km on paths in the high mountains and ends at the ruins of Machu Picchu, the birthplace of a wonderful civilisation that never knew how to write. The reward for the effort is mainly the view, but there is a golden rule that those who arrive having walked the entire route get to enter first and can enjoy the archaeological site with only fellow trekkers for a few hours. Later in the morning the gates open for the other visitors.

During the four days of the walk, you are assisted by a plethora of porters, each carrying 20 kg of food, tents, pans and whatever else you may need. Don't even think about going it alone. You wouldn't be able to carry everything you'll require, and in any case, these people live off the work you provide. If they are happy, why should you be embarrassed? They are so well organised that they manage to cook a hot meal every night and, in the morning, I would find a tiny bowl of hot water to wash my face in, much to my delight as it was cold at night.

I was starting to get really fit and was able to keep up with the porters on the ascent, although I was only carrying 5 kg with me. On the descent, on the other hand, it was impossible to stay close. How they managed to launch themselves over that impenetrable terrain without ever falling I have no idea. However, I was the first to arrive at the final destination for one simple reason, the porters hold to some silly superstitions particular to themselves and so they don't go in, believing it to be bad luck. Some have never seen Machu Picchu despite having walked the trail hundreds of times.

Conversely, for me, seeing the place could be considered tremendous, good fortune, and the only difficulty I had, common to many travellers, was that of deciding how long to stay and admire such a marvel. How many days does it take for you to have had enough and no longer be amazed? As a child enamoured with the foreign number plates it had taken thousands, but as an adult, there's definitely a lower limit. With safaris for example, from the excitement over the first zebra to the boredom with a lion about ten days had passed. Imagine that with ruins that obviously don't move. However, even after almost two years, as the attractions and scenery kept changing, the 'WOW FACTOR' was still high every time.

In **Bolivia (43)**, I landed at El Alto airport, which is over 4,000 m high, ready to move to even higher altitudes to chase flamingos and visit a salt desert. In those days, I chewed coca quite legally, and perhaps, due to this alteration, I seemed to see the most beautiful but also the ugliest women in the world. Without being disrespectful, quite simply the beauty standards of the indigenous people are the opposite of ours, and for good reason. Since life is extremely hard, a woman is considered beautiful if she is strong, and able to carry heavy weights in a world without roads and wheels. These women work from childhood, rarely have the opportunity to wash and have a high mortality rate during childbirth. They always keep a hat on their head which they believe to be traditional, although it was in fact introduced by the Spaniards, towards whom they still hold a grudge. They are also systematically mistreated by their men. In fact, as you may have guessed, the typical image of living in a paradise in the middle of those beautiful mountains, far from the stresses of the modern world, just doesn't carry any weight.

Upon entering **Chile (44)** I was effectively back in a kind of Europe, in the sense that there is not much that is indigenous in that country. I had broken my laptop screen by dropping the backpack containing it from the table on which I was hurriedly filling out immigration forms, so I spent the first day looking for a way to replace it. Having found a retailer who could get the part for its weight in gold, I began a leisurely tour of the country. There was money for the repair in the famous contingency fund, so I was not unhappy about it.

A few days later, the spare part had indeed arrived, and the computer was ready and fully functional. The repairman, whilst picking it up, tripped in front of my eyes and crashed to the floor along with my computer. The screen was more broken than before! It was one of those situations where you're really annoyed but you just can't stop laughing. He wasn't hurt, but he was mortified. In the end, I didn't pay for the repair, but since I really needed a laptop, because my documentaries were on it, we made a strange deal that he would transfer the saved videos to another computer of his own, of a lower standard than mine, and give it to me in exchange for the broken one. I had no objection as I would walk out of the shop with something that worked. In fact, I did actually wonder if there was a worse laptop than mine. I had deliberately chosen a low quality one, along with my mobile phone, so as not to be a temptation for anyone.

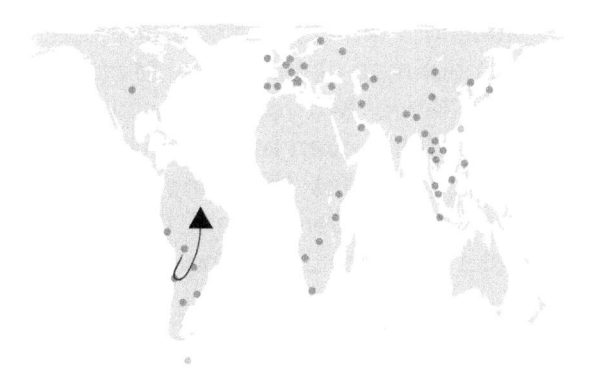

The year was coming to an end, and I was itching to go to Easter Island, which belongs to Chile, but the cost of flights was prohibitive. My Spanish had allowed me to exchange a broken laptop for a whole one, but my flight home, booked a year earlier, left from Rio so it was time to switch to Portuguese, a language I understood nothing of. I confidently went to **Brazil (45)** and like any good Italian, my hands spoke for me and often managed to make themselves understood, though not even numbers shown using fingers or hand gestures are universal.

On one of my first excursions, I met a bejewelled lady, who had felt inspired when, on recounting the tragicomic episode of my laptop, I had concluded that I was keeping it because I preferred traveling with nothing that was worth stealing. She told me that she was in complete agreement and in fact all her jewels were worth very little. I nodded, but I wanted to answer harshly 'That's smart, but do you really think that whoever wants to rob you knows that they are worthless?'. If they steal something of little importance from you in the hotel while you're out for a walk, the reasoning makes sense, but if they rob you on the street, you still experience a violent crime, and the value of the objects counts for little. On the contrary, you also risk having things you care about stolen from you, like perhaps your mobile phone and passport, just because they are attracted by the fake sparkling jewels. You should never call attention to yourself, although it is good to have a nice large denomination note hidden in your pocket so that if you are robbed despite your precautions, the criminals will be satisfied, and you will be safer. They're risking trouble, possibly jail, and if they get nothing, not even enough for a fix or a drink, anger and despair could lead them to punch you, or worse.

My advice to those with a backpack would be to use jewellery in the opposite way to that demonstrated by this lady. Some tribal or fabric bracelets, in my opinion, symbolise an exhibited poverty, as if to say I am a tramp with no money, I have nothing worth stealing. I didn't have one of those bracelets, but I looked like a poor man all the same. My blue sweatshirt, worn almost every day for two years, would have been unacceptable in Rome. I didn't even have a shirt with me, my underpants had more scribbles (from the various laundries writing the hotel room number in pen) than any free fabric left, and my socks had the classic holes. But it was my gear that I had grown fond of, and I didn't want to change.

I returned to Rome on a low-cost flight that I wouldn't wish on anyone, because 12 hours in those conditions are just too much, but I didn't mind the discomfort at all. After experiencing such privations at various points on my journey, I could get used to sleeping on a wooden bench with the light on in jail if I needed to.

The second year was over, and I was beginning to feel more confident. I felt that this school had been useful, and I could be moderately satisfied. The days had often been intense, and I had developed incredible stamina even though I was mentally tired in the evenings, because speaking in another language and being constantly culturally stimulated is exhausting. I had begun to learn a lot of things, even trivial facts, about 50 or so countries. The number of books I'd read and documentaries I'd seen by the end was impressive, but then again it had been my full-time job. And speaking of work, all around me, in the off-season, all I had seen were hordes of elderly tourists. I was so privileged! I could travel now, at my age, without waiting for retirement. More to the point, as everyone was so keen to remind me, would I ever have a pension since I had only a few years of contributions? Well, I would have to think about that in a few months. Looking for work at the beginning of summer makes little sense, much better to try in September…

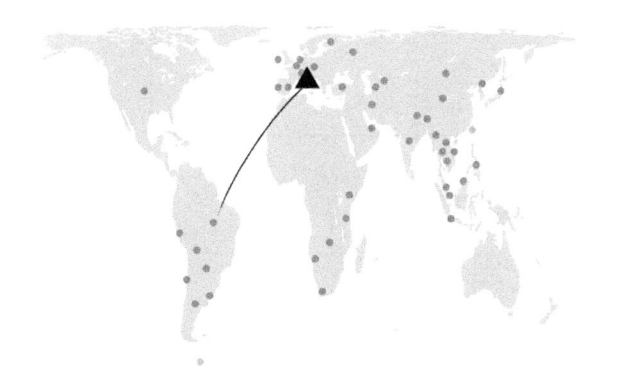

YEAR 2

SPAIN	TURKEY	UZBEKISTAN
RUSSIA	VIETNAM	CAMBODIA
UNITED ARAB EMIRATES	TURKMENISTAN	SOUTH AFRICA
NAMIBIA	MALAYSIA	PHILIPPINES
SINGAPORE	BRUNEI	INDONESIA
ARGENTINA	URUGUAY	PARAGUAY
PERU	BOLIVIA	CHILE
BRAZIL		

45/193

YEAR 3

Not wanting to stop just yet, I came up with a cunning compromise with myself which essentially entailed continuing to travel until the end of the summer, another four months longer than planned. I was so into the idea of 'school' that I visualised the next year as not starting until the autumn term…

I went to the Caucasus and visited **Georgia (46)**, **Armenia (47)** and **Azerbaijan (48)**. Apart from underestimating certain aspects of the mountains, for example, I would seriously advise a calculation of at least one degree drop in temperature for every 200 m of altitude, I had also overlooked the pitfalls of going from Armenia to Azerbaijan, two opposing nations. In fact, there are no direct flights and to get from one country to the other I had chosen to fly via Moscow, thinking that making a stopover in Russia would solve any problems, despite this involving travelling over 4,000 km rather than a few hundred. Instead, in Armenia, I suffered a long delay due to numerous questions and absurd demands, and finally was only given a boarding pass for Moscow, despite the fact that my journey continued with the same airline.

In Russia, the conflict between the two countries was of

no interest to the airport staff, but I still lost hours because of the Iranian visa in my passport. I was detained for further checks, and it took some time for an English speaker to arrive. I showed photographs of my trip to Iran to clarify the fact that I was merely a tourist, and finally got my new boarding pass for Azerbaijan where, as you may have already guessed, the fresh Armenian stamp caused me more trouble. After various questions and searches, I was allowed through, as long as I gave up my shoehorn as they had never seen one and according to them, it could be used as a weapon!

These minor difficulties with immigration rules were only just beginning. My two-year electronic visa for the US had expired and I applied for another one. This time the application was rejected because I had been in Iran, and I had to return to Rome to be interviewed in person at the US embassy. I took advantage of the enforced trip home to also apply for a visa for Tibet, which leads me to a necessary word of caution.

Whereas obtaining a Chinese visa is simple it's better not to declare that you are going to the autonomous region of Tibet because this will complicate the procedure. Only after having obtained the Chinese visa should you apply to the Tibetan agency to get their permit as they have an interest in you visiting the region and will handle the paperwork competently. This way, as long as you are not a journalist or political activist, you should have no problems. And provided you are not applying for entry during 'sensitive' periods such as when the Chinese government expects protests from Tibetans. During those periods, Tibet is closed so that any cruel repression cannot be witnessed.

In the meantime, since the Iranian stamp created so many problems, I contacted the Israeli embassy because I was afraid that this infamous stamp would be an obstacle to entry. Fortunately, this was not the case, although I had to prepare myself for lengthy questions and scrutiny upon arrival in Tel Aviv. This was something I was beginning to get used to, always remaining optimistic since I have a good Italian passport that arouses hardly any suspicion of terrorism and raises a few laughs about pizza and spaghetti. In addition, my surname is Ferrari, which at once makes way for the classic joke that no, I don't own one, and if I did, I would surely have arrived by private plane, yet here I am travelling around by bus…

I had thought I was ready for the interview at the US embassy, but I had completely overlooked the issue they were concerned about, which is traditionally associated with an Italian passport, namely clandestine entry or overstaying one's permit and then looking for work. I was a man who had no job, and no home or dependants in Italy, in short, the number one suspect. Surprised by the refusal and annoyed that I hadn't even thought about it, my reasonable objection, was that those trips, which were clearly visible from my passport, showed that I had certain financial resources at my disposal and was obviously not someone desperately looking for a job. They replied that they were willing to give me the visa, but on condition that I came back with something other than stamps in my passport. I could either get married, buy a house, or get a job. I played a huge bluff and said I was planning to start work very soon and was already in advanced negotiations. Years of poker were coming in handy. They gave me an appointment two weeks later.

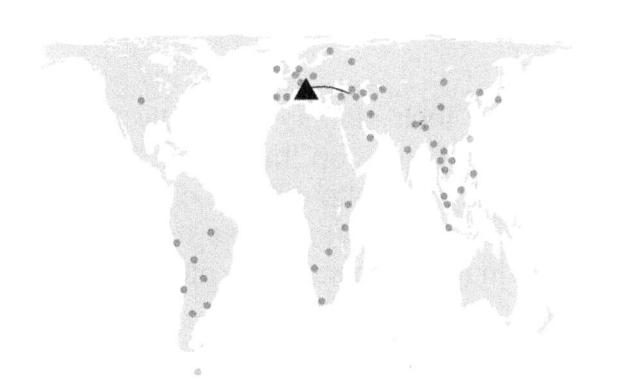

In the meantime, I got my Chinese visa, forwarded the documentation to Tibet and booked my trip to Israel and Palestine. I decided to forgo America as I didn't want to wait for the response on the US visa before beginning the planning and there was a high possibility of failure.

Two weeks later my fears had vanished because I had obtained my visa instantly, having chosen the simplest option. I had been hired on a permanent basis thanks to the help of a friend, only to resign afterwards. I had abandoned the planned trip, but my intention was to go to the United States to do something other than the usual visit to Las Vegas.

This time I was interested in the central states, those of the Bible Belt, which is a kind of imaginary band that unites the regions where the Bible is an indispensable point of reference in daily life. I was looking for a small town where I could spend a few weeks and experience a mentality that was so very different from my own. To this day, when someone comes back from the United States and enthusiastically tells me about their experience of discovery, I put them on the spot by immediately asking, 'What is the smallest village you visited there?'

The United States is huge, spanning everything from skyscrapers to religious communities, Indian reservations, *Inuit* in Alaska and Polynesians in Hawaii, but without going into detail, there are two significantly distinct realities: the coastal areas and the interior. This is a huge generalisation, but it gives the idea.

The big coastal cities and their states, especially California, are the most innovative places on the planet. In addition to technology, they also propagate culture, civil rights blossom here, along with the open-mindedness that often extends to the entire West. In the interior, on the other hand, society is traditionalist, and deeply Christian, to the point that in some schools Darwin is not studied and people believe in Noah's Ark. People cultivate the land and live in small communities.

It is important to bring this into focus, especially because travelling around the world one often comes across people who either love or hate the United States. And they do so for different, indeed conflicting reasons! In fact, there are those who hate America because it is so modern, without identity, a melting pot, a forerunner for limitless freedom, sexual display and of course capitalism and big finance. All of these are thinking about the coastal areas.

Others despise that same America because it is too religious, and fanatical, with people who want to go around carrying guns, who don't possess passports and don't know that Europe is not a single nation.

Even for those who admire America, this double mindedness applies. There are those who extol its integration, its excellence, its production of culture, its scientific discoveries, and its world-leading universities. The few who love the America of the central states, appreciate their devotion to work and how they are practically the only place on earth to defend Christian values in the world; perhaps they are the last strong religious outpost in advanced and secular countries.

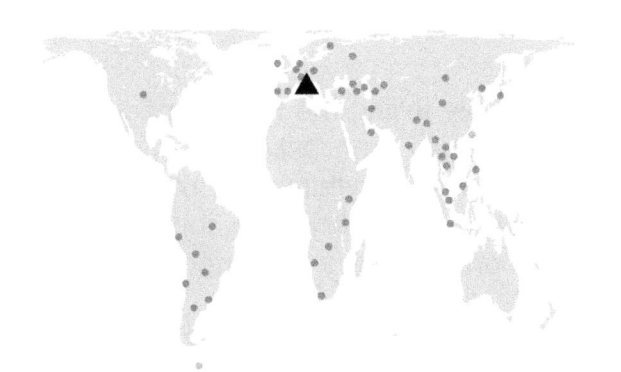

I left for **Israel (49)** but first I put some thought into what the best way would be to present myself at the border. After much deliberation, my battle plan was very simple: tell the truth, namely that I had been travelling for over two years, that I used to play poker, and that I had been to Iran out of curiosity. Of course, I would appear unusual, but in the end, that was how it was. I printed documents to support my answers to the possible questioning.

The incriminating stamp was spotted immediately as expected. They didn't bat an eyelid at the poker, nor at my quest for adventure, indeed my passport spoke for me as it was crammed with stamps and had few pages left. Moreover, I had just obtained a visa for the US, so I had passed an important screening. But they still kept me in a room for several hours.

At intervals, someone would come in and ask me slightly outlandish questions. The first was a woman who handed me a piece of paper and asked me to write down my grandparents' names. It was an easy task, even though they are long deceased, and I don't think any of them were on Facebook or the internet to check this out, so maybe the only information needed was to see that they had an Italian name. Later a young man came and again very politely asked me to make a list of the things I had in my suitcase. Had it been a school assignment I would have been delighted, as it's the one subject in the world that I'm most knowledgeable about, I would have chosen it myself as a favourite topic! But here, now? Would I appear suspicious if I was able to be so precise?

Faithful to the idea of simply telling the truth, I made as complete a list as possible. They then asked me if I had done my military service because everything was folded and rolled up so neatly. In Israel, military service is compulsory and long, and it is common practice for young men to leave for several months once their service is over. They might have imagined that I was doing the same. What I had not anticipated, and what perhaps made the wait so long, were the questions about the entry and exit stamps on the same day for the United Arab Emirates.

Now, as mentioned, I have a friend there, so on several occasions when I would transit from Dubai, I would take a long flight connection and meet him at the airport or somewhere nearby for a few hours. Hence those stamps. Eventually, I was let through and given a sheet of paper that was valid for entry so as not to leave any traces in my passport, thus avoiding getting a tourist into trouble if they wanted to travel to countries hostile to Israel. At this point, I thought my battles with immigration were over, but little did I know how many more adventures, or rather misadventures, I would have in the future.

Tel Aviv is a wonderful city and so well organised that it makes you want to live there. Jerusalem, on the other hand, struck me as being very small. Did all those countless things I have studied and pictured actually take place on this tiny pocket handkerchief of land? Was it the famous promised land?

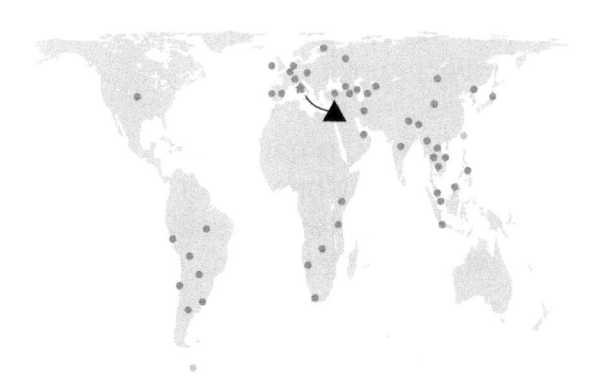

As already discussed, we can imagine America as being divided into two distinct areas, but Israel shows an even more pronounced contrast. On the one hand, it has a modern, educated population, full of initiative, and then, in comparison, there is that significant segment of the population that lives by scrupulously following religious precepts, the orthodox people, who are poorly educated, and have birth rates higher than many African states and no awareness of the rest of the world.

I found a very cleverly organised tour: I would go around with an Israeli and a Palestinian guide each giving their respective versions of the facts in different places. Both were extremely polite and respectful people, who were used to working together. I visited **Palestine (/)** which I do not count in the 193 nations because it is now a 'Permanent Observer State to the United Nations' and not a member. I slept at a hostel run by a man with a distinct Indian appearance. His grandfather, indeed from India, had come here at the time of the British protectorate. He had obtained a Jordanian passport, while his son had an Israeli one.

Jordan (50) itself was a pleasant surprise, being well prepared for tourism, and offering every service. My arrival coincided with the period of *Ramadan*, the Islamic month of fasting, so I also participated in this experience of self-denial, which includes no water but is also intermittent since you can eat and drink as much as you like after sunset. I took part for the whole week with the exception of the day of the visit to Petra, an important archaeological site, when I had to walk more than 20 km in the sun so I would sneak into the bathroom and secretly have a drink of water.

At night I joined in the enormous, organised banquets in the company of my guide, ate to my heart's content and binge-watched TV shows until I collapsed. To some extent it's like our Christmas time when all the big films come out and we visit relatives and spend time with family. In a hot country, however, much of the day is wasted sleeping or dozing so as not to suffer from the deprivation. Perhaps in the old days, the rule allowed one to feel close to the poor and better understand their suffering, but today, for a whole lunar month, very little work is done, and everyone hauls themselves around wearily.

At the taxi rank in **Morocco (51)** I was literally dragged from one place to another by someone trying to get me into his car, causing me to fall to the ground. Secretly I felt like *Jessica Rabbit* when she asks if anyone has a light and I soon realised that it was better to take a cab that passed by on the street, so that at least there was no fight for the customer. I've often reflected on taxis, regardless of the country, and my initial instinctive hatred has mellowed into a more rational appraisal.

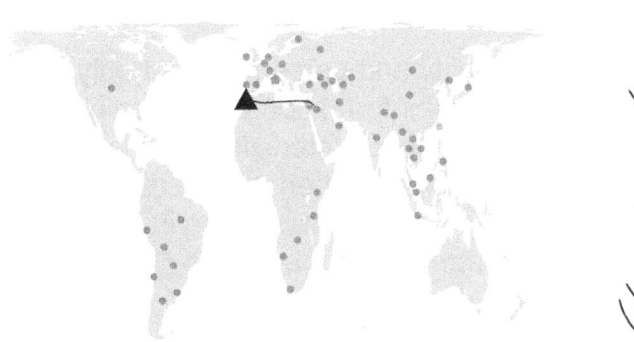

The way the job is structured, there must be a strong, sometimes irresistible temptation to rip someone off when the driver sincerely thinks he has a rich person on board to whom the loss of a little extra cash was of little import. In some cultures, there isn't even any shame in cheating a foreigner. Taxis are always on the move, so they don't have to build customer loyalty, there are often no fixed fares, the tourist doesn't know the route and the game is based on lack of understanding of the language. It's a business in which there are few professionals, many drivers being unqualified since at the end of the day, all you really need is a car. Certainly, this overcharging is dishonest, but as well as taking the extra €5 from the contingency fund so as not to get angry, try to remember that for any job you do in Italy you earn perhaps ten times more than someone doing the same job in that distant country.

If that's still not enough to reduce your ire towards the profession, there is much more. You are honest, and therefore perhaps a little timid towards the taxi driver, but in actuality, it's primarily the cabbie who is afraid of the customers. The nature of the job requires them to go wherever is requested, often alone and outnumbered by two or three people sitting in the back, added to which they carry a lot of cash, making ambushing them very easy. On the other hand, if the taxi driver asks you if they can pick up a friend of theirs who is going the same way as you, that puts you at a numerical disadvantage and for your own safety you should refuse even if he offers you a discount.

I flew to China and then on to Tibet, a place so mysterious and isolated that it was once thought that paradise might be hidden there. Often limited knowledge inspires people to build a very idealistic picture of a place in their imagination, which tends to remain later, so this land is still perceived as mystical and fascinating, despite more recent reports of its baggage of isolation, backwardness, and xenophobia.

This tension between reality and perception, not only remained after the British spread information at the beginning of the 20th century, but perhaps even intensified, to the point that Hitler's henchman Himmler imagined it to be the cradle of the Aryan people, writers such as James Hilton in *Lost Horizon* set the conquest of immortality there, and Hollywood saw Tibet as a place of central importance to the world. And of course, many genuinely believed that the 'abominable snowmen' lived there.

Tibet is actually an objectively inhospitable place for all humankind because of its geography. Nature is beautiful there for a few months of the year and you can experience clouds hovering just above or below you, but even in summer, such elevations are an obstacle to life. Giving birth at altitudes above 4,000 m is strongly discouraged, for example, and living permanently above a certain height is very hard. Yet even the geography has been reinterpreted and the numbers romantically changed into the attractive descriptor 'The Roof of the World'. But then, the cold mathematics does indeed show the average altitude to be higher than the summit of Mont Blanc (4,808 m), which is traditionally considered the Roof of Europe. Tibet is the highest plateau in the world and is home to some of the tallest mountains on the planet. It also boasts ice, crystal clear lakes and a sandy desert at an altitude of 4,000 m.

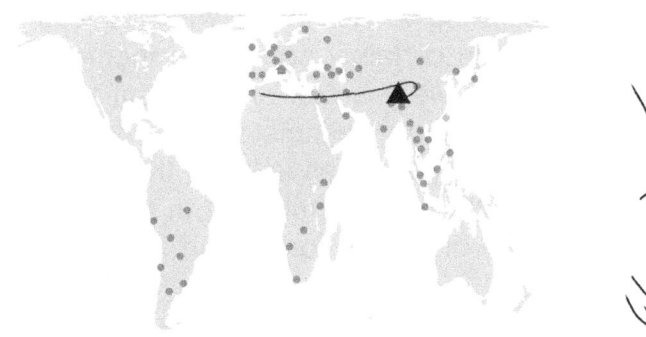

I arrived on the 'sky train', so-called of course because of the elevation at which the railway is built. During the journey you can take in breathtaking scenery as you ride the ultra-modern train along state-of-the-art rails through stations built at an altitude of over 5,000 m, some of them fully automated, needing no human personnel. It's a miracle of engineering, since taking trains across mountains poses great problems, not only due to the necessity for tunnels, but also because the steepness of the incline that they are able to ascend or descend is limited, requiring large turns to reduce the angles. Only in roller coasters or cartoons do trains go down steep inclines! During the journey, they pump oxygen to help the passengers and perhaps this hyperventilation prompted me to read the entire *Dream of the Red Chamber* which occupied me for the 48 hours on the railway. It was a good choice also because other books, whether on politics, religion or even merely containing a picture of the Dalai Lama are forbidden.

I had prepared well for the trip, having done a lot of homework, and was beginning to orient myself somewhat, culturally speaking, in this complex territory. From a physical point of view, I wasn't worried, having slept at 5,000 m in Bolivia with no ill effects and walked at 4,000 m in Peru. However, as a precaution, I took diuretics as recommended. It's not clear what the mechanism is, but they do help prevent altitude sickness. The other popular advice is to stay hydrated, so between drinking lots of water and taking diuretics, I arrived at Everest base camp having taken numerous toilet breaks. There I unfurled my pretty coloured flags, leaving the wind to pray in my place and apologised deeply within myself for a wrong perception that I realised I had embraced as I had grown up dreaming of a Tibet free of China.

For the first time following a visit somewhere, I was changing my mind, although certainly not on the methods used to invade Tibet, which were brutal and unjustifiable. From 1950 to the present day, some estimate the number of dead to be as high as one million. If, as is likely, they were many, many fewer, still nothing would change in terms of ferocity, violence, and total disregard for human life. Even without reliable numbers, to understand the horror the Tibetans must have experienced, one only has to remember that China is a nation that had no qualms about shooting its own students for protesting. Imagine the force of repression against Tibetans, who are sadly despised, and who have been openly rebelling for decades. This was clear to me.

What I had never realised on the other hand, was that communist China had brought civilisation and perhaps even freedom. Paradoxical but true, and I had needed to come face to face with it to realise it. They had built hospitals and schools, sent the monks to work and abolished slavery. In fact, the monks had controlled the economy as well as the religion. Trade took place in the monasteries that owned the land where you were forced to work, and they were also special banks. They collected compulsory and voluntary offerings. It was a tradition for Tibetans to give everything they had managed to save, only to then find themselves begging, perhaps even at the monasteries, where they could borrow money, but with interest. In fact, the system was a vicious circle that forced people to work for and depend on the monastery. Apparently, during some periods, one out of every six men was a monk and therefore refused to work because those who embraced that choice could not and should not toil. Elsewhere they would beg, but in Tibet the monks would force others to 'give'. For those who rebelled, there were terrible forms of punishment and torture was widespread. With the new Chinese master, namely the Communist Party, things are arguably not as bad. They'd tried to limit nomadism, but it is still widespread. Life expectancy has risen a lot and infant mortality is just slightly higher than in the rest of China. As they had been trying to dilute ethnic Tibetans to make them a minority in their region, during the years of the one-child obligation, minorities, including Tibetans, had been exempt from the rule.

Now, with economic prosperity, China has been able to really improve the whole territory, not just the capital, Lhasa. The Chinese are creating dams, wind turbines, tunnels, and road networks, as well as planting trees to increase oxygen, improve the landscape and mitigate the wind.

For the first time in my life, I saw the other side of a coin with my own eyes. When I had read about this, I'd assumed that the Chinese were the ones extolling their achievements for their own ends. Of course, Hollywood has had a lot of influence in making the world aware of the atrocities and in demanding an independent Tibet, but the truth is that Tibet is Chinese. There's no point in dancing around it. In a nutshell, I had changed my mind.

I flew to Nepal after hours of stringent checks at the airport, this time not so much for me but rather to prevent the escape of Tibetans from Nepal to the area in India where the Dalai Lama is in exile. In Kathmandu I could access Facebook again, at which point I realised that my cover image was still Tank Man, the mysterious hero who had stood in front of the tanks in Tiananmen Square with his shopping bags. If they had typed my name online at the Chinese visa office and found the picture, I would have risked not receiving travel authorisation. Or they might have first looked deeper into my itinerary, which was bogus! It turned out fine, but it was a huge mistake.

Next, I arrived at the last country on the programme, **Ethiopia (52)**. It was one of the most intensely beautiful trips ever, essentially a dive headlong into a world of the past where they cultivate the fields with a plough, donkeys are everywhere, and there is no widespread use of fertilisers, so the productivity of a field is very low. You can see the hard work that is put in for so little fruit and can better understand the stories in historic novels that tell of anguish over the harvest, the hunger of the peasants, and the suffering of backs broken down through fatigue.

Roadside shops display platters, glasses or other objects so that the illiterate can see what they are selling without reading the sign. The money is the dirtiest in the world as few people have a bank account in which to deposit or from which to receive new notes. Those sheets of paper go round and round and when you use one, you know it has been in dozens of people's underwear. As a visitor, it is a culturally rich country, but the poverty is a constant punch in the stomach. Tourists are given great consideration and smiles, and they always receive special treatment, perhaps out of kindness or maybe fear, and partly because they hope to get something in return. But it's certainly not because they live in the idyllic place that travellers imagine. If they were in paradise, they would smile at each other all the time, but in fact, they do so only to you.

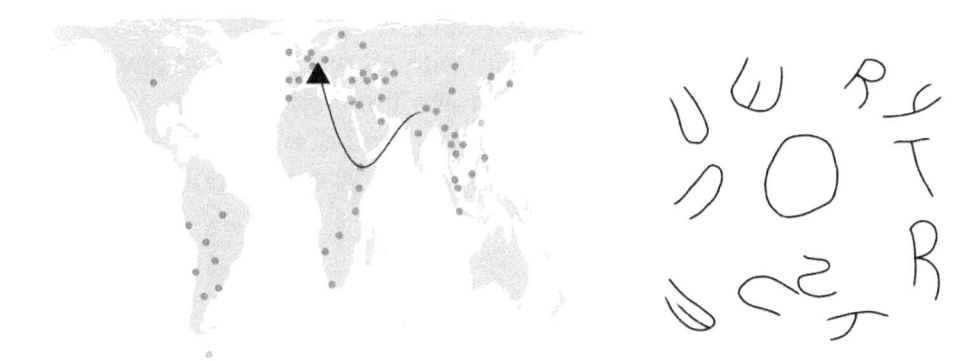

There was a hitch on my way home as my return flight was via Istanbul and just a few hours before boarding they announced a coup d'état in Turkey. My sister was still awake in the middle of the night because she was nine months pregnant and couldn't sleep, and she called me to say the Istanbul airport had just been closed. We solved the problem over the phone by booking a flight that got me home earlier than planned which was a good thing because not 24 hours later my second little nephew was born.

I mused on the fact that in ten years the child would be of legal age to work in Bolivia, and in Ethiopia, however illegal, he would probably have ended up in the fields even before the age of ten. I mentally repeated the phrase 'He's so lucky to have been born in Italy' which I found tiresome but increasingly true.

I was pursuing a degree as a globetrotter and now that I was back home, I wondered whether 28 months of travel school had been enough. I had taken 163 planes, slept 33 nights on trains, camped for 7 weeks, spent almost 1 month on a ship, and read at least 1 book on each of the countries visited.

I had learnt to open up to the locals, yet would still spend my time mainly with Westerners, especially if I met any Italians. I justified myself by thinking of motorcyclists who greet each other having only owning a motorbike in common. It was understandable that I was more likely to say hello to someone with whom I shared language, tradition, and habits. And I enjoyed that moment of peace that came alongside the perceived laziness of clinging to those who are predictable, and easy to cope with. A chat with Italians becomes a short rest from travelling, while with others you must always be alert and attentive. But to make the world a better place you have to travel and talk to those you don't know. Just as in order to make the roads less angry, every motorcyclist would do better to greet car drivers…

I've learnt to be confident over the years, having not had any bad experiences in hostels. I've slept alongside strangers all the time and never had anything go missing. I've perfected my English so well that I now understand the lyrics of songs and in fact, no longer like them. It would have been better not to have understood, and sometimes I would prefer not to and wish I could delude myself like the tourists who say they have found some famous paradise in a random corner of Africa or on a remote island.

While a heavenly place for me was not even on the horizon, I had understood the trick that some people use to achieve success in finding this. They project themselves as part of the elite of the place, in the month with the best climate, on the day of festivity and general merriment. Then they compare the pleasure of that special moment with the normality of their life elsewhere, and paradise appears! But I cannot do this.

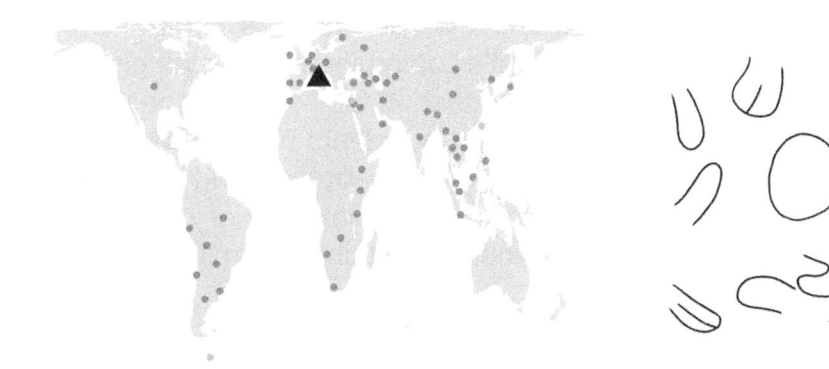

These are the same tourists who photograph a smiling child in Africa and think he is happy all the time, the same ones who immediately imagine great wisdom in the face of an exotic-looking old man because they see a deep, thoughtful gaze. In reality, if you're photographing him in a tourist place, he's probably thinking about what to sell you so that he can afford to take something home for dinner, or looking at what he perceives to be the tourist's immodest clothing and feeling shocked because in his life of limited opportunity he has gained no understanding of how the world elsewhere has changed.

Will this school of travel coming to an end for me leave a sense of discipline for life or will I soon be back to being the wimp who washes his socks as soon as he gets them off his feet? I was already putting on my flip-flops in the shower in the changing room of the swimming pool in Rome that gets cleaned all the time, while I had gone barefoot in the public toilets in Cambodia without a problem. Did I need a different environment to be different? Or maybe that was the beauty of it, having to adapt all the time?

I would certainly need to readjust to get a job. After finishing travel school, I would officially be unemployed and the only people optimistic about my future economic situation were the airline marketing departments, who were always ready to suggest that I travel business class. So, albeit without any clear ideas, I had taken a small office for myself where I was not doing much. The world of poker no longer interested me. Sometimes I was bitter that everything had disappeared so quickly, but more often I was grateful because without that money I certainly couldn't have left with such a light heart.

I was bored in Rome, but I was enjoying feeling safe. Except in very rare cases, the worst hazard is being pickpocketed on the bus, and that's something I had never given proper consideration to in the past. In fact, now maybe I felt too safe. For example, most car accidents happen close to home, partly because that's where people spend most of their time, and also because of the relaxation of being almost there. You feel safe when everything is familiar. I now considered myself 'at home' wherever I was in Rome. The smog and asphalt of the city, as ugly as they were, had come to feel like my protective shell.

With the new knowledge I had acquired, I followed foreign policy more closely, partly because I couldn't take any more of the news from Italy which was mainly accidents, tragedies, and the obituaries of anyone who had had a moment of notoriety in their lives. Perhaps this flood of bad news amazed me because when travelling one is taken to the opposite extreme as the world of tourism tries to show only beauty. Besides the holiday from work, they also try to sell the holiday from bad news. Even some documentaries are trying to sell a holiday, and so they enhance what is beautiful or only select what is appealing. Preparing scripts is easier when there is nothing negative to frame and explain. You can make almost any place look great with pictures anyway.

In contrast, printed travel guides can only use words, so when there really is nothing worthwhile, they are forced to clutch at straws and write that the big attractions of that place are 'vibrant cafes' or 'pretty restaurants'. If they then go so far as to open with 'despite the bad reputation, however...' don't even think about setting foot there. They must complete the guide, but you have the whole world at your disposal, so choose wisely. And maybe it's good to think before booking from those who exaggerate. Is it possible that this particular tour is the only 'real Brazil' or 'the most authentic Asia'? Are you sure that that place is 'the navel of Africa'?

I myself, in choosing some of my organised tours, had been carried away too much by sensationalism. I have realised that pursuing and understanding other peoples' traditions is important because that is the only way to succeed in doing better than them, learning and progressing. It is in traditions, customs and fashions that one can see how a populace likes to represent itself, how people see their past, and how history and myths can merge. Lies that are created over time and repeated become the new reality. Mind you, I have a strong impression that travel operators edit for their own use and consumption, too often offering a distorted, or at least blurred picture.

Here in Rome, for example, I am able to see this for myself as the fake gladiators receive more photos and enthusiasm than the ancient streets. These tourists will go home telling their friends and relatives about lions and tigers and not about how the Romans instituted the law. Was I visiting other countries in the same way, that is, spending too much time on their real or supposed 'gladiators'?

Or worse, perhaps I was behaving like an English tourist I had met in Israel, who came to Italy every year to watch the Sienese horse race, an event he loved with all his heart. The occasion is awesome, it exalts tradition, people love and cheer for their colours, and the city is in celebration, this is true, but on reflection, it is not pure love at all. There's hatred between the districts that goes so far as to celebrate the defeat of others, there is envy, bribery is made a legitimate instrument of competition because money can be offered to other jockeys, superstition is everywhere, and horses are blessed with holy water. I could see the good and bad of the Palio horse race or the Corrida bullfight, but in foreign countries, did I have the cultural tools to appreciate and exercise such a critical spirit? Was I able to recognise flaws and imperfections in a flower I did not know?

Some folklore events are treasures and it's there that a remote culture of past rituals and thoughts is hidden. Dreams, fears and hopes of yesteryear are in there and much of that information is mysterious even to local experts. But, for the person who seeks to learn at the school of travel, was I overlooking how the mediocre life of a Chinese office worker is more representative than a carnival masquerade involving a few hundred people? Did I know more about the normal lives of hundreds of millions of people after 28 months? Yes, but I had a strong doubt that I had not done enough. What did I know about the places where the bad news really is majorly predominant, the places where tourists don't go?

The globe-trotting degree that I felt was mine, based on the many countries I had visited, was perhaps not deserved. I had to sweat harder to achieve it, rethink my whole concept of travelling, go deeper and, at home also, work towards the goal now that I was no longer overwhelmed by planning the next day.

It was the right time for this, both personally and for those around me because there is a unique acceptance of differences in a person when they have just returned from a long trip, indeed there's actually an expectation from others that you will come back changed. In fact, if you leave for a long time and come back exactly as you were before leaving, people will think that you have been ignorant and learnt nothing. Change becomes a sign of seriousness and intelligence. If, in the course of your normal daily routine at home, you change your mind on major topics and values in life, you can sometimes be accused of being illogical, yet after being away this is expected.

Perhaps this opportunity to reflect freely without being judged for changing your view is one of the greatest qualities to be attributed to travelling. The only obstacle left is ourselves. We can dismantle and rebuild our beliefs thousands of kilometres away from home, and once back we can reinvent a better version of ourselves.

The final expenditure was €105,000, which was quite close to the €100,000 allocated at the start. Let's say I had spent an extra €5,000 from the contingency fund, for something that was not really an emergency. Perhaps the famous master's degree I had thought of years before would have cost me less and who knows what it would have given me in return. It was a legitimate doubt but one that certainly did not bother me, as I was reasonably convinced that I had chosen the right school.

Attending the opening ceremony of the Rio Olympics had been more fun than previous ones because I now knew the flag, language, population, religion, a bit of history, main tourist spots, key statistics and even a few bizarre and curious ones for some of the countries. I observed the faces and costumes of those who paraded, and sometimes I recognised athletes who had the features of a visited or studied minority. I was overwhelmed by the deluge of information and colours that remained involuntarily in my head. It was a feeling of pleasure, albeit mixed with the fear of the confusion being created there.

The news had recently appeared in the newspapers that a young student had invented a new word in the Italian language: *'petaloso'*, meaning full of petals. It was such a beautiful adjective that it had been accepted by the *Accademia della Crusca*, the highest authority in the field. Here was the word I was looking for: the world is a 'petalous' place. Every petal is slightly different, but they all belong to the same flower. It had taken a primary school pupil to help me visualise my memories in this way and manage to put them in order. And there were many more nations, or petals, still unknown to me.

I renewed my passport because the old one had almost run out of pages and decided to have eye surgery to remove short-sightedness. I'd been thinking about it for some time and during the trip my glasses had attracted negative attention. I strongly believe that we still tend to see the 'four-eyed' person as the perfect victim, and this can attract trouble. They were also uncomfortable and contact lenses were an unwanted complication. At one point someone had watched in amazement that something would come out of my eyes if I rubbed them. To be able to see so well again was a wonder, and who knows how much more pleasure I would now be able to have in those open spaces.

YEAR 3

GEORGIA	ARMENIA	AZERBAIJAN
ISRAEL	JORDAN	MOROCCO
ETHIOPIA		

52/193

YEAR 4

Many people would ask me about my trip, when actually, rather than wanting to hear me recount my experiences, they were desperate for an opportunity to utter the magic phrase 'I love travelling too,' in order to tell me about their own adventures. A popular question was whether I'd experienced the so-called *'mal d'Africa'* or African blues, usually followed by the intimation that they too missed it, both subtly communicating that they had also travelled in Africa and leading neatly into a tale of some adventure rich in imaginary dangers. But my answer was always 'Never.' I had felt no nostalgia for Africa. Perhaps I had stayed too short a time, but I doubt it, since a few months was almost certainly above the average amount of time one of these suffering travellers would have been able to spend there. Or, on the other hand, it could be because I had continued my journeying after the long periods in Africa and had seen so much nature elsewhere.

But now, shut away in my office, I felt nothing. In fact, right there in my tiny little room, I reflected that I probably wouldn't even suffer from the famous mid-life crisis, a condition that in my opinion afflicts those who have already made most of the important or perhaps final decisions in life. They've chosen whether or not to get married and to whom, where to live, what job to do, and if they'd like to have children, and are now wondering whether those were the right paths to take. I had made none of the big decisions. In fact, my mid-life crisis at its worst had taken place in a hostel, when the person accompanying me to my dormitory bed had made a point of letting me know that I had the one on the bottom since I was the oldest in the room. Considering that it had been some time since I had had any fun peeing in the communal showers, it seemed that I had indeed become a bit of an old man.

For a while now, I had mainly been wandering around my own neighbourhood, so much so that the longest journey I had made was to the **Vatican (/)**, a country I could reach on foot. This tiny land with less than 1,000 citizens, all men, is a Permanent Observer, like Palestine, but not a member of the United Nations so it isn't included in the count. I had visited the Vatican Museums on a school trip as a boy, but now, as an adult who had travelled, I appreciated the enormity of the collection of art from all over the world. Some see the evils of colonialism in the overflowing museums, others the greatness of Western civilisation, which is among the few capable of appreciating, disparaging, and cataloguing the cultures of others, continually making comparisons. Missionaries around the world were constantly collecting, buying, preserving, seizing, and stealing things to bring back to Rome. Everything is collected here for me instead of me having to travel myself.

I was not homesick for Africa, but I was bored after having had so much continuous action for months. No place is paradise, but what came close to heaven for me was moving from one place to another. The idea of continuing to travel was all-pervasive. Initially, I had left quickly, making a rough plan of action that had improved over time. But it was only now that I felt I had sufficient knowledge to return to the field, to study and to gain as complete a portrayal of the world as possible. I still had to visit many places and of course, this would require money, which I had, but it was no longer the money for the master's degree, it was my savings, my peace of mind. Could I spend it all like that when I no longer had any income?

To cut a long story short, I always gave myself the same answer, 'Yes, I could!' I was sure it would be money well spent as it was investing in myself. Phileas Fogg had almost been out of money before he found out he had won the bet, and at today's rates he had bet over two million pounds, everything he owned. There was also the possibility that I too could turn this expensive adventure into something profitable, like one of the expeditions of yesteryear perhaps, where you stake everything, travel for years and then hope to bring back something of value that repays the effort. No gold or spices, but lots of information and experience to maybe… write a book! This was what my (semi-) rational side was telling me, but in reality, I had quite simply become addicted to travel, it had become a vice. I, who had approached poker without allowing myself to get carried away, who knew when to get up from the table, had spiralled out of control with travel, a dependency not much considered by the scientific community. I'd said one year, then it turned into two years, which was quickly exceeded, and now I wanted to start again, this time without even setting an end point, as it was pointless to keep giving deadlines that I did not meet. I had said €100,000, yet now here I was gambling everything in a way that I would never have done at the poker table.

I headed to the travel vaccination clinic first, where they asked where I wanted to go. Mockingly I replied, 'EVERY-COUNTRY', which they took seriously, injecting me with everything as if I were a soldier who must be ready to be assigned anywhere in the world. That evening I couldn't raise my arms due to the various shots, but by the next day, I was fine. The second port of call was a computer shop. I'd realised in the past few months that I couldn't brag that I'd bought the worst laptop in the world anymore because the one from the Chilean repairman was even more useless. I needed a new one, and yet, to my astonishment, I had to admit that I had grown fond of that piece of junk. When you only take a few things with you on a journey, each one becomes important.

It was time to take my passport to the Indian embassy as I wanted to pick up where I had left off. Before the main adventure outside Europe, I went to see a friend in **France (53)** who I tried to involve in the trip to India, but the most I managed to achieve was to visit **Monaco (54)** with him, with the casino as our destination just to remember the old days. After that, I finally got on a plane to **Slovenia (55)** to visit another friend. Flying almost felt like a new emotion after a few months of abstinence. I really love the aeroplane, where you are over 10,000 m from the ground, seeing for hundreds of kilometres from the window, and travelling at almost 1,000 km/hour. Eating seems so good too, whether to alleviate boredom, or because the food often seems to me to be seasoned with clouds.

I got the visa for India on my own this time, even though tension over a case involving two Italian marines accused of accidentally shooting two Indian fishermen had made applications submitted by Italians more complicated. I would visit the mountainous areas that are now the refuge of the Dalai Lama in exile from Tibet, arrive in Amritsar, the sacred city of the Sikhs, and then go south, primarily to Kerala. Finally, I would travel to Mumbai, where I would stay in a very luxurious hotel called the Taj Mahal after the famous mausoleum. I'd booked a room for $250, a monstrous price by Indian standards and the most expensive I had ever paid. But there was an ulterior motive behind this one night of seeming extravagance as it allowed me to join the guided tour that the hotel offered at 5 pm every afternoon. At dinner time, however, I had a problem as I was not allowed into any of the restaurants because I didn't have a shirt or proper trousers. I was a welcome guest at the hotel in my traveller's attire, I'd walked from the pool to my room in a swimming costume without a problem and taken the lift in my bathrobe, but I had to eat somewhere else. As I returned, a swarm of beggars materialised around me when they realised where I was heading. I was out of the habit of seeing hungry children and when you then have to say 'No' and return to your luxury room, you feel even more disheartened. As if a refusal made in front of an expensive hotel has any more impact on someone who is starving than the same denial outside a cheap hostel!

The Taj Mahal hotel is unique, whereas the hotel rooms of the big chains usually look so similar that no one pays attention to the details. I was so accustomed to the constant change of accommodation in the previous years that even on this occasion I didn't look at the paintings that hung there. For me the room was just a facility, it gave me no aesthetic pleasure. Had it not been for the guided tour, I would never have come here. The next day I went to my subsequent accommodation in Mumbai, which cost less than a tenth, but still had one much sought-after element of privilege that was probably not experienced by many of the inhabitants of this crowded city: my own bathroom.

I flew to **Sri Lanka (56)** and during the journey, a printed newspaper was distributed on board. In the obituaries, they expressed the wish that the deceased would reach Nirvana, a new angle that made the ever-present string of deaths in the newspapers seem a little more bearable to me. As a lover of gaming, I was fascinated by the fact that the number draws reported were for the Buddha lottery, but the most absurd news story of all recounted the number of elephants that had been rescued whilst swimming in the open ocean, perhaps pushed out to sea by the current.

From my miserable little room, I could hear more noise than I'd endured in Mumbai where the horns never stop, and here it was doubly annoying because they were doing renovation work a short distance away. The workers would set up shop on a tiny table in front of their scaffolding every morning. They would climb up, and get on with their ear-splitting toil, but if a customer passed by, they would come down and sell him a coconut. What a brilliant way to supplement your income! Initially, I was amazed by those little shops around the world in out-of-the-way places that only sell water, soft drinks, crisps, sachets of shampoo, a few phone top-ups, biscuits and little else – basically just non-perishable goods. A woman usually sits inside all day doing some chores, occupied with the same activities she would do at home. With a small amount of money, anyone with a street frontage can start up an enterprise that appears pointless as it earns very little money, but it is in fact better than nothing.

At the beach, whilst jogging after sundown, I found myself surrounded by a pack of dogs. They were small to medium-sized but there were about ten of them and I didn't know what to do. There weren't any stones or anything else I could throw so I ran into the sea to try to get out of their territory, hoping that they would then lose interest.

I had to swim with one hand because the other was busy keeping my mobile phone out of the water and kept hoping that someone would come to rescue me as they had with the missing elephants, but no one was nearby. After a few seconds of indecision, I slipped off my shoes and socks to keep myself afloat. This farcical scenario with a frightened man keeping his arm outstretched holding his mobile phone as he kicked to take off his shoes eventually ended well as the dogs didn't follow me into the water. This would be the first of many bad canine experiences on islands, and in fact the smaller the islet, the more intense the problem. Especially at night the neighbourhood becomes theirs in a way that I would never have expected. I understand that it's difficult to get an idea from a simple story, but apparently, they reproduce quickly, join together in packs that fight each other and take over entire areas, making them extremely dangerous.

Back in India for the umpteenth time, I found myself

assailed at the station by requests for money, this time from an enormous group of people with the most striking deformities I had ever seen. Evidently, there are those who seek out these unfortunate people in the villages, put them on trains and take them to the city. They move between stations, temples and mosques, some being pushed in a wheelchair by another person who perhaps also has problems that make them unable to work. It's a full-blown organisation, exploiting displayed pain to make money.

But what other sources of income could such unfortunate people have in a country with little institutional support? Their families aren't always helpful. Perhaps to really judge I would have to know how they are treated and how they divide the money they receive, but that is information I will never have.

In any case, I gave nothing as usual, not because I was afraid that the money would end up with the exploiters, but because giving charity on these occasions is dangerous. You are surrounded by so many who ask in good faith because they see your generosity, and it's easy for some ill-intentioned person to creep in amongst them, and then between a tug and a plea, the risk of being pickpocketed escalates.

I had lost my train ticket in this chaos and was stopped on the way out for a spot check. Certain of receiving a fine, I was surprised to be asked how much the ticket had cost for the route I had claimed to have travelled. When I answered correctly, they let me through.

From there I flew to **Bangladesh (57)**, a country a quarter of the size of France but with three times the population. There are more people here than in Russia. I spent about ten days with an exceptional guide who genuinely put me in touch with the local people as much as possible. I visited one of the largest brothels in the world, with hundreds of women and girls offering services starting from 50 cents. Whole families live inside the brothel and as soon as a customer arrives, the woman stops her domestic activities. Children are born and raised there. I spent a day in the ship cemetery where the carcasses are dismantled and recycled by a huge number of workers. Every family in that area has suffered a bereavement or has an amputee at home who was the victim of a work-related accident.

I wanted to visit a huge *Rohingya* refugee camp nearby. Unfortunately, this population is mistreated by everyone. They have been violently expelled from Myanmar because they are Islamic and, according to the Myanma, not native to the country. And so, they are forced to make a risky journey to poor Bangladesh, a country that is not in a position to help much. In order to enter the camp, my guide and I stationed ourselves in one of the many makeshift bars on the nearby road. Pretending to want to rest, we waited for an hour and it was them who came up to me and asked who I was. I said I was in the area to visit the longest natural beach in the world, an uninterrupted 120 km. They suggested that I should be careful because it was a dangerous area and after some small talk, as expected, they invited me to see what the situation was. Now I was in the clear, I had been invited directly by the people who were making the area unsafe! I left a donation at the end of the visit, stating the amount aloud so that at least the village head who had pocketed the money couldn't claim that I had given a different sum.

As I left, I saw something that left me more horrified and saddened than by all the demands for money at the station in India. A few metres away from me, a naked child, about three years old was crawling around on his hands and knees, all alone, continually putting things he found into his mouth. He had no eyes.

Now in Rome, my world is made up of a very few people. Most of them grew up in a good neighbourhood and are university graduates. I live in a bubble of well-being. In just a few days I had become aware of hundreds of women forced to take steroids in order to gain weight to please truck drivers or sailors, inexperienced workers risking their lives for a scrap of metal, and hundreds of thousands of refugees in a country that is already poor itself. Yet as sad as these things were, on this occasion, though reeling from the reality of so many needs and so few solutions, it was the single tragedy of the abandoned blind child that had completely shocked me. I was struck by the similarity of my experience of deep sadness for the person who had eaten the dirty leftovers of my chicken leg left in the car to be cleaned, when again I had not cared as much that around me so many seemed even poorer and in trouble. As I travelled, I was meeting people in a condition that hardly exists in Italy, and, if it did exist, I wouldn't be in contact with it.

Quite reasonably in Bangladesh, some people looked at me in amazement when they found out that I was a tourist, probably thinking that if I was lucky enough to live in such a nice place, why on earth would I come there? It was difficult to explain that I was curious, that I wanted to see with my own eyes and that certain hardships, when you know you will soon be somewhere else, become experiences, even entertainment.

On the bus, everyone was ready to find me a good seat, but the real fun was in travelling on the roof. And on the train, I had my reserved seat but chose to stay near the open doors because I had never travelled that way before. Of course, it's dangerous, but less so than it looks, as the train goes about 20 km/hour, and the bus maybe even slower.

There is so much chaos on the streets that you need a conductor on board to act as a helper for the driver. This is a boy, sometimes a child, who gets out to check if there is enough room to pass, talks to the other cars hoping they will move over, and helps with manoeuvres, especially reversing. Sometimes they don't have shoes on their feet, and I doubt they go to school. On the train, you see a lot of people inside the locomotive because the train drivers supplement their wages by pocketing the money from these extra passengers.

On the boat, my guide had booked me the only single room and I had my own personal helper to serve me meals and keep an eye on me. The boy could not get over the fact that I was always absent from the most privileged place on the ship, but for me, the curiosity and novelty were in being out and about, walking among the chickens, marvelling at the amount of luggage.

As soon as one person asked me something, a huddle would form. I was an attraction like any other, and in fact, here crowds formed for everything, personal space doesn't exist. If two people talk together, those nearby blatantly listen in, without doing anything to hide it, indeed they will join in the conversation. Physical contact is inevitable, constant, and accepted. After just a few hours together on the ship, previously unacquainted people appear to me like a group of high school kids on their way out of school, with their hands on each other's shoulders, slaps, half-hugs, and their legs stretched out over another's knee.

Just as I was starting to feel like a good person because I was joining this bath of humanity, from the fifth floor of my hotel room I watched an enormous downpour, so heavy that it was difficult to see. I could, however, make out people running haphazardly from all sides, the makeshift vendors intent on rescuing their goods, and rickshaws opening their already-soaked hoods. For some reason, the scene amused me, perhaps because I had just returned and was revelling in my lucky timing. Or maybe I was enjoying the sound of the rain beating down on others. I was listening to the sound of my own selfishness.

Yet another passage to India was next, and inevitably during the flight my neighbour had taken possession of the armrest. Now I could easily have put my arm on top of his without him complaining, and perhaps that would make more sense than adopting the approach two Japanese people might have, which would be for neither of them to use it at all so as not to appear intrusive.

I often reflected on how to behave, and I was continually trying things out. In these *no gap* societies where there's never a space that's not immediately occupied, you have to get a bit pushy, or you lose out. In China, if you get distracted for a moment in the queue, they pass you by, and in

India, you need to jostle a little. And anywhere in the world, you have to carve out your own space in hostels and dormitories, never asking other people for it. If it's reasonable, you put your things there, turn off the light, open the window and so on. I also felt very experienced in knowing when it is good to say goodnight or not, but even more complex was knowing how to say whether you feel like chatting or really want to sleep.

I arrived in Goa where I played poker to see how I would feel. The answer was simple: bored. In the months off at home I had never played because I knew I was no longer having fun and to earn money you need time, perseverance and commitment. But here I wanted to try because the environment was completely new. After all, Goa itself is special, it was Portuguese until 1961 and has maintained its unique character. In contrast, a city where everything has changed in a very short time would be Dubai, in which I arrived for the usual plane transit. Until a few decades ago, it had been a desert that was used just to refuel planes due to its strategic location, but hardly any passengers travelled there. Today, however, it has boomed to become one of the most visited places in the world.

I reached **Egypt (58)** where two people were waiting for me holding a sign with my name on it. I don't usually book the transfer from the airport to the accommodation because it costs a lot, it can be hard to meet up, sometimes I haven't yet bought the local SIM card and a phone call to the driver doubles the cost of the transfer, or there's a possibility that I'll be very late, and I don't want to keep people waiting.

More often, it tends to be the person who picks me up who is late because they think it takes a long time from landing to getting through to arrivals, whereas in fact, I jump out of the plane, crack the joke about pizza, spaghetti and Ferraris at immigration, and then have no luggage to collect. But this time, mindful of how I had been manhandled into a taxi in Morocco, I had booked a transfer when I bought my plane ticket. In the run-up to the trip, I had repeated over and over, 'I pay a little more, but I save myself the worry.' I was pleased that I had persisted in my reasoning, but then two cars appeared. Maybe I could get into one and put my suitcase in the other! After a pleasant bit of banter, I chose the driver who spoke better English, so for that person, having a skill became a drawback. The other driver could go straight home, while he first had to deal with the traffic in downtown Cairo where I was staying.

About 100 million people live in 5% of the total area, but coming from Bangladesh I didn't find the country crowded. The real nightmare was the insistence on selling. I don't shop, I only carry hand luggage, I don't return home, in fact, I don't even have a house. I hadn't bought anything frivolous since the kimono. Moreover, I hate haggling, and feel uncomfortable when they charge huge sums and then reduce them by a lot. We have outgrown this distasteful custom at the market, but we maintain it in court, where it is acceptable behaviour to ask for millions in compensation only to accept perhaps just a few thousand. Another curiosity is how the carpet is the only object that crosses borders and carries this culture with it. In fact, in Western shops, where prices are usually fixed, they are sold with a sign advertising an astonishing 80% discount. There are no such signs on souvenirs in Egypt, but one thing I have understood about bargaining, is that when the tourist says, 'He asked for $100, but I only gave him $20', he has forfeited the bargaining. He has lost because he started from the price he was asked. The tourist looks at how good he was at haggling, but it is not he who saved $80, it is the seller who cashed in $20. He lets the tourist boast and he is satisfied with the money.

For me though, the worst deal of all came every morning when a neighbourhood crank would come over immediately on seeing me and ask, without haggling, if I would send him stamps from Italy for his collection. Each time I explained to him that I wasn't going home, and he would make the face of someone who couldn't remember my answer. Yet he would remember that I was Italian...

I took the longest commercial flight on the market at that time and from Dubai, I arrived in Auckland, **New Zealand (59)** in about 17 hours. I was going to spend a few months in Oceania without much of a clear programme. I had picked this plane and the one returning from Australia to Poland, letting myself be guided by the prices.

Almost at the opposite side of the world to Italy, there are frequent, efficient buses available to travel around the entire length and breadth of this country. The road trip through this unique landscape is pleasant, with no advertising hoardings.

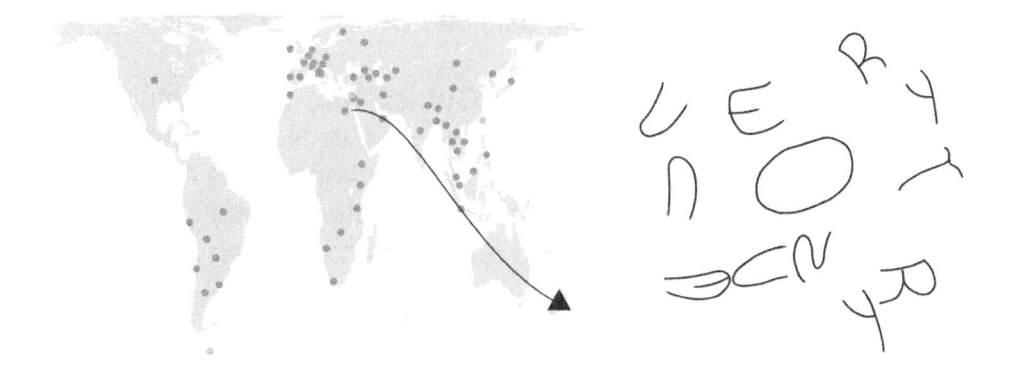

The South Island is so sparsely populated that the bridges have only one lane on which both directions alternate. It struck me how there would often be a caravan, camper van or some other form of camping equipment parked in front of the isolated houses. What need do they have for that kind of holiday when they already live in the middle of nature? Then I realised that there was simply nothing else to do! Any trip requires time to get to the airport and then hours of flying and huge costs. Moreover, for those who have a farm and animals to look after, holidays almost don't exist. We complain that technology makes us constantly available and therefore working, but here we realise that being a farmer or a shepherd is an occupation that keeps one's whole life on the job.

To visit the Maoris, I hired a person who was supposed to act as a cultural guide, but I found myself caught up in the usual tourist shenanigans. I learned ten steps of the dance made famous by rugby matches where you frighten your opponent by showing your tongue and threatening to eat him. I tried cooking in a hole in the ground. In a nutshell, I was engulfed by every imaginable Polynesian stereotype. As we left, I was invited to go to the bar, which we found closed, so the guide managed to get us a drink while we were waiting for it to open. At least he had been good for something, although maybe that was also part of his routine with the customers. However, my theoretically non-touristic adventure was just around the corner as I was soon to go to Papua New Guinea. When I mentioned this to a rather elderly American lady who had lived in Australia and was sitting on the same bus as me, she said she would pray for me…

The flight to **Papua New Guinea (60)** with a return to Australia cost me more than the one to New Zealand. In fact, it was the most expensive I had ever bought at almost €1,000. This country has the most isolated capital city in the world, Port Moresby with no real roads connecting it to other cities and only forest around it. It's the same for a few other cities in the world, for example, Iquitos in Peru which has to be reached by boat because it is surrounded by the Amazon rainforest, or Petropavlovsk in Kamchatka where you have to fly in because it is located in the middle of nowhere.

If the capital is isolated, imagine what the other areas are like. This huge island has high plateaus and mountains that rise to 4,000 m, and it sometimes snows, which is quite rare so close to the equator. There is forest everywhere, so much so that only the Amazon and Congo exceed it in size. Many isolated tribes live in remote areas in the interior, with so little outside contact that different languages have even developed between neighbouring tribes. There is such variety that today Papua is the nation with the most languages in the world.

The tribes live a long way from the coasts because it's cooler in the higher lands and more importantly, there are fewer tropical diseases. The island is volcanic, with fertile soil and plentiful water everywhere, and one of the two great rivers overflows every year, which has a beneficial effect on crops. It's easier to survive in the highlands than it is on the coast, and it's unnecessary to form large communities, quite the opposite in fact, villages are isolated and even kept hidden intentionally because each tribe is a potential enemy. There are constant wars, and the feuds, vendettas, and hatred are fierce. The more remote one is, the safer one feels. Until the 1930s, hundreds of thousands of people in the highlands of Papua were still living as if stuck in the stone age, and no one in the world had heard of them.

Port Moresby is one of the most violent cities in the world because the worst things in such a backward society are concentrated here. Young people with no future, excluded from the tribes, try to make a new life for themselves and risk becoming criminals because it is extremely tempting to go from boredom and unemployment to being an 'esteemed' gang member. Tribal fights escalate because no one is on their own turf anymore, it's an everyone against everyone else situation. Human life is worth little, and people easily slip into superstition and witchcraft. Secret societies and violent initiation rites still endure, and unfortunately beating women is the norm. Barbed wire is everywhere, and if you call a taxi from the hotel they ask if you want it standard, with an escort or with an armed escort. A significant portion of the population is constantly in a state of stimulation from chewing on the betel nut fruit.

I stayed only one day in the city. I was picked up from the hotel in one of their cars and the driver confirmed what I had already read about for myself: the gangs, called *raskol*, which literally means rascals in the local language, have shocking initiation rites, usually raping a woman in the street. Besides stealing, their modus operandi is the use of violence, even if it's unnecessary. One of the most frequent crimes is car theft, which is why you should never stop if someone on the side of the road asks for help, unfortunately, it's better to keep on driving. If you encounter an obstacle, it's best to speed up since they go so far as to throw themselves into the middle of the road, risking their lives to force the car to stop. And you are not allowed to open a gate yourself because they may be lurking there, waiting for someone to get out of the car. The market is also a place of unavoidable encounters between different ethnic groups and there are many women, which consequently means that the ladies' toilets are the site of frequent rapes.

I met an American girl as crazy as me at the airport in this unromantic city. She was going to see the mask festival that I was intending to go to and was staying in the same hotel. Who would have guessed at that moment that I would visit 15 other countries in quick succession with her?

The domestic flight is a geography lesson. From the window, you see with your own eyes the grandeur of the mountains, the looming clouds, and the green of the vegetation that covers everything. You land in Rabaul, a city recently destroyed by a volcanic eruption and now partly rebuilt, and the festival site is nearby. It's an occasion when the various tribes get together, perform, dance and earn money from ticket sales and the market that they set up. But since the tribes loathe each other, it's clear that they are being assembled by a manager, a neutral man, probably Australian, who does the organising. And so begins the struggle for visibility. The traditional costumes, already flamboyant and beautiful, are revamped to be more attractive, and appealing, ensuring that more photos will be taken. Where I was, the tribe that danced with fire was excluded from being with the others because it received too much attention, so they organised a small counter-festival of their own (at night of course) nearby.

To attend you had to drive there in the dark and my car was pelted with stones by members of the rival tribes to discourage participation. I went anyway and during the performance I was in the very front row, and an organiser came and told me to watch out for flying sparks and the risk of my hair catching fire. I was surrounded by dozens of local children with thick hair that he did not care to warn but after all, only I was his customer…

During the day, the town was full of people, so I walked around freely. Taking advantage of the fact that it was always raining, I had taken the largest and sturdiest umbrella I could find, so I didn't give the impression that I was afraid of anything, but I did have a strong stick available for every eventuality. I also had a brief experience of village life, since over 80% of the population here is not urbanised. The children use tiny boats with outriggers to reach the only school, which was on a small island. But those days were a long way from being the plastic, metal and electricity-free environment that I had perhaps imagined. Did I want to play at being an anthropologist from another time?

I doubt it was the lady's prayers, but the fact is that I got out of the country safe and sound and went to **Australia (61)** where I had already been as a student but having had no money back then, had travelled very little. Now there was both excitement and apprehension as I contemplated the 5,000 km of road that lay ahead of me. I also wanted to visit what was left of the hostel where I had slept for months in Sydney. That was a disappointment. It had become a real hotel and there was nothing left to stimulate any memories in me. Even the stairs where our possum had lived were no longer there.

In Tasmania, a large island to the south, I went to Port

Arthur, where there used to be one of the cruellest penal colonies. The British would send criminals to Australia to rebuild their lives in dramatic conditions and the most unfortunate would end up in Tasmania, with those who had rebelled and committed more serious crimes ending up in Port Arthur. In short, the worst of the worst came here in a kind of slavery, for once perpetrated to the detriment of whites. Today it's one of the most developed and civilised places in the world. In fact, they are the best possible proof that the theories on the heredity of criminal behaviour are hogwash.

The western part of Australia, on the other hand, is empty. You have to go there in person to realise that you are in the middle of nowhere. As with the Gobi in Mongolia, the Sahara, the desert in Namibia, even the long days of staked-out safaris, and the final 55 hours of the Trans-Siberian Railway, with my travels in general, it can be said that without experiencing the great boredoms, one loses perspective on reality. Collages of wonderful photos assembled after a long journey, or an adrenalin-fuelled video with constant changes of location, or even this book with one adventure after another, are misleading. In between, there is boredom, time, and effort. And a lot of thoughts.

In the centre of Australia there's a town where many Aborigines live. They walk around barefoot and follow their own rules. It is a most violent and dangerous place, and especially on Friday night, which is payday, it's best not to be on the streets. Many spend their money on drinking and the result is widespread violence, especially domestic, they beat their women. They possess the oldest culture in the world, so the ability to survive, developed in such harsh surroundings, is to be admired, but they carry with them some now unacceptable flaws. It would be very easy for a tourist like me to exercise tolerance when in their home, but that would be an acceptance granted at the expense of the weakest. I've developed the idea that people should be judged on how they treat women, rather than on smiles, invitations for tea or souvenirs.

Going to *Uluru*, the huge sandstone monolith sacred to that people, allowed me a less harsh opinion. It was nearly 500 km from the city I was in, through the desert where living conditions are extreme. There's no farming as nothing grows. There are no animals to tame, and to hunt what few there are, they have to set fire to large areas, destroying nature and taking enormous risks. But worst of all, you are covered with flies for many months of the year, literally swamped, and nothing will keep them away for long.

In such conditions, surviving is already a miracle. In fact, now I think back to the images of the past, in which some of the men had people fanning them, and I have a better understanding – it's not so much the heat, it's the insects that are hell! It's the same for both men and animals, and the latter don't even have hands to swat them away and their tails don't reach every part of their bodies, which explains their desire to stand next to train tracks or with their bottom on the side of the road where cars pass by. There is a bit of entertainment to be had maybe, but mainly they are making use of the continuous and effortless fanning that wafts the insects away as the vehicles rush past.

I camped in winter, so the conditions were better. There were only spiders at night, as well as a huge group of noisy tourists from Hong Kong who had wanted to be far away from there during the celebrations imposed by the Chinese regime to 'celebrate' the 20th anniversary of the return of the former British colony to China itself in 1997.

The discomfort you face is well rewarded though, as the monolith is enormous and magnificent, changing colour continuously as the sun sets. Climbing the monument was allowed just for entertainment, but the hike is arduous and long, to the extent that certain bodily necessities are necessarily performed up there. Imagine how an Aborigine would be treated if they climbed St Peter's or the *Kaba'a*. Yet in reverse, it was allowed. From the desert, the stars were beautiful, with no clouds, no lights, and little trace of humans. That place has become sacred and indeed couldn't be otherwise, just like the sky was for the Mongols. The Aborigines that I met boasted that they had always had a healthy and loving relationship with nature that Westerners cannot understand, so I listened in silence to an idealisation of the past, before the 'discoverers' of Australia arrived, that had no basis in fact. Certainly, I do not doubt that there was much love for nature but combined with fear, which would be entirely justified. It's horrifying to imagine living in those places without modern means. If, on top of that, hostile people come from far away and dump their criminals there, try to drive you out and take over the land, then the scene is just bleak.

The return flight was to **Poland (62)** where I had arranged to meet a Ukrainian girl who was studying in Italy. We visited Auschwitz together, but then I went alone to another tragic place, Chernobyl, in **Ukraine (63)**.

Despite the sinister name, the visit was easy and safe. There are plenty of agencies that will organise the whole package for you, allowing you to retrace the dramatic moments of the accident. Radioactivity is minimal, to the point that thousands of people have been living there permanently for years.

In one of the buildings symbolic of the tragedy, they display the cradles abandoned in a hurry and rusted by time. This was heartbreaking for me. I was too young to remember the days of the disaster, but I remembered that when I was 18, my then-girlfriend's parents would host one of the orphaned children for a few months a year as a way of keeping them away from the radioactive areas. They ended up adopting him. That had been such a beautiful and important event, but I had not given it another thought. It had taken seeing the cots for it to come back to my mind.

From Kyiv, I went to Moscow, a route that makes an impression now in the wake of the war, and then took one of the longest domestic flights that exist, approximately eight hours long, to get to Magadan, a city in the far east of Russia. Picking me up was a kind and very considerate man who candidly confessed to me on the way that he had just been released from jail, which didn't bother me in the least. However, when he suggested a few days later that we go to meet his fishermen friends to bet on some games they'd invented with the fish, I declined because I imagined it would be some scam that he had learned during his imprisonment...

Speaking of prison, this mining town is infamous for having been one of the great centres of imprisonment during the Stalin era. There is little left to be seen of that tragic past, and in fact you could understand more from reading Applebaum's books, just as you have to read Hughes' *The Fatal Shore* to understand that the whole of Australia was a huge prison.

To find some wooden shack or *gulag* turret in Siberia, one has to venture out for hours in a special vehicle with six wheels, each one taller than me. It could knock down trees to open up a path. I camped at the location, and we had to take shifts on bear patrol. I had flares that spewed smoke and made noise in case I spotted one in my hour of lookout duty near the tents. While I was reasoning about how strange it is that evolution has led us to snore so loudly as to communicate to the predator that we are asleep, and usually pretty chubby too, the trouble came, not in the shape of bears, these were mosquitoes.

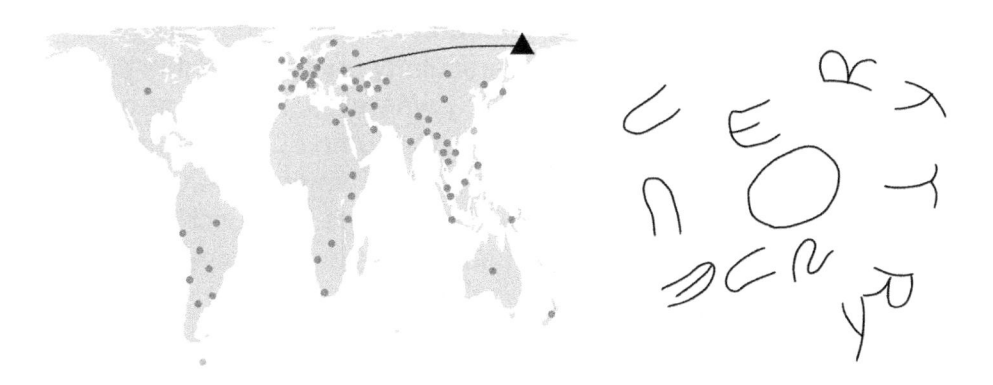

They flew in formation like a swarm, and I was tempted to set off a rocket at them but controlled myself with difficulty. I fought with honour, killing many, but the next morning my feet were so swollen from the stings that I had difficulty putting on my shoes, and I'd been fully clothed while they stung me! My comrades had also suffered injuries, one of them having his eyes practically closed from too many stings on his eyelids. Some political prisoners had been tortured or even driven to death by being tied naked to a tree and left to the mercy of the mosquito plague. During my night of torment, while making notes on my mobile phone in preparation for this book (and perhaps attracting even more with the bright screen), I hastily wrote 'Mosquitoland'. I think that gives the idea aptly enough.

Back in town, we got drunk in the evening to take our minds off the itching. We drank so much that pure vodka, as they say locally, seemed to have a taste, some kind of flavour. That's a sign that you're really far gone as it's just water and alcohol. And in our condition, I would say that not feeling itchy anymore should also have been a fair indication.

The next morning, we were still off our heads and trying to catch foxes using frankfurters as bait right in the garden under the Mask of Sorrow monument, a memorial to the millions of victims of Soviet communism. My guide swore he had caught foxes that way in the past. He was conducting this tour for the first time and had found six customers, so he was happy with the profit. On the other hand, he had listened to our conversations, with our tales of travelling and living in normal places, for a whole week. He spoke good English but had never been out of Siberia and must have been thinking about the long winter months that awaited him in the cold and dark. Living in Magadan is unpleasant, even for someone who was born there and knows nothing else.

I've mentioned how I was fed up with going to places that were beautiful but not representative of anything, organised carefully for tourists, but certainly not reflecting a nation. Now, I realised that I was instead tending in the opposite direction and focusing in on particularly ugly and terrible places in a kind of horror tourism. I was attracted by the damaged petals. I think it's right to go to some of these places in order to keep a memory alive, even if sometimes very little remains of the original, as in the *gulags*. In Auschwitz you are moved, in the Cambodian extermination camps, there are still piles of skulls, in the Australian penal colonies you relive the same pain. In your own small way, you find yourself completely immersed in the tragedy that happened. In contrast, I fear that at Chernobyl, the main focus is a dramatization of the tragedy. Tourists seem to care little about the deaths and the despair, they are just looking for a selfie in a radioactive place.

From Moscow, I flew to Oslo where I stayed for a few days before heading 2,000 km north of the capital to the **Svalbard Islands (/)**, which belong to **Norway (64)**. The world's most important seed repository is located here. All nations have sent specimens so that they can preserve crop diversity in the event of catastrophes. To date, Syria is the only one that has requested something back in order to be able to replant in its homeland following the destruction of the war. The store is deep inside the permafrost, so even if the refrigerators broke down or the power went out, everything would be preserved by the natural cold.

These are such remote islands that until a century ago no one had been able to live there permanently. They are a polar desert, and hardly anything grows there, but whalers began to arrive because of the high peaks that could be used to locate prey in the sea, and good landing places to drag them ashore once they had been caught.

The handful of people who live there today must carry guns because of the polar bears, and fortunately, others took care of watching out for them for me. My last experience as a Siberian bear warden had seen me succumb to mosquitoes, but I did want to meet a polar bear, and I succeeded. I was able to observe four of them safely from a small boat that stayed at a sensible distance.

I continued to **Greenland (/)** on the same ship from which the rubber dinghies had set off on the ice 'safari'. It is among the worst-represented lands on traditional maps, to the point that it appears almost as large as Africa while it is a good 14 times smaller. But even with this 'downsizing' it remains the largest island in the world and belongs to Denmark.

An indigenous population, the *Inuit*, has existed here for a long time. We used to call them Eskimos, but that term is offensive because it literally means raw meat eater. This is true by the way, but since freshly killed prey has a body temperature above 30°C when it is maybe -30°C outside, the sensation of hot food is there even without any cooking. It is clear, however, that pictures of bloodied faces sinking their teeth into meat arouse contempt in those who do not stop to think and have the privilege of cooking a steak in a frying pan. In Siberia, the *Chukchi* are the laughingstock of Russians' jokes for the same reason.

My passport was stamped in Greenland because the country had left the European Community in 1985 just so that it wouldn't have to follow the new rules on hunting and fishing, restrictions that made sense in most of the world, but not in Greenland where there is a small population whose whole life revolves around animal products. They warm themselves by eating and burning fat since there is no wood, they wear skins, and are an almost completely carnivorous populace. After all, with no agriculture, how else could they survive?

Today there are special rules for the *Inuit* concerning hunting and fishing and they are given quotas. Where I was, they could hunt up to 35 polar bears a year. They can hunt certain animals but only for their own consumption, not to sell their meat and skins. Other animal products have labels attached explaining why they killed the animal. Yes, the *Inuit* found themselves having to explain to some Greenpeace supporters, whose experience with animals sometimes goes no further than the goldfish bowl inside their house, why they hunt and fish!

The environmentalists say they respect their culture but do not want them to hunt. Missionaries say they respect their culture but want to make them convert to a new God that suggests completely different beliefs and rules of life. I, on the other hand, am less hypocritical and openly say that I am very happy that the *Inuit* children go to school, have a permanent home, no longer leave their elders to die, and have a parliament and laws similar to those in Denmark.

Living in Greenland is hard, with the cold, the darkness of the polar night, and the *piteraq* wind that blows at up to 250 km per hour. Those of us used to places with a temperate climate may understand the challenges presented by ice, but we overlook the impact of wind on everyday life. I personally had had some small experience of it in Mongolia and Patagonia, and it's true, the wind makes some places unbearable.

I was able to visit Ittoqqortoormiit, a small village of about 400 people, considered to be the most isolated in the world. It's the only real settlement in the whole of East Greenland, which has the most inhospitable coastline because it isn't washed by the warm gulf stream. I spent the afternoon in the company of a Danish policeman who was in the mood for conversation. He would stay on duty here for a year and was from Denmark because it's important for the policeman to come from outside to exercise authority. An *Inuit* would find himself in trouble since he would inevitably be related to someone who would expect to be favoured. Whatever he did, however he behaved, he would be seen to have switched sides and consequently would always be regarded as a traitor.

I had a strong sense of the cruelty of nature whilst in this village. I was visiting on the finest summer's day and yet life appeared to me to be as wretched and insignificant as it could be. Everyone is unemployed and supported by Denmark. Among the *Inuit* in general, there is the highest suicide rate in the world (although part of this is culture and not total despair as some old men let themselves freeze to death in solitude so as not to burden others or inhibit their journeys). The number of abortions is high, and alcoholism is rampant. Previously, as nothing grew here, there was no way to produce alcohol and they also seem to lack a certain enzyme that helps metabolise it, which means that they suffer even more bodily damage than would be normal for a European. They smoke and consume a lot of coffee (often laced with the usual alcohol). They are severely criticised for all this, but I, on the contrary, do not feel like moralising since these are among the few (bad) habits that provide relief in an empty existence spent fighting against nature in the darkness of an endless winter. In my life, I have smoked, drunk, tried drugs, gained weight, and been lazy despite numerous opportunities and beautiful sunshine. I cannot even imagine how it would be there.

The guide in Magadan had only felt depressed after prolonged direct contact with foreigners which had given him a better understanding of the wonder of everyday life in places with a mild climate. For an *Inuit* I imagine that a YouTube film would be enough to feel the misfortune of being born on the ice, even though climate would be the hardest thing to understand from a video. For those who have never experienced the pleasure of 25°C on the skin, it is easy to see that you are walking around in a T-shirt, but impossible to really imagine the feeling of comfort and warmth in the open air. In the past, there were fewer instruments of comparison which perhaps lessened the suffering.

On the other hand, I saw the most beautiful sunset of my life as I left Greenland. Nothing obstructed the unique view of a fireball descending into a sea full of ice crystals, except the overbearingness of a photographer on board who was not satisfied with there being only our ship as far as the eye could see, he wanted the sunset all to himself. He reminded me of my last neighbour on an aeroplane. On a packed flight, he was the first to put his briefcase in the overhead compartment that served three whole rows and then he closed it.

When the sea turned completely orange, I and many others strolled back and forth because visions like this, in a completely isolated place, make it possible to forget the problems that plague the world. Perhaps this is the only advantage of living in a remote area. Even the Islamic terrorism that was raging at that time, no longer concerned me while I was on the deck of that ship.

Initially, Svalbard had seemed like an open-air geology book to me, because in the complete absence of vegetation, one can appreciate each layer of rock with ease. The transit between Iceland and Greenland was also instructive because the ice on the route forms hexagonal patterns, which is the most stable composition in nature with its 120° angles. I had already seen the same phenomenon in salt deserts and with solidifying lava.

In **Iceland (65)**, an island that is considered to be a seabed brought to the surface, remaining almost as it was millions of years ago, I saw a double rainbow, an inverted rainbow called a circumzenithal arc, and I was also lucky with the northern lights. It was one WOW after another, and access to this world's beauty was being made available to me by modernity, tourism, the aeroplane, and big tour operators. But it was clear that some of it is only wonderful as a tourist, a protected visitor who has shelter, and is transported by someone, in a sturdy vehicle, truly a privileged spectator. For those who live there, these are hostile environments.

The number of inhabitants is a good initial parameter to understand the bountifulness of a land. You can take the most beautiful pictures in the world while visiting, but if hardly anyone lives there, there must be a reason. There are about 60,000 people in Greenland and the island is more than seven times the size of Italy. This also applies in reverse. Moscow has a climate that we would describe as uninhabitable, whereas in fact, it is a city where over ten million people live permanently, so the climate is evidently not as terrible as we think. In any event, since I have been travelling, I have come to admire those who work outdoors anywhere in the world.

Very few people, only about 300,000, actually live in Iceland, despite its being very civilised. Visiting has become more popular than it used to be, and there are low-cost flights and tour operators available. This is apparently thanks to the eruption of a volcano that blocked air connections throughout Europe and brought attention to the small island. The boom in tourism goes hand in hand with traditional activities in a bizarre way as both the whaling ships and those offering tourists a whale-watching tour departed from the same pier. Who knows if they were sharing information or spying on each other!

Denmark (66) is the key country to better understand the history of my recent destinations and so I flew into Copenhagen. The city is quite disappointing, on top of which the famous statue of the little mermaid is really small. But the location is interesting because Copenhagen sits on an island jutting more towards Sweden than its own nation. It's an indication of how Denmark, which boasts the world's oldest flag and perhaps monarchy, was a great power in the past. The Vikings, navigating the rivers, took possession of Paris, conquered England, arrived in Kyiv and founded the capital of Estonia. In more recent times, Denmark possessed, among other lesser-known lands, cities in India, some territory in the Caribbean, a piece of Ghana in Africa and was, unfortunately, active in the slave trade. That is until it made the mistake of allying itself with Napoleon. As a result, in

1815, when Europe was redrawn, it lost a lot of territory as punishment. For example, Norway, was ceded to Sweden and later became independent in the early 1900s and was assigned the island of Svalbard because it was a fledgling nation that didn't trouble anyone.

The crossing by ship between Greenland and Iceland took place through the Denmark Strait. Iceland had initially been colonised by Irish monks who had sought to isolate themselves to find God far away from everyone, just as the early believers did in the desert in Egypt. The journey from Ireland was dangerous, but it represented a test of faith. However, the real colonisers were the Vikings who moved to Iceland or perhaps sent their slaves. The island remained Danish until 1944 when the Icelanders took advantage of the German invasion of Denmark and with British help, they became independent. It was from Iceland that the colonisation of Greenland took place. Probably around the 10th century, the Vikings reached this immense island (which they perhaps considered an archipelago, the ice making it difficult to realise that it is one huge mass). For some reason – still unexplained today – they called it Greenland. Obviously, it is a land of ice, but that name already belongs to Iceland. Yet while Iceland was uninhabited back then, Greenland may not have been!

From Copenhagen, I flew to Ukraine to the girl I was seeing and together we visited the most beautiful parts of the country and also Budapest in **Hungary (67)**, where I again ran into the problem of not having anything decent to wear, only having expedition clothes. In European cities, I really was a fish out of water, and she reproached me for dressing like a tramp. She was right, but luckily in Eastern Europe men dress even worse than me so my suit blended into the crowd...

Still wearing my horrible suit, I went to Central America

for the first time. I landed in **Mexico (68)** and the already lengthy journey was prolonged by hours of traffic congestion on the way to my accommodation. Sometimes the last half hour seems to drag in comparison to the time before. The 12 hours by plane are planned and personally, I enjoy them. I organise myself and I know exactly what is going to happen. Whereas the traffic at the end in this case, or even a long queue at immigration, I would perceive as unfair and therefore frustrating waits.

I was here to visit as much as I could of this huge country, including the Guadalupe Cathedral, which is the most visited Marian shrine in the world and whose existence I had only discovered while studying an itinerary. American Catholics go to venerate Mary's appearance to one of the first converts in 1531. The event is considered especially important because Mary manifested herself as a *mestizo* or mixed-race woman. At the time, colonisation had just begun and there were very few *mestizo* people, so the apparition was taken as a symbol of possible future integration. It was the first time I realised how important it is for distant peoples to have a God brought by others that manifests or reveals himself directly to them.

I had mountains of books to read and was starting to fall behind again, which is a big problem, especially when you visit different cultures within a matter of a few weeks, scrolling centuries forwards and then backwards to each monument, with no clear context. You inevitably create a mishmash in your mind. It took me a few books before I came across a sentence: 'In Egypt, the pyramids were funerary, here they are ceremonial [...]'. In this case, I had already moved on to the details without having focused on the basic concept.

I had arrived in time for the Day of the Dead, which is observed in a very original way in Mexico – you must celebrate, and obviously, you do so at the cemetery. People get drunk on the graves, you dance, someone plays music, and you talk to your ancestors. They say that it's the dead who come to visit, so it's nice to be there and bring food and drink for them. In my experiences with Buddhism and Hinduism, I had created offerings and cooked for spirits and deities with my own hands to take part in the feast, here I just bought some crisps.

It was nice to experience the cemetery in this way and not at all disrespectful. In Cambodia in the extermination camps there is a sign stating clearly that it is forbidden to smile during the visit, and in Auschwitz everyone expects seriousness and rightly so. These are places where the horror goes beyond death itself and you suffer on discovering how deep the evilness of man is. In cemeteries, a different attitude may be acceptable.

The more you make places serious and difficult to be in, the less they will be frequented because the visit requires effort. Perhaps in a small way, this is what those who demand that you wear your best clothes to go to church don't understand, as you only end up going on Sundays. In a mosque, they invite you to go if you just want to stand in a corner and chat on your phone. So, if you can drop by for a quick, comfortable greeting, or even for a simple walk as in certain cemeteries or temples in Japan, attendance increases. In Germany, they allow people to eat and use their phones at holocaust memorials, so that remembrance, though lacking the full attention it deserves, is a daily occurrence.

In general, the choices around the world vary widely as to how much to expose or conceal death. In a museum in Sri Lanka, I witnessed something that made me stop and reflect. There was a picture of piles of naked bodies that had been slaughtered during the terrible civil war. The fatal wounds, and even their open skulls were clearly visible, while they had put a black stamp on their genitals. Death had to be shown, but a corpse without underwear did not.

Crossing the border to **Guatemala (69)** was very easy. A month of travelling around Mexico had hardly improved my Spanish at all. It's funny how a poor knowledge of the language limits you to the point that you need to dive into your books in Italian to unfold your thoughts, occupy your mind, and create an imaginary dialogue with the author. In my head, I would once again be able to use adjectives, the exact word instead of 'the thing', and a few adverbs. Otherwise, if you're always travelling around alone, your thoughts and words become more and more limited. You become like a child again, only communicating in order to ask for something or to get basic information. And then I couldn't take any more of hearing the accursed *entonces* (Spanish for then or so) every five words…

The place where I slept was busier than a kindergarten.

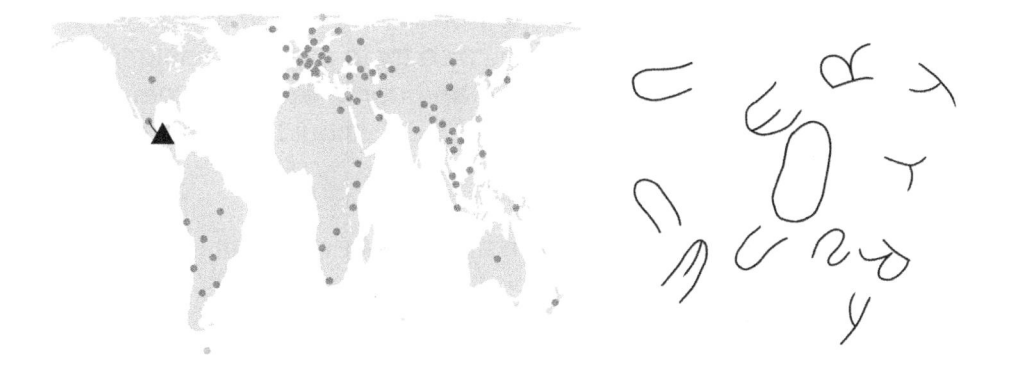

It was very noisy, with so many childhood songs and nursery rhymes which you will never know no matter how well you learn a language as an adult.

A group of German women in their forties was also staying with me in this house full of many related families, and they were enthusiastic about their choice. They took one photo after another with a dozen little kids, along with videos of them playing in the garden or with something improvised, constantly praising the close-knit family, old-fashioned toys, and happy children who weren't slaves to technology and television.

I understand the photos and the fun with lots of children because in Germany it would be impossible to go into an actual kindergarten, take ten of the tiny students and play with them at will. But this is an environment and a lifestyle they could easily embrace if they really wanted to, but they have no intention of doing so, despite their grand proclamations.

None of the three of them had any children, but if they'd had offspring of their own in that place, I strongly suspect that they would have spent their days telling them not to play with that bottle that might cut them, not to chase each other with sticks, and to stop mistreating animals and getting into fights. Not only that, but from their stories, they had already taken trips together at Christmas. So, they had been the first to run away at one of the few times when the family traditionally gets together in Germany.

I too am very much at the front of the queue to run away as soon as possible, but if you also try to avoid a christening, have a hard time at reunions, and don't like your extended family's enormous meal tables, why should anyone else's celebration be so different?

Also, hierarchies apply in these places so that in the end

the head of the family rules, and everything takes place within the boundaries of sometimes quite cruel traditions. The women who took care of the lodging had probably had an arranged marriage, had to live with relatives, and were spending the years of their youth continually pregnant. If you start having children at 15, you cannot develop your own personality. If you quarrel with one of the thousands of relatives, you are forced to hang out with them every day and to keep your head down. There is widespread domestic violence, verbal and physical. Photos surrounded by women and their many children, with the caption that they have serenity in their eyes, don't make you laugh as you would at the guy who says he wants to open a beach bar in Brazil. They are simply nauseating.

I arrived in **Belize (70)** where at last English was spoken. I only stayed briefly but it was here that, a few years later, I would end up buying a small island, together with 75 other serial travellers. We put up $3,000 apiece and own a little area of land a short distance from the capital that can be reached by a fast speedboat ride. For now, we can only camp there but in the future, we hope to build a small hotel. In general, the entirely utopian idea is to turn it into a micronation with its own rules. There are already some in the world, who knows, our **Principality of Islandia (/)**, as we have christened it by democratic vote, may succeed... (Of course, I don't yet count it among the nations).

I entered the United States for the first time since I had

obtained my visa and was stopped briefly because, on the monitor of the agent checking my passport, it appeared that I had been denied an e-visa. What a discovery! That was why I had the non-electronic visa issued by the embassy.

I stayed in Miami for a few days, having secured very cheap accommodation, for which I soon discovered the reason. The other 'tenants' were people with obvious problems or on the fringe of society. They were drug addicts, the mentally deranged, and even prostitutes clearly working in that very place. They all knew each other, meaning that I was the only short-stay guest. In such an environment you only need to take a walk in the garden to socialise, as they are often out there smoking since even in what is virtually a brothel, where drugs are freely used, it's forbidden indoors. I haven't smoked for a long time, but I took a moment to find an angle to talk and establish a rapport. I said that I played poker for a living. I hadn't talked about my past for a long time, and now I was lying about still playing. Maybe in their eyes, I looked like someone who had been badly damaged by gambling or was just there because my wife had kicked me out of the house…

Going to **Haiti (71)** was more frightening than the sleazy hotel. It's a really messed up nation. They'd had the courage to rebel against France, proclaim the first black republic and abolish slavery, even promising freedom to anyone who reached the island. I really can't understand why Hollywood hasn't yet made a great film about this historical event. Since then, however, everything has gone wrong and today it's the poorest country in the western hemisphere. It was the American girl, who I had arranged to meet up with here for the first time since Papua, who gave me the courage to get around without any problems. At a table in a restaurant, when someone asked how we had met, as we were clearly of two different nationalities, I offered to pay for their lunch if they guessed right. I don't think anyone would have imagined that it was at an airport in Papua New Guinea.

I was in awe of this girl. She managed to do most of what I did and yet had a normal life. She was very organised, working without wasting a minute, and then she could turn off the computer and devote herself to the trip. Of course, she had no family, so she only had to look after herself, but I couldn't even do that. In any event, managing a top-level job whilst travelling to the most remote countries in the world is not easy.

Our Haitian guide kept telling us that everything was peaceful in the country, but the barbed wire on every window, even those of poor houses, spoke volumes. In countries where people don't have bank accounts, paradoxically cash can be found in the houses. Everyone keeps what little they have under the famous mattress. In fact, at the exchange office, a $100 note is worth more than five $20 notes, a common occurrence in this type of country. Money has to be kept safe, and if you have to run away it has to be hidden, sewn into something or even swallowed, $100 notes are a very functional little treasure.

The area surrounding our bunker hotel was full of people who slept in the street, stoned or drunk. I judged them less and less after my experiences with insects. Imagine being desperate and also having those mosquitoes around all night. It would be impossible to sleep without help.

Some people decide to get a tattoo on the final day of a trip, but the two of us decided to get married using a Voodoo ritual! The experience became expensive because it was still a kind of wedding, but not a tourist one. The ceremony is copied from a standard wedding, but more fun, complete with an oath, an exchange of faith bracelets and a ritual sacrifice. This is followed by a solemn drink, accompanied by a lavish meal of fantastic lobsters at $5 each, which is very cheap because it is the 'slave' food in Haiti. Lobsters eat rubbish from the seabed, so they are despised. My guide was the only person in Haiti who was on time for the ceremony, his infallible method being to have his watch set 1 hour 22 minutes fast…

The marriage obviously had no value so, uncertain whether to start a serious relationship, I continued alone to **Cuba (72)**, which, when put that way, doesn't suggest I was seriously interested in a commitment. Cuba has had a lot of sex tourism in the past. It's less so today, but the island certainly extols some vices, for instance, lengthy explanations about the manufacture of cigars, rum and cocktails are among the most common tourist attractions. A cigar or a cocktail may make you feel special, but in my everyday life I find that smokers say cigars are great but then smoke cigarettes. Even with the overly fancy cocktails, I get the impression that they give more pleasure to the eyes than to the palate.

In general, the tourist industry on this island subscribed to the popular idea that you had to visit as soon as possible because everything was changing. I think the tour operators played on it a bit to create urgency, so you felt the rush and would buy the travel package, however, some rules were indeed constantly changing. What never changes though is the allure of Cuba that delights everyone.

The other thing that shows no sign of changing is the dictatorship. My guide was more objective than I had thought possible under such a vicious regime though. During our solitary journeys by private car, he would indulge in accurate analyses and even offer some direct criticism. When he asked me what I thought, he feigned curiosity, but I could tell he had heard the same concepts a hundred times before. Instead, my comment that I had never before seen a country that had remained so poor despite having no illiterate people, left him open-mouthed. I had turned his way of looking at the issue upside down.

The journey to **Ecuador (73)** was very long. As soon as I arrived, I obviously went right to the Equator, which gives the country its name, and took part in the various little games that are organised there with the water discharge rotating in one direction or the other at a distance of a few metres, and then straight down without spinning at the exact point of the equator. In reality, this is achieved by skilful pouring to create the rotations and using water that has stood in a basin for a long time to demonstrate how it goes straight down.

It might have been possible to visit the indigenous communities where they performed religious rituals, but they said they were very possessive of them, so no one wanted to explain anything to me. Deep down I understand that they do not want to reveal their beliefs to those who, like me, are there ready to judge. They were mocked enough in the past when the Europeans came to conquer and bring the gospel. The natives had found a simple solution to keep them happy, namely, to become Christians on Sunday and then remain faithful to their own religions during the rest of the week.

State laws are only partially enforced in the communities, enabling certain traditions to be kept alive, but more importantly, making the laws understandable and perceived as just. There are none of the white man's quibbles, no need for a lawyer who humiliates the man who feels innocent, and there is no corruption. In essence, they follow a law of retaliation that is clear, straightforward, and accepted by all.

I was familiar with the Indian reservations in America because I had visited some of the casinos that have been established there under special rules. Alongside the right to offer gambling, people who live in those places have language schools, tax advantages, and alcohol-free areas. But here in Ecuador there is a wider reaching exemption from state rules. They have the right to abandon a guilty person in the wild, and for some transgressions, there are lashes, sometimes imposed by a relative so that it is clear that the family agrees with the punishment.

I had a very good guide, who understood how much I wanted to discover a new reality but had no desire to give me satisfaction. He knew that I would have condemned the rules, so he got away with saying that his people respect the laws when they leave the reserve but are free inside. In his view the environment in which they live has protected them from the outside world, but I think that sometimes it has isolated rather than protected them. The arrival of others brings trouble, but also ideas, comparisons, novelties and improvements.

Speaking of isolated, the **Galapagos (/)** are aptly named islands, described as a kind of Noah's ark because they are home to some unique species which thrive in this remote place. I had found a week-long cruise, with a naturalist on board, at a reasonable price and finally, my dream of visiting was realised. I was sharing a room with a Japanese man who immediately grabbed the best bed, but I found a paper crane that he had made on mine, so I cracked a smile.

It was here that I experienced a new way of interacting with animals. You could approach them calmly as they have evolved far away from humans and predators and don't fear or attack you. Just like the penguins in Antarctica who feel safe on dry land they aren't frightened by the presence of humans. I started with the usual 1,000 photos of iguanas and then I didn't even notice them anymore, just as I had with zebras on safari. Giant tortoises facilitate the easiest 'safari' in the world as they are notoriously slow and not dangerous. Sailors and pirates used to take these animals on board and keep them as a living food supply since turtles can survive a long time without eating, and then when it was time, they would cook them. In Papua they regard the pig as a living refrigerator in a similar way. They feed it, storing their leftovers inside, and then when needed they eat it all by killing the pig. In general, many animals are seen as walking food or tools to turn grass into meat.

I had read a few stories about people who isolated themselves in these places, even an Austrian baroness with her lovers. And so, I asked myself why a person is considered a romantic, a dreamer, or at worst a loner or an eccentric when they take refuge in nature, while on the other hand, someone who chooses isolation in their own home, with the technology at their disposal to communicate and be entertained, is just considered anti-social. Today, our survival no longer depends on the herd and cooperation between everyone, so why this hatred towards those who isolate themselves in nameless places?

Around New Year's Eve, the American girl, or rather my wife according to Voodoo, had her holiday again and so we decided to meet in **Lebanon (74)**. It was a very long journey for her coming from San Francisco but only took me three hours since I had come home to Rome for Christmas. Lebanon is really interesting. It was deliberately created to offer refuge to religious minorities otherwise persecuted elsewhere. The country is mountainous, which once constituted its best defence. France wanted Christians to be protected and sheltered, so it tried to gather them there. At the end of World War I, the overwhelming majority of the population in Lebanon wanted to remain under French mandate. The Lebanese emigrated en masse following the directions and opportunities offered by the French, and throughout French-speaking Africa, trade is still conducted by them.

The port of Beirut is an important world thoroughfare used by France in particular and developed as a base to reach Indochina (Vietnam, Laos and Cambodia, formerly French colonies of course), which is why Beirut was the 'Paris of the Middle East'.

Today in Lebanon there are as many as 18 official religions that try to coexist and there is an institutional framework that should help peace. The president is always Christian (Maronite), the prime minister is Sunni, and the president of parliament is Shia. This is to avoid disputes and to reflect the theoretical demographic weight in the political one. But no censuses have been taken for a long time because if they were, the balance of power would change. Everyone knows that today the Shias are in the majority and in fact they have created, especially in the south, a state within a state, run directly by militias and very closely linked to Iran.

Changing religion is almost impossible as ethnic affiliation comes with religious belief. Imagine if you want to give up your religion, being forced also to relinquish your Italian citizenship, your family and circle of friends, being seen as a traitor to the cause, and disowned by your mother. Our guide, however, was secular and chameleon-like, just as capable of snatching permission to visit from *Hezbollah* terrorists as of humbly knocking on the door of a convent. He had learnt to constantly change his name so that he could always present himself as being of the 'right' religion with the girls he wanted to pick up.

I already had a girlfriend, and we celebrated the New Year in a way that only the two of us could conceive – planning a crazy itinerary and booking flights for €5,000 each to remote Pacific islands.

The year was coming to an end, and I was about to invest a lot of money, time and effort to get to some objectively quite insignificant little islands, while there were still so many important places I had not visited. But I had mentally divided the world into geographical areas, which were homogeneous from my perspective, and I wanted to visit a few places from each of them. Did I need to visit them all? What was in my head? It's difficult to reconstruct with certainty, however, the choice was also driven by the fact that the American girl would change jobs in March and before starting the new one she had managed to carve out a window of almost two months. We wanted to maximise that time and go somewhere remote and new for both of us. In fact, I couldn't answer the question of whether I was going for the islands or for her with any certainty. From time to time, I would be following her lead, but also the idea of the little islands was one that I had brought up and pushed myself.

Of one thing I was sure, I wasn't giving myself a date to quit. I still had money, but I hadn't earned anything in years, I hadn't even done my tax return. I had no house of my own, no utilities, and I hardly ever got any mail. All I had left was a mobile phone contract and a bank account. Had I died that day, my paperwork would have taken up a single afternoon.

MONGOLIA

RANGOON

CHINA

CARNATIC

GENERAL GRANT

YEAR 4

FRANCE	MONACO	SLOVENIA
SRI LANKA	BANGLADESH	EGYPT
NEW ZEALAND	PAPUA NEW GUINEA	AUSTRALIA
POLAND	UKRAINE	NORWAY
ICELAND	DENMARK	HUNGARY
MEXICO	GUATEMALA	BELIZE
HAITI	CUBA	ECUADOR
LEBANON		

74/193

YEAR 5

When I'm at a restaurant in Italy, I have no interest in other people's conversations, whereas when I was travelling, as soon as I heard my own language spoken, my ears would tune in and I'd want to listen. Why this sudden curiosity? Was it a search for companionship perhaps, or a yearning to feel that I have someone familiar in case of need? Or perhaps it's simply loneliness? All the serial travellers I've met on the road keep a diary, partly because there's so much to remember and communicate when you travel, but more predominantly, I believe, because you can feel so lonely. I was also a constant note-taker, despite being fortunate enough not to feel particularly troubled by isolation. And yet I couldn't help but at least wonder, 'How do others see me'?

Most of the Westerners I met must have thought I was running away from some bereavement, trauma, or love affair. Or that I was maybe a bored billionaire or a drifter who couldn't stay long in one place. I was well aware that this wasn't true of me, but every now and then a doubt crept into my head. Could I perhaps be someone who had a hard time finding where they fit in the world? I had in fact met people like that. Once, I'd got to know an American, who had been born in a so called 'normal' situation, and yet had ended up in a quite 'abnormal' location for no clear reason. He'd slowly deteriorated, and the geography had made his condition apparent as he had moved from a coastal state to increasingly remote places, eventually ending up in Alaska. Was I in danger of becoming this person? That was certainly a risk, and worse, I had the potential to fall so much further. He had hit rock bottom with Alaska, while I had the whole world in front of me, and there were still places far worse than Alaska to 'not' find my place in the world.

For anyone other than Westerners and a few other exceptions, excessive though my generalisation may be, the idea of simply travelling alone without a specific purpose is inconceivable. One travels for business or religious reasons and the few who can travel far from home or abroad for pleasure don't usually go alone. I would see deep curiosity in the eyes of those who came in contact with me, but it was rare for anyone to ask directly. I often gave away snippets of my life as I pleased, sometimes fabricating things out of thin air, mainly because telling people I played poker either risked portraying myself in a bad light or else required lengthy explanations. This way I could reinvent myself as the person I wanted without feeling like a liar. Little did I know that I would soon find it necessary to become a glasses salesman, an oil consultant, and even a missionary! In general, if you sense the curiosity of those who have noticed your presence in a particular place, all you have to do to satisfy them is to ask, 'Is such and such a location or monument in that direction by any chance?' You already know the answer thanks to Google, but your question has now told them the reason you're here.

Indeed, Google, and efficient services in general contribute to the reason that some countries are perceived as cold and aloof, since every piece of information can be found on the Internet. The route planner shows the way, enabling you to find a dedicated shop for every need, a number is available to call in an emergency, and consequently, the reasons for talking to others are drastically reduced. It's rather like the difference between a luxury hotel and a hostel. In rich countries everything is organised and offered professionally. Similarly, when you need something in a hotel you would only ask a member of staff for help and not another guest, whereas in a hostel it's different. Some service is available, but you help each other, and you spend time together rather than closing the door and hiding away. Hotel guests aren't mean, uncaring, and aloof, and neither are the Swiss or the Norwegians, they have simply delegated much of their national hospitality to professionals, just as hotels do.

The climate also plays a role. In cold weather, everyone spends time in their own homes or at least in enclosed spaces, where you must ask permission to enter. When it's warm, there tend to be more communal spaces and they are open to all. So, in warm countries, as in hostels, there is a higher level of contact between people, which can have negative implications, because now you have to tolerate those things that you find annoying. Being together is fun but creates friction as one person takes advantage of a situation, another crosses a boundary, and keeping it all in check becomes more difficult.

To continue generalising, in impoverished countries, life is lived in the company of others for entertainment, something that is needed less elsewhere, where there is so much amusement offered for those who will pay for it.

I took advantage of the passage to Rome from Lebanon to request entry to Ghana, a country that requires you to apply for a visa where you reside. I carefully organised what I would do while waiting on the infamous small islands trip and went to **Germany (75)** for the first time in years. Berlin struck me as being a very different city from the one I had known, which wasn't surprising since my Erasmus trip dated back to 1999. When I returned, my visa was ready.

Before I left again, I took my passport to the Eritrean embassy. I'd obtained the documents needed to apply for one of the most complex visas ever and had taken obsessive care in arranging everything. Being Italian is a great advantage in this circumstance, as relations with the former colony remain decent and the embassy in Rome is one of the few to authorise visits. Nevertheless, it would take at least 30 days to process, and I would have to collect the visa in person. The only good news was that I could keep my passport with me in the meantime as they only wanted to see it at application and collection. With the way I had organised my travels, it was a real problem to go back to Rome. This ridiculous situation meant that I would literally have to go around the world to pick up my visa!

In the interim, I went to **Ghana (76)** where I was confronted for the first time with places associated with the slave trade. For Europeans, this West African coast had been the closest black African destination. The winds were good, the landings many and then from here it proved convenient to start Atlantic crossings to bring slaves to Brazil and the Caribbean. About 4% of the total number ended up in the present United States, though I had thought it was much more. And almost none were sent to Europe.

The symbol of this filthy trade is the infamous Elmina Castle, where first the Portuguese, then the Dutch, bought slaves from African tribes. The castle also bears witness to a ridiculous rivalry between Europeans in Africa. Despite there being only a few people in those huge areas, they fought each other. The dual soul is highlighted by the two reconstructed churches inside, one Catholic, the other Protestant built after the handover to the Dutch.

In 1957, Ghana was the first black African country to gain independence. The leader, Nkrumah, who had previously been arrested by the British, was allowed to participate in the elections, which he won. He was released from jail and found himself leader the same day and very soon Prime Minister. He gave his independence speech in a polo field where entry had previously been forbidden to Africans. The British colonists accepted the result. Today, I think it is more common throughout the world for the reverse to happen and for a prime minister to end up in jail.

Nkrumah dreamed of a united Africa under his command, and had a huge complex built to house all the African leaders and foreign ministers, spending a fortune on something that was only used for four days. It's painful to visit these 'wedding dress' buildings that have so much invested in them but are only used for one big occasion. And speaking of brides, in order to be seen as the leader of all Africans, Nkrumah asked Nasser to choose an Egyptian wife for him, so that he could visually represent black and Arab, Africa's two dominant souls. He ended up as one of many communist dictators, dressed like Mao and died in exile despised by the people.

I went on to **Togo (77)** where I ventured into the villages. Five years of French at school had yielded more or less the same fruits as my super two-week Spanish course, and I spoke badly. I had made fun of the Germans in Guatemala, but here, in more or less the same way as they had, I felt really happy in one village because I was surrounded by children. Soon dusk fell and everyone gathered under the only working streetlamp in the centre of the square. I was the guest of honour, thanks to a generous donation from my guide. I had dinner, which was followed by singing and dancing. Very few tourists passed through that village. Some of the children had deep scars on their faces as scarification is still legal. Circumcision is sometimes performed on boys in front of the whole village, and they have to prove their resistance to pain. Perhaps at one time, it prepared you for the constant wars and feuds, but nowadays how does this serve any purpose?

Anyway, I was enjoying myself and tried to insist on sleeping there, but my guide was adamant that no accommodation was available as no one in the village had a mosquito net. Initially I had the suspicion that he was using my security as an excuse because he wanted to sleep in a hotel. By the 100th mosquito bite, however, I was quite happy to go to an inn, however expensive. Of course, the bathroom drain was blocked, and it was disgusting but at least it had protection from the dreaded insects. In some parts of Africa, there are very few facilities, which means that you only have two options – either camp or go to the only hotel, which usually costs as much as if it had five stars, but actually ranks somewhere between two and four as far as services are concerned. These hotels can be found almost everywhere as they are the venues used for weddings, receptions, hosting businessmen and occasionally a rare tourist.

Did I feel happy in this crowd of children because I was alone? If the three Germans had been with me taking selfies, would I have been thinking about how to make fun of them instead of enjoying the moment? At least I had avoided the hypocrisy of envying the conditions of the place or extolling that lifestyle. Was I happy for myself? Yes. I had enjoyed a fun evening with a thousand screaming children, then I had slept comfortably, and this was far removed from my usual way of life.

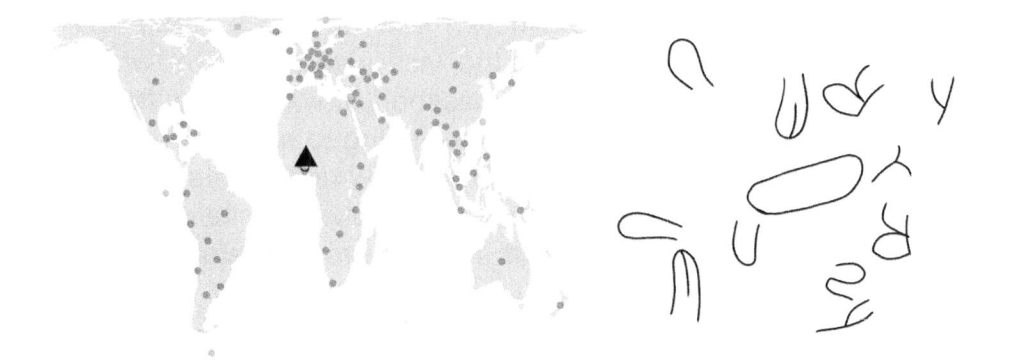

Another border and I found myself in **Benin (78)**, a country where Voodoo is the official religion. Besides marriage, what else remained to be experienced? Well, healing. In fact, according to Voodoo, illness passes from a human being to an animal that is sacrificed, an animal that is ritually purified at the expense of the sick person. The idea is that an evil spirit, having taken possession of a body, doesn't go away unless you offer something in return to be tormented and killed. The most widely practised sacrifice is that of the chicken for three reasons. Firstly, it is the cheapest animal and is easy to transport. Secondly, when the chicken's head is cut off, it runs around headless for a few seconds before collapsing on the ground, which is macabre to see, but is obviously interpreted as 'acceptance' of the body for the evil spirit that possesses it. The third reason is that it lays eggs, and one is usually collected before the sacrifice in order to proceed to divination, that is, to understand what illness the patient is suffering from and cure him with prayers or herbs. The egg is perfect since there's usually some residue of blood inside, always some mark, and a flow of liquids that can say what one wants to hear. The fetish market is also related to the healing process and is in fact a kind of pharmacy, consisting mainly of dried animals, herbs, and jars with chopped body parts inside, all to be swallowed or used in magical rituals. Not far away, however, a billboard pointed out that the clinic they were advertising was a Western one...

After a quick passage through Spain, my flight would take me back to Guatemala where I had already been. That itinerary was cheaper, so I was saving money by restarting my American travels from there. I stayed well away from the accommodation from the time before, with the toxic large family gathering. This country had once been ruled by Union Fruit, Chiquita. The company had been involved in coups, and was a symbol of corrupt United States' governments, which had led to the coining of the expression 'Banana Republic'. I was looking for a banana boat myself, but for a very different reason. I had read that they would let paying passengers on board the ships, thus becoming pioneers in tourism, and I needed transport.

I didn't find anything like that though, and continued by land to **Honduras (79)**, where I entered with a group and was disappointed because the visa was collective, which meant they didn't stamp my passport. It was a blow for an enthusiast like me, but I was beginning to resign myself to not having a complete collection. Israel doesn't stamp, and neither does North Korea. Obviously, having an Italian passport there was nothing from many European states, but I had obtained the Danish one thanks to Greenland.

In the various villages in Honduras, it's common to walk around with a big hat and a gun on your belt, even when you go shopping. Furthermore, wherever I arrived with my big tour group there seemed to be hardly anyone around. Were they all inside the houses secretly watching the strangers from the windows in the manner of the old Western films?

In **Nicaragua (80)** the price was exactly the same for a four or an eight-hour tour. The guide I had hired confessed candidly that he wouldn't find another client if he only worked half a day, so he was happy to stay with me as long as possible. People who don't have much to do tend not to value their time. Anyway, that idle afternoon was useful. We met a Sandinista revolutionary who gave a very biased reconstruction of facts, bordering on the ridiculous, but then again, we'd contacted him on purpose. The jail I visited, where they used to keep the Sandinistas imprisoned, has been cunningly turned into a museum of 'Nicaraguan myths and legends' and in doing so, the stories of the torture that had actually taken place are mixed with legends and lose their intensity.

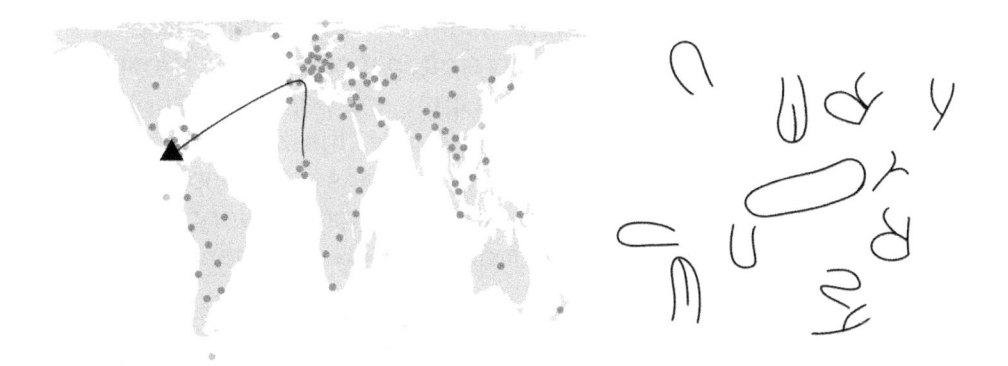

In **El Salvador (81)** I met a gang member who was now dedicated to making money by telling anecdotes to tourists and showing the places where graffiti is being removed (a sign that the government is back in charge in those areas once controlled by the gangs). Roads can be similarly representative of the prevailing authority. As long as they are paved there is some government entity in charge of them which therefore then oversees the area, but once the dirt road starts you are outside of that influence.

It was interesting that these tattooed and bejewelled men always talk about the great values that drive them: family, honour, and loyalty. It's all dressed up in religiosity, to the point that perhaps the only accepted way to get out of a gang without retaliation is to become a priest. Likewise, in Italy our criminals, particularly the mafiosi, are usually religious and believe in the same values in their own way. At the end of the day though, these mainly translate into blind obedience to the will and orders of the head of the family.

Gangs aside, however, some of the values that ostensibly sound reasonable and good need to be seen in context because the negative implications are often just around the corner. For example, tourists are fed the great warrior tradition of the people, their men and their courage are extolled. Today though, this is no longer necessary for the survival of the group, and if that value remains central, women and all non-warriors hold a subordinate and miserable position in society. A young man can't look up, can't even ask questions if he hasn't comprehended an elder's order, and you see that women eat only what is left over. Preserving family unity sometimes means prohibition – marrying a member of another village or going to work elsewhere are not permitted, and people of different religions cannot live nearby. Too often living in harmony means excluding diversity.

Finally, even when there seem to be no hidden implications, I wonder more and more often if outside the Western world these wonderful values that are portrayed apply to everyone. Because, in my experience, the word 'everyone' sometimes includes only men, or perhaps only people of this ethnic group or that religion, which of course is very different from the 'everyone' that is understood by the listener.

In some years, the numbers of murders and violent acts in El Salvador and Honduras have been the highest per capita in the world, making the alarmingly bad statistics of Johannesburg pale into insignificance. Certainly, here too, the numbers should be weighed, because most of the deaths are among gang members themselves, however, as in South Africa, even when situations that would never be encountered by tourists are discounted, the risks remain considerable. **Costa Rica (82)**, on the other hand, is a peaceful, neutral country without an army. It once attracted religious fundamentalists who didn't want to be forced to do military service, while today it draws pensioners from the United States. The cost of living here is low for those with an income in dollars, and there is lush nature and a pleasant climate. We often read about brain drain in the newspapers, but pensions on the run are spoken of very little, yet this is a phenomenon that is on the increase worldwide.

While I was climbing a beautiful volcano, the American girl informed me that she had interrupted her work a little early and wanted to join me. We met in **Panama (83)**, where we were able to travel the entire canal together.

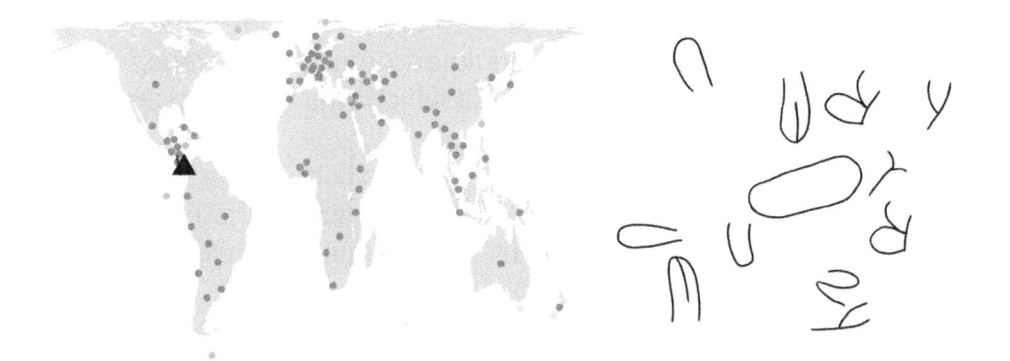

This was a remarkable experience as it's one of the great junctions of the world. You have to admire the human ingenuity that has managed to connect two oceans by cutting a strip of land, taking advantage of the presence of a lake in the middle. Many men paid with their lives for that construction and much of the credit for the success is due to the discovery that it was the usual damn mosquitoes that brought trouble. In fact, the workers died mainly from illnesses and not from accidents at work. By reducing their numbers, life would be more bearable and the environment healthier. After a huge clean-up operation, with fewer mosquitoes around, the dream was realised.

Our next stop together was the famous **Easter Island (/)**, which belongs to Chile. The American girl's last-minute flight had cost her a fortune, whereas mine had been bought by a Chilean man I had previously met (not the computer repairman/destroyer!) who was connected to a Chilean website, and therefore had lower prices available to him. Prices for international tourists are inflated, as the island is a destination for the rich.

The giant statues are fascinating, but boredom soon sets in. In books, every anthropologist or archaeologist expounds his theory as to why they were erected. Very simply, without knowing anything, I think they carved them to feel less lonely. This theory is a personal one and therefore quite unverified, but more credible and proven theories exist as to how men arrived on this tiny piece of land. Notably they reveal that it was the Polynesians who found this needle in a haystack (their expertise also enabled them to find atolls, which are coral deposits that lie just above the surface of the water and are therefore very difficult to spot), the self-same people who discovered and populated other small islands but missed out on gigantic Australia which was much closer.

Today, Easter Island is notoriously isolated from everything, but taking into account the size of the earth, it's relatively close to Hawaii. In fact, together with New Zealand, they are the most far-flung lands reached by Polynesians. If you draw a line between Hawaii, Easter Island and New Zealand, you can see that it creates an imaginary triangle which is known as the Polynesian triangle.

Our adventure in the tiny remote nations of the Pacific had to begin in Hawaii. United Airlines has created a route that connects numerous islands via a ticket called the *Island Hopper*. It's a single expensive ticket, but one that allows six trips on those little-used, remote routes.

I had to go through Rome first because the visa for Eritrea had to be picked up in person. This meant that I had to do the whole round-the-world trip again in a few days! From Easter Island to Santiago de Chile was almost five hours, then I had a 12-hour flight to Madrid, then Rome where I immediately rushed to the Eritrean embassy to have the visa physically affixed into my passport. To keep calm I repeated to myself how lucky I was to live in the city with the highest number of embassies in the world.

Then, from Rome, I flew to Hong Kong in about 20 hours, where I stayed one night in a capsule hotel, thus maintaining the ambience of an aeroplane. In the novel, Phileas Fogg embarked from here for Japan which took 13 days, while I needed two hours to reach Manila and with a further three, I finally arrived in Palau.

The American girl would meet me there from Honolulu. At

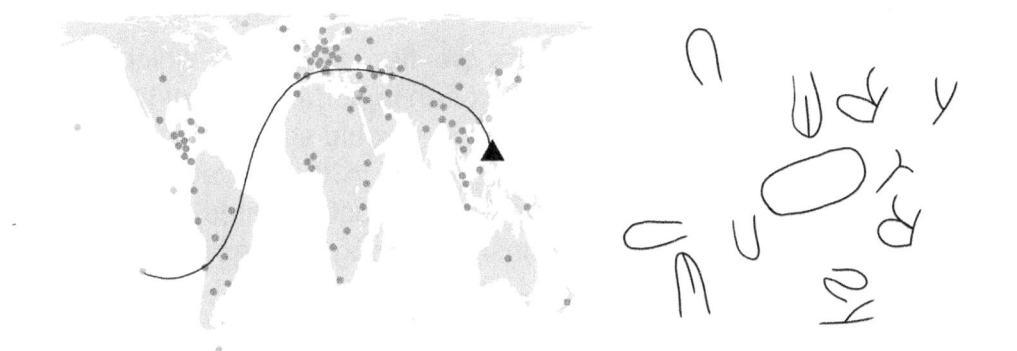

the airport on Easter Island, while checking in for Santiago, I jokingly told the stewardess my situation and had an incredible surprise when she upgraded me to business class. I think she did it out of human pity. I very much enjoyed the first leg in these huge seats, which, as is well known, are basically a nice restaurant with an open bar. The difference between business and economy is sometimes more than €100/hour if you want to compare prices that way. Honestly, if I had a free upgrade to business class, and then someone offered me that amount to sit in their seat in economy, I would gladly accept. Not exactly straightforward reasoning maybe, but I would never pay for business class out of my own pocket unless I was really rich.

When I arrived in **Palau (84)** my love of stamps was very well satisfied. Indeed, they insert a long text, like an oath, which they ask you to sign in your own passport. It's a declaration in which the tourist pledges to respect nature. Having set foot on the ground, on the one hand I felt like a cyborg because I had extraordinary stamina, and on the other I took note of how determined I had been to do anything to get that absurd visa. The American girl was already at the hotel waiting for me, but just as the hostess had, she took pity on me and let me sleep for many hours. On waking up, yet another flight was waiting for us, but this one was better than business class as we had it all to ourselves. A tiny plane, without doors for a full view, would fly us over the lagoon, where I saw the bluest water of my life. Here too, as with the Namibian desert, the sea is the archetype of what a child aspires to draw.

To get out of the country we flew to Guam, which is American territory and the site of an important military base. From there my *Island Hopper* ticket would start with the first destination, the state of Micronesia. In the United States however, the concept of transit is not contemplated. You enter their territory, so you must go through immigration and the various controls, and then you can resume your journey, which is why you may have had to collect your luggage when you landed in America even though your journey was continuing. And of course, you must have everything in order with the entry requirements. In my case, more time was lost, because my visa was now in my old passport and so a further inspection was needed to find out why I had changed a passport that still had so many years of validity. Running out of pages does not happen often, but it was at least an easy reason to explain.

I bought a huge map of the Pacific Ocean. For years I had kept the inflatable globe with the Pacific side facing me, but most of the names on the islands were new to me, or at least I didn't remember many of them from those early days of travel dreams. We arrived in the **Federated States of Micronesia (85)**, where we would visit two of the four main islands. On the first one, we found ourselves in a hotel with a group of Russians who had come specially to explore the wrecks sunk during the Second World War. They are really dangerous dives and of course, taking things away is forbidden but I guess that was part of the fun.

We then went to Pohnpei, where there is a kind of 'Venice of the Pacific'. All over the world, as soon as something is built on water, it's dubbed as some form of Venice, so I took little notice of that aspect. It had been a difficult search to find a guide here, and once we arrived at the moment for the tour to begin, I realised how futile this quest had been. Rather than guiding and explaining, she said that she wouldn't follow us into the ruins because it was bad luck! How many times should I already be dead and buried with all my violations of taboo spaces?

But a real bit of bad luck was just around the corner. On the way to the airport, we discovered that the United flight to our next destination had skipped the island and would continue to do so for the next few days. It had rained too much, even by the standards of one of the rainiest places in the world.

We repeatedly missed our flight, to the point that our travel plan, so meticulously researched in Lebanon, was about to fall apart right then and there. The connections between these islands are very limited, but we'd left ourselves room for manoeuvre and had already researched alternatives in our nerdy Excel spreadsheet.

But now we were in a fix, and when we finally managed to leave to go to the **Marshall Islands (86)**, we were only able to fit in a brief visit. We had to continue within a day otherwise the domino effect would come into play, and we would have lost everything we'd planned. Maybe I will return someday, despite the fact that these islands don't have a lot to offer. The friend I had found on Facebook to obtain information joked that this country was used by the United States as a firing range to test atomic bombs and other weapons, so it is easy to imagine how desolate they are.

Having greeted the airport in the capital, Majuro, in *Iokwe* the local vernacular, literally saying, 'You are a rainbow', we continued on to **Kiribati (87)** which was the moment I had been most looking forward to. Kiribati had been written so clearly on that inflatable globe that had sat in front of my eyes for years. It was my fairy-tale land, and I felt like a child who had been told, 'Once upon a time there was a kingdom far away...' and then was actually taken there. But I was far too old already to believe in paradise on earth.

A devout Catholic, officially registered online as a tour guide was eagerly awaiting us. She was the one asking me the questions because she was so curious about Rome. In a few months, she would finally go to the Vatican on a trip organised by her parish, spending her entire life savings. She took us to various churches, got us into parliament, and enabled a conversation with a minister. At her behest, we were taken into a school, where, without bringing any gifts or treats, we were assaulted by hordes of screaming children who were so happy to see foreigners that they offered us their smiles for nothing. It was one of those experiences that test a couple's determination not to have children.

Then we went to see one of the places where the Americans defeated the Japanese with the help of a little ruse. Being familiar with the obsessive precision of their enemies, they had counted how many toilets had been built and were able to work out exactly how many Japanese soldiers were present. Curiosity aside, these islands would give a history aficionado a true sense of the violence of the battles that swept across the Pacific front during World War II. I'd studied those events in school, I knew about Pearl Harbour and then the two atomic bombs, but I had overlooked how in between there had been numerous naval battles, or more accurately battles in the skies, with planes taking off from ships, perpetually moving across the vast expanses of sea. In such a large ocean, each small island was crucial and was referred to as an unsinkable aircraft carrier. Still today, they are indispensable for the control of the sea and the skies.

The woman also showed us parts of the island that were sinking due to climate change, lamenting as she did so that the polar bears' problems came before their own in the Western news. Maybe she was right, but rarely have I seen a person with a car that emitted blacker smoke or who felt as comfortable throwing all their litter to the ground as she did.

We'd talked with a priest about the fact that in these islands the word mountain was untranslatable and how missionaries didn't know how to render Bible passages. Now, however, we were confronted with a new type of mountain in the shape of ever-increasing heaps of rubbish. Especially in the capital, where more than half of the total inhabitants live, there is a high population density and dirt is everywhere. In such remote places getting rid of the rubbish is difficult, and in fact, the relics of the World War II are still there after decades. Of course, it won't be the refuse that sinks the islands, but my engagement with the ecological nightmare waned the more I watched my guide at work.

I had long since given up on the idea of a dreamlike paradise and I don't believe it is true that there is more equality between people on an island. On the contrary, hierarchy is everywhere. Women are not even allowed to go to the centre of the *maneaba*, the huge hut where social life takes place. Violence is rife, vices abound, boredom oppresses, and tragedies are recurrent. Even today, with modern equipment at their disposal, a fisherman can still go out to sea and then simply not return just because he hadn't wanted to listen to the weather report, didn't feel like filling up his tank, and said that what little petrol he had would be enough. Everyone has his own method, his own superstitious rituals on how to fish and getting drunk at sea is customary. In Papua during the mask festival that brought together distant tribes, an NGO had been handing out cartoons of a very hasty 'dumb fisherman' who set out to sea without caring about basic safety procedures. Now I understood the importance of this.

Of course, life is simpler, you walk barefoot, the sea offers wonderful views, and the starry sky is fantastic. But it really is a life that looks downright miserable. The heat is unbearable, there are mosquitoes everywhere, and this faraway kingdom of mine with such a curious name has very little to offer. Even the food is bad. The population is fat, due to their eating sweets and various junk foods from abroad. Locally there is the fish I used to eat every day. Kiribati, with its many widely scattered islands, has an exclusive fishing area that is enormous in relation to the country's size. Being here I became more aware of how essential fish is to feeding humans, although it makes one smile to discover that the most consumed fish in the world is cod because it does not taste like fish! As I continued to fly over the Pacific, it was easy to appreciate that all the land devoted to agriculture is a small fraction of the fishing area offered by the oceans. And it is interesting to note that fish, as well as humans on the land, are concentrated in certain areas despite the vastness of the space available.

It was a short passage to the **Solomon Islands (88)** which are Melanesian, and therefore similar to Papua New Guinea, the country where we had met, so we spent very little time there. Discovered in 1568 by a Spaniard who had heard from the Incas in Peru about islands brimming with gold, he named them the Solomon Islands in honour of the famous biblical king, who apparently owned large gold mines in Ofir. Then, for about two centuries, the islands were never found again, despite the fact that there had been numerous Noah's ark-style expeditions with married couples, animals and seeds on board in order to be able to populate them. In those days it wasn't easy to find an island because the calculation of longitude was still approximate. In 1885 they were divided among the European powers, in fact only the Germans came here.

They remained little explored until World War II when the usual battlefield airport was built here as well. In my guide's joking opinion, the road hasn't been maintained since then, and indeed I had never seen a road this vital in such a disastrous condition. The route from the airport to the city is the most important in an entire nation. Kings, prime ministers, and guests from abroad are obliged to cross it, so you try to make it the best it can be. If that road is rubbish, then things can only get worse.

Dodging between the potholes, we reached this cursed airport. There was only one flight to leave the island that suited us, and our anxiety was considerable. In fact, on the famous Excel sheet of flights and back-up plans, we'd written here in huge red letters: no alternative. If the flight was cancelled, we would be in trouble. We arrived so early that we were the only ones there. Half an hour later a man arrived with a huge bunch of keys and slowly started to open the doors. I was fascinated by the key rings that jingled with every step, dangling dozens of keys with incomprehensible numbers and acronyms on them. They have different coloured caps that only the owner knows but then he doesn't always guess at the first attempt either. Those keyrings open stories and adventures as much as doors. Now we had the whole terminal to ourselves, and we challenged each other to a wall-to-wall race on our wheeled suitcases.

An hour later the place came to life. Luckily, the flight departed on schedule, and we arrived in **Nauru (89)**, the least visited country in the world. We were the 16th and 17th visitors despite the year being a quarter over, giving a final projection of about 80 tourists in 12 months. We slept inside a sort of container rented to us by a Pakistani. We tried to run around the island but were interrupted by the usual dogs chasing us. You had to walk with a big stick and carry stones in your pocket. There were no amusements, and even bathing wasn't recommended due to the strong currents – you have to go to a spot protected by concrete barriers that turn the huge ocean into a bathtub.

Unlike the other island nations we'd seen, this entire country consisted of one single island of just over 20 km^2 and with about 10,000 inhabitants. There was very little to see, but even on this remote patch of land a lesson was available to be learned. Soon after independence in 1968, thanks to its many naturally occurring phosphates, Nauru became one of the richest countries in the world. They managed this wealth recklessly, immediately squandering it all. In an attempt to recoup these losses, they then tried to make a profit by allowing the Russian underworld to use the nation as a tax haven.

Currently they are trying to survive by giving Australia the use of parts of the island as a detention centre for illegal migrants. That's why there were Pakistanis in this remote place running that unusual sort of hotel. Another illegal migrant, an Iraqi, was improvising as a barber so I had my hair cut. Three days on the island had been more than enough and then here we were back at the airport, once again hoping that the outbound flight would leave. The connections were operated by the national airline, Air Nauru, founded during the golden years of phosphate mining. At that time, they had bought as many as six planes that could carry 10% of the entire population at once. Having an abundance of money, the islanders would frequently go shopping in Australia, squandering money, and getting swindled.

Nowadays Air Nauru flights are unreliable for a number of reasons: a minister can commandeer the plane for state business if he wants to; if there is a medical emergency or a boat is lost, they go searching for it by air; or maybe a part breaks and you have to wait a week for it to arrive from Australia.

Thankfully, we left without any problems and reached **Fiji (90)**. This country is half Polynesian and half Indian because the British brought workers here from India and today you can feel the tense atmosphere between the two communities. It's the home of the University of the South Pacific, where the ruling classes of these micronations gather to study, which means that those who will someday have senior roles within their respective island nations get to know each other as youngsters. Households that have a member serving in the military or working in the United States also tend to already be acquainted with each other, because they inevitably meet in Hawaii.

The distances travelled each time are immense. Truly the water is the great protagonist while the land occasionally peeks out timidly. The Pacific alone is larger than all the landmasses of the globe and is home to some 25,000 islands that together occupy less than 1% of the ocean's surface.

About halfway through, it was time for a first assessment of the value of going to these little islands considering the cost, time, and effort. The answer was very straightforward, it wasn't worth it. There are obvious differences between Polynesians, Micronesians, and Melanesians, but having seen one island per geographical region, the others are mostly repetitions. The American girl and I had made fun of the tourists in Panama, intent on shopping and buying yet another handbag thinking they needed it for some tiny, insignificant detail. But in fact, that's what we were doing with the islands. We were buying a new, very expensive handbag every time, expecting it to have something unique and important. And yet, perhaps like some of the handbag shoppers, we were having the time of our lives!

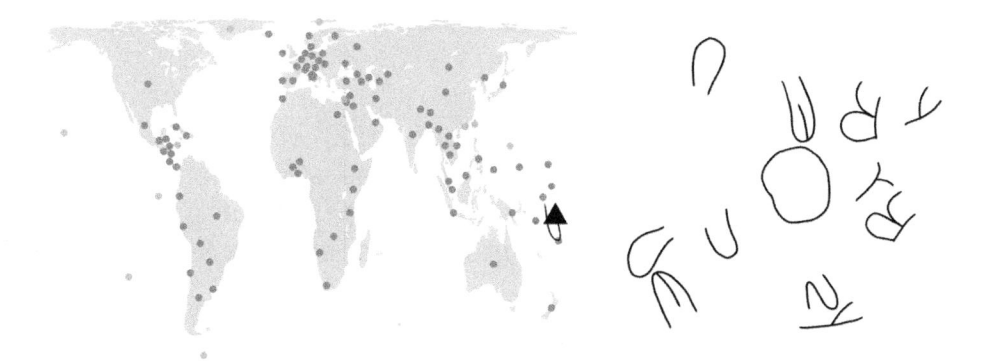

A 20-minute internal flight in Fiji takes you to the only airport that has flights to **Tuvalu (91)**, a country so small that the airstrip is an essential space for the islanders and many activities take place there. We too would go out onto the tarmac to jog at sunset. Then, twice a week when a plane lands, access is closed to people, and everyone moves to the arrivals area to celebrate the big event. Along with the two of us, there was another tourist on board who had come to buy stamps. These had been one of the island's few incomes until the internet provided them with a stroke of luck whilst assigning exclusive domains to the various nations. Tuvalu became the proud owner of the .tv domain, which has since generated the country large amounts of money for licensing it out to TV streaming services. With $100,000 in its pocket, the small country was finally able to pay its membership fee to the United Nations.

During the weary days on the islands, I asked the American girl to explain to me a world I was not familiar with, namely that of Silicon Valley. She had just left her job at a biotechnology company in San Francisco and had a picture on her mobile phone capturing the moment when she rang the famous bell on Wall Street as her company went public. She would unveil this environment to me as we went about our various domestic activities, which made me feel like those Zen monks who talk about the highest of concepts as they peel potatoes. I was fascinated by this high-level person who could make important decisions over the phone whilst simultaneously learning how to put a worm on a hook. And indeed, here you ate what you caught, along with a couple of coconuts that were always available. On every island, the thought was the same, 'Here we lead a life that is as simple as it is boring'. If you had to choose between stress and boredom, the decision felt harder than I could have believed. Boredom destroys you.

Our next destination was **Tonga (92)** where we arrived squarely on Easter Day. A woman was waiting for us, and hastily took us to the rented flat, then without giving us any warning about the surroundings, she left. Everything was closed! Even on a normal Sunday, one must devote oneself entirely to church, to the point that all other activities are forbidden, including sports. Imagine the situation at Easter. For dinner, we were forced to knock on the front door, and ask for something. Strong religiosity characterises the island: they are almost all practising Christians, but the struggle between the various denominations is fierce. The Mormons in particular invest enormous resources, and their missionaries cycle around constantly promising economic benefits to those who convert. Their dream is to turn Tonga into the first Mormon nation, and they could succeed, because if the king converts, it is possible that many will follow him.

Our guide for the next few days was an Englishman who had lived there for 30 years. He tried to set up a meeting with some nobles but without success (for the king himself you have to pay). He was very frank in describing a society stratified into castes and dedicated to food to the point of having one of the fattest populations in the world. Each chair was made to hold the weight of two normal people.

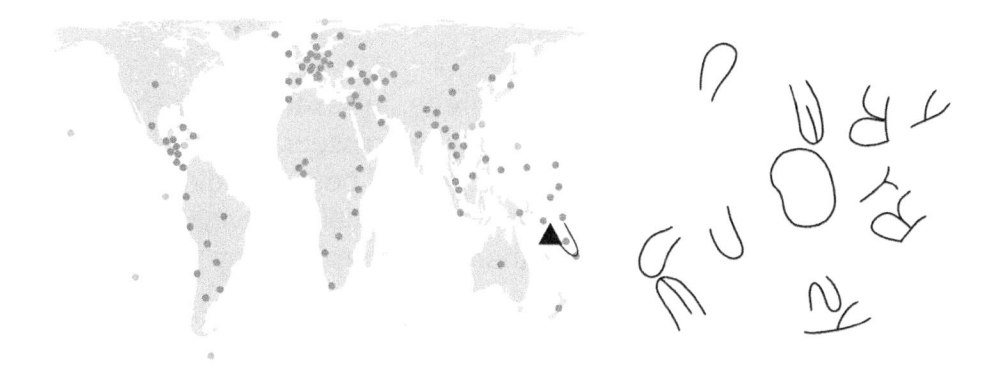

In **Vanuatu (93)**, on the other hand, tourism is developing, and many Australians go there on holiday. Even on the official immigration sheet, there were advertisements about what to do and where to sleep. From the capital, we took a further flight to the site of an active volcano, where it was possible to climb to the summit and observe lava explosions. I keep the picture on my desktop, so I relive the same thrill every time I turn on my computer. I took a well-focused picture at a reasonable distance, whereas other tourists were intent on taking selfies, walking on the edge, and jumping with fright at every noise or puff. Basically, in a split second, with just one slip, they could fall inside and die.

A cargo cult was born on this remote little island during World War II. The local Melanesians, who still lived as if they were stuck in the stone age, came into contact with European and American soldiers who received an abundance of goods directly from the sky via military air drops. They had deduced that the pilots of these planes were the ancestors of those strange men who received food in abundance, without having to hunt or fish, and so they began to build small runways similar to the real ones where the planes landed, to organise religious rituals that mimicked military exercises and to pay homage to the same flag as the soldiers.

But what caught my attention, more than the wacky religion, was the presence of Japanese technicians, intent on explaining to the Melanesians how to build their huts more efficiently and sturdily using local materials. How satisfying for me. Whenever I would hear people eulogising ancient techniques, which are still considered unparalleled, something inside of me would say 'That surely can't be the case'. Indeed, it is admirable what has been achieved and handed down over time, but today we can easily do better. And this applies to every past culture, even the mysterious pyramids. Of course, we don't know exactly how the Egyptians of the time built them, but there's no doubt that we would be able to build them now.

The same is true in other areas, for example, when one reads that the *Inuit* are the best connoisseurs of ice. Or that in Namibia the desert peoples are the best at finding water. And yes, of course the Polynesians excel at navigating with canoes and knowing that there was land nearby thanks to the waves, the reflection of the clouds, and the flight range of the birds. Even just concerning ourselves with people already encountered in the narrative, we become aware of a pattern of generally held belief. But let's be clear. What is meant in these cases is that these are notable achievements in situations where the use of technology was not available. There's no getting around the fact that, with modern tools and knowledge, you can always do better in any field.

Our final country on the continent of Oceania was **Samoa (94)** where we ended up in an awful hotel that was so dirty, we decided to leave. We had swarms of gnats in the room swirling above the bed, bugs everywhere, and we were tired after weeks of constant touring, so for once, having realised we had gone too far in being 'local', we went to a hotel and slept comfortably. It was a bittersweet feeling as we left – though, because the girl working in the garden had such an incredulous look on her face. I could imagine what was going on in her head. The room for the serving staff must have been far worse than ours and she actually lived there, whereas we couldn't bear to stay there even a few nights. Unwittingly, we'd hurt her and although she hadn't asked me for an explanation, I told her that it was our honeymoon and therefore we wanted something special, which coaxed a relieved smile from her.

The Oceania continent was completed. It represents a tiny percentage of the world's population, about 0.5%, and has only 14 nations, but it was still quite an achievement.

The map I bought in Guam now had lots of nice little crosses over the islands visited, a bit like playing Battleship by myself and trying to sink some land. Most importantly, those huge spaces featured on the inflatable globe I had kept on my desk for years as a boy had finally been filled in.

We returned to Australia and then said goodbye to Oceania for good, continuing on to Bali in Indonesia. From there we had a further flight to **East Timor (95)** where we found accommodation in none other than the honorary Mexican consulate, which rented out rooms on the side. On an excursion to the coffee plantations, a tourist couple from the Czech Republic joined us. Such encounters inevitably turn into accounts of the most incredible adventures, because those Europeans who holiday in East Timor have obviously already seen a lot. They were serial travellers, collectors of 'handbags', just like us. They seemed to me to be arrogant, annoying, and superficial. Were we two also like that? We had fallen into the comparison trap, that is, this irrepressible desire to immediately share the most remote and difficult experiences. We wanted to impress each other, to give a good image of ourselves, and to compare to find out who had done more. In that car where we sat, we were not exchanging information and emotions, we were just measuring our egos.

Of course, first with poker and now with travel, I get into circles where you find a particular type of person. Some of my best friends and the people I admire most have played poker professionally, but in the player category, to be honest, the average level is low because it is traditionally a fringe activity. With travellers, on the contrary, I feel pretty confident that they are above-average people. Travelling implies having curiosity, a desire to discover and a willingness to take the initiative. Those who travel a lot are usually more educated and open-minded than the average person.

But how do we categorise those who travel 'too much'? Is there a number of trips beyond which one goes to excess and thus breaks the positive mechanism? I can't answer for others, but for me as a pupil in travel school, the learning curve was still uphill and the more I continued, the more I discovered. 'Too much', if there is such a thing, was far away…

Certainly, this last nation, East Timor, was also below average, as were those recently visited. In describing the country my guide said that it exports oil, but my homework was much more forthright – 90% of the nation's exports are oil. It sounded to me like the times in school when they used to talk about spice expeditions in the old days, in other words, telling the truth but neglecting the scale of the phenomenon and how important it once was, almost on the same level as oil is today.

Timor also has some agriculture as a few Australians living there are focusing on coffee production which is exported, but there seems to be no nation in the world more dependent on a single export. Australia, aware of this and feeling guilty for having abandoned them to the Japanese in World War II, has renounced all claim to the oil and is trying to help build a new nation.

The independence from Portugal proclaimed in 1975 by a communist government was followed by an invasion by the Indonesians, supported by many western countries to remove the communist threat in the heart of the archipelago. After a long and bloody struggle, there was finally a referendum in which the population voted for independence, and so East Timor became part of the United Nations in 2002. Of course, it is good that each population has the opportunity to decide for itself, but can Tuvalu and Nauru, with their 10,000 or so inhabitants, have a vote at the UN on par with India on certain issues? Pluto has been downgraded from a planet, should we perhaps do something similar with my beloved Kiribati islands? These little nations put their vote up for sale to the highest bidder and provide a poor show.

On our return to Indonesia, the American girl flew off to start her new job. Neither of us had formally asked if we were in a proper relationship, but the anxiety of the question hung in the air. Sooner or later, we would have to talk, but for now I stayed in the country and went to Komodo, the home of the famous dragon.

My flight from Bali was direct to **Greece (96)**, as you can imagine, because it was cheaper. And while I was visiting the Meteora, which are monasteries built on top of high rocks, I wondered if I wanted to start this relationship. I admired the girl, and we had a stimulating intellectual interaction. In recent years I had known mainly young, poorly educated or even half-literate girls, without great dreams, crushed by poverty, laziness, and the absence of stimulation. They just didn't understand why I was travelling, and spending my money in this way, but she obviously supported and even nurtured my curiosity.

Other people had no idea where my next destinations were; with her the evenings were spent discussing how to get to Timbuktu. We would share our ideas on how they should load the plane by first boarding people at the window instead of using seat numbers. We wanted to revolutionise announcements at the airport. She would then explain the modern, progressive mentality to me and in return I was a dedicated tour guide. By then I had been studying full-time for years and had picked up the pace in doing my homework: so that I would arrive at the next destination prepared. For each intended location I was able to give her a picture of the situation from various points of view and she would take notes as I spoke because she wanted to verify my statements, the dates I brought up, the comparisons with countries I had already visited. She rarely caught me unprepared because she didn't take into account that the time she was devoting to work, I was devoting to this. I was becoming something of a true professional. Famously, convention dictates that it takes 10,000 hours to qualify as an expert in any field of human knowledge, and I had already far exceeded this on the trip and was only halfway through the adventure.

We were a phenomenal travel team, but honestly, I was confused. She had managed to keep her feet on the ground, she had a career, she was very well-rounded. In short, she was a bit too serious for me. If I had wanted a normal relationship, I would have chosen her. But I wanted nothing more than adventure, fun and of course, the school of travel. I wanted to continue to travel full-time and have experiences, which tended to be on my own. Basically, I needed her in five years' time, but she wanted me now. She'd broken up with someone who had also been a constant travelling companion who had worked at the United Nations, after a long relationship which she had been very committed to. Now she wanted to speed up. So, when I was confronted with an offer to move to San Francisco, or to try living together for a while in Portugal, in an environment more familiar to me and congenial to her because her family had emigrated from there, I said no. We never saw each other again in person.

0% ▬▬▬ 50% ▭ 100%

I had some time before my next booked tour, so I went to **Bulgaria (97)** where I appreciated the custom of eating a big salad as an appetiser. If it hadn't been for the addition of vodka, I would have taken them for health conscious. You fill up immediately with vegetables so then you eat less. In any case, the yoghurt is actually better than anywhere else.

In **Romania (98)** I went to visit the famous Dracula castle and then I was ready to embark for Istanbul. From there I reached **Tajikistan (99)** where I began the adventure of the 'Pamir Road', over 1,200 km at dizzying heights coinciding with an old stretch of the Silk Road. I had come from coral atolls bathed in blue, and ocean as far as the eye could see and now, I was about 2,000 km from the sea as the crow flies. This transition from one reality to another was not disorienting; on the contrary, I was happy, but between one breathtaking view and the next, unfortunately it was diarrhoea that kept me company, not leaving me in peace for a moment.

Hygiene in these places is poor, but especially at over 4,000 m where the water does not boil at 100°C so there is no chance of eliminating all germs. You just have to put up with it. I was certainly not the only one suffering in the group, and between photos and various emergencies, the necessary toilet stops were frequent.

A Bulgarian woman, an air traffic controller, had brought along a Polaroid camera that printed photos in a couple of minutes. It was a great idea, and people were finally really happy having lenses pointed at them all the time. There was a queue to get a photo of yourself. Mothers with children were hurrying to her, everyone wanted that print to hang in the house, to send to their distant father. An elderly woman shyly asked for the photo and then begged her to wait a few minutes as she wanted to go home and do her hair first. A gentleman showed up in what was clearly a good suit he had just put on and asked one of the men in the group if he could have the photo as he didn't want to address a woman, especially a western one directly, as they are seen as very loose. By their standards this was invariably true, as you only have to have had more than one partner in your life to be considered depraved.

About ten days later I was in **Kyrgyzstan (100)** where the wonderful, paved Pamir Highway ends – or begins. True nomads still exist in the country and many walk around wearing an elongated white hat. It is one of the national symbols and they are keen to explain that the shape resembles that of the mountains, snow-capped of course. This hat is particularly eye-catching, even absurd, yet on reflection, wherever I've gone, the local headgear has seemed ridiculous, including our own. But I realised that what was important wasn't whether a hat was 'normal' or not. I was just grateful that I lived in a climate that was mild enough not to need to wear one.

Now, apart from tiny Bhutan, Tajikistan and Kyrgyzstan are the countries most covered by mountains in relation to territory. About 90% of the area for both and the average elevation is around 3,000 m, which is difficult to live on and in consequence a huge number of men go to work abroad, mainly in Russia.

There is very little arable land, so the diet revolves around animal products, making it hard for a vegetarian to eat, and almost impossible for a vegan. Even for those without strict dietary requirements, the food was monotonous and in every house that hosted me, dinner was always exactly the same. The service was identical each time and the drinks and courses were served in the same order. A foundation run by the local Islamic sect, the Ismailites, trains local families to reach certain standards of service and hygiene. Then it finds them customers, tourists like me who have ventured to the Pamir. In my experience, these families follow the guidelines so closely to the letter that everything looks the same.

The foundation also offers English courses, and as soon as we were able to exchange a few words, my question to the locals was always the same, 'What is your favourite food? The answers were invariably 'Meat and milk', which made me happy since there's no sense of deprivation in someone who is used to a diet rich in meat and dairy products.

The monotony of the simple food wasn't a problem for the Kyrgyz. Getting married, on the other hand, could be much more complex due to the lack of choice. I had noticed on the smaller islands that had populations of a few hundred people or less, that almost everyone was related. Incest is a big problem and to find a partner they have to go to other islands, inevitably taking the woman away from her environment and family. Marriages are arranged by the elders of the various islands, who actually trade young people.

Here in Central Asia the environment is completely different. There are many more people in the high mountains, but it is also difficult for nomads on the move to find a wife, so the solution is to kidnap her. This terrible custom (*ala-kachhu*), absurd as it may seem, is still widespread in Kyrgyzstan. It's formally forbidden, but it's tolerated, even recommended for a happy marriage. Imagine being caught, blindfolded, tied up and taken away, only to find yourself married to a man you don't know. Your life becomes a servitude to him and his family. What a nightmare. Nowadays the newlyweds usually at least know each other, but it is still barbaric.

We take our right to be able to choose freely about a relationship for granted, not having to follow rules of religion, profession, income, not having to go to the imam, the priest or the teacher to ask for an opinion on the partner, not having to look for a virgin girl or haggle with the father. We are making huge steps forward, but in the world today, arranged marriages, where there is essentially a market for brides, are still widespread. In India, the world's largest democracy, almost all marriages are arranged and respect caste rules.

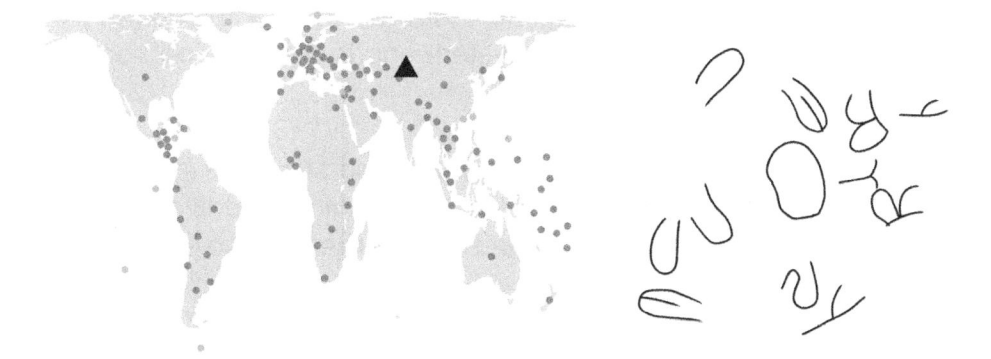

As I travelled, I focused on the fact that if I ever get married, I don't want to enter the house carrying my wife in my arms, because that seems as if she is my property. Nor do I want the bride to be accompanied by her father and brought to me. It is a tradition that no one pays attention to, but this symbolic passing from father to husband speaks volumes.

I celebrated my reaching country number 100 alone in a very sad room where the power went out for the whole night.

To go from Osh, the Kyrgyz city at the end of this incredible journey, all the way to Asmara takes a lot of patience and imagination. But with five flights and a one-night stop in Dubai I managed to get to **Eritrea (101)**. I had flown much further to get the visa!

The former colony retains something of Italy and in every bar in Asmara I felt like I was back in my childhood days. The furnishings and posters were those from when I used to queue for packaged ice cream as a child and would carefully ponder the options. Choosing the ice cream was a big deal! Even the prices on display were still in lira and my memory went back to counting the coins to see if they were enough for what I wanted. Forty years ago, people had paid less attention to children in the queue, so adults had usually walked past me. Now, standing there in front of those billboards, it was me who looked like the aggressive one, even though I had done nothing and would never push forward. The Eritreans would let me pass in front. But why? More regurgitation of colonial values? More likely they are so oppressed by the regime that they think a European in their country is part of the system and therefore a person to be feared.

The poor Eritrean citizens were forced to serve in the military for very long periods, some for their entire lives. They enjoyed no freedom at all, and the internet was so slow as to be unusable. It was kept that way on purpose, which means that there was complete censorship, but when people accuse the regime of blocking access to the Internet, they were able to reply that it existed and was available. It's a bit like the sham elections with which dictators can say that people vote in their country. As a tourist, I had everything and saw that others had nothing. This country was a disaster, and the dictatorship was so suffocating that some compare it to North Korea.

It was only for me and the few other booked tourists that they operated a non-electrified train built by the Italians that ran from the present capital to the port of Massawa, the capital in colonial times. A height difference of over 2,000 m required a great deal of engineering, and no railway has been built since. In the ruined city of Massawa, I was again gasping under a stone-cracking sun while still feeling the cold of the mountains.

I was in a non-stop whirl; all my energy was involved in doing and venturing out even more. The only thing I was passionate about was my school of travel and I wanted to gobble up information about the whole world. I had passed the 100 countries visited threshold and there were no longer any big holes on the map.

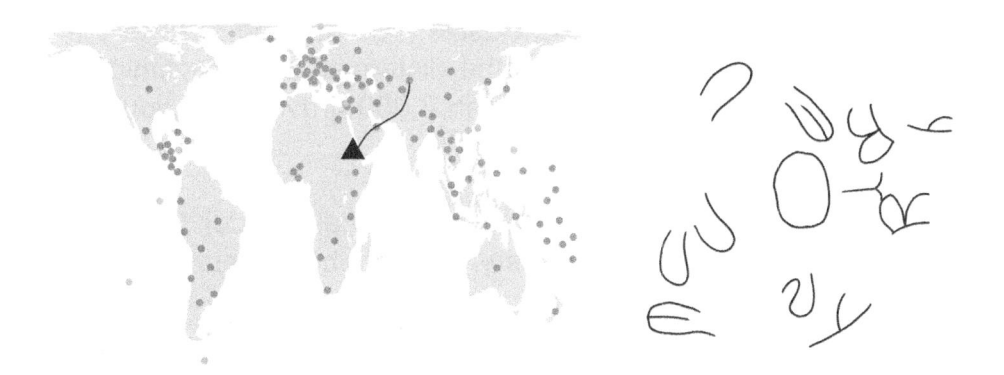

On several occasions I had begun to dream of actually visiting every country in the world and some mornings I got up determined, telling myself that I must go everywhere. 'Let's take the map again and work on it, a way must be found' I would tell myself. After all, I had already faced some dangerous places, I had an idea of what awaited me. But I had yet to explore the most difficult countries and no matter how optimistic I tried to be; the goal was as yet far from being achieved. The physical, mental, and economic effort to visit nations that were heavily discouraged was such that, at times, a new trip added a nation to the tally, but made me feel the full weight of the challenge.

In particular, Afghanistan was the nation that worried me the most, for a simple yet difficult-to-guess reason. It's the first in alphabetical order, so any plan inevitably leads you to start there.

Meanwhile I found a way to go to Saudi Arabia, the only country in the world that doesn't accept tourists. These days the rules have changed, indeed it has become really easy to go, but in 2018 the most viable route was through a business meeting. I found an agency that suited me and started processing my documents. In the meantime, I travelled between Slovenia and **Croatia (102)** and then stayed in **Bosnia and Herzegovina (103)** and visited Srebrenica.

A genocide had taken place there, right in the middle of Europe, during my adult years, yet again I knew very little about it. Information is readily available everywhere, but going there in person is conclusive. You see the sites of the massacre, you understand the distances, and the timings. You contemplate the more than 8,000 graves, and you will never forget what happened.

This horror had taken place practically under the eyes of the Blue Helmets, the very people who are supposed to keep the peace on behalf of the United Nations. This is the same organisation that I have taken as a benchmark for my nation 'counter'. There are 193 members. If you ask anyone how many nations exist in the world, you will get the most varied answers, but no one can answer with a number less than 193. Some argue that there are more. Some tend to include the Vatican and Palestine because they are Permanent Observers. Others add Kosovo and Taiwan, or others. I think 193 is the simplest and most straightforward answer to date.

While I was in **Serbia (104)**, another 'visa' I had applied for while in Greece a few months earlier was finally approved. I was now authorised to go to **Mount Athos (/)**. This monastic state of over 300 km² is all within Greece and has existed for over 1,000 years. It has its own rules, to the point that you need a pass to enter and only ten non-Orthodox men a day are admitted.

Some monks spend their entire lives uttering *Hesychasm*, the prayer of the heart, which is performed with the repetition of a single phrase and is such an enveloping way of praying that it involves the whole body. The breath and heartbeat harmonise with the words, as the body and mind both ask Jesus for forgiveness. I stayed for four days and spent the nights watching them pray obsessively in a truly evocative setting. I had only one meal a day, long walks, and an omnipresent preoccupation with death. Despite the territory being in Europe, these monks forbid the entry of women and even female animals are kept away. Was it really possible that such determined men need only look at a woman to no longer find God?

It was time to go back to Rome as the documents needed to apply for a 'business' visa in Saudi Arabia were ready. As much as my life may seem to be a continuous mindless game, from a logistical point of view there was always organisation to be done. From home, I also applied to participate as a spectator in an astronaut launch and to board a cargo ship. I had no lack of ideas and was determined to spend all my money if necessary. My blue sweatshirt, a friend for a thousand adventures, was beginning to come to the end of its life. It was in disastrous condition even by my vagabond standards. Luckily, I found one of the same brand in just a slightly different colour. Still, I was sorry to see it replaced as it had been my 'Linus blanket' for four years.

In **Saudi Arabia (105)** along with my new sweatshirt came a new identity – I was an eyewear salesman. I'd chosen glasses as my 'business' because I had a friend with an opticians practice in Rome and I'd obtained some headed paper from him. The number of his shop was my contact address and obviously, if the embassy had called to check, the response would have been that I worked there. I'd also spent an evening being briefed on his work.

The only worry was about my beloved luggage. It is not normal to go to Arabia on business and show up looking like a vagrant, albeit in a new sweatshirt... As usual, I did not wear a suit, shirt, or tie. Had I been asked why I had no suit I would have claimed that I was going to buy one there, something traditional to be considerate towards my potential partners. After all, Western smart clothes are pure conventions, there is nothing logical about wearing an uncomfortable tie or having a collar. Other things are objectively valid: trousers are more efficient than any other clothing when it comes to sports, activities or fighting. I state this with conviction, after all, in armies all over the world one wears trousers when in action and traditional clothes on parade. But loose-fitting clothes that let the air through are comfortable when it is as hot as in Arabia, and in addition, they fit you for your whole life. In the West, as soon as you change size, you have to revise your wardrobe.

In the men's toilet I made the terrible gaffe of drying my hands on the white headgear of a man who had unrolled and hung it up. I apologised several times, but the guy was more amused than angry. That white headgear is useful against the sun and is held in place by a rope of goat hair that can be used as a kind of brake for the camel. What is neither clever nor funny are the women's clothes. We are in the desert, and they force the women to cover themselves completely with heavy black robes, made specifically to conceal them and make them lose all desire to move.

Now the recently visited Mount Athos was clearly an absurd legacy of the Middle Ages. If someone wants to isolate themselves to pray, they are free to do so, but to forbid women to enter a huge territory within the European Community is madness. Here in Arabia, they adopt a different but equally despicable solution to keep the sexes apart: men isolate their families instead of themselves, they go around freely while women are mostly at home and need a male guardian to go out.

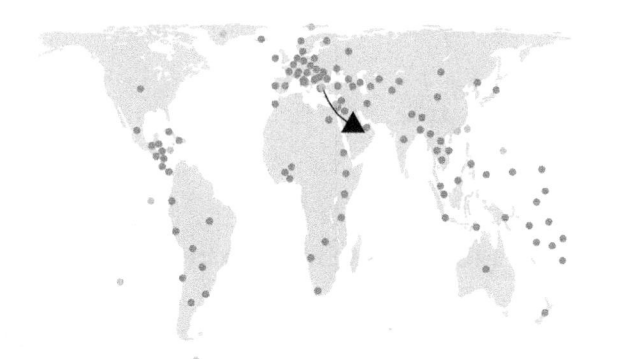

But for once, despite being a man, I too was faced with a prohibition that is inconceivable in the modern world. As a non-Muslim, I couldn't enter the city of Mecca. In general, a country like Arabia amplifies a notion that I was in the process of formulating. When doing your homework, it is crucial to delve into religion, because only by getting into precepts and beliefs can you find the key to understanding the non-obvious behaviour you are witnessing.

I visited **Kuwait (106)**, a truly unremarkable place, a small stronghold held by the ever-cautious British, separated from Iraq in order to have further access to the sea. The most entertaining part of the visit was going to see a camel race. This animal, more precisely a dromedary, is considered a marvellous gift from God and in the Koran, it is named before heaven and earth. It's the ship of the desert and it allowed the Arabs, the first to domesticate it, to transport goods over long distances connecting far flung worlds.

Camels are also considered attractive, and beauty contests are organised for them, with competitors even going as far as to perform cosmetic surgery to enhance certain features. A very good-looking or fast specimen can be worth millions of dollars. Truly, different peoples have different tastes. There are competitions for the most beautiful carp in the East, or closer to home, for dogs and cats. So many people like horses that they ended up being perceived as sexy. Indeed, the horse is your sports car, your armoured tank, your most trusted friend, an extension of you. Many great men of the past have statues made of themselves on horseback. It's the same feeling with the camel for an Arab.

Next, I went to **Bahrain (107)**. Now, while in the big and influential Saudi Arabia many things are forbidden, in this small kingdom one can let off steam. If you will, it's the place where fringe activities are facilitated, and Saudi Arabia tolerates them as long as they take place abroad. This small island is joined to the huge Arabian Peninsula by a bridge, so for those who live nearby, especially in Dammam, getting to Bahrain is very easy.

That bridge is the key, as the small nation is not part of the Holy Land that is home to the two holy cities of Mecca and Medina, so some things become tolerable. American military bases are here, alcohol is available, prostitution is rife, cinemas show uncensored films, and women walk around freely and dressed normally. Lots of Saudis come over at the weekend and go wild. In the busy lobby of my hotel, I realised on the first evening that I was looking at a woman again. I hadn't seen a female face for a couple of weeks.

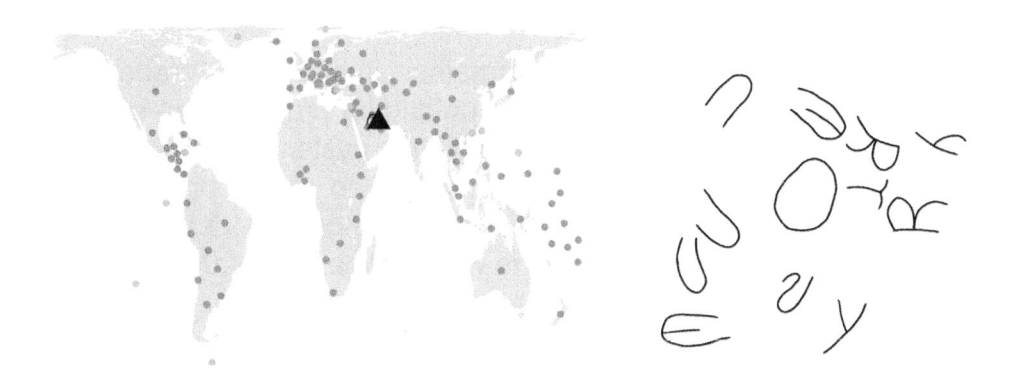

Here again, the existence of a small nation is due to the British. In 1820, annoyed by the constant attacks of pirates, they closed an agreement with various small states in the Gulf. From 1853 onwards they called these countries 'Truce States', which was a truce from piracy. The British guaranteed protection from the Ottoman Empire, and in return, the bloody piracy, which had always had the support of the local emirs, was kept under control. After World War II however, the British wanted to withdraw completely and no longer offer protection. In 1968, despite the oil that was there, they announced that they would leave, but they were asked to stay as Bahrain feared, with good reason, that a race would ensue for its conquest by Arabia and Iran. The other truce states joined together to achieve greater size and resist the invasion, and what is now the famous United Arab Emirates was born, consisting of seven separate entities, including Dubai and Abu Dhabi. But Bahrain didn't get along with them, and neither did Qatar, both remaining independent because the British played pre-emptively and made agreements with Arabia and Iran to cede some territory, on the promise that they would not conquer any more.

In **Oman (108)**, a country very well equipped for tourism, I had some classic desert experiences. In the *souk*, or market, I was about to buy something frivolous – a man's suit that has a flap designed to put perfume on so that it smells good all day. In Islamic countries it is men who wear perfume in public, and women only in private. Above all though, I was busy trying to figure out how I could visit neighbouring Yemen. It seemed virtually impossible with a civil war raging, supported by foreign powers, primarily Iran on one side and Arabia on the other. Not coincidentally, these were the same two nations that had fought over Bahrain in the past.

Meanwhile, I flew to **Malta (109)**, where I awaited the arrival of my ship for five days. It was behind schedule, but on the upside, some gaming companies are based there, so I had the chance to pass the time with a few friends. The long-awaited embarkation was exciting. I would finally experience the open sea continuously for a month. This too is what exploring the world is all about.

In the 1950s, the first container ship changed trade by speeding up the loading and unloading process and eliminating the theft of goods. Today, this system is a universal standard, even more so than that of an airport or a chain hotel room. 90% of international trade moves by sea, in fact, it's these ships that move the world. Mine had 11,000 standard containers on board and only 22 crew members, mostly Filipinos.

This time, however, despite the photos of my beautiful classroom, there was little connection. They only invited me to pray in their rooms on Sundays and for the odd game of PlayStation, oh and one of them cut my hair in exchange for a Mars bar. Perhaps they were afraid that interacting with me might give the impression that they were not working since I was the only passenger. The captain had given me the freedom to go everywhere, as long as I did not disturb anyone's work, which, in a situation where you never leave their workplace, is a rather contradictory message. I thought about joining the sailors during the port stops, but they were so short that they didn't even have time to leave the harbour, and therefore there was no way to socialise then either.

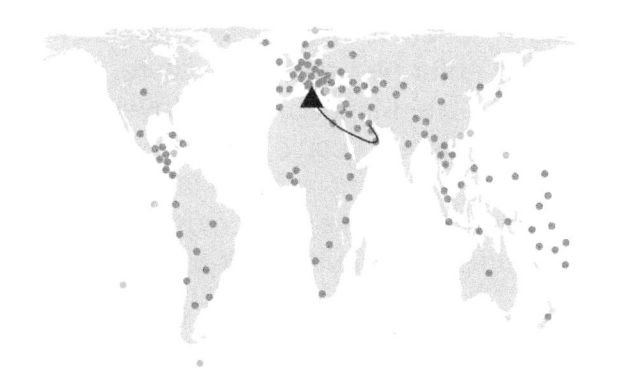

The container has simplified and reduced the loading and unloading process to the point that being a sailor no longer has the same fascination. You don't see the world, there is no more drinking and dancing in ports, no more girlfriends in every country. Indeed, with rare exceptions, the crew didn't even have time to go out to find hookers, an occupation that I had been convinced kept sailors busy at every stop. But this was fine by me, I spent hours on deck watching the ocean: this was travel school. It was an experience of profound solitude and introspection.

The cabin was larger than a hotel room, and there were no pictures on the walls to ignore, but it had what I needed, as well as a 'view' of the containers. During the night everything disappeared, even the sea, and I could admire the stars. I had come for the water and was falling in love with the sky. From the middle of the ocean, you could look up without any light altering the view. Our immense ship did not show a single light, everything was shrouded in darkness. And these stars don't speak, yet they shine in such a way that they really seem to want to say something. It was only when I was there that I was able to finally comprehend the blue sky of the Mongols, the monolith of the aborigines, and the feeling of serene death on the ice. Now, for the first time in my life, I had an understanding of the stars, of horoscopes, of seeing them take shape in the body of an animal and communicate with you.

I fought boredom by sorting my travel notes since there was no television or internet. I even missed the chaos of the hostels, nights with people snoring or moving around all the time, the sound of zips in the morning, and the hustle and bustle to the bathroom. But this absence of distractions came in handy when writing the book, which was started in the middle of the ocean.

Mainly, however, I entertained myself by going to the bridge. I stood beside the captain during the transit of the Suez Canal, another major junction in the world besides Panama. I watched the ship enter port and manoeuvre, we passed through the Strait of Bab el-Mandeb, and I stayed on watch for a few hours at night to see if I could fulfil a task that was clearly not for me. While it was impossible to fall asleep during the bear watch in Siberia because of the mosquitoes, and at Athos you had to stand singing loudly until dawn, here the temptation to give in was fierce. All the instrumentation which emanates light from the monitors was covered so that the eyes could get used to the darkness and be able to spot danger. All that remained was total silence and the stars. If the sailor on duty didn't touch anything for a few minutes, some sort of alarm was triggered as a precaution.

But the most interesting days were those transiting the waters near Somalia that were infested by its notorious pirates. Bulkheads were erected around the ship to prevent anyone from climbing in, powerful water cannons were installed on each side to counter the assault with jets of water, and the speed was increased to generate a repelling wave. I also had to turn off the lights inside my room at 9 pm and I had practised how to reach a sort of fortress inside the ship where I could hide to avoid being kidnapped (it was very simple, even in the dark and in panic, you just had to run and turn to the right each time, you couldn't miss it). We would have continued to control the ship from its heart, even if the pirates had reached the highest deck.

But all this was mainly done to fulfil insurance obligations, and the risk of an attack was close to zero. The ship was flying the British flag and not the famous Liberia or Panama and apparently pirates attack ships with flags of convenience, knowing that no one will come to their rescue. This freighter paid millions in taxes in the UK and would certainly have received help from the British navy based in Djibouti and probably also from others that often sailed nearby.

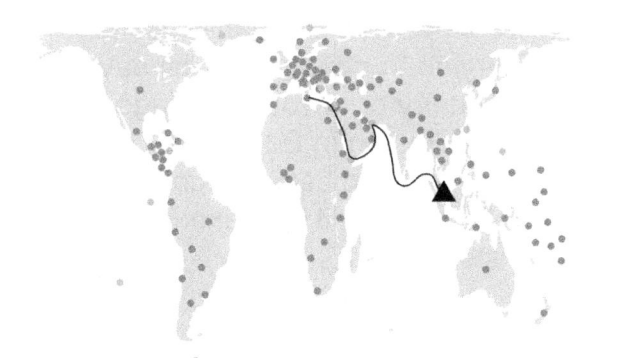

In short, the only unwelcome guests on board were the Saudi authorities on arrival in Jeddah who at times could be overbearing. To prevent problems, the captain had asked me to put my computer in his room. He had assumed that it was full of porn and as a passenger, I could be checked out, whereas such rudeness wouldn't be tolerated towards the captain. I couldn't go ashore for those two days because tourism was forbidden in Saudi Arabia and my 'business' visa had already been used up. As I no longer even had a computer on board, I reread *Endurance, Shackleton's Incredible Journey to the South Pole*, an adventure book that I adored, to prepare myself in the near future for weather that would be even colder than I had experienced in Antarctica.

After a month on board, I disembarked in Kuala Lumpur wearing a company T-shirt that the captain had given me, knowing that in the port they would take me for a real sailor returning home after months. Contrary to their expectations, I flew to **Kazakhstan (110)**, despite contending with many difficulties due to the changed schedule. The ship had arrived in Malta five days late, forcing me to change my return flights, and the journey had accumulated two more days, so my schedule had been disrupted again and I only had access to the internet at the destination port. The arrival in Astana (now called Nur-Sultan) meant a transition from equatorial heat to the early winter cold of a city where it easily reaches -30°C. Only Ulan Bator in Mongolia is considered colder among the world's capitals.

Kazakhstan is as huge as it is unknown. When I was in Kenya with my friends, in order not to be constantly pestered by layabouts on the beach trying to chat you up by saying something nice about your country or in your language, we replied that we were from Kazakhstan in Borat style, so no one ever knew what to invent. If Iceland became more popular with the explosion of a volcano, here it had taken the film, but there were still few tourists.

I visited a very moving Soviet concentration camp for the wives of political prisoners. Some of the photos on the walls recorded the women wearing beautiful dresses because they had been tricked into showing up at the place where they were supposed to meet their husbands on their return from the *gulag*. Instead, they imprisoned them on arrival. Imagine the frustration of being in a trap, not being able to see the man they loved again and ending up in the *gulag* themselves. My visit took place during a snowstorm which added drama to the horror.

My guide, a very young boy, was dressed poorly and wore the same outfit every day, just as I was doing since I wore the only warm, heavy things I owned. But I was a minimalist traveller with hand luggage and felt no deprivation, just as those who always dress the same out of simplicity and free choice do not. He appeared to me to be buried in his clothes and didn't appear to have chosen this for himself. Sometimes clothes allow one to distinguish work from leisure, they add some nuance to the personality and mood of the moment. Every now and then I tried on traditional dress to more easily imagine my life in a place, while I met numerous tourists who did the same, just to put a picture on Instagram. Who knows, a little money for a change of dress might have broken up the monotony for him as well.

In any case, it was so cold that you only went out for a few hours a day, and the rest of the time I spent in the hotel with a sauna and Turkish bath in blissful warmth, rereading

Hopkirk's *The Great Game* while waiting to finally be allowed into Baikonur, the world's most important cosmodrome.

Just a few days and I would be lucky enough to be at the launch base to witness the departure of the astronauts to the space station. This huge centre, twice the size of Luxembourg, has been the scene of great tragedies and enormous successes. It was from here that Gagarin and Tereshkova set off on their missions in competition with the United States, one of the few things we could call a positive outcome of the Cold War. Upon the break-up of the USSR, Kazakhstan, in addition to returning the nuclear weapons, agreed to leave Baikonur in Russian hands in return for payment of rent. The US also reduced its investments, and it is a pity that there are no diamonds or gold on the moon, otherwise we would know a lot more today. Getting in, however, had been very complicated. Months earlier, when I thought I had made it, they had cancelled the launches due to technical problems and then postponed my entry twice more for unspecified reasons. But my tenacity was rewarded; after all, more people have been in space than have visited every country in the world!

I met the Italian astronaut Parmitano, who was in reserve on that occasion and finally, witnessed the launch from more than a kilometre and a half away, feeling the heat on my skin, which was pleasant since it was -20°C in the cold steppe. After the first ten anxious minutes, we got the news that everything was going well, the command of the operation had passed to Moscow and the high-risk phase had been successfully completed. I celebrated as if I too had a part to play among those professionals I was watching with admiration as they worked.

Between the cargo ship and the rocket, I had taken a close look at the technology of large vehicles. An iPhone is more aesthetically pleasing because it must appeal to the general public, while on the control deck, the bridge was basic and the facilities at Baikonur were ugly. But these instruments are only used by experts who appreciate their real qualities and are not bewitched by the design or shiny buttons. A small joystick adjusted the controls to move a ship almost 400 m long, and a single grey button gave orders to millions of horsepower to propel a rocket into the sky.

I was incredulous, on the other hand, that even in such modern and rational environments, people fell into the most primitive superstition. Drops of liquor were thrown from the ship into the sea to keep the waves calm, and even more remarkably, an orthodox priest had come to bless the spacecraft. Now, I can understand the holy water sprinkled on the horse at the Palio race in Siena and I found it quite natural that the famous hot-air balloon (which I had not taken) in Burma was inspected by a monk who set the lucky take-off time, but for the rocket, I just didn't get it.

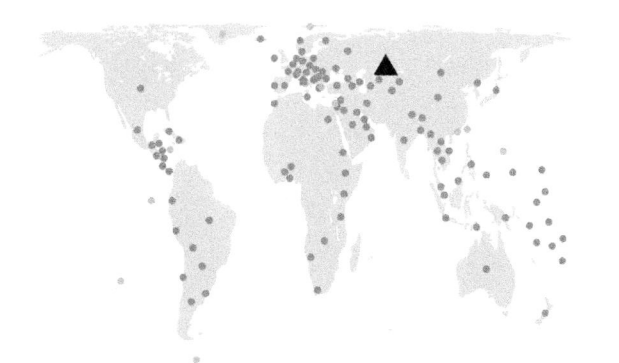

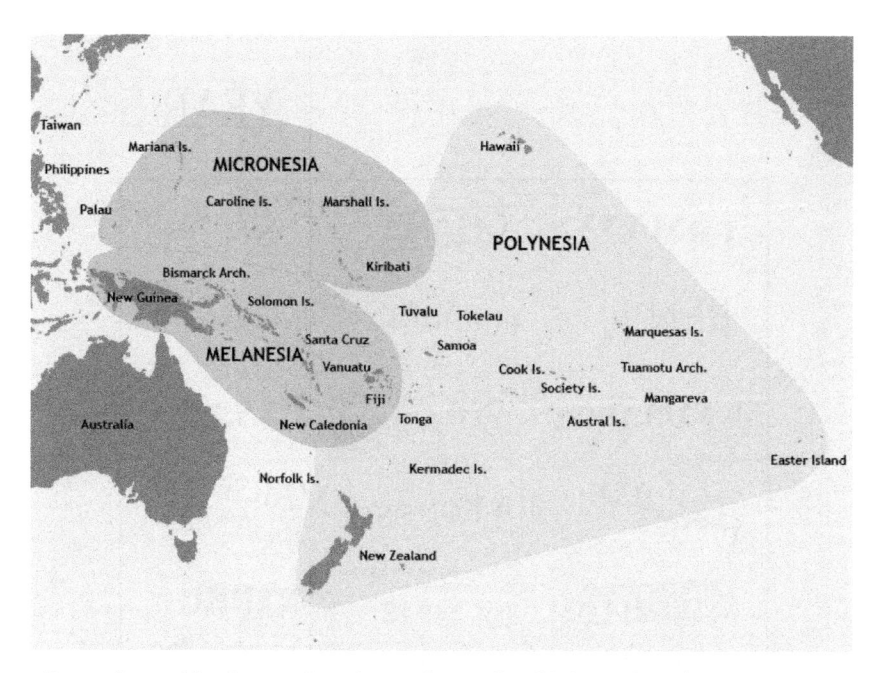

Oceania and its four subregions: Australia, Melanesia, Micronesia and Polynesia. The Polynesian Triangle is drawn by connecting the points of Hawaii, New Zealand, and Easter Island.

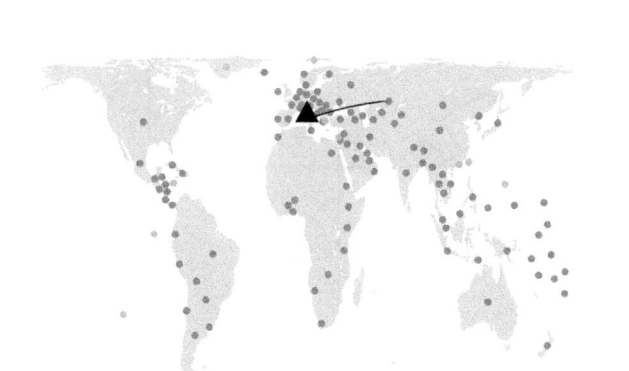

YEAR 5

GERMANY	~~GHANA~~	TOGO
BENIN	HONDURAS	NICARAGUA
EL SALVADOR	COSTA RICA	PANAMA
PALAU	MICRONESIA	MARSHALL ISLANDS
~~KIRIBATI~~	SOLOMON ISLANDS	NAURU
FIJI	TUVALU	TONGA
VANUATU	SAMOA	EAST TIMOR
GREECE	~~BULGARIA~~	ROMANIA
TAJIKISTAN	KYRGYZSTAN	ERITREA
CROATIA	BOSNIA AND HERZEGOVINA	SERBIA
SAUDI ARABIA	KUWAIT	BAHRAIN
OMAN	~~MALTA~~	KAZAKHSTAN

110/193

YEAR 6

Back at my parents' house for Christmas, as usual, I was busy organising the next stages of my journey. I needed to make the most of the few days in Rome and my passport was already waiting for yet another visa for Russia. When returning home after long periods, travellers often recount the same feelings: regained comfort and security, the ease of being in familiar surroundings and, of course, meeting loved ones. And then comes the description of a psychological 'down' associated with returning to normality. Being back is suddenly boring. However, I experienced none of this as my visits to Rome were short and I was always focused on the next adventure, which meant I enjoyed the comforts, family, and friends.

Although managing the return was very easy, I had to deal mentally with the farewells that would follow one after the other, to the point that I had turned them into a sort of routine. Almost every day on the road I would meet people that I would never see again, and constant, tiny moments of grief punctuated my days. But what I systematically worked to counteract wasn't the sadness, but rather the temptation that occasionally assailed me to not invest time and energy in others. If you start thinking that you will never see them again, you lose the desire to get to know them.

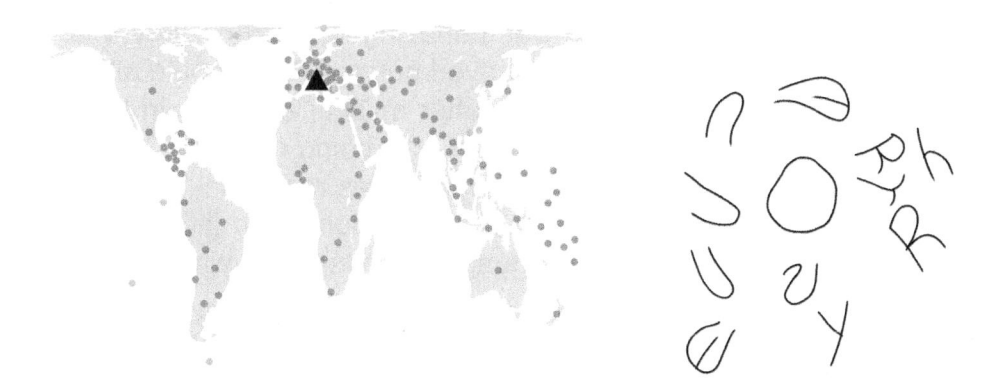

Social media can help in this regard as you are able to maintain some contact with lives that have briefly brushed past you, sparking a small hope of perhaps seeing each other again one day. I had begun to have friends from all over the world and these lives that flowed in such distant places were intriguing. I myself was a pretty nosy guy, but my travels definitely also attracted attention from others, meaning that I was probably an object of curiosity in my own right. In truth, I felt like the famous man who constantly rattles his big bunch of keys and has an interesting story to offer behind every door he opens.

Not having to move all the time is relaxing, but what really gave me peace of mind at home was no longer having to obsess about my passport. When travelling I was constantly on the alert as to where my backpack was with all the documents inside, sometimes waking up at night to check it. Losing my passport would mean interrupting the trip and having to rush home, losing a considerable amount of money, not to mention enthusiasm, as a consequence. Booking and organising visas, permits, and flights so far in advance, everything is associated with your passport and nothing else could be used in its place.

While at home, I witnessed another strange phenomenon as minor aches, pains and discomforts magically appeared. Why did I suddenly get a stiff neck just now, when I never had one after whole days on the bus on bad roads? How could I have a digestive problem after a normal meal when I had none after eating street food in third-world countries? I guessed that my mind was behaving in a bizarre way and was telling me that having arrived home safely, I could allow my body to feel unwell, look after myself, and stay in bed. The slightest sign of discomfort was being relayed. On the road, this wouldn't happen unless I was really sick. I would suppress the fear of being ill whilst alone with little assistance and no common language to understand what a doctor was saying, and the release was in letting go at home. In essence, while travelling I had more confidence in my body, indeed I had felt safe enough to make a reservation in the most intensely cold inhabited place on the globe.

Having obtained my visa, I went to Russia in early January. Again, I took a domestic flight from Moscow lasting many hours, crossing six different time zones to arrive in Yakutsk, the coldest city in the world. And I was purposefully visiting it at the most extremely wintry time of the year.

Now, if you played Risk, you would probably have gathered your plastic tanks and attacked the famous Kamchatka from these places on the map, allowing you to reach America... Sakha, (named Yakutsk in the game after the capital), on the other hand, is a less coveted board game territory, but in the real world, it is the largest administrative unit that exists. It's as vast as the whole of India although only one million people live there. The second largest is Western Australia, the one with the big nothingness, the emptiness, and the suffocating heat as soon as you leave the coast.

In contrast, in this Russian republic, the temperature was -44°C when I arrived, and the good part was that there were plenty of people around. Almost 300,000 people live in this city and during the long winter they lead an almost normal life. For example, they wait patiently for the bus while their eyebrows freeze, unable to play with their mobile phones because taking off their gloves is inadvisable, and besides, battery life isn't great at those temperatures.

In Rome I had gone to a specialised shop to look at some technical gear. According to the salesman's advice, the total expenditure for the equipment amounted to over €2,000, including boots, a jacket and various layers of clothing to wear underneath. That was a considerably higher figure than I would have spent on the entire 10-day trip, including flights and I was reluctant about the purchase, having seen too many tourists wandering around with paraphernalia that was as expensive as it was excessive.

There were ordinary people sporting ultramarathoners' backpacks, which would allow them to drink while continuing to run, a feature that is ridiculous when simply walking in the mountains. Who knows how many folks have got carried away and bought gear that is way out of proportion to their real needs, which then ends up becoming a hindrance, much as a large suitcase can. They purchase a thousand useless gadgets when a good pair of shoes would suffice.

But was I overdoing it with those items? In the end, however, trusting the tour operator's suggestions, I only spent €120 for a thermal shirt and long johns to add to a super all-in-one jumpsuit I already had. The rest I would be able to buy locally, plus the Russians had vowed that they would bring me extra clothing.

At -40°C even a few minutes in the open air without the right clothing will leave its mark, especially on someone like me who is not used to it. When I had gone to see Father Christmas in Finland, I had made the decision to travel with only hand luggage and I had thought that this would be the coldest place of my adventure. My packing choices proved successful, but how wrong I had been about the place that claimed the trip's record low temperature.

They were true to their word and on arrival greeted me with a giant jacket to add to what I had put on before I got off the plane, but a slight headache came on immediately. They took me to the hotel where my guide unsheathed a huge knife with which he first took the measurement of my feet with all my socks on, then skilfully carved a kind of thick carpet and 'sculpted' me some boots. And the cost of these custom-made shoes? Just $10, rather than the $800 the shop would have charged.

These were the advantages of going with a competent local person, while the disadvantage was not being able to understand each other. The person at the agency I had booked with had warned me and asked me numerous times if I felt up to being in such a situation, but I hadn't hesitated. I was becoming more and more adventurous, I mean, people spend every single winter there, surely I could survive a week without being able to speak Russian…

When the other members of the tour saw that I was alone, didn't know a word of Russian and only had hand luggage, they regarded me with curiosity. I would have done the same, because with a scene like that you have to work out whether you're looking at a tough guy or a big fool. I had a week to make them understand that I was neither one nor the other, but just a chilly man, in his sixth year of travel school, so by now with a huge jingling key ring, but who in this circumstance could not open any doors or tell any tales.

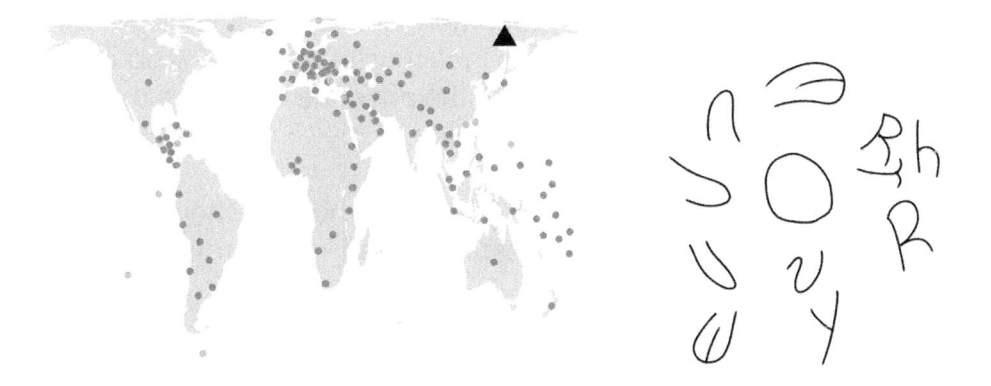

Yakutsk was only the starting point. To get to the so-called Pole of Cold two days of driving awaited us, on frozen riverbeds and roads where ice crystals are constantly stirred up, shaking and dancing, just as I had seen sand do when driving in the desert.

The latitude isn't quite extreme enough for full polar night, so the sun comes out for a few hours a day, but it doesn't heat things up. I had written in my notes here that the sun was 'broken', but this is obviously not a situation that can be 'fixed'.

Sakha is so large that a lot of the land lies at a great distance from the sea, which is why it's so cold. By the coast, the large mass of water that makes up the ocean mitigates the temperatures, cooling in the summer and warming in winter. Inland Sakha suffers from the absence of this effect from the sea, rendering both seasons' temperatures more extreme. In winter, the icy cold of the North Pole is pushed towards these inland areas by the winds, where it remains trapped. Summers are so short that the joke I was greeted with was that winter lasts 12 months here, and the rest is summer. To make it clearer, we can think of the desert, a place that is, by definition, without water, where it doesn't rain and has a dry climate. It's very hot there during the day with the sun beating down unimpeded and at night it is suddenly cold, as I had learnt in Mongolia where it snowed on me in the middle of summer. In fact, with no water vapour to release the accumulated heat, the absence of the sun quickly renders the place freezing cold.

When we arrived in Oymyakon, we had reached what is considered to be the coldest inhabited place in the world.

It's a village of a few hundred people which once recorded -71.2°C, or so they say (other communities dispute this and claim the title). However, one thing I do know for certain: in the three days I spent there, the temperature reached -58°C, and the bathroom was located outside. Going to the toilet therefore meant experiencing a temperature change of 83°, because the little house that accommodated us was well heated and boasted +25°C.

In Italy we are obsessed with temperature swings that are supposedly the cause of colds and unwellness, whereas in that place I experienced the body's ability to store heat and use it to resist the cold. The phrase 'being chilled to the bone' took on new meaning at -50°C as you realise that the cold is gradually penetrating your body. Once well warmed up at home or in the car, even I didn't suffer for the first few minutes outside. But, of course, when everything is so extreme, you had to get fully dressed to go to the bathroom even if you counted on being back in five minutes.

I wore boxers, thin socks and a T-shirt so that I could change this sort of underwear every day, while the rest of the clothing was specialised, and I had to wear it all the time. I sported a full thermal suit, then an additional T-shirt and the specially engineered long thermal underwear bought in Rome, two pairs of cashmere socks brought from Mongolia, double gloves, a pair of tracksuit bottoms previously worn on my hot dates in Ukraine, and ski trousers on top. For my upper body, I always had with me my 'Linus blanket' sweatshirt which was a replica of the first one. Then followed a double fleece sweatshirt, and finally a giant jacket and boots, much of this gear provided by my guide. I got rid of the face mask early on because it accumulated too much ice simply by breathing. In the 15 minutes it took to get dressed I reflected that at these temperatures wearing clothes is a necessity, there is no pleasure in it. Being a stylish country like Italy requires a good climate.

If getting dressed was challenging, getting undressed to go to the bathroom was even more so. The outdoor toilet is a nightmare. The water usually used to flush would freeze and break the pipes, so the toilet cannot be cleaned or emptied in winter and it's best to keep it well away from the house. Without going into details, I will just mention that the entire experience proved quite tragicomic. I had to take off my gloves to undo the zips of the clothes I was wearing, then proceed with my bodily needs, put my clothes back on and only then could I put the gloves back on. As a result, my hands were sore from the cold and scratched from the frantic contact with the zips I was trying to manipulate as quickly as possible. It was a complicated exercise in itself, made even more difficult by hands that lost their feeling quickly. You can be sure that nobody reads magazines in the bathroom here!

I would stop drinking at 6 pm because I was terrified of having to go to the toilet in the middle of the night, having to get fully dressed, and sneaking past the dogs sleeping in front of the door. If you're getting any strange ideas, you should know that I shared a room with the rest of the group, so even without me speaking Russian, the lady who was our host had made herself understood. We were permitted no resort to an emergency bottle, so we got dressed and went outside. The last time I had peed where it was not permitted, in Mongolia, I had been punched, so the best solution was to go to bed thirsty. To make up for it, I ate a lot because that's essential to keep warm. Mayonnaise, which is high in fat, was added to every food, and then there were all sorts of jarred foods that you find in Russia because nothing grows in winter, so they have to preserve everything from the summer before.

We also did some experiments, such as making vegetables explode by hitting them with a piece of wood because the water in them is frozen, driving in a nail with a banana so hardened by the cold that it could replace a hammer, and hanging a wet T-shirt outside that a few minutes later you could rip it with your hands. We threw hot water from a thermos flask into the air to see it immediately freeze and fall down as sleet. Even vodka, despite being so alcoholic, becomes a block of ice at -29°C and can't be drunk outdoors.

At this point, all that remained was to get back in the car for two days and head for Yakutsk. When I arrived in town, once I had verified that the bathroom was heated, our final dinner was punctuated by beer and vodka, with no fear of nocturnal peeing. So much vodka in fact, that I realised that some of my fellow travellers were slurring a few words in English. It had taken alcohol to dissolve that shyness that prevented them from trying. In the end, the departure was a little mournful as always, and I was sorry not to see them again. I have laughed in the past about people who briefly meet someone they cannot communicate with and write on Facebook that they have become best friends. But if you experience adventures and difficulties together for days, a bond is created regardless of the lack of words. In fact, my verbal communication had been practically non-existent and yet I was sad about the separation. I could only remotely imagine the brotherhood created between soldiers over time, through hardship, while talking in the same language.

My next destination was Morocco because I wanted to visit the **Western Sahara (/)**, which is essentially a big chunk of desert that would like to gain (and partly already has) independence. Algeria supports the fighting Front, probably in order to oppose the hated Morocco and obtain access to the Atlantic via the new state. But without getting into geopolitical issues, I, who stand as a staunch defender of democracy and am in favour of populations governing themselves, had an inconsistent thought here. I was happy that the most populous colony left in the world, with some half a million people, was still part of Morocco. I had the clear feeling that independence, which I imagine is really wanted by the people living there, would lead to the creation of a fundamentalist Islamic state, and that concerned me. You could feel an atmosphere steeped in religious oppression, hatred for women, and backward thinking. Even my guide, in excellent English, was indulging in some dire statements.

As a colourful side note, I entered the only restaurant that served alcohol one evening and ordered a glass of wine. The waiter arrived accompanied by a huge blackboard on which the menu was written. He placed it in front of me waiting for me to decide what to eat. But it wasn't that they were so anxious to receive my order, they simply used the menu as a screen as they didn't want other customers to see the wine.

The extreme heat, for me coming from Sakha, was a pleasure. My small suitcase had everything I needed to sustain me even on this occasion, and a climate change of about 100°C was no problem.

I had a hard time crossing the border into **Mauritania (111)** because there are several kilometres of no-man's-land where shady dealings take place and it seemed that all the old Mercedes 190s, practically the only car circulating in the entire country, had gathered there. It was hard to know whether or not to trust anyone offering a lift. I am usually happy to receive help on the road from strangers, but not at or near a border, so I set off alone in the sun, with my little suitcase full of thermal underwear and Mongolian cashmere socks. I didn't want to have to worry about what a driver was carrying or what trouble he might be in, and I already had some explaining to do about the ridiculous contents of my luggage.

The frontier is where tourists run the risk of real trouble, so you shouldn't rely on anyone who suggests crossing together because they know how to do it and can help you. And obviously never make yourself available to carry a suitcase or put an envelope in your backpack, not even a letter from a fellow traveller who begs you to give it to someone just across the border who is waiting for it. Don't join a group you don't know and also beware of anyone who might impersonate a customs or immigration guard. If in doubt, insist on going into their office or some official place.

The Islamic Republic of Mauritania is the last country in the world that still has a society based on slavery. After Saudi Arabia and Yemen, under international pressure, abolished it in 1962, Mauritania persisted until 1981. To make it worse, enslavement only became a crime in 2007. But the law is as yet unenforced and about 20% of the population is openly enslaved. Mauritania is one of the countries where the Arabs came into contact with black Africa, so the unwritten rule, as you can imagine, is as follows: those who have very black skin have a high probability of being enslaved, while the descendants of Arabs or presumed Arabs, who are less dark, are almost always the slave-owners.

Out of the blue, I received a terrible phone call from my sister begging me to come home because my mother was not well. When you're far away such a request is devastating because your mind races and you think the worst. In a disrupted phone call, where it was difficult to understand each other, my questions were answered evasively. With my heart in my mouth, I rushed to the small airport nearby to try to buy the first available flight to any European destination, from where I would find my way home. There was a flight leaving for the Canaries at a price of €300, but it had to be paid for in cash and in local currency. I had enough euros, but no one was able to change the money for me and there was no ATM. I left my suitcase at the check-in desk for safekeeping, took a taxi to go and make a withdrawal, then rushed back to the desk and finalised the purchase.

The security officer had witnessed the scene and knew the reason for my hurry, so he let me jump the queue, but not out of kindness. In the curtained area that they use to search veiled women away from everyone's gaze, he began to ask me for money to get on the flight. It was real cowardice, but I was emotionally fragile, I needed to catch that plane and I didn't even have the strength to fight. Fortunately, his colleague came to my rescue. He opened the curtain, waved me through and wished me luck with my troubles.

I arrived in the Canaries in the evening, and the first flight to Barcelona was the next morning, so I spent hours on a bench without being able to sleep. It was easier to phone from Spain, so now I knew for sure that she was not dead, but the situation wasn't good. I arrived home exhausted in the afternoon and a horrible time began. The diagnosis was advanced cancer, and she had a matter of a few months. I was heartbroken and the journey I was on suddenly made no sense, but only two weeks later we were given some hope. It was a metastasis of the same cancer she'd had treated 11 years earlier, which wasn't as bad as a new one. From then on, we received only good news, and she began a long course of painful therapies that eventually saved her life.

A month later I was on the road again, but with the intention of returning home more frequently. The person who was closest to me during that time was the American girl, who was experienced enough to talk to about my case and was helpful in understanding how to proceed from a medical point of view. Then, once the situation was moving in the right direction, she helped me to find the strength to leave again.

My time in Rome was spent mainly between hospitals and consultations and I was really grateful for the medical opportunities that were being provided. I had come from

Mauritania and Western Sahara where I had been taken to see the potions that could be created from what the desert offered. Those magical concoctions, basically a kind of tea, a few coloured berries, combined with amulets, were man's reasonable need to cling on to whatever he has. I'm sure I would have done the same in a place where there is practically nothing, so the peremptory statement that 'The desert gives us everything', I interpreted like this: 'What little we have all comes from the desert'. This is probably the same mechanism by which so many turn to religion, although even in the blackest despair, I had felt no urge to pray. Now, however, I had the opportunity to return to my beloved India for the *Kumbh Mela*, the largest religious gathering in the world. I wanted to experience it for myself and see if a spark of spirituality would be ignited, given the situation I had experienced and with the help of such an engaging environment.

I arrived at Prayagraj emotionally shaken and perhaps seeking comfort, but my first encounter with the pilgrimage site provoked annoyance. I was overwhelmed with requests. Some people would actually board my bus, which had its doors open, to offer me accommodation, and place themselves at my service. I had to move away from the window and not let them see me.

I'd booked a luxury tent near the river where you immerse yourself and was soon surrounded by gurus proudly walking around naked. They don't use their genitals for sex, so why should they be ashamed? I found myself submerged in a river made up of bodies, not water. It was apparently the largest gathering ever, with millions and millions of people. I only lasted a few hours on the first day and so the next I hired a guide, hoping he would better explain the things I didn't understand, but it was impossible to communicate on the ground, everything was so complicated.

On the third day, I found a smart guy who offered to take me around, organised a ride on the river in a small boat, and then, I'm afraid I ran away. I couldn't take it anymore. I was exasperated by the demands for money, I had experienced the stampede and was not surprised that people had been trampled to death or that in the past, without any communication, some had lost sight of relatives or children, never to be seen again. I had felt more at peace hugging and contemplating a tree than I did in these rivers.

I suggested to a young man who had a taxi that he should take me as far as Varanasi about 100 km away. I'd chosen him because he had driven carefully and even swept out the car whilst waiting for me. A man who takes such obsessive care of his vehicle may not give a damn about me, but he wants his taxi to arrive safely at its destination! Other cab drivers in this country where life sometimes seems to flow so slowly, become incredibly hurried on the road and jeopardise their asset, the car, to save a few seconds.

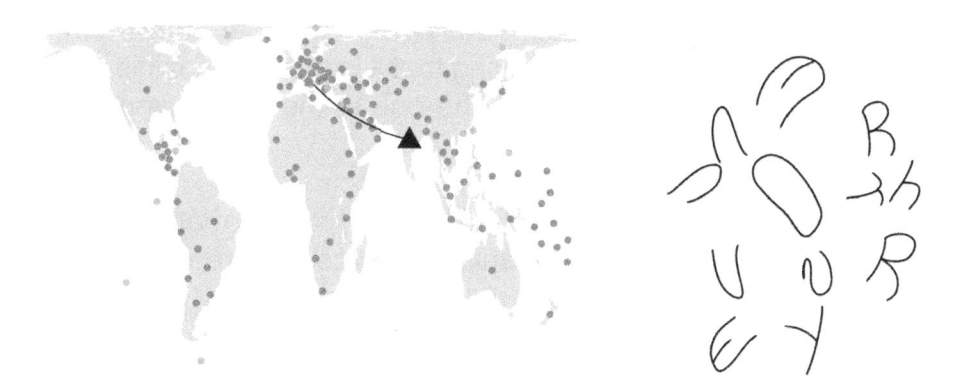

When we arrived in this holy city, the cautious driver insisted on staying with me, which made very little sense because I wanted to get around on foot or by boat and there were plenty of local taxis available. After a lengthy friendly discussion my resolve failed and, in the end, he stayed with me for three days. He slept in the car, and of course was my driver but also an impromptu guide. We went boating together at sunset and he took me to see the cremations which we alternated with a visit to the cinema for a three-hour long film packed with lively dancing.

The taxi driver offered to take me to an Ayurvedic centre because he sincerely believed that they might have something for my mother's condition that we had talked about. But I really didn't want to do that. I had started to explain to him that if these people really had effective remedies against cancer, they would certainly not be there selling them for pennies, they would be in the West to collect the Nobel Prize. Plants that have been proven scientifically to work are already being used for medicines all over the world. When he then argued that this medical tradition had existed unchanged for thousands of years and therefore, I had to trust it, I left him speechless by replying that I wanted medicine that evolves and improves.

This is one of the fields where continuity and tradition do not seem an advantage to me. But surprisingly, it was he who made me gasp, because he told me that these forms of treatment cost ten times less than going to a real doctor. Having one's urine smelled or tasted costs a fraction of the analysis in a real laboratory. India is the largest producer of actual medicines in the world, but in that discussion, which had gone far beyond my simple refusal to buy anything for my mother, I was completely overlooking the fact that so many do not have access to modern treatments and turn elsewhere. I felt as stupid as a person in a car showroom looking at a VW Golf and saying that it is not true that this car has a good engine because the one in the Ferrari is more powerful.

In the end, I was very happy that I was not alone. My new friend was good company, and I was sorry that he slept in the car, but it was his choice and by now I had learned that what embarrasses me is perceived differently in certain places. His strategy for staying was all based on not needing to reimburse expenses, so paying for his hotel would have been a move that would only have made the hotelier happy. Instead, by giving half that amount as a tip, I saved the other half, and he was incredibly pleased because with that money he could pay two weeks' rent.

Using our own frames of reference in that context isn't the best choice. In general, with menial but legal jobs that are normal in the place you visit, don't feel guilty. Take for instance the porters in Peru who seem so burdened, or the people who clean your shoes, or the rickshaw-peddlers in Bangladesh, it isn't by refusing these services that you will save the world. The person who takes care of your tent and the frying pans for your dinner would be carrying the same weight for a different job and earning less. Or worse still, they wouldn't have any work.

The best choice in my opinion is to gratefully acknowledge the effort, to pay the right amount, and indeed possibly leave a tip, because that is a form of appreciation for a job well done. A handshake or a pat on the back is fine for friends, but not for the porter. And if you think you have established a friendly relationship there, remember that they rightly have other priorities and until the school fees are covered, they are out there smiling at you mainly for their children.

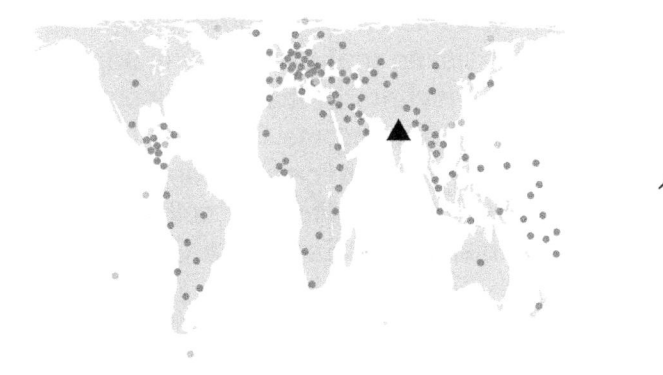

I no longer had a problem with guides who would watch from afar as I ate at a restaurant during lunch in the middle of a tour. They didn't want to sit with me and enjoy local specialities at high tourist prices instead of receiving a tip (the traditional choice of gratuity being one or the other). They were more than happy to go around the corner, choose what they wanted and chat with their friends on the phone for a tenth of the cost.

Anyway, not only was I without an eating companion, but I was also not sharing much of my pain, and in truth, I was perhaps adding to it. I had thought that the pilgrimage might help me, that maybe seeing that others were experiencing the same distress would help with acceptance. But in the end, I was having the opposite reaction and I felt pity for myself and for them. Would it have been better to return to Antarctica in order to have a vision of peaceful death? Or perhaps set out on foot as we had in Santiago? By leaving the chaos and going to Varanasi I was experiencing a bit of the transcendent because in that city one is constantly surrounded by death since the devotees come specifically to end their days in a holy place. But above all, I was consoled by offering the river mountains of candles placed on top of leaves. Seeing a small light floating uncertainly and drifting away gave shape to an idea of slow and peaceful detachment.

Although I had visited India frequently, I was always amazed both by this omnipresent religiosity that conditions life and the fact that it is the world's largest democracy. In books, some authors describe this union as them accepting modern Western rules but insisting that spirituality is something of their own. They are teachers of that, not disciples. Perhaps it was also this that attracted me from the beginning. What the books fail to convey with catchphrases, however, is the strange relationship with European colonialism. Now the British, or rather initially the East India Company, committed huge abuses, plundered and exploited, and even deliberately starved them. But on the other hand, they laid a solid foundation, brought schools, facilities and infrastructure, and the use of English. I had assumed before the travel school that everyone resented the colonialist, but this is not the case, and I would also find this to be true in Africa, where the colonial crimes were yet more notorious.

I went back to Rome for a few days and then was happy to go back to Ukraine where I would meet the girl I was seeing. In a nutshell, I was moving from a crowded bathing frenzy to an intimate relationship, but those were days that gave me no distraction. My mother's hair was starting to fall out, she had strong side effects that were affecting her skin, and she was in pain, but on the other hand, relief was coming from the prognosis because the therapy seemed to be working well. In Rome I obtained a visa to go to **Sudan (112)** and, despite rumours of an imminent coup d'état, I left without a second thought. The problems I was really afraid of were at home, not at my destination.

I had joined an international group who, like me, wanted to visit the pyramids. They are smaller than the Egyptian ones, some without the tip because an Italian had blown them up in the hope of finding treasure. We were the only tourists and camped nearby, in a magical if incredibly windy atmosphere.

To my great delight, I was able to take part in the dances

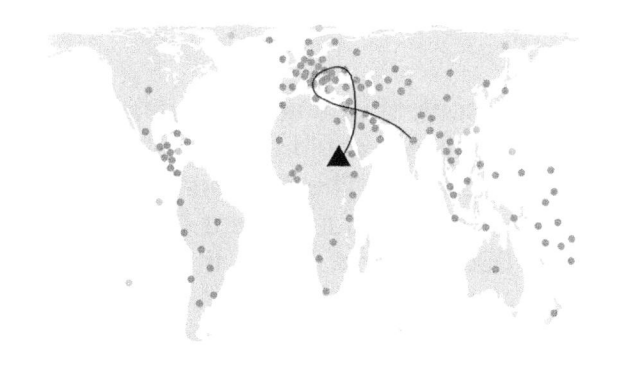

of the Dervishes. They are fanatics who still have enormous power in the country, and I noted that certain dynamics are always the same. In every religion, people with physical and mental problems gravitate towards these ceremonies and find their place there, becoming protagonists, performing some function, and feeling accepted.

My guide was an emancipated woman, even though she grew up in a house where her father had four wives and 40 children. During the ceremony, she had to keep herself in the background because women are not allowed to take centre stage. But by then I knew for myself how those ecstasy-inducing wild dances work: spinning around quickly intoxicates – just like when you were a child, jumping on the bed, you couldn't hold back your laughter and excitement – the music accompanies and beats the rhythm and doing it all together doesn't make you feel embarrassed.

However, with my new foreign friends, the entertainment consisted of getting into the taxi in the worst condition, taking a photo and winning the money we had put up for grabs. Our guide acted as judge. Many of the objects that are no longer used in the West come back to life in other countries, and this is especially true of cars. In Mauritania there were almost only very old 190s, which on the one hand shows the strength of such a prestigious brand, since everyone wants to be able to say they have a Mercedes, and on the other creates a virtuous cycle, whereby every mechanic now knows how to repair your car, and where to find the spare part. There's also no need for sophisticated software to detect most problems.

The winner of this bizarre contest was an Englishman in a Toyota where the yellow paintwork could barely be made out between the rusty metal sheets. The dashboard hung down towards the steering wheel, the fuses were exposed. The car had covered 700,000 km and I think they hadn't washed it for at least 500,000. The contest aroused hilarity even among the drivers, indeed, they happily posed with the car and laughed about it. After all, having a car, albeit a dilapidated one, is a luxury in Sudan. But were we, unintentionally, joking about poverty?

I set off home with some trepidation, because just as I was checking in for my flight, the coup had actually happened. The whole airport was at a standstill, everyone watching the TV to see what was happening and to follow the new leader's speech. He didn't say that the borders were closed, so the flight left as usual a few hours later and I stayed in Rome for the now familiar days of chemotherapy.

After that, I decided to go to **Kurdistan (/)**, a de facto nation but formally part of **Iraq (113)**. The visa is obtained on arrival as is normal in countries that do not enjoy the recognition of others, just because they aren't official and so don't have embassies that issue visas. At most, they have some representation such as Somaliland in London or Kurdistan in Washington. Now the US invasion of Iraq was a failure, based on false assumptions, and yet here the stars and stripes flags fly freely and Americans are welcomed with open arms as liberators. I found an exceptional guide there who took me around churches, mosques, and synagogues, and also to the poor Yazidis, who are always persecuted because they are accused of worshipping the devil.

The most moving place, however, was Halabja, where

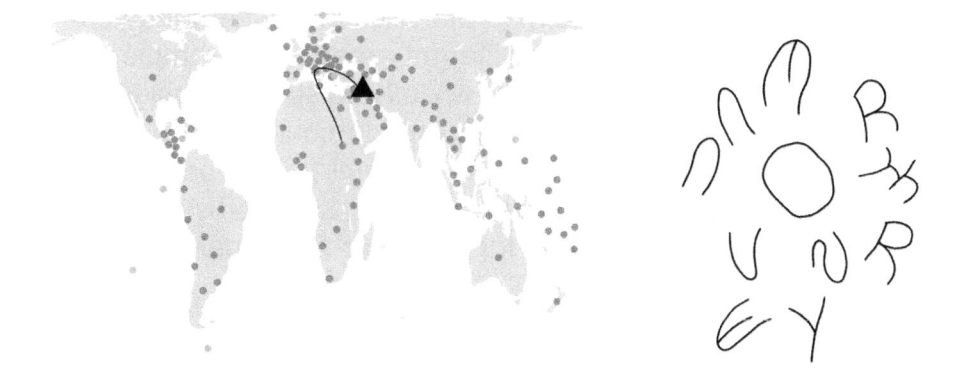

Saddam used gas to exterminate 5,000 Kurds. The Kurdish civilians had no experience of defending themselves against such an attack, so many were found dead in basements because they reacted the way they would to the bombings; by going into the ground. Apparently, it is better to get higher and it's possible that going up to the top floors would have been enough to save themselves as the gas is heavier than air and tends to sink. Unfortunately, the gas is deceitful, it has an intense and pleasant apple smell that makes you want to breathe deeply. The chemical attacks are called 'bird rain' because they are the first to die and they act as an alarm. You may survive, but everything will remain contaminated for a long time and places become uninhabitable. In short, even without much knowledge of the historical framework, it quickly becomes evident that in Kurdistan, America is a beloved nation, having invaded Iraq and killed its genocidal dictator.

Officially I was in Iraq, which is one of those countries considered very dangerous to visit. The Italian Ministry of Foreign Affairs website had advised against going, but without distinguishing between regions. If there is a dangerous area, the whole country automatically becomes dangerous, which has implications for standard travel insurance. Mine, on the other hand, explicitly covered countries that were not recommended and I soon learnt that in order to find out the real risks, I had to use different tools.

Other European countries offer a more accurate service than the Italian one because they create different degrees of alert, plus they offer a map of the country where they associate different risks with different areas. For example, all the advice is not to go to Iraq, while Kurdistan is considered a visitable place. In the former French countries, it's good to go to the site run by the old colonial power, because it has up-to-date and reliable information, and staff still on the ground. The same applies for England. Switzerland has its own site in many languages, and the United States offers an excellent service, although perhaps some of the dangers specifically concern those with American passports and in some areas, an Italian would certainly run fewer risks.

Kurdistan wasn't dangerous. In saying this I wasn't making the mistake of relying on the superficial feelings of a tourist who is only staying ten days. Nor was I relying on my guidebook's accounts or the local taxi driver's unfailing eagerness to tell me how the world works there. I was informing myself through expert evaluations, web searches, and available facts. My personal experience, which is statistically insignificant, was only one of the parameters. However, I'll leave this point there, because a strong desire to go and see even objectively risky places was growing in me. Or rather, I was developing the conviction that I wanted to go everywhere, dangerous or not. Every petal in this flowery, perfumed world attracted me, including those that were withered, dry or had little colour. Until now I had enjoyed looking at other people's photos of the places I had already been to. I relished reliving my own trip in this way and making comparisons, but particularly there was the irresistible temptation to say, 'I've been there too' and disguise this outburst of protagonism behind some advice or compliment for someone else's trip.

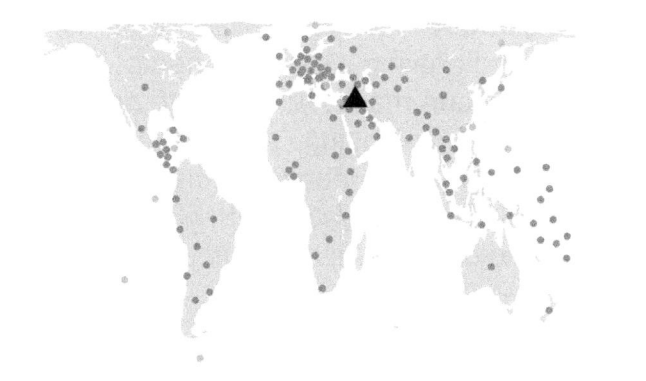

From now on though, I was only interested in photos of the places I hadn't visited. I was past the stage of 'I've been there too' and I wanted to see everything and to hear the stories on the ground. My travel school was entering another dimension where the objective seemed so important to me that taking risks became acceptable. I now had basic information on every single country. Doing a rough analysis, and despite the fact that so many countries were strongly discouraged on world sites, there was a slight chance of succeeding. I was prepared to take risks and the money I needed no longer mattered, I had enough to finish the trip and then start from scratch. At the end of the adventure, I thought I would find a job in a travel agency or maybe open one of my own.

I returned home (more chemotherapy) and renewed my passport because all the pages in the second one had also been filled in just over two years. My mother was physically ill, but the prospects were beginning to look good. In fact, the doctors were optimistic that the tumour was shrinking to the point where it could be operated on and removed. I was elated and full of energy, so, with this enthusiasm, I set out to find a possible way to go to Afghanistan, the country that seemed to me the most dangerous.

I had learnt how to manage risk during my time playing poker, and one of the most important rules in that game was to choose the table well and then be aggressive, without fear. So, you are cautious and prudent in the selection phase, looking for a table where you would play for sums appropriate to your wallet and against weak opponents. But then, once the decision has been made, you have to go on the offensive without being afraid of losing. You win by playing on the attack. Now, though, I was managing the risks in the opposite way, essentially telling myself that I wanted to play on the most difficult and dangerous tables in the world, and then trying to be cautious once I was seated. In poker, this would have been a losing strategy, but with travel it made sense. Here it wasn't about winning money, it was about bringing your hide home and risks were only to be taken as long as they were reasonable in relation to the prize, not just for the hell of it. My award was cultural – I wanted to collect unique and unforgettable experiences. Previously my main fear had been losing my passport, while now it was losing my life, but that was alright. To be honest, with myself and with you, I distinctly remembered making fun of those who travelled for a challenge, yet now there was clearly that stimulating and perverse fascination in me too.

I contacted the photographers who were publishing from Afghanistan, and looked through the acknowledgements on documentaries for the names of the local guides they had used until I found a highly reputable person who was about to organise none other than a marathon. I liked the project so much that I volunteered to raise funds for this special event, and in doing so I made a commitment to myself to train to be able to finish the race, which would take place at an altitude of 3,000 m. Most importantly, I reaffirmed my clear determination to go anywhere, no more excuses or fears, my travel school would have no borders, and I wanted to play the whole field. The idea of being cautious having arrived in the place also went out the window, as a marathon added risk on top of risk.

With Afghanistan, every website advised against going

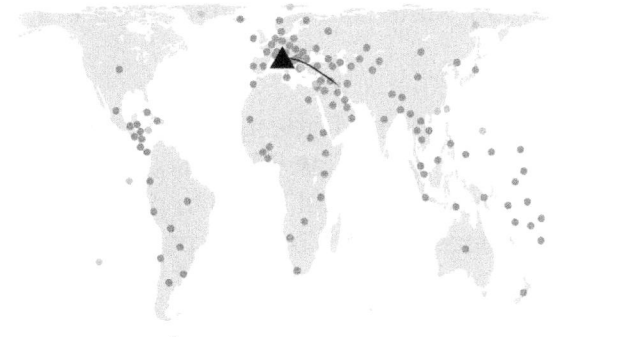

in all possible ways. And it was easy to go beyond words and find figures which were difficult to refute. For example, the official figure for the last available quarter, before I left, counted 1,174 dead and 3,139 wounded among civilians alone, which excluded the numerous people who were fighting. The marathon was in essence about challenging the Taliban, because such an activity can be organised to emancipate girls through sport.

In a country where women are forbidden any physical activity, imagine practising athletics, and then doing it without wearing a *burqa*, because with your face covered you wouldn't know where you put your feet. Through running, a woman gains confidence in her own capabilities, she realises she can do it, she may even overtake a man in a race. Above all, completing a marathon requires long and constant training, so it means that the girl has to leave home to run alone, without a male guardian. This is where Free to Run, the non-governmental organisation behind the event, for which I am an ambassador, achieves the real challenge. It looks for girls who want to participate in such an extraordinary experience and assists them throughout the year, convincing families to give them the chance by using financial incentives and providing study materials, training, and even a safe place to take refuge in case of trouble.

The marathon was in October, still four months away. Like the girls, I too had to train. I began preparation and, in the meantime, visited **Moldova (114)** with its fantastic wineries, and then went to **Transnistria (/)**, another territory that functions as an independent state, but is formally a part of Moldova.

Do visit these 'de facto' nations if you get the chance. They are among the most interesting as it is difficult to appreciate how they really function without going in person. It was here that my small suitcase, which used to be the envy of *Mary Poppins*, left me without clothes for the first time. Compounded by my eagerness to go running every day, I had managed to get everything dirty and in the unexpected cold, I had found myself in trouble. I went to reception and asked if they had anything I could borrow. I was taken to the storeroom where there was a collection of lost property that customers had forgotten about maybe years before. I had a new wardrobe in no time and was finally fully dressed as a man from the East, albeit with my usual sweatshirt over the top, of course.

I went on to **North Macedonia (115)**, to **Kosovo (/)** another nation that shouldn't be counted because it is not a member of the United Nations. It is not recognised by giants like China and Russia who don't accept its independence lest they have to recognise other separatists elsewhere, or rather, at home. In fact, not even Spain recognises Kosovo because of its own internal separatist issues. In contrast, American flags are everywhere in Pristina, the capital, just as they were in Kurdistan, and as soon as people realise you are a tourist, they hope that you're American.

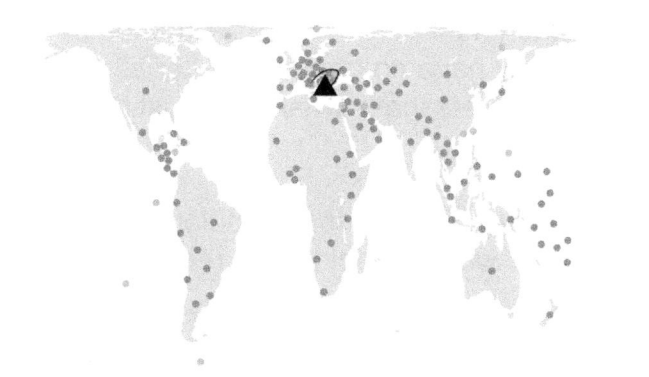

In **Albania (116)** I ran on the beach, in **Montenegro (117)** in the mountains. In Croatia, I managed to complete a half marathon for the first time. Once I returned, it was time to grow a beard to blend in a bit, start fundraising for Afghan women, and apply for a visa. My online appeal was a success, and in a few days, I had met and exceeded the target of $6,500 that I had agreed with the organisation. But after collecting the required documents and turning up at the embassy with a big smile on my face in readiness for the 'Ferrari' jokes, I was brutally informed that the tourist visa for Afghanistan was no longer being issued. It was too dangerous to go there, and they didn't want the responsibility. So now what? They were destroying my project and extinguishing my enthusiasm, but more importantly, I'd collected money that I wouldn't know how to give back. I'd asked for these donations by inspiring confidence and guaranteeing that I would go in person. Now I would look like a fraud.

I didn't lose heart, however, and discovered that the other Afghan embassies in Europe couldn't issue a visa to an Italian passport because Rome alone was responsible. I'd always felt privileged to live in the city with the most embassies in the world, but this time it was the worst location for me. I had to get out of Europe to have any hope. I would have to pretend that I was travelling constantly and that I couldn't pass through Italy to apply for a visa there.

After some research, I found written instructions that in order to proceed in this manner, the Afghan embassy in Rome would have to send a document to the other venue in which they state that they would not object to another location authorising me. I tried to request this document by phone numerous times but never received a reply. Obviously, I couldn't go and ask in person because that would be nonsense, it's issued remotely to people who can't get back to their country of residence. So, I did what I would do playing poker and prepared myself for a bluff. I would say that the embassy in Rome had let me know that they do not issue that document, but they have no objection. After all, by never responding to my requests that's what they must have meant, right?

I got my ticket to Dubai and went to the consulate, ready to lie about the clearance whilst keeping my return flight ticket well-hidden as officially I wouldn't be returning home for months, which was of course the point of asking them for a visa. The result: 'The consulate does not issue tourist visas at this time'. They clarified that it was a temporary thing, and I would just have to visit them again in a few weeks. To add insult to injury, the official reminded me that if I passed through Rome, there was an embassy there... My celebrated budget for unforeseen events, which I had replenished when I left again in the third year, took a nasty blow.

Back in Rome, I organised myself to tackle the problem more thoroughly, setting out to get the visa for Pakistan as that is the easiest place from which to get the Afghan visa. I asked the person who would take me to the marathon to help me organise a tour of the country to maximise my chances of getting the visa in Karachi. And as a backup, being a good planner, I booked a flight to go from Dubai where I would stay for five days in order to try again for the visa there.

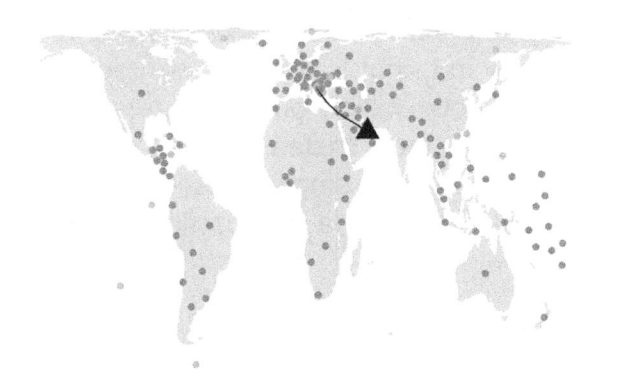

It was an expensive plan, that's true, but a devilishly shrewd one. I would visit a new country for 15 days, hopefully get my visa, and get acquainted with the person who would have to take care of my safety at the marathon. I worked up my courage by telling myself that if I managed to go to Afghanistan and run through the mountains with the women after they had abolished the tourist visa for Italians, I could succeed against any obstacle.

In the meantime, to use a terminology dear to poker, I raised myself again and went to apply for a Chinese visa as well because the tour in Pakistan would end at the border with China. I soon discovered that something new was now required. I was asked for a sheet listing the countries visited in the last five years, complete with the date of entry and exit.

Before tackling the problem, mindful of the fatal mistake I made with Tibet, I went onto Facebook to check that I didn't have any images posted that would be disagreeable to the Chinese Communist Party, and then I presented myself at the counter with my two complete passports and the third current one, showing that they covered the last five years and together had about 100 pages full of stamps. I explained that I would like to go all over the world and was not able to fill out that sheet, but I had photocopied every page of the three passports and was ready to attach the bundle of papers. The clerk, a little bewildered, went behind the counter with my passports and photocopies, only to return five minutes later saying that there's no problem, no form for me. Finally, some good news!

I flew to Dubai first, and rushed to the Afghan consulate, which by now I knew well, and rejoiced to hear that the consul was in his office. I waited three hours for my turn, handed over all the obsessively prepared documentation, and then an hour later I was called as the consul himself wanted to talk to me. I feared the worst, that is, that he wanted to inform me that he was perfectly willing but that I needed the infamous clearance from Rome... Instead, without even looking me in the face, he asked me a single question, 'First time in Afghanistan?' I answered with a monosyllable and got the go-ahead.

WOW! I didn't even have to bluff. And I now had four free days in Dubai that I could devote to running. Because I had finally obtained my visa, my mind now turned to focus on the marathon as I had to be able to finish it. During the long hours on the move, I had realised that when you have time, determination and money to spend, many things become possible. Who knows what strength and accomplishments a rich and persistent person can achieve.

With my mind set on the marathon, I was taking the Pakistan trip in my stride. There are plenty of flights from Dubai as many thousands of Pakistanis work there and much of the trade between this country and the enemy, India, takes place in the United Arab Emirates which act as neutral intermediaries. I had chosen the cheapest flight to get there and found a dead fly in my lunch box. A few rows behind me a gentleman asked if the rest of his meal could be packed to go, which was the first time I had heard such a request. I thought he must have wanted to have the remains analysed! The poor hygiene of the place coupled with the altitude of the mountains perhaps promised intestinal problems, but on arrival 'diarrhoea' was not on my agenda, or at least I needed to eat something on the way so I could feel guilty for being the cause of my own troubles…

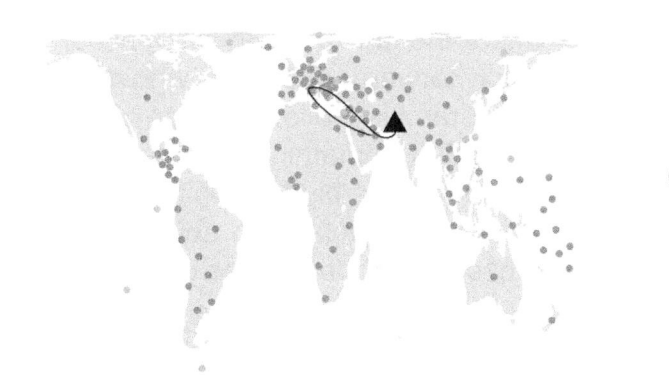

I entered **Pakistan (118)** via Karachi. My accommodation was terrible, but I had chosen it on the basis of its proximity to the Afghan consulate where I was glad I no longer needed to go. I took a walk around the neighbourhood looking with amusement at the papers I had brought filled with phrases written by my guide in the language to attract the goodwill of the officials. I had a fake itinerary in Afghanistan to make it look like I was only going to the two safest places. I didn't have to mention running, and I'd even received advice on how to dress.

We really had tried everything in the hope of pulling the rabbit out of the hat, however it seemed that the consul was a sociable type. He would offer you tea and then decide on your visa after a chat on various topics. I wanted to pass this test and studying had become easy for me, having genuinely become interested in the country out of curiosity. Where else do you find a nation of over 200 million people created solely to be 'not part of' India due to their hatred of that country and the fear of living with rules inspired by a religion other than their own? About a million people had died in the terrible violence that followed Britain's withdrawal from the colony's territories in 1947. Two different nations were formed: India on one side, Pakistan on the other to give the Muslim population a home. This partition gave rise to one of the largest migrations of men, as those who were Muslim sought to move to Pakistan while the Hindus moved towards India.

Today Karachi is a huge, crowded city, and people from the countryside continue to flow into it. Evidently, life is even worse away from the chaos, otherwise, people would return to their villages. Pavements are few and far between, and always full of goods and obstacles to the point that you end up walking in the street, where the law of the fittest applies. Buses and cars push their way forward, and those who hesitate never get through. The hierarchies follow the size of the vehicles but there is a trade-off. If something were to happen, the blame would be placed on the biggest which therefore means that they have to be careful not to abuse their privileges. The continuous use of the horn serves to warn of danger and to reiterate this jungle law. Should a foreigner then be involved in an accident, he wouldn't stand a chance, it would be his own fault.

The demands for money would be insane, even simply for killing something like a hen because people would invariably claim that it was their most beloved animal, perhaps the famous goose that lays golden eggs. Injuring another person can lead to lynching, so if you have the unwise notion of driving alone, in the event of an accident, drive straight ahead, stop at the first police station and tell them what happened.

Unfortunately, some people live out their religion with the same aggressiveness. Apart from the hatred for India, Islam is the only thing that unites this country that is so internally diverse. A large part of the population experiences the religious realm with excess, anger, and fanaticism. Every now and then I think about how easy it must have once been to find cannon fodder for an army among the religious extremists.

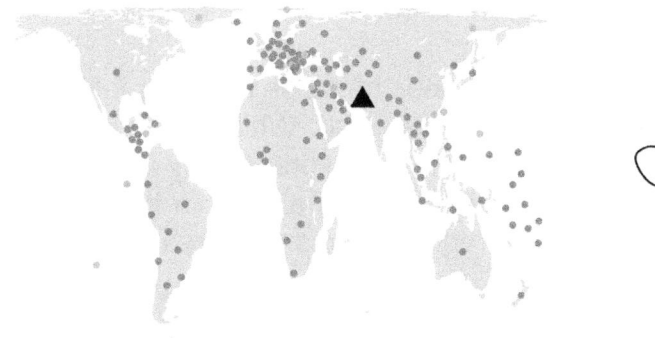

On my way to the border with India, I took part in the flag-raising ceremony, where each nation watches the other so closely that the soldiers even brush arms. They engage together in strange movements performed by the tallest and most imposing in the army to project an image of strength and dominance towards the enemy. War occasionally crops up in Europe, but it has virtually disappeared from our lives and at most is experienced in tiny doses in sporting competitions. Whereas here, war is still a serious everyday affair, and only in this instance is it perceived as a game or as a kind of competition. A few years earlier I had pretended to cheer and dance with the Indians on their side of the border, yet now, to support my host country I had to pretend to shout '*Allahu Akbar*', because in Pakistan as you can imagine, war is completely fused with religion.

The tour began in Lahore accompanied by one of the marathon organisers. After all those messages for the visa, we finally met in person. In Pakistan, he was my main key to understanding the local culture, but later in Afghanistan, he would be the protector of my life. The tour took me to visit Abbottabad where Osama bin Laden had been hiding, but there was no trace of him left. They tore down his palace to prevent various types of processions of supporters or opponents from happening. Some even consider him a martyr capable of dispensing blessings.

Then we travelled along the Karakoram Highway, the only international route higher than the one I had tackled in Pamir, between Tajikistan and Kyrgyzstan. The Khunjerab Pass stands at over 4,600 m and marks the highest manned border post in the world. Intrepid men work there, who have oxygen pumped into their cabins during the long days. You enter China from this point and move the clock hands forward three hours because Beijing has imposed a single time zone for the entire nation, meaning that in these remote areas, just like in Tibet, thousands of kilometres away, you have to comply, using a clock that is perhaps unsuited to your geographical locality.

Border controls are meticulous because they fear infiltration of Islamic terrorism from Pakistan. While in Tibet they banned books on Buddhism and censored every image of the Dalai Lama, here they confiscated a book in Italian on the history of Islam in the region. It wasn't a great loss, I'd grown bored of reading it, but I had jotted down my thoughts there, so I quickly snapped a photo of the last page, which came out blurred. My book clearly had a historical slant but still did not pass the scrutiny. There was, however, something that made it across the border and will stay with me with no need for notes, and that was the incredible hospitality I received in Pakistan, equal only to that of Iran.

The mountains were also incredibly beautiful. The view of Nanga Parbat from Fairy Meadows is unique, although the road that takes the Jeeps to base camp is so dangerous that on the way back, I left a few hours earlier and walked down. The excuse was that I wanted to do some training, but the truth was that I was afraid of those roads. And I had made the right decision. Back in the city, I discovered that the accident and fatality figures on those climbs and descents are mind-boggling.

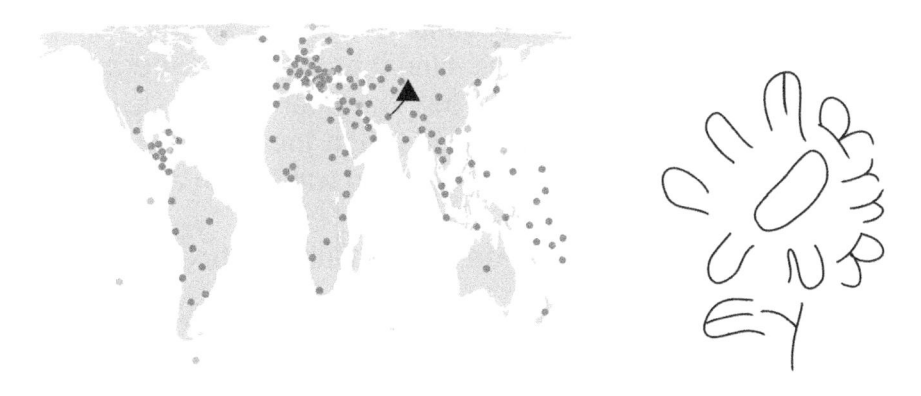

On the other hand, it's very safe to go and look at the Rakaposhi, a 7,788-metre-high mountain that plunges almost 6,000 m from the summit to the viewpoint (itself at an elevation of over 1,000 m), casting a majestic shadow. And so, the collection increased. Like the blue sky in Mongolia, the monolith in Australia, the ice in Antarctica, the stars from the dark cargo ship, and the orange sunset in Greenland, this mountain conveys sacredness and places a representation of God before your eyes.

In China I got another piece of good news. I was unstoppable, like a volcano in full eruption, and my visa application for Iraq had been approved. No Kurdistan this time, I was going to tour the whole country. I was playing on all fronts and so I organised this further trip and bought the plane tickets, coordinating them with those I already had. From Kabul I would be flying to Baghdad via Fiumicino, which was a decidedly unusual flight plan, but at least, if someone had asked for an explanation, I would have been in Rome!

In the meantime, I was touring *Xinjiang*, this Chinese region that borders Pakistan and is considered their Far West. Five times the size of Italy and sparsely populated, it has high-altitude lakes, deserts and mountains rendering the land beautiful but inhospitable. Here, China has been placing the local population in re-education camps, which are essentially prisons. It appears that one million *Uyghurs*, the local Muslim ethnic group, have their freedom continually restricted, and are even tortured. I wasn't shown anything, and whereas in Tibet at least the guide let himself go, here the person who was obliged to accompany me never opened up.

I thought it was time to leave China and India since I still had over 70 countries to visit. The challenge I had undertaken was amazing but there was a compromise to be made and I needed to prioritise a few uninteresting countries. In this book, I've been counting countries since the beginning, but it was around this time that I started to become obsessed with one number, 193. The goal was to visit the 193 nations that exist in the world, and then I would have the rest of my life to continue exploring without an abacus.

At last, the big day came. From Dubai, I boarded the

plane to Kabul, and I was relaxed, despite the fact that there were mainly American soldiers on board, who at regular intervals were entitled to leave for Dubai where they could switch off and feel safe for a while. Perhaps I'd unwittingly discovered another reason why that city is so full of prostitutes! Still, I was prepared and excited at the idea of being the only tourist on board. On leaving, I was heartened that Kabul was simply a destination like any other on the airport board, and there were no fewer than three daily flights scheduled. It was the first time I had been advised not to talk to anyone on the plane, not to say where I was going or how long I was staying, not even to other Westerners. Whereas in the past I would ask questions about places just to say where I was going and chat, now I had to mind my own business at all costs.

In **Afghanistan (119)** Kabul Airport is among the safest places and during my visit in 2019, it was still run by Western forces. It was a kind of *matryoshka* nesting doll, made of protected zones inside other zones, inside other zones and so on. The final terminal is a long way from the first entrance and only accessible if you have passed security at all the other checkpoints. The numerous checkpoints, bland as they are, increase protection as a terrorist with a bomb on him would find it difficult to keep his nerve at each gate. Bomb dogs sniff out men and luggage, and there are areas where you have to leave your bags and wait at a distance for them to be searched, and then again, and again. You have to have a lot of patience.

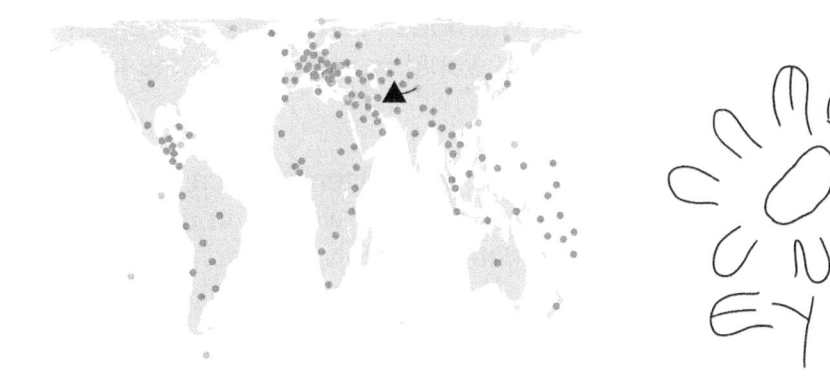

At immigration, I left my address as the name of a big famous hotel, which I would not go to later. I changed clothes and put on something local brought by my guide whom I would see again after having parted company at the border between Pakistan and China. I would stay in a different place every night as a precaution, and the best thing was that I didn't know the name and address of my lodgings, I just had a phone number for emergencies. There were other Westerners in that unmarked hideout, so it was better that only a few trustworthy people knew exactly where we were. In the worst-case scenario, a kidnapped person couldn't reveal their whereabouts even if they wanted to. My guide, who knows how to behave and how to find the route, would always be with me.

Between the beard that I'd let grow and the suit, from a distance, I looked as if I would merge in well, although I saw a child leave like a shot and come up to me to beg, even in the midst of so many people. The disguise worked, yes, but only partially. While for a man it is a question of proximity or distance, for women things are more complicated because a Taliban is like an expert hunter stalking prey, and a Western woman would be immediately recognisable, even under a *burqa*. You just have to observe how she moves in the presence of men.

As is sadly well known, life is terrible for women in Afghanistan. Their bodies don't belong to them, they are the property of their husbands, their families and their tribe. A man's honour is deemed greater the more submissive his woman is, indeed, a man who doesn't dominate his woman doesn't deserve respect. He would be despised in the tribe and seen as a weak loser.

Afghan women are worse than illiterate because they only spend time with and talk to other women in the same condition. A typical uneducated woman, unfortunately still common in the world, at least learns something by being around people who have different experiences. Perhaps they gain something from their husband who has more access to information or has attended a few years of elementary education. In Afghanistan, outside the family, women only associate with each other. With this spiral of enforced ignorance, the feeling of one's own inferiority is confirmed and strengthened. A woman who is kept in the dark, and punished for every word or question, can only lose self-confidence and shut herself away in her thoughts.

The marathon, in its own small way, sought to go against these awful viewpoints. The race venue was a mountainous region in the centre of Afghanistan where the *Hazara* ethnic group lives. They are hated by the Taliban mainly because they are Shia and not Sunni, that is, they follow a minority stream of Islam. It is the *Hazara* themselves, therefore, who are trying hard to keep the Taliban off their land.

Furthermore, it was here that the terrorists had destroyed the two giant statues of Buddha, and the race thus became, symbolically, a small revenge. To increase the security already provided by the locals, the date was kept as hidden as possible and the organisers themselves referred to it as the 'secret marathon'. They made a film with this title. The entire area had been cordoned off and secured with the help of foreign forces. Some employees and diplomats had been invited by the embassies to participate as a further show of support.

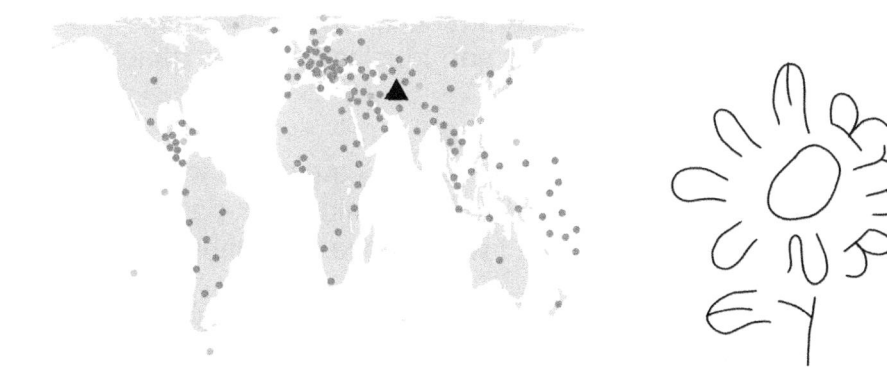

Now though, it was necessary to get to the *Hazara* territory. It might seem easy because it is only 200 km from the capital, but getting out of Kabul by car is risky. There are very few roads, and once foreigners have been spotted, it is easy for a Taliban to report the sighting and suggest to his accomplices that they wait for them on the way. The safest method is to fly. I was lucky, my plane left without a hitch and returned to Kabul with only a 24-hour delay. Others saw their flight cancelled, as often happens, and had to face the road.

An unmarked car was used to maximise security, with a lead vehicle carrying an Afghan man and a woman in a *burqa*, equipped with a telephone to communicate. Had there been anything unexpected, they would have suggested turning back. Roadblocks are dangerous because you never know if they are being operated by the good or the bad guys. As well as the Taliban, who actually controlled the area, there was a risk that the blockades were made by common criminals, so the danger at each checkpoint was either that they would simply be robbed, or worse, kidnapped.

Being inconspicuous, it was less dangerous for the girls to get to the marathon site and a fantastic experience for them, being away from home without their parents for the first time. As a fundraiser, I was able to spend the days leading up to the race with them, which of course was quite emotive as I was able to communicate well in English with some of them. They had incredible stories to share and there was a great atmosphere of fun but combined with trepidation because if the Taliban had spotted us, they would have stormed in and cut off everyone's head immediately. Women dressed normally in the company of a non-Muslim man, wild dancing, even music....

During those days there were many questions for me, by far the most popular being, 'Can you help me get a scholarship to go to America?' And I would have done that willingly, but I had no idea how it worked in the United States.

Mostly local men and women participated in the marathon, in addition to the girls brought by Free to Run and then 14 foreigners, including myself and those from the embassies in Kabul. In total, almost 800 registered and keeping so many people running, girls and Westerners in plain sight for hours, was in defiance of all kinds of restrictions but also a risk. In the other places I had visited, everything was done in small groups and very rapidly so as not to give anyone a chance to organise themselves for an attack. A whole marathon, though, can't be completed quickly.

Around 40 Afghan women completed the 42.195 km course. Twelve of the girls at the finish line were from the Free to Run organisation, it was a fantastic achievement. The first year, in 2015, only one managed to finish. Moreover, this year, no women were insulted, no stones were thrown, and no death threats were made against foreigners. It was quite a success.

In my own small way, training in the most diverse places in the world had paid off and I finished the marathon with a time of 6 hours 40 minutes. The winner took 3 hours 25 minutes, and the fastest woman 4 hours 52 minutes.

In some respects, a marathon is more a journey in itself than a run, but in this case, it's a race towards emancipation.

- *Do they want you to walk slowly and one step behind them? – You can overtake them in the race.*

- *Do they want you to be so unrecognisable under your burqa that when you leave the mosque (where you pray separately) they don't even recognise their own wife waiting for them? – You go running dressed in sportswear.*

- *Do they want you to make no noise, not to laugh? – You let out a huge shout as you cross the finish line like we did.*

And so, if I took some risks, fine. Gender equality is not just a Western women's right, it belongs to every woman on the planet. It's the most important cause in the world, it affects half the population.

Having finished this beautiful adventure, which for the first time had actually earned me the support of those who opposed my travels to dangerous places, I was ready to pass through Rome, from where I would continue on to Baghdad. I left the airport for a few hours, not so much to pass by my home as to start the new journey from scratch. Being continually on the move, having to say I was coming from Kabul and wanted to go to Iraq, all for tourism had been overwhelming even to me. In short, had I been an official at the transit gates, I would have double checked me too! Yet it was nothing but the truth.

Back at the airport, I was ready with my prepared documents. The Iraqi permit was a piece of paper sent by the Ministry of Tourism, written only in Arabic, with a few stamps. It was scanned quite badly and was actually a pre-authorisation that would be converted into a visa in the passport at Baghdad airport. Now, with such a piece of paper, the concern was that I would be banned from boarding in Rome because airlines receive hefty fines if they let passengers travel without the required documents, and I couldn't expect the gate crew to recognise a document written in Arabic.

The flight had a stopover in Istanbul, so at the Fiumicino desk, I only asked for my boarding pass for Turkey (I thought it wasn't even worth trying in Rome since in Istanbul they would surely have an office capable of evaluating the documents). To my surprise, the check-in clerk told me that I was flagged and kept me waiting for well over an hour while everyone passed me by, then came back and handed me the boarding pass for both Istanbul and Baghdad! Excellent! And I had thought that the steward would come back with two security staff instead…

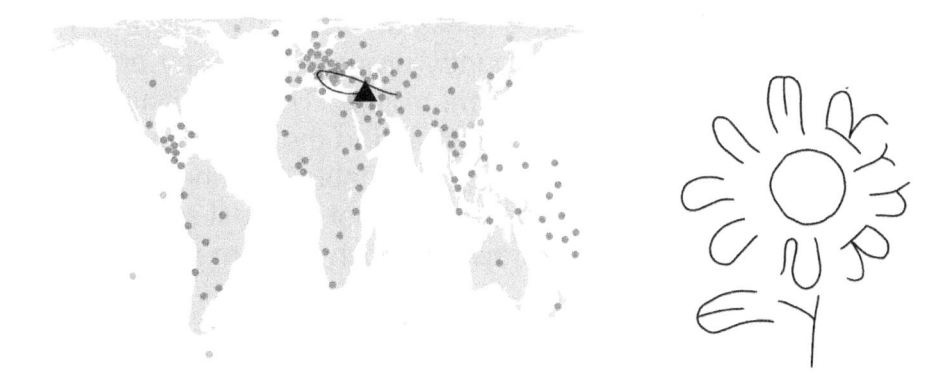

Once the minor anxiety about boarding was removed, along came that about the journey. Yes, I had come from Kabul, so I was accustomed to constant stress, but it had been eased by the thought that I would die a hero in Afghanistan, a champion of women's civil rights. The newspapers would have spoken of a brave young Italian who had gone to demonstrate against the Taliban. Now, in Iraq, had I been kidnapped, wounded or killed, the headlines would have been quite different: 'Hardened gambler loses his final hand against fate' or 'You don't bluff with ISIS'. Essentially, I would have died an imbecile, being just the classic fool who thinks the world is made up of good people and that the dangers are an exaggeration of journalists who want to sell more copies. Ultimately, as in poker, if you succeed you have been brave and determined, but if something goes wrong you have been naive, deluded, or rather someone who has gone looking for trouble.

I wanted to be objective, and I assure you that despite appearances, I am not someone who enjoys danger, nor am I reckless. I would go so far as to call myself a cautious person, but I understand that people may not believe me as when you look at the facts, all the evidence goes against me.

I was already feeling the physical tension on the plane because the arrival is quite something. On the final approach, the plane descends on a bizarre circular trajectory that makes you feel a little nauseous. It's called a 'corkscrew landing' and is used to avoid missiles.

From Baghdad airport in Iraq, you can only exit in an authorised vehicle which will have previously been thoroughly checked and will then never leave the airport area again. These cars only shuttle the several kilometres between the arrivals area and the exchange zone where normal taxis will be waiting to take you into the city. The large distances are due to the same logic seen in Afghanistan; they help to ensure maximum security.

A member of the Ministry of Tourism was with me all the time and took care of the endless bureaucracy involved in moving around. Iraq is a country divided into many areas under the jurisdiction of different militias. These militias are the ones who fought and contributed to the liberation from the Islamic State, so it is understandable that the central government that has been formed cannot now just say thank you and ask them to withdraw. So, each of them maintains control, is responsible for its own territory, and ensures that nothing happens, least of all to a Western tourist, whose troubles would end up in the newspapers.

Each militia competes to demonstrate its hold on the territory and its ability to guarantee the safety of all the people under their protection. I was 'handed over' numerous times from one militia to another. My escort was constantly changing, with soldiers at each checkpoint who were excited to be assigned to me, providing them with a different day at last, in contrast to their usual pastime of sitting lazily by the side of a road and stopping cars. This made for a nice human adventure, as some soldiers spoke a little English and there was a mutual curiosity to get to know each other.

On the other hand, however, the waiting time was always very long, with small relocations lasting hours. A piece of paper would be missing, or an authorisation, not to mention the prayer times when everything stopped, and I would feel like a parcel left in the sun for hours waiting for someone to pick me up. One day was wasted because one militia would not hand me over to the other, saying it was late and my new guardian angels would not be able to get me to safety before it was dark.

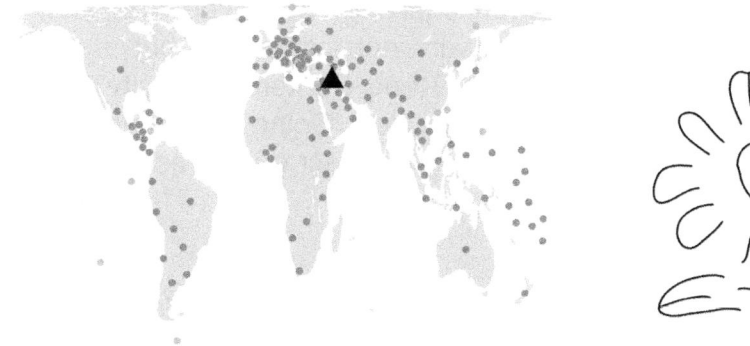

I seemed well protected as I had entrusted myself to a very competent person and had taken as much care as I could. I walked around with the Koran in my Kindle underlined and annotated, ready to show that I was about to convert. I had studied Islam passionately, I knew how to pray a little in Arabic and move my body properly, I knew how to do ablutions in both Sunni and Shia ways, but none of this really made me safe.

The truth is, the only place with very little danger was a fortified area, called the 'green zone', and not because of the natural surroundings. It's a large area in the centre of Baghdad controlled by foreign powers. But a tourist has no access to it and those inside rarely leave. The American embassy had grown to over 10,000 people, and boasted a Burger King, along with every service imaginable. People have to live there for months, in danger, between barricades and the sound of bombs. Everything has to be provided for them. The green zones, often made in the middle of the city, are so large that they obstruct the urban network and create terrible congestion. The airspace is manned, with huge airships visible in the sky whose job it is to film what is happening and prevent trouble. But in the end, just as in Kabul, here among the destroyed buildings and the stationed soldiers, there are women going to buy bread, and children running to school. For me it was an adventure, for them it's simply home.

I visited the holy cities of Karbala and Najaf, and went to Babylon, where the workers at the archaeological site were glad that so many things are in the museum in Berlin, otherwise everything would have been destroyed. I climbed to the top of the minaret of Samarra, and personally photographed the ziggurat that used to be on the cover of one of my history books at school, but the real challenge was to get to Mosul. My escort kept saying we were not authorised, but at the last-minute permission arrived and I entered the city in a sort of tank in order to be protected. Going unnoticed was impossible, so we might as well protect ourselves as best we could.

My hotel was in a street closed to traffic, with rooms on the two upper floors, but for additional security, I stayed instead in a corridor that started from behind the reception and was basically the owners' private living quarters. Holed up in that small, hidden room, I thought of the foreigners who had left their respective countries to join the Islamic State. What could have driven a boy born in Belgium to come to Iraq to fight and kill? Probably, apart from the obvious religious intent, there was also a bit of that gang motivation here. From being an apparent nobody, one becomes a person of value, and if you survive and the Islamic State establishes itself, you will then have a position of great respect, wives and sex slaves, money and authority, and you will be one of the founding fathers of this new reality.

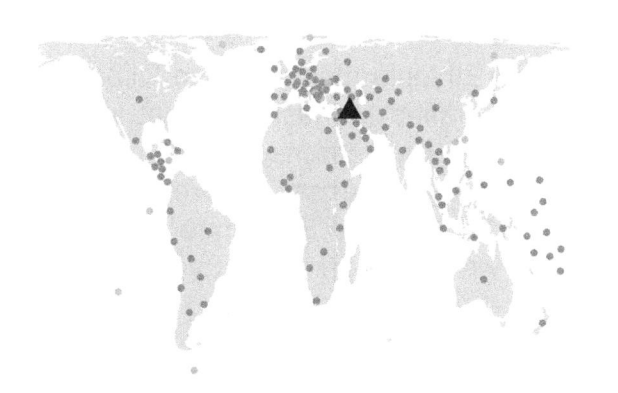

In Mosul, I asked to visit a church where one of the last remaining priests was hiding. They don't usually open their doors to strangers, but they couldn't turn away a guest from Rome and they let me in to visit the tiny Christian community. They too had a meagre and shabby militia, which would be completely incapable of protecting anything. They had obtained economic but not military aid from abroad. The priest told me, in decent English, about the atrocities he had suffered, and having to celebrate mass alone. He showed me secret places where he had hidden Bibles and relics to prevent their being destroyed and finally pointed out the bullet holes inside the church.

My mother underwent a successful operation, though I certainly couldn't take credit for keeping her calm while she had waited. Once her convalescence was over, I left for **Djibouti (120)**, a small nation strategically positioned on the Red Sea where they subsist by renting space for military bases to other nations. Italy is present, and the only real Chinese base abroad is also here. This peaceful invasion by the military has created a price distortion, making some goods and hotel rooms very expensive. In fact, the few facilities capable of providing decent levels of service cost a fortune; a car with a driver can be hundreds of dollars for a day and the prices of imported goods at the supermarket are skyrocketing.

To save money, thanks to the advice of a tourist I met in Sudan, I got in touch with a kind of hotel that was very cheap, where no soldier or supplier of the various armies would want to stay. From the signage to the food, to the décor, everything was aimed at a Chinese audience, with our correspondence being in Chinese thanks to Google Translate. Structures of this kind are proliferating, especially in Africa, some having a casino and prostitution inside, in any event I saved money. I dined at the table with the other guests, some who had been there for years, without understanding a word, but after a week in Sakha with the Russians, this didn't seem so strange to me.

I was happy to go on to Ethiopia then because Djibouti had little to offer. I visited fortified monasteries that were difficult to reach because they were perched in this mountainous country surrounded by its once warlike Islamic neighbours. They were hidden because this rendered them hard to destroy, and some were so high up that you had to use a system of pulleys to enter. There was often only one path to walk up to these incredible entrances and a group of children would ask for money in return for being 'protected'. Just to clarify, the protection served to avoid trouble from them throwing stones at unprotected tourists.

I entered **Burundi (121)** on a bus that several cyclists had grabbed onto with their hands to be dragged along. The country is all hills, and with heavy merchandise on their bicycles the climbs are very hard. But clinging like this to the back of a huge vehicle is very dangerous because you can't see anything and so you are caught off guard by any unexpected events.

My first dinner here cost €1. In Djibouti it had cost 30 times that, but this is considered the poorest nation in the world, at least according to the Gross Domestic Product index. Now as mentioned previously, this index has some debatable entries in it, but it's easy to understand that despite low prices, you are in poverty if you are forced to live on a few dollars a day, and you descend to absolute poverty if you have even less.

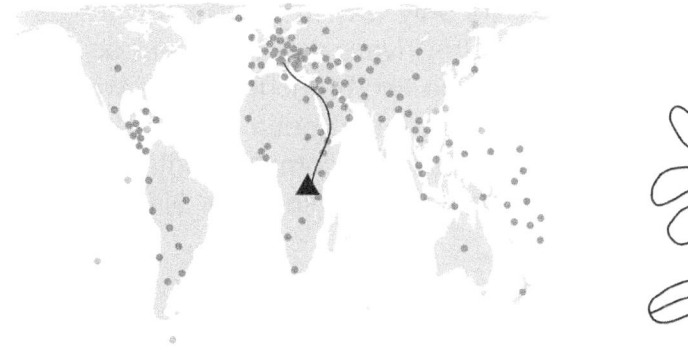

In Burundi, the situation is so tragic that living on a few dollars a day puts you above average. Not only that, but some people here, like elsewhere, don't have access to money. They may have their own fields and survive without going hungry, but the problems remain. For example, you cannot barter a chicken with the teacher of the school the children attend, you have to pay in cash. In the hospitals, they want money, not eggs. You sometimes see women trying for hours to sell four bananas on the street or some vegetables, because they need money. And unfortunately, even such bad vices as alcohol and tobacco are also paid for with coins. Ultimately, living like this, without money and without a state that can help when a field doesn't produce enough or there is an adverse weather phenomenon, you go hungry. Your entire network of friends and relations, with their potential assistance, usually find themselves in the same plight at the same time and are not able to help.

I visited a maternity ward in the company of an NGO who asked me for a contribution to buy a mosquito net. Even in this hospital, in the end, the number one enemy was always the accursed mosquito.

In the past I had looked for the source of the Blue Nile in the disappointing Lake Tana in Ethiopia. The longest river in the world has many tributaries, the White Nile being one of the main ones, along with the aforementioned Blue. Conventionally this has its source in Uganda, but in Burundi, they also say it starts there. Chasing these places is not just geographical curiosity, they are important areas. Explorers dedicated their lives to these discoveries because away from the coasts, Africa was impenetrable, with no roads, and often dense vegetation. The only way to get to know it was to understand the paths of the rivers and use them as access routes. I'd seen where the two branches joined when I was in Khartoum in Sudan and it had been interesting, but in Burundi there was a ridiculous tap, complete with a series of fountains to mark that particular origin of the Nile, which amused me greatly.

I crossed the border into **Rwanda (122)** where I arrived well informed about recent history because by now homework was a constant task, keeping up with it by reading and watching documentaries. But no matter how prepared one may feel, seeing the images of the genocide that took place here in 1994, committed by one ethnic group against the other, to the sound of bludgeoning and singing the praises of the Bible, still feels like a punch in the stomach. In 100 days, nearly a million people were killed in a barbaric manner.

Travelling is an exercise in understanding others, but what happened here remains truly incomprehensible. Since then, however, the situation has changed, and the nation is now at the cutting edge in all of Africa in terms of security, cleanliness, and foreign investment. Rwanda is trying to become a kind of Singapore. It's one of the easiest countries in which to open a business, the state encourages trade and services, and corruption is low. But just like Singapore, democracy is lacking, and freedom of expression and criticism of the government is limited.

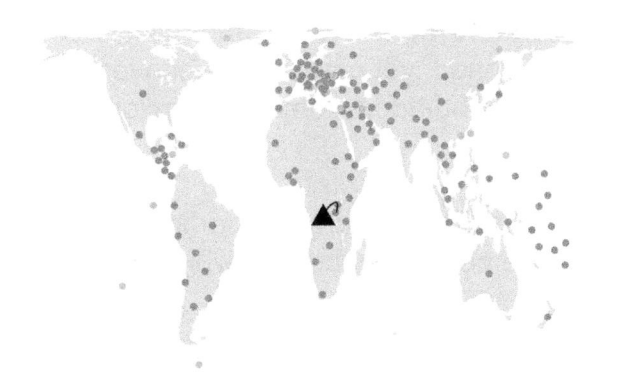

About 80,000 people a day cross the border with Congo, which is one of the busiest frontiers in the world. Joining this human river in procession from one side to the other, I entered the **Democratic Republic of Congo (123)**. There are numerous connections between North Kivu, the region in which I was setting foot, and Rwanda, as can be seen from the number of border crossers. These days, it's little Rwanda that exploits Congo and its resources, which is unfortunately a constant for that poor country that has had to suffer far worse in the past.

After Napoleon, Europe 'invented' Belgium, which was first put under Dutch rule, then became an independent nation. The young state, once free, had a king who in turn wanted to conquer something, and Africa offered the opportunity. This king moved deftly on an international level, and complicit in the rivalry among the other great powers, he succeeded in being awarded the huge newly created Congo, 75 times the size of his own Belgium.

The colonialists carried out unspeakable atrocities in this nation, including cutting off the hands and feet of child-slaves who didn't work well. Then came the Chinese to train rebels, and Che Guevara to fight and a part of the long-distance struggle between the United States and the Soviet Union was consummated here when, to ingratiate themselves with the dictator of the day, the Americans organised the boxing match between Muhammed Ali and Foreman with Congo, then Zaire, as the host. It was the most famous match ever contested, called *Rumble in the Jungle*. The year was 1974, and it took place in the middle of the night so that it could be on prime-time TV in America.

Virtually the entire nation revolves around the river and its basin. Just as discovering the headwaters of the Nile was important for delving into new parts of Africa, here it was critical to understand the course of the Congo River. In school I remember studying by heart the tributaries of Italy's longest river, the Po, even divided between left and right, but hardly anything about the Congo, yet now I was discovering that this river has numerous tributaries, some of them longer than the Po itself.

This huge forest gave shelter to many of the fighters in the disputes that took place across the border, which is why the town of Goma, where I was, has a huge population density, being the only place that offers shelter from armed rebels. To complicate matters, in 2002 an eruption destroyed the houses, so people live in makeshift dwellings created on top of lava, with no toilets, hastily built and then made permanent. People live cramped together, and sanitary conditions are terrible. Perhaps this is one of the causes of the Ebola outbreak that has been recorded. In Goma I had a further experience with a city divided by checkpoints, but this time sanitary ones, where it was compulsory to measure your temperature and wash your hands.

I was there to organise a visit to Virunga, the huge national park, which is impossible to control due to its size and the terrain, and therefore full of rebel groups. When you hear about poor dead rangers, it is because they clash with these rebels who are hunting for food or poaching to resell the rare species to some rich Chinese person. The rangers who escorted me were heroic because they genuinely risked their lives and sad to say, two years later the Italian ambassador and an Italian policeman were killed there. I rode with the rangers in a Jeep driven by a man wearing a tattered Barcelona T-shirt who looked like he was dying. On board was a nursing woman and finally a chicken. They were full of courage, but it was a poorly presented group.

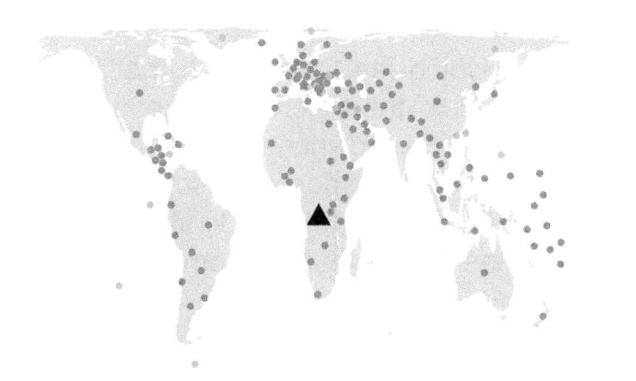

I spent the night in a lodge where I got a shock because as soon as I fell asleep, I heard someone trying to force open the zipper of my tent. It was a lad whose job it was to bring hot water bottles to the guests. He was very late, but he couldn't have imagined that I would have gone to bed so early and padlocked my tent. Fair enough, in those places it's normal to walk around with a machete, but waking up because an armed person is trying to get into your tent is never pleasant.

The next day I paid $200 to visit the mountain gorillas, of which only 1,000 remain. You'd be right if you think this seems cheap for such a privilege, but few people come to Congo, because most travellers prefer to go to the two neighbouring countries for the exact same experience because they are much safer. In Uganda, permits cost four times as much and in Rwanda much more. To reach the gorillas you have to walk, often in the rain which makes the vegetation so lush. I had the hems of my trousers tucked inside my shoes and a second sock on top as an anti-ant measure, a bit of sun cream sprinkled with mosquito repellent on my visible skin, and the whole thing topped off with a silly hat.

The rangers led the way, already aware of the primates' whereabouts as they needed to protect them from poachers. They also ensure that the precious animals do not cross the border! They are worth millions and each of the three nations holds on to them tightly because a family of trespassing gorillas impoverishes one country and enriches its competitor. For the first time in my life, I put on a mask, not for myself but to protect the animals from our diseases. Of course, I had no idea that this would become obligatory in the near future.

Nor did I imagine that I would feel at home in that forest. The gorillas, accustomed to the discreet presence of researchers and travellers, welcomed those who ventured there in peace. They offered a unique spectacle, sometimes walking upright and displaying their adaptation to life on the ground, just like us. And, rather like humans dream of doing, they ate all the time!

History in books has been part of our lives for millennia, while the study of our 'living history', that is, of these primates, only began a few decades ago. At the end of my sixth year of travel school, I can say that it was by far the most incredible experience I have ever had.

The wonder continued, and the next day I was intent on climbing to the top of the Nyiragongo volcano located nearby. I spent the evening watching the light of its continuous eruptions from afar while reading *Congo* by Van Reybrouck. I scorched my shoes that I had left too close to the fire to dry them after being caught in the rain on my way to see the gorillas. The laces had melted, but the next day I was still ready for the most beautiful and frightening spectacle of nature I had ever seen. The route up was fairly easy, albeit long and obviously had to be traversed in the rain. In about six to eight hours, you reach the top, which is where you will sleep, so you also need porters. They didn't have anything to eat or drink; everything was for me, but of course they would try to highlight this in such a way that you would be prompted to share. They would get food and water in the camp at the top of the volcano at the end of the day, but eight hours of walking is a long time.

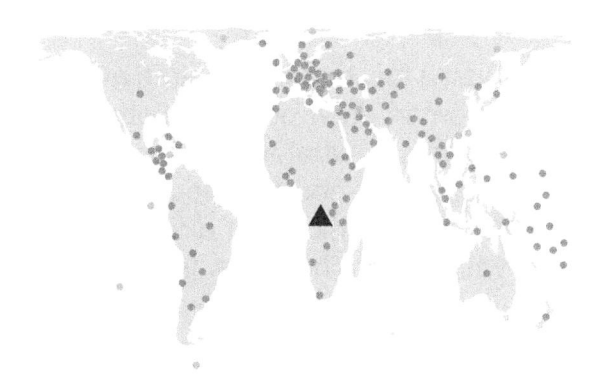

How should one act in this situation? This is a more complex question than it seems, and similar scenarios had arisen for me previously. Initially I had thought that it was okay to eat the minimum and be generous. In fact, I wanted to face the experience under the same conditions as the porters and several times I carried baggage myself. But then I changed my mind and aimed to eat only the most 'delicious' things, so that I was half content and yet felt good about my conscience.

Ultimately, as always, the important thing is to leave a decent tip, which will make the porters happier than having received cookies, apples and juice while working. By then I had overcome any discomfort or stress in these situations. I was no longer a tourist who wants to signal his generosity, nor one who has to play Superman to show that he too can carry things without help thus causing them anxiety that their work is unnecessary. In the past, according to their stories, some explorers wanted to show themselves up to the task and refused help, putting the expedition at risk by doing so.

In addition to the porters on this hike it was mandatory to be escorted by the usual rangers to guard against rebel groups that might be lurking at the top. On the other hand, there is nothing at all to protect you from the volcano, not so much as a railing or a sign. It's worse than Vanuatu. A single overly risky selfie can cost dearly. The bubbling lava can be seen with the naked eye even during the day, but it is at night that it glows, expands, spatters and makes noises that pierce your ears.

There's a huge lava lake just a few hundred metres away as the crow flies. If a fireplace can draw our attention and your gaze is lost in the fire, imagine what it's like here. At night you can stare at it for hours and hours without getting bored, you lose track of time. If you look into it directly, the skin on your face flushes, whilst your shoulders freeze because you are about 3,500 m above sea level, experiencing cold and heat at the same time, just like in Bolivia. Similarly, the temperature becomes cold as soon as the sun goes down, so that the rain you were caught in on the last stretch becomes a problem. As soon as you get there it's important to change or dry off at the fire because it drops below freezing at night, even in summer. At least, once you're at the top, it doesn't rain anymore since the clouds are down below.

I put on my flip-flops to walk down because my shoes with the burnt laces were now also wet. I gave everything up to a porter and attracted even more attention by opening my beautiful sun-blocking parasol, just like a little Japanese girl. I didn't have to prove anything more to myself, I didn't have to be first in my class, I was going to every place and climate on earth. And the descent was fun, with the powerful tool that was my French, I was taking the mickey out of myself, and everyone was laughing. I could understand what the porters were thinking at that moment, but we had developed a sense of complicity and they were curious as to what a single person from Italy was doing in a place frequented by rebels in the midst of an Ebola emergency.

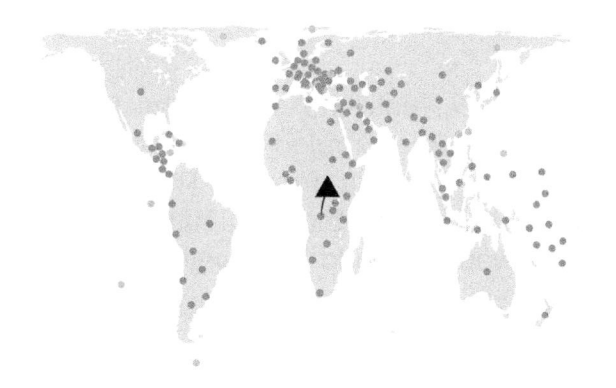

It was certainly not the best time to visit the Congo, but the experience had been excellent. Recently, literally on my own skin, I had experienced the cold of Siberia with temperatures lower than the daytime temperatures of Mars, felt the heat of the desert, of rocket engines and an active volcano, seen lakes at altitude where the blue of the water joins the blue of the sky, and completed a marathon in the Afghan mountains. I had been drunk on physical exertions that had made me happy.

I went to **Uganda (124)** to visit yet another source of the Nile and participated in witchcraft rites on an island to which I was dragged by a very beautiful and intriguing girl I had met on Tinder shortly before.

The ceremonies and rituals were ridiculous to me, but the purpose was curious, namely, to have the evil eye removed. Now, although once more aware of the enormity of my generalisation, I think that this widespread belief that one's unhappiness and misfortune is the fault of others is one of the great evils of Africa and sadly other nations too. Witchcraft experienced in this way drives you to evil because you dream about others not succeeding, rather than pursuing your own fortune. Is this one of the merits of monotheistic religions? Everything comes from the same God, good and evil, so it's pointless to be upset with others…

I continued to Tanzania where I stayed a few days waiting for one of the few flights available for my next destination, the **Comoros Islands (125)**. They comprise one of the least visited countries in the world and not surprisingly, they are a sad and desolate place. The archipelago consists of four islands, but one, Mayotte, refused independence and chose to remain French. Since then, thousands of people from the already small population have drowned trying to reach this island, which is surrounded by shallow waters that make navigation dangerous.

Despite their independence, until the end of the Cold War, the other three islands were still ruled for a long time by a group that could be traced back to France. They were mercenaries who covertly supported the legitimate president, thereby offering the western world a convenient vantage point over neighbouring Mozambique, which was the hideout of many African communist guerrillas. The leader of these mercenaries, Bob Denard, dreamed of turning the Comoros into the first modern pirate nation, along the lines of the epics of yesteryear when pirates were the true masters of so many islands.

But today it is the rubbish that is in charge. Everything is dirty and broken down, and of course those who can, go and work elsewhere. On the flight from Dar es-Salam, I was the only one without suitcases and boxes, while for the rest, who were returning home after working abroad for a long time, the symbol of success was to show off objects and gifts. Multifunctional rice cookers, iPads, the latest model of toaster, really, the amount of luggage they had to take on board was shocking.

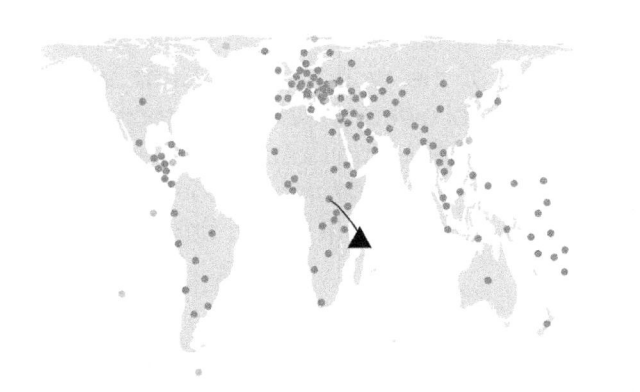

To give (or perhaps more accurately sell) a bride, the father often asks for a giant TV set instead of cash. A migrant spends what he has earned on these gadgets and returns home triumphant. You see, money in the pocket is less impressive, success must be shown off. I had to stand for hours in the check-in queue to realise what was going on, I had never thought about it before, and yet it's clear that in places like this there is no Amazon to deliver what you want. And whereas in some parts of the world for those living in the village a short visit to the city means returning with something, imagine coming back here after years abroad. The importance of the event could be seen in the clothes chosen for the flight, only the best, not the comfortable ones usually donned for a journey. The arrival must be triumphant. You must be elegant and well made-up, as that's the image of yourself that will remain in the photos and in the minds of people who only see you once every three years.

In spite of the fact that the country count wouldn't increase, I decided to visit this famous **Mayotte (/)**, the island that was still French. As expected, the people who populate it are exactly the same as those I had just greeted in the Comoros, but the support offered by France makes it possible to go to school, maintain the infrastructure, be less overrun by rubbish, and have more protection. The laws are secular with no inclinations towards *sharia* and outdated traditions.

During the short plane flight, it made an impression to think that so many Comorians would be willing to risk their lives to reach that island. I had found a bed and breakfast that looked good but had no reviews. I took a risk however and landed on my feet. The host was preparing to run for mayor of the small town near the capital. He took me to see the famous foreign legion stationed there and strutted around with me to show everyone that he had a foreign guest. I was a bit like a state-of-the-art blender to show off.

In **Reunion (/)**, another French territory, I was finally joined by a friend. It had been a long time since this had happened and together, we flew over the Piton de la Fournaise volcano, one of the most active in the world, on a scenic flight which was another great thrill. France had owned major interests in this part of the world before Suez was opened, and these territories allowed ships bound for India to break their voyage and carry out repairs and supplies. For centuries, there have been people in Reunion who seriously search for treasure buried by pirates, but to this day that remains the stuff of legends.

I also managed to find time to explore the islands of **Mauritius (126)** which are about 200 km away. Like Fiji, they are half-populated by Indians brought there by the British as workers with punishing contracts. Their expenses were entirely covered, particularly those of the long journey, but then they were required to work without pay for a certain number of years. Today these islands are a dream destination for Italians. They have beaches where one can relax, lush nature, luxury resorts, and are well equipped for tourism. For me, on the other hand, they were too comfortable, expensive and too much of a holiday destination to be very exciting.

I met up with my friend again in **Madagascar (127)**. I had come from either current or aspiring French territories, whereas this huge island now seemed to resent the colonialists. Feelings had apparently changed over time, and one could see the evolution through the artwork. In the museum, the king of the time who welcomed the Europeans was depicted by the French as a half-naked savage. This was followed by portraits of Malagasy kings and princes in suits and ties commissioned from painters to emphasise and exalt their civilisation. When relationships with the colonists had broken down, the kings went back to being proudly painted naked.

The island is famous for its exceptional biodiversity, in particular lemurs, which are both friendly and cute, although some are considered bad luck and are killed, and others are eaten. The most persecuted lemur of all though, is the aye-

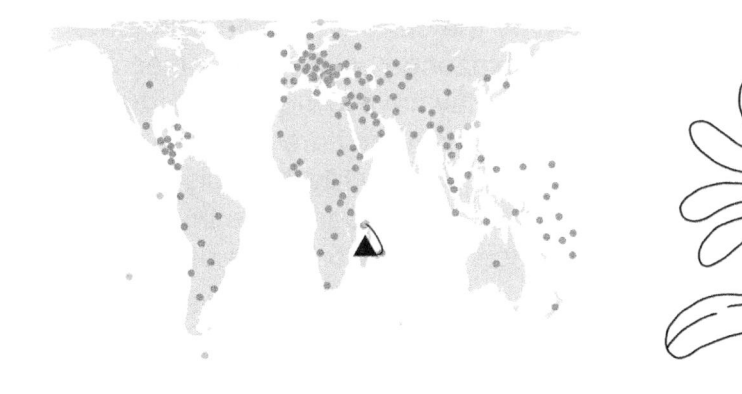

aye, which roams about at night, a bit like our owl in Italy. The hatred it unleashes is fierce because it has one finger that is much longer than the others and according to popular belief, seeing it pointed at you is tantamount to a death sentence.

At night, Madagascar's animals give incredible concerts, especially the frogs that croak continuously. There are over 200 species and some tourists come just to track them down, through the water, braving mud and disease, stings and sleep, just to spot one. I thought only scientists would go that far, but after the birdwatchers I met in Paraguay and the frog watchers, I think some enthusiasts have comparable determination.

The animal that most influences life on the island, however, is the zebu. Every part of its body has a use, even its ears and lips. This seemed normal to me for behaviour in an inhospitable place, as I'd seen the *Inuit* do the same with the whale, which they turn into furniture, or with the reindeer, whose bones they use to make bait or to light fires, and in Tibet, where not even the droppings of the yak are wasted but are burned for warmth.

The zebu constitutes the real wealth for the families of some tribes and the horns are used to adorn graves to display the rank of the deceased. So, here too, someone wants to be the 'richest man in the cemetery' despite the fact that the country is incredibly poor. One only has to take a quick tour to realise how many people's everyday wear consists of the T-shirts given to them by the current election candidate, with his or her big face emblazoned on them. In other very poor countries in Africa, they may have low-quality shirts that are faded and tattered, but at least they are fake Barcelona or Real Madrid kits! On top of the poverty, the cuisine is always the same, monotonous. The Malagasy are the biggest consumers per capita of rice in the world and depend on zebu, a bovine for their meat.

The roads are among the worst I have ever seen, and torrential rain accompanied our long hours in the car, but for once I was not alone. We chose the plane to visit the famous Avenue of the Baobabs, thus avoiding a few million potholes, and we observed the huge expanse of red earth that seems to be the result of environmental disasters committed by the locals many centuries ago. This huge island is unfortunate, but it had, and still has, luxury resorts in the north that were successful in the years when Madagascar tended to be communist and wanted to conceal from the locals the luxuries it had in store for Westerners seeking relaxation and good weather out of season. After all the effort it entails to reach such remote places, locking oneself up in a resort seems a real shame to me, it's missing the point of travelling.

However, my school for that year was over and I had even more ambitious plans for 2020, I thought nothing could stop me. Like everyone else, I never in my wildest dreams imagined that travel was about to be banned.

YEAR 6

MAURITANIA	SUDAN	IRAQ
MOLDOVA	NORTH MACEDONIA	ALBANIA
MONTENEGRO	PAKISTAN	AFGHANISTAN
DJIBOUTI	BURUNDI	RWANDA
DEMOCRATIC REPUBLIC OF THE CONGO	UGANDA	COMOROS
MAURITIUS	MADAGASCAR	

127/193

YEAR 7

As soon as I returned to Rome in December, I went to apply for a visa for Nigeria. The procedure usually takes a few days, but the officer explained that it would take a while because Italy was refusing visa applications from Nigerians and so there would be some retaliation. Even with this kind of tit-for-tat reaction which would temporarily block my passport, my goals remained ambitious however.

A truce had been announced in South Sudan, so I wanted to exploit this precarious peace. I had made contact with a Filipino woman who had been working there for ten years in a large hotel and could get me the authorisation to finalise my visa on arrival. At the same time, I had applied for Syria, another piece of paper that takes an inordinately long time.

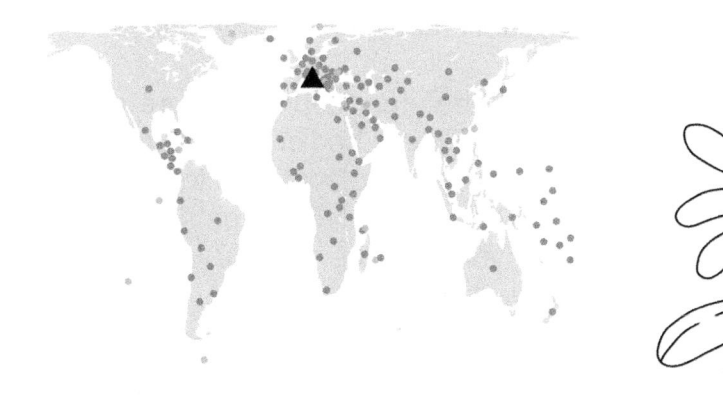

I'd then arranged for an appointment in Cameroon with both the consulates of the Central African Republic and Chad. These two countries are among the few that do not offer this service in Rome, so Italians usually have to go to Paris. A new country was obviously better for me to visit than France, and in addition, Douala, the big city in Cameroon with many consulates, would be a good place to try to get a visa for Equatorial Guinea, one of the most closed countries in the world (the embassy in Rome has a consulate, but it seems to reject requests). Finally, I was organising to go to Somalia where you get the visa on arrival but only after proving that you have an armed escort.

It was a great programme, but it had its first setback when the visa for Nigeria was finally ready. The printed dates had already expired and obviously would need to be redone. I protested, saying that I urgently needed my passport for work, but to no avail. The procedure started again, and the approach of Christmas made it even slower. The person who had custody of my passport had gone on holiday, and the substitute on the first reminder phone call replied that they didn't actually have it! I was already imagining the worst since all the procedures in process, as usual, were linked to that passport, so I rushed to the office in person, where further searches were made, but in vain. Perhaps, having made a mistake with the visa, they had separated my passport from the pile, leaving it to end up who knows where.

Fortunately, they called me the next day saying that it had been found and they would try to rush it through. In the end, I got my visa 25 days later, or more precisely, I got two, one with a huge stamp on it declaring it invalid, and on another page the valid visa. At that point, I was finally able to hurry to the Cameroon embassy, as the country I was heading to in order to obtain three more visas, in turn, required an entry visa for Italians! My mind was more stressed by the bureaucracy than by the dangers of the trip. I left with so many documents, passport photos, photocopies of previous passports, vaccination certificates, forms, various stationery, dollars, euros and pounds, ready to fulfil any request.

Now apart from Syria, all the other countries were relatively close to each other. In the past I had chased flight promotions, being willing to yoyo from one continent to another to save money. This time I was trying to focus on a specific area, but this choice, so rational on the surface, simplified things less than one might think. In fact, some African countries are so poorly connected to each other that to go from one neighbour to another you are still forced to pass through Paris or Amsterdam, and by land, some of the distances are immense.

My first flight was to Uganda with Qatar Airways. The airline hadn't offered a good price, but, with minimal expense, the connection to Doha could be turned into a tour of the country. If you arrived with the national airline you were entitled to stay up to three nights in a four-star hotel for €20 a day and visit the capital on a tourist bus, so I took up the offer and split the flight. Upon arrival in Doha, **Qatar (128)**, everything was simple. I was transferred free of charge to my chosen hotel, paid €60 for three nights, spent two days relaxing by the pool and had an afternoon on a guided tour.

The city oozes wealth thanks to oil and natural gas. Until a few decades ago, the meagre population engaged in piracy and pearl harvesting, there not being many options as the entire country is a desert. Today, skyscrapers, artificial islands, a splendid airport, luxury hotels and the famous *Al-Jazeera* news network have sprung up using the profits from extraction. The discovery of oil, here as elsewhere in the Middle East and the Arabian Peninsula, has given rise to large population movements from countries without resources. In Qatar, as many as 90% of the residents are foreigners, mostly men and unfortunately treated very badly.

Immigration is managed through a system called *kafala* which requires a sponsor, so that it is guaranteed that you have a job and a place to live upon arrival. In fact, the patron, that is, the person who pays to get the visa, has unbelievable rights over the immigrant. He can withhold his passport for a long time and can refuse to pay him, so that the worker is essentially being extorted.

Officially, Qatar doesn't trade in slaves, but it lets people buy visas that allow them to be treated as such. Any disagreement is invariably resolved in favour of the sponsor, who is Qatari, speaks Arabic, and is an observing Muslim. Moreover, salaries are sorted by nationality rather than by job, for instance, a Pakistani will have a different pay scale from a Filipino, an Indian, a Somali, and so on. It's a scandal that such a system is still in place.

The workers who died in the construction of the stadiums for the controversial 2022 World Cup have recently come under the spotlight, but women are also heavily mistreated, especially those serving in private households. In fact, the mentality is still so primitive that the domestic worker is a veritable slave, and easy sexual prey, to be used at will. Some embassies go so far as to advise their female compatriots against accepting work even though they know how necessary that income is.

Of course, as in Dubai or Saudi Arabia, the only ones who are treated well are the professionally qualified Westerners who enjoy handsome salaries. From a pure tourism point of view, Dubai, Abu Dhabi, Doha or Manama offer entertainment, shopping, restaurants, and luxury, but you will be surrounded by tourists and expats and could be anywhere else in the world. If it is the school of travel you seek, in this part of the world it is preferable to go to Saudi Arabia, where you will receive less but will at least be among locals.

The second segment of the flight continued to Entebbe in Uganda where I had recently been. I had already made acquaintances through the online dating app Tinder, which helps in new countries and works almost everywhere. Even in Afghanistan, where I had opened it purely out of curiosity since I would never have been able to meet any girls for security reasons, (not to mention the fact that I didn't know where I was staying), one of my travelling companions told me that he had managed to find women online one night as there were some foreign female soldiers on bases in and around Kabul!

This time, I visited the Aero Beach with a girl I had met, again online. It's a small beach on Lake Victoria where aircraft wreckage is on display. Apparently, among the remains there is something traceable to the famous Air France flight 139 that was hijacked in 1976 by Palestinians in Entebbe and liberated by the Israelis in one of the most successful operations ever.

Special forces secretly flew to Entebbe from the Middle East, bringing with them a person who would impersonate the giant Ugandan dictator who had authorised the landing. They put this actor in a Mercedes similar to the one actually used by Idi Amin and took the terrorists by surprise. They freed the hostages, killed the hijackers and flew away. There was only one death among the Israelis, the commander. Maybe there was nothing left of the plane, but we were walking on the spot where it was liberated.

The Ugandan girl had never heard of this story and didn't really understand why I had invited her there. Perhaps it may not have seemed ideal for a first meeting, but what really blew her mind was hearing my plan for the next day, to fly to South Sudan. So many of the refugees in Uganda had fled from that turbulent nation, so why on earth was I voluntarily going to stick my nose into such trouble?

I couldn't answer that I was trying to go all over the world because, however true that was, I would have looked like the stereotypical 'dickhead trying to impress a girl'. So, I simply said that I was briefly in Uganda in transit to Juba where I had business. In fact, I explained to her that I actually hadn't even wanted to go to Uganda!

The plan had been to use the more reliable Ethiopian Airlines to reach South Sudan and so transit from Addis Ababa. But after I had booked my ticket on the website, I had received a phone call from the airline asking me to go to their office with some identification, and pay in cash because credit cards were not allowed for that flight. According to them, they had experienced so many frauds involving airline tickets to that destination that they did not even trust an Italian customer, who was paying from Italy using an Italian credit card, reachable on an Italian number, and who had already flown with them numerous times. So, I had given up and chose the flight from Uganda. For that girl, my explanation only reinforced her diagnosis that I was a madman, since even Ethiopian Airlines, with its absurd rules, seemed to be warning those who wanted to fly to South Sudan.

I have long since absorbed the shock of being older than

the founding of some countries, but this nation could be my daughter! It is the youngest in the world because it was only in 2011 that it finally managed to become independent from Sudan. Historically, the colonialist Europeans have been accused of drawing Africa's borders wrongly, without respecting ethnicities, religions and geography. This accusation is correct in the case of South Sudan, while in general for Africa I have the impression that we confuse tyranny with a lack of logic. The mission to create borders – which certainly nobody had entrusted to Europe – was impossible, with thousands of ethnicities, hundreds of languages and dozens of religions. To draw consistent lines would have meant creating thousands of nations. As proof of this, once it became independent, Africa changed its borders very little, and didn't remove much in the way of entry visas between one country and another, despite considering them a horrible racist white man's rule.

There were only a few tiny exchanges of territories between neighbours. Cape Verde and Guinea Bissau preferred to separate immediately, while any further attempts at independence by regions, for example Biafra and Katanga, were stifled by bloodshed. The only two successes were achieved by Eritrea separating from Ethiopia in 1993, and, as a matter of fact, South Sudan in 2011.

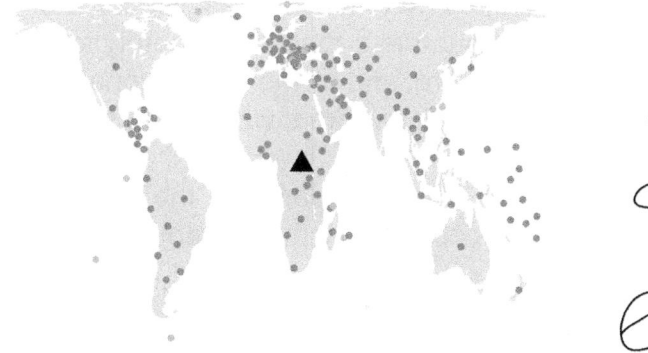

In the latter case, as previously mentioned, the two nations are very different, Sudan being partly Arab, completely Islamic, and predominantly desert. South Sudan, on the other hand, is greener, isolated during the rainy season, Christian and Animist, and populated by tribes with a deep resentment towards the Islamic Sudan that used to come there to take slaves.

Even today, it is disgusting to discover that people in Khartoum refer to the South Sudanese using the term slaves. The Europeans, besides having made a huge mistake in uniting them, established an unprecedented multi-level colonialism in these places: in essence, the British had control over Egypt, in co-ownership with which they ruled the Sudan. The latter imposed its fierce control over the South, which was then part of a nation where it counted for practically nothing.

On arrival at the airport in Juba in **South Sudan (129)** there were more humanitarian flights than scheduled ones, greater numbers than I had seen even in East Timor or Haiti. The entire capital had been built with foreign aid and the prices in Juba, as in Djibouti, were very odd. In a sea of poverty, the few good hotels stand out, costing an exorbitant amount, and likewise, the few services that existed required excessively high payments. But all this allows a sizeable group of Westerners to live there.

I had experienced 'fringe' management before, zones of tolerance on the part of governments where laws are flouted. Here, the way these 'fringes' operated was the complete opposite, and a bubble of almost normal life had been created in a disaster area. This may seem unfair, but it is a superficial feeling of annoyance. Without these measures, hardly anyone would be willing to live there, and all the professionalism and expertise of the international workers would be lost.

The nation really needs this help because the wounds of the past have been compounded by the tragedy of a civil war, which erupted at the time of independence and has left hundreds of thousands dead and millions displaced. The Ugandan girl was so incredulous about my visit because she knew these numbers well. The war and troubles, though lessened, still remained, and now the two factions had agreed to a 100-day truce. I was taking advantage of the moment to reduce the risks. I told you I was cautious, didn't I?

At immigration it would have been rare for them to see a lone tourist, so they didn't let the opportunity pass them by and asked me for my visa money plus an unspecified service charge, then for an extra $50 because my passport didn't seem to be in 'good' condition, and finally for more money to register me with the police, which I would have had to do again elsewhere, obviously paying once more. Everyone who was on duty at the time seemed to agree that a person without a diplomatic passport and who wasn't working for an NGO could be harassed. There were cameras but no one cared, so I fought to limit the damage, but certainly not to win this war that was already lost.

There was absolutely no point in becoming outraged or judging too harshly when this behaviour, although clearly wrong, also had some excuse. Those people at border control were probably paid a pittance, and indeed they may have had to pay bribes themselves to get a job that was unpaid but put them in a position to earn money by soliciting bribes from visitors. In some countries, policemen are paid a token salary, and for the last two hours of their shift, they stand on the street threatening to fine anyone who refuses to leave them a donation. In large, busy cities they sometimes supplement their wages by offering themselves as special 'taxis' that can overtake all other cars.

Given the ongoing hostilities in the country, taking photos was theoretically forbidden, unless, of course, you paid for permission, so I kept my mobile phone locked inside a zipped pocket in my backpack, to avoid constant demands for money to allow me to use it. I only have one photo of this trip, the one of the Nile crossing the city, taken from the plane as I was landing.

Several brave and resourceful humanitarian workers slept in my hotel. The tragedy of this nation has greatly affected the international community, which has allocated it a lot of money, and the desire to bring one's own religion has also proved just as strong. In the contest between Islam and Christianity to obtain new believers, played out to the sound of cheques being written, this is fertile ground for NGOs, especially American ones, which pride themselves on staying longer than the others. Initially, they help in emergencies like everyone else, and then they stay to evangelise.

But regardless of religion, just like the civilisers of yesteryear, some aid and development workers today are convinced that they are in the right by introducing Western values that are at odds with the local culture. This strikes a chord with me because rationally, I realise that they too will be judged harshly in the future for doing this, and yet I can't help but agree with them. Today, as in the past, there is of course another substantial group of people on the ground, ranging from entrepreneurs and businessmen to traders and then to all kinds of exploiters. If I had been born with this desire to travel a hundred years ago, I wondered which category I would have fallen into?

Nomadic tribes around Juba still live in total symbiosis with their long-horned cows, which in my naivety I thought were bulls. I had my first real experience with a savage world here. They wash with the cow's urine, and also drink it, they blow into the rectum and vagina of each of the cows to increase milk production, and they sprinkle themselves with ash and excrement to keep insects away.

The cow conditions their entire life, it's their only wealth, and in fact without cattle, you can't buy a woman and you are worth nothing. The cow doesn't get to be a deity like in India, but the worship is total.

When I was there, had it not been for the small mobile phone some of the tribesmen had in their pockets and the fake American basketball team jerseys, I would have lost all reference to the time I was living in.

The inconvenience was not camping amidst the cows though but having to pass through the numerous checkpoints to get to the campsite, each time requiring exhausting bargaining about how much I had to pay to be allowed through.

I passed the last checkpoint on the way back, border control at the airport, then, I took a final glance at the billboard inviting everyone to stop cattle theft and caught a flight to the **Republic of Congo (130)**.

When I had phoned the embassy to gather information, they'd greeted me by saying, 'We are Congo Brazzaville, not the other one,' sure that I had made a mistake, but I had dialled the right number, and I did want to go there. The capital was named after Brazzà, an Italian who had explored these lands on the right bank of the Congo on behalf of the French. Stanley had done the same for the infamous King of Belgium who would go on to commit such terrible colonial crimes, but Pietro Savorgnan di Brazzà didn't go down in history as a criminal. Quite the contrary, he adopted local girls and defended the native inhabitants, and is still considered by the Congolese to be a benefactor and a man of great worth.

The country is proud that the capital is named after him, yet I don't remember ever hearing his name in school, while I learnt the name of every Roman emperor by heart. Once the era of great sea voyages was over, it was the people who ventured inland using rivers, braving disease and clashes with local populations, overcoming unimaginable obstacles and tackling areas of the world that were still blank on maps, who were considered courageous explorers. In short, people like Brazzà, Stanley and Livingstone, the latter who ventured out with his pregnant wife and children in tow.

Brazzaville is relatively small and neighbours the gigantic Kinshasa, the capital of the other Congo (Democratic Republic). No one has a precise idea of the population of Kinshasa but there are certainly more people who speak French there than in Paris. Apart from the exceptional situation of Rome in relation to the Vatican City-state, these are the two capitals closest to each other, less than 10 km apart in some places.

I took an excursion on the Congo River, but without crossing any borders, as I had already been on the other side. To get to my next destination I would need to fly.

Cameroon (131), which literally means 'shrimp', received its name from Portuguese sailors who decided upon the name after seeing the abundance of crustaceans in one of the rivers they explored. Subsequently, it was a German colony and then later was divided between France and the United Kingdom. Its territory extends northwards with a strange tongue of land that was created to allow Cameroon to have access to a portion of Lake Chad, once a lush body of water. I travelled to Douala, the most densely populated city, which overlooks the sea and is home to the consulates.

The stay in Congo had been very relaxing after the continual tensions of South Sudan, however now it was time to face new bureaucratic problems. The person I was in contact with to help me find what remained of the brief German colonisation, offered to go on my behalf to the consulate of the Central African Republic. That way he would speak in French and crucially, if something went wrong or there was some unforeseen request or question, we could take our time and find a solution.

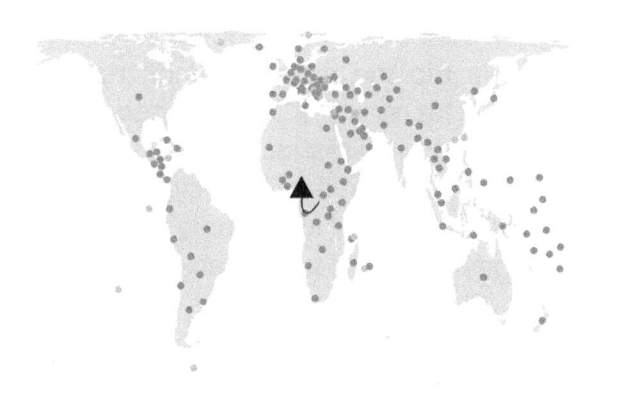

Everything went smoothly, so I invited him to do the same with the Chadian embassy. We had another success in record time with no fuss, and, having paid for an express procedure, the visas were both ready in a few days. I also wanted to try for Equatorial Guinea but gave up because the available flights created an insurmountable obstacle.

Just like the other two on the schedule, that country was not well connected. The few existing flights departed from Cameroon so I would have needed to return to Douala, but my entry visa for Cameroon was single and I had already used it up! For the Central African Republic and Chad, I was able to get around the problem with a little contrivance, namely by staying in transit. On my return to the country, I would prove that I had another flight to a foreign destination in the next 24 hours and thus didn't have to go through immigration.

As I landed in Bangui in the **Central African Republic (132)**, I was still a little apprehensive because the Douala airport doesn't offer any facilities and my transit would force me to stay there for 18 hours on my return. Basically, I was more worried about a temporary inconvenience than about entering one of the most dangerous countries in the world.

If you haven't ranked it among the riskiest, that is probably because terrorist attacks in Afghanistan are reported in the newspapers, sometimes on the front page, while very little is known about the Central African Republic. Even in my own small experience, my friends and relatives were all worried when I was saying goodbye before going to Iraq, while when I announced this trip the most common reaction was 'Have fun in Africa'. The reality is that the frequent clashes between Christians and Muslims causing hundreds of deaths are ignored by the newspapers. The civil war is ongoing, and the numerous UN forces are unable to guarantee security and are themselves victims of attacks. Armed rebel groups and gangs of criminals roam the territory, and Russian mercenaries aggressively look after their nation's interests. Quite a pretty picture!

I'd chosen my accommodation carefully and would sleep in the Swedish honorary consulate. For weeks I had been in contact with the consul, a lady who was obviously Swedish but had lived there most of her life with her family. She only hosted people who were staying at least a few months, so a tourist booking for a few days wouldn't usually be her client, but my persistent emails eventually worked and, perhaps intrigued to see the face of someone who comes to such a place as a tourist and says he wants to visit every country in the world, she agreed to have me. I had then hired someone who had worked in a national park and now lived in the capital to take me around, as venturing out alone would have been a real gamble. He picked me up from the airport with his six-year-old daughter in the car, which wasn't particularly professional behaviour, but immediately made me calm.

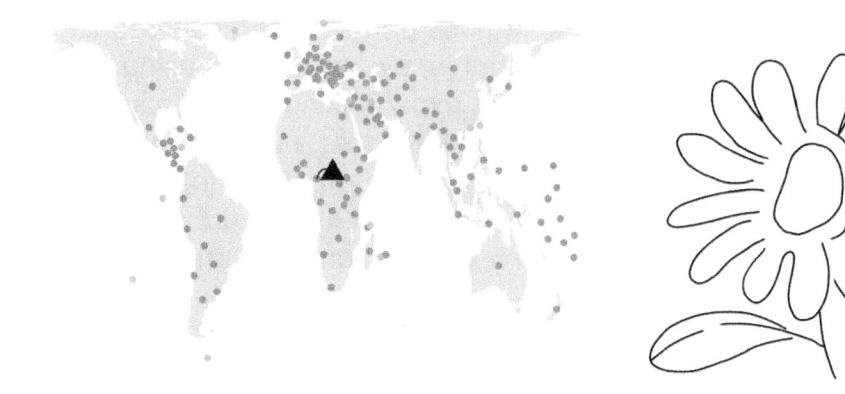

I proposed a stop at the 'good' bar, which I had read about online, to mark our first meeting, have something to eat and buy the little girl an ice cream. They presented me with an astronomical bill of about €20 for a packaged ice cream, two small desserts and a bottle of water. Apparently, I was in one of the so-called 'white' areas that survive in Africa and in this bar 50% of the customers were white. On the plane that had taken me there, as often happens, 75% of the passengers were white, and inside the consulate 100% of the visitors were Westerners and it was forbidden to bring in guests. Discrimination is perpetuated by money, not skin colour.

One ethnic group that is still openly despised and segregated is the Pygmies. They suffer incredible mistreatment and humiliation here in Central Africa just as in Congo, Rwanda, Uganda and wherever their communities survive. I visited them by crossing a road that was considered safe because it was guarded by Russian mercenaries. I have seen roads and vehicles in worse conditions, but never 20 people inside a hatchback before. They travel on the roof or clinging to the doors, even on top of wooden planks that cross the car from window to window. Many animals are transported in dire conditions because in societies with few refrigerators they have to be slaughtered at the place where they will be consumed. I used to entertain myself trying to count all the living creatures in the cars, but it was difficult to be precise. Once I saw a family with six children and their parents on a motorbike and to this day, eight on two wheels is my personal record.

The encounter with the Pygmies was a superficial experience. There were a few sketchy dance steps, two demonstrations on how to shoot with the bow, and some photos to show how short they really are. I got only the usual theatre performance, from which one learns nothing. It was here that my guide uttered the famous phrase that these people 'Do not understand stress', but in my opinion, not using the word stress doesn't mean not experiencing it. The pace of life may be less hectic, but I believe that anxiety is greater when you don't know if you will eat tomorrow than when you have to answer 100 emails. My books had provided me with a better picture than any explanation I had on the spot.

Perhaps a few hours in someone's company doesn't leave you with much, especially if you can't communicate directly.

We had to be back at the consulate by 7 pm, with each of the huge Jeeps parked so that we could quickly escape through the gate in the event of an assault. They were all in single file, nose forward, and tank full, in perfect readiness for any eventuality. So the parties on Sundays were held at childish hours, from 2 pm to 6 pm, after which we rushed inside before dark. At the table I listened avidly to the stories of aid workers dealing with malnutrition, disease, domestic violence and superstition.

People still go to jail in this country for the crime of witchcraft. Some prisons are overflowing with alleged witches, sometimes incarcerated by personal choice, taking refuge there to protect themselves from the fury of their own tribe, which sees them as the cause of all evil. In Saudi Arabia too, people still go to jail for witchcraft and in fact you will hardly find anyone willing to perform as a magician or conjurer to avoid any risk of being misunderstood. If that is the level in Arabia, where people study for years and have knowledge of the world, imagine the situation here.

On the third day, after having gained some confidence, I asked my guide if we could visit the neighbourhood occupied by the Muslim minority in conflict with the Christian majority. To my surprise the answer was 'Let's go, pull your hood over your head and do not get out of the car under any circumstances'. The conditions, if that were possible, appeared even worse than in the rest of the city.

Getting out of the country was easy, no one asked me for money, and I landed in Douala where unfortunately I had the confirmation that I could not leave that part of the airport until my departure some 18 hours later. The airport is small, and not equipped for transiting passengers. There is just one very long corridor leading from immigration to the boarding gates and I was a prisoner in there, as no tolerance was given over the rule which then might perhaps have allowed me to go and buy something in the vicinity of the airport. Inside there was only one small shop that would soon close, so I rushed to buy several bottles of water; I had food and built myself a kind of mosquito shelter. In essence, I was camping in an international airport.

There was no one there, even at immigration, which was my boundary line, everyone had left for the night. But the order not to go out had been given to me and to avoid trouble I didn't cross that imaginary border. I was delighted when someone came to get me in the morning. Since there was no transit desk, they escorted me to the check-in area, took my boarding pass and I was taken back to the terminal I knew so well. I needed that kind of help to explain to immigration why I was passing through without a visa. And so, I took the flight to N'djamena, the capital of **Chad (133)**.

I had made arrangements with a driver for a transfer to the hotel because I was going to land quite late, but no one turned up. When I called, he candidly told me that he had forgotten, yet I had sent him a message the day before. But I still hadn't paid him, so he lost the money he had so tenaciously bargained for. Previously, I'd given in to his exorbitant demand because he had been the only person I could find who had references, which meant I had been prepared to pay approximately the equivalent of a local's average fortnightly wage ($50), for a couple of hours' work at most. I was frustrated because after 24 hours on the road I had no desire to look for a late-night lift, but I was also amazed by the incredible capacity that this driver showed to not give a damn about anything or anyone.

My frustration wasn't a question of money as my contingency fund still existed and came to the rescue in times of discomfort, and in fact in this particular case the lack of transport would save me money. On long and complicated journeys like mine, small problems are constant, things never go perfectly, and you have to solve everything yourself. In the long run it's exhausting. I was envious of those who travelled with others on evenings like these and would have liked some companions with me to deal with inconveniences such as finding a taxi or spending the many hours lying on the ground in the airport among the mosquitoes.

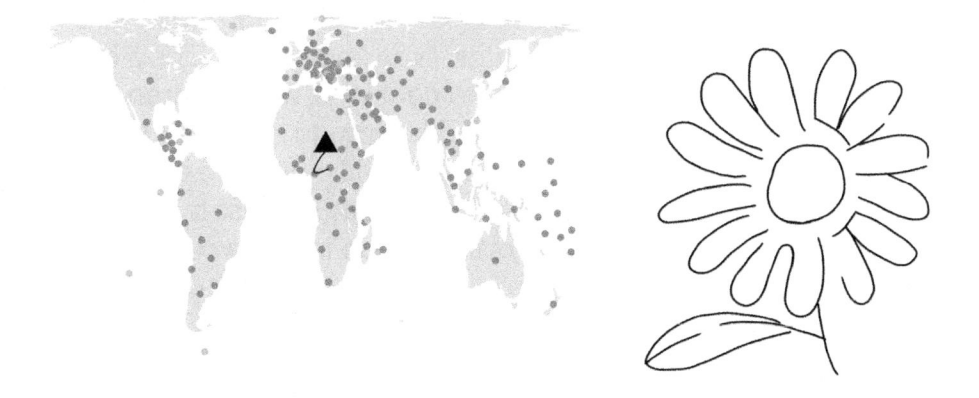

With companionship one loses flexibility, but most of the silly drudgery of travelling, the kind that wastes time while teaching very little, is removed or at least alleviated. Ideally, one should alternate between different ways of travelling. On your own you discover yourself because you do exactly as you please, without having to accommodate others or find compromises. It is a triumph of one's selfishness, which, by manifesting itself, allows us to analyse what we really want. Travelling alone is an introspective adventure with the additional exercise of putting yourself to the test. But as adults, when you have learned how to deal with certain situations and have already experienced moments of self-love, it is also nice to travel as a group again as you did when you were a teenager.

Travelling with friends is great on account of the fact that at a certain age, the time you spend together is less and less and you just end up exchanging the classic tired questions like 'How's the family?' or 'How's work?' without even expecting a real answer. But when you are travelling, the spectrum of conversation and sharing widens, and in this new context, you are finally able to talk to each other about things that aren't conditioned by current affairs, the latest political statement or the football result. These are topics on which we often don't truly converse, because we have switched to autopilot, always having a preconceived opinion and never changing our minds after listening to others.

The next day, while I was still irritated by the minor difficulties of the journey, I saw a refugee camp along the road a few dozen kilometres from the capital. These people were so desperate to escape that they had come to Chad, one of the poorest countries in the world, where you can't count on anyone's assistance. They were impoverished people fleeing the civil war in the Central African Republic, my previous destination.

The biggest worry in my head that day had been the further night in Douala airport that awaited me soon, because I had to pass through there before flying to Nigeria, and of course a night without a bed and in the company of mosquitoes is unpleasant, but that corridor in the airport was better than where these unfortunates lived every day. They had marched for weeks in the sun to get there, with children and every little possession they owned in tow, to a horrible place. Yet they were not going back, so the hell they were escaping from must have been worse. I went with interest to visit the inevitable market that always springs up inside a camp even among refugees who don't own very much.

On arrival in Douala, I spent the night in my usual corridor, fiddling with my mobile phone cable, which seemed to be losing its efficacy and didn't want to charge. I felt a chill when my plane was scheduled for a considerable delay, afraid that someone would completely lose it with me when they found that I had been in transit for more than the maximum time allowed. If the flight had been cancelled now, I wouldn't even know how to look for another ticket without a charged phone and the Internet.

Finally, I proceeded to Nigeria where I would join an international tour group. The timing was perfect because even though I had promised myself that I would stop complaining, I was actually fed up with coping with the petty troubles. Now I wouldn't have to worry about anything for a while, a tour leader would struggle on my behalf.

I landed in Lagos, **Nigeria (134)**, a mammoth city consisting of the mainland and two poorly connected islands. The few bridges are congested, the traffic is the heaviest I have ever seen, and the lagoon is among the most polluted places in Africa. The population is said to have exceeded 20 million, giving the city the record for the largest number of English speakers, just as Kinshasa holds it for French.

Here resides the most prolific film industry, called *Nollywood* from the union of the words Nigeria and Hollywood.

They are low-budget productions, with bad special effects, but if you think about it, the early *Star Wars* films are almost laughable today, yet they still appeal. The plots are very different from ours, aimed at people who are sometimes illiterate, with unusual rhythms and using unnatural language.

In part I had already had the same experience with *Bollywood*, which takes its name from another city with 20 million inhabitants, Bombay now renamed Mumbai. India boasts the largest film industry outside the United States, and it too uses tricks to reach a huge audience ranging from the Indian graduate to the peasant.

In both of these thriving entities, a film does not belong to one genre alone. The films are lengthy epics full of suspense, drama, romance, beautiful actresses, humour and crime, all of course interrupted continuously by wild dances in which the actors are all on stage at the same time without following any kind of logic. It's good to forget our own habits in order to appreciate it, and not to expect coherence or realism. Instead, you have to enter into the film, take the part of one side or the other, and let yourself be carried away. Going to the cinema here is still a big event and no one would accept it if the film finished after only an hour and a half.

Everything in Nigeria is incredibly slow and chaotic. We are not at Indian crowd levels, but the numbers are impressive: about one in six Africans is Nigerian. To form an idea about West Africa, or indeed about the whole of Africa, you can't ignore this country which is a huge patchwork of ethnicities with over 250 different languages. The British in these areas tried to aggregate as much land and population as possible with an anti-French motivation. In 1914, the governor united North and South, his wife made up the name, and voilà: Nigeria was born.

The North is difficult to visit as those lands are victims

of Islamic extremism and therefore off limits to tourists and those coming from other regions. Religiously speaking, the country is split between Christianity and Islam, yet it is fifth in the world in terms of Islamic population and interestingly, the top four are in Asia but none of them are in the Middle East (or Near East as is used today). Before the school of travel, I would never have imagined this to be the case. Indonesia is first, followed by Pakistan, India and Bangladesh, while the most populous Arab country by number of Muslims is Egypt.

Prior to researching Nigeria and then seeing it for myself, I frankly had held a negative impression of it because of the famous scam emails that are purported to be from kings or princes promising fabulous gifts on the condition that you send money first. It isn't actually these kings who send the emails, but they do exist and still play important roles in society. They settle petty disputes, administer land, commend worthy people, advise on marriages and present themselves in exactly the way we would expect a king to appear. To be credible, recognised and feared, the pageantry, deference, colours, and clothes, everything must be aimed at projecting authority. Even the guards stationed in front of every building or shop, or simply in front of the petrol pumps, have huge rifles, which I imagine are difficult and inaccurate to use, but in this society what counts is to display as much strength as possible to deter any ill-intentioned people, of which, unfortunately, there are many.

The scam mentality is really widespread. Some Nigerians, only a minority, let's be clear, believe that cheating the foreigner is perfectly acceptable, indeed desirable, and this has made them unpopular with many countries, especially African ones. However, I was untroubled, since, being by nature cautious, I had a good guide to protect me and the group. The ten days passed quickly, and I continued on to Abidjan in the **Ivory Coast (135).**

This nation is affluent, and people live in much better conditions than in the neighbouring countries which lack resources and access to the sea. Immigrants are numerous, especially from Burkina Faso, which creates major ethnic tensions in the country. The rules on who is really a citizen have changed over time and have affected even those with valid papers. All it takes is for one of the parents not to be Ivorian for political restrictions and discrimination to be triggered. On arrival at the hotel, even I was asked to write the full names of my mother and father.

In Yamoussoukro, the administrative capital of the country, I visited the basilica intended to emulate St Peter's. This is a small town about 250 km from Abidjan, the most important centre. The cathedral was erected here because this was the birthplace of the man who was the nation's ruling president for over 30 years. The building is gigantic, surpassing St Peter's in size, and has a copy of the canopy over the altar inside, along with a statue of the Pieta. It is both splendid and ridiculous at the same time, provoking tears rather than laughter because it is said to have cost 50% of one year's budget for the entire nation. It would be outsized anywhere, even for the Pope, and here Christians are in the minority and there are fewer Catholics. Secretly I managed to get a photo of the stained-glass window, commissioned by the president, where he was portrayed prostrating himself before Jesus as he passed on the donkey.

In the meantime, news of a mysterious virus in China

was increasingly appearing in the newspapers. I didn't pay much attention to it initially, but I was getting phone calls from friends and relatives telling me to be careful, the reasoning being that Africa was full of Chinese and therefore they could be infected. As well as the general concern that medical care would be lacking if I fell ill, I was perhaps, like everyone else, somewhat dazed, but honestly, since I was going into considerable danger by choice, a virus that was only present in China simply wasn't at the forefront of my thoughts.

Instead, what scared me was entering Somalia a couple of weeks later to run in a charity marathon. I had received the necessary documents well in advance but had only been told a few days before that I had to arrive on a certain Turkish Airlines flight from Istanbul. Since a single armed escort would be waiting for the nine runners, they all had to arrive together. The price of that ticket was considerable, but luckily the plane had a stopover in Djibouti, so I managed more cheaply by buying just the last leg. I now had two weeks free to organise and I was certainly not going to spend them in Djibouti where there is nothing to do, and everything is expensive.

Back in my beloved Ethiopia, I visited the Danakil Depression which is considered the hottest place in the world going by an annual average. Standing for a couple of hours in the sun was enough to realise how inhospitable it is as a place. You could hardly breathe. Seeing that some people survive in the surrounding area by collecting salt, shaping it into large bricks and transporting it on camels was impressive. Afterwards, I went to the Omo Valley to visit the tribes that, so they say, are still living as they used to.

I had already travelled enough to know that paradise on earth does not exist, either on mountain tops or on remote islands, and even less so where people live who we consider to be hardly 'contaminated' by the modern world, such as the tribes of South Sudan or the Pygmies. But I had arrived here with high expectations because the photos immortalised smiling faces, beautiful women, and statuesque bodies. The story goes that in the villages, everyone shares what they have, and people are very close to each other. In reality, however, it is immediately clear that there are those who command and those who serve. Women are mistreated, openly beaten, and labelled as property.

Tourists rave about this experience because it is one of the few relatively accessible places where they can feel part of a world that is thankfully disappearing. The more resourceful live with the tribes of the Omo Valley for a few days by camping in the surrounding area, but for most of the tourists, this sense of belonging takes the form of a few pretty pictures. Cameras go crazy at being surrounded by ten practically naked young girls, and tourists with huge lenses feel the thrill of being in the midst of warriors in loincloths.

These photographers, in addition to swollen breasts, scarification and painted faces, try to convey happiness by capturing a smile. Now, if people back home end up believing this because of a single shot, imagine how these locals must misinterpret reality. They only see people with large budgets on holiday having a good time. They probably consider us luckier than we really are. But even if they were able to gauge this correctly, consider how envious they are knowing that we are free to travel, never hungry, and talk about economic recession instead of famine. They see that we enjoy watching them prance about for us, that this intrusion into their lives is only a passing amusement for us. They know that our praise of their culture is a sham, we speak many fine words but then in reality we willingly live differently.

These tourists do not even grasp the contradictions in the different judgments. They condemn night-time beatings in a barracks, or toothpaste in someone's shoes on the first day of high school, as terrible acts of hazing, while they are quick to congratulate poor boys forced by their elders to jump bulls naked in order to be considered men. They preach gender equality in the West but here they are amused by female mutilation, by women deforming their bodies to please a controlling man. The famous saucers in the lips, which cause them to lose teeth and eat liquid for the rest of their lives, are photogenic objects rather than torture and sliced vaginas are called 'tradition' instead of horror.

The average tourist winces in annoyance at one single issue, the demands for money to take pictures. That breaks the charm of the untainted people. When people who are apparently so primitive and naive, use the normal rules of the rest of the world, they lose their appeal as savages, which was the only thing that made me happy in this human zoo. They do well to ask for money, just as you would have to pay in a museum, at a festival, or on safari. They've understood that everyone wants photos, so they ask for money to pose, which is why they are made up and dressed in their best every day. Such dynamics as money and commerce have always existed everywhere. Why are we surprised?

By then I was an over-the-top traveller and yet I had never criticised mass tourism, which is by no means ignorant nor necessarily disrespectful of places, but rather allows many to see the beauty of the world. At most, I had sometimes mocked tourists who believe in heaven on earth or think Bhutan is the happiest nation in the world. Now, however, I felt real annoyance at these tourists who were disappointed by the requests for money. Dear dumb tourist, you have arrived here quite comfortably in your Jeep, you want to meet some savages who have to pose for you, you want to rub your giant camera in their faces, and to take a few selfies to put on Instagram to make yourself look adventurous and open-minded, but you don't want to pay? You have no problem paying for your hotel, restaurant, plane flight and guide, but for some mysterious reason paying the savages is disturbing, even if it's a tiny percentage of your total expenditure!

Still reeling from the experience, I returned to Addis Ababa where I avidly read the news: Covid had officially arrived in Italy, South Korea and Iran. Somalia had closed its borders to anyone who had been to China in the last few months. In Nigeria, there was apparently the first infected person on African soil, an Italian traveller himself. I had received a visa for Syria but now Lebanon had banned Italians from entering the country and my visa was only valid at the land border with Lebanon. I was screwed, but there were still a few weeks to hope, in my naivety, that the prohibitions would be lifted.

Italy was considered a risky place, but I had been away for almost two months. On the African continent, all the nations I had visited had required visas and affixed stamps, so I was able to prove that I had not been to Italy. I had the idea, as a precautionary measure, of photocopying the relevant pages of my passport and preparing a summary sheet in which I listed the date of entry and exit from each nation, with the number of the page where I could see the original stamp next to it. I had reconstructed the number of flights and the places where I had stayed.

Djibouti, where I was returning for the second time, was full of Chinese people. Predictably, they were asked to form a separate queue when we landed, so I tried to blend in with the others, but when it was my turn at the health check, I was told to join the Chinese... It was a long wait in the blazing sun, and I was the last in line. Everyone was asked to identify on a huge map of China where they had come from, where they had moved to, and a list of all the people they had come into contact with, and then there was endless paperwork and questioning about where they were going, with whom, etc. With me they didn't really know what to do since the Italy problem had only just erupted, but my paper proved effective and within minutes I was free to go to my hotel.

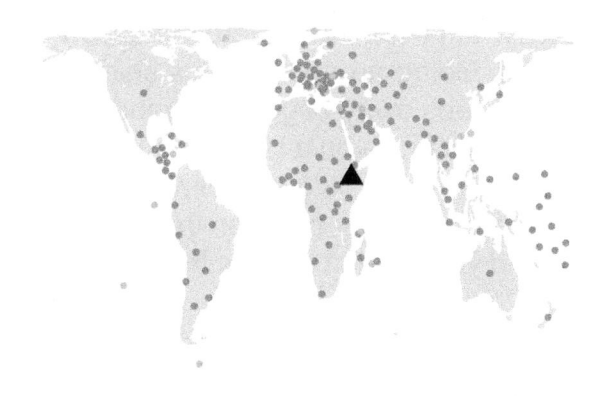

At this point, it was I who was a little afraid because I was about to go to a hotel full of Chinese people who had just arrived. And apparently, we were all intimidated, since for them, I was the threat coming from Italy! The manager waited for me at the door and asked me if I had Covid. I presented him with my nice collage of dates and stamps, and he was satisfied.

He was the brother of the person who had taken me in on the previous trip and I was glad they had swapped places. He spoke English so he took me around. I spent an evening at the harbour with his friends, then visited two lakes, whilst frantically reloading the page with the entry requirements for Somalia every hour, hoping that there would be no new bans.

My mind was focused on Somalia. The news from China in the previous month about the virus had been scarce, and then there was so much censorship and control, one couldn't trust it. Italy was the first free country to experience the virus, but from Djibouti it was difficult to fully understand what was happening. At the airport I boarded the Turkish Airlines plane to Mogadishu in **Somalia (136)** without any problems.

Even on arrival, no one cared about Covid. My nice sheet documenting my movements remained in my pocket, while they wanted confirmation that my armed escort was ready in order to issue the visa. There were nine of us for this race, we recognised each other quite easily, and the escort was actually lined up outside, eight people spread out over two pick-up trucks with rifles continuously cocked.

In Afghanistan I had opted for a disguise and tried to be inconspicuous, in Iraq I was with the militias, here the escort was private and very flashy. Going around like this shields you from petty bullying and keeps away beggars, layabouts, and troublemakers, but it also makes you a target. You don't go unnoticed, and it becomes implausible to claim to be a mere tourist. And you have to wonder how far the escort would be prepared to defend you. I didn't believe they would allow themselves to get killed for me. The guards of the president of the United States are chosen from thousands of applicants, they are loyal, well paid, with many privileges, with a life annuity for their loved ones in the event of death in the line of duty and, above all, they've had a lifetime of training to be ready for the ultimate sacrifice. I've known my bodyguards for two hours, we speak different languages, they get $100, and they don't give a fig about me...

The airport is located within the green zone of the city and is run by the Turkish military. Somali politicians feel safer there than in parliament and sometimes schedule risky meetings at the terminal instead of in a government office. Whereas in Baghdad and Kabul these safe zones were reserved only for diplomats and special personnel, in Mogadishu they are open to those who pass certain checks and pay for protection: in essence, these safe zones are not really so safe. Nevertheless, efforts are being made to prevent attacks.

Cars authorised to enter must be carefully inspected and must be driven by an identified driver who has been given the password for the day. These cars don't even have a number plate, they are recognised through phone calls to trusted persons who vouch for them. There are often long lines of cars waiting under the sun with their bonnets and boots open ready for inspection and with the various escorts in tow trying to keep up with operations. The green zone closes at 5 pm so there is a need to hurry.

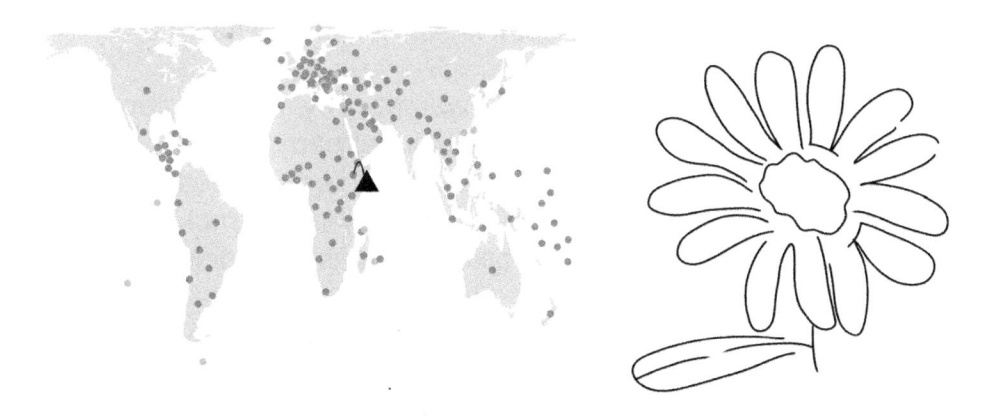

Once past these numerous checkpoints, there is then hotel security where every laptop must be switched on and each phone has to take a photo in front of a staff member. Dogs sniff luggage and backpacks, and there is only one metal detector making the procedures very slow. It would be difficult for a person to trust another someone else's escort, so they all remain outside. The hotel has armed personnel to protect everyone.

While, again, in Afghanistan I had chosen a hidden shelter, here there are only a few huge hotels, in full view, but fortified. Mine, one of the best, had high concentric walls because terrorist techniques were sophisticated. The most frequent attack scenario initially involved a car full of explosives, without anyone on board or driven by a suicide bomber, crashing into the wall or gate. Then followed the attack through the hole created by the explosion. It sounds like a cheap war film, but unfortunately, it was a reality. Fifteen people had been killed in the last attack on my hotel, despite all these precautions and the various walls.

Somalia is truly the prototype of a failed nation, where the government has no control over the territory. In such situations it is the tribes that are in charge, and gangs are formed in the pay of the warlords. This is why the pirates act from here since once they return to land, there is no authority to pursue them. Islamic extremists spread terror and, like a normal mafia, demand money by offering protection. So, the visits to the Italian colonial remains were swift as well; nine escorted foreigners inevitably attract attention and as soon as a crowd builds up, it is a good idea to move away.

Everything is destroyed by war, poverty and malpractice, everything is discarded. As we have already seen in Papua New Guinea with the use of *betel*, here *qat*, makes most of the male population euphoric and they are completely addicted to chewing it. The people with guns, including all eight member of my escort, were also intoxicated.

Despite all this, I was here to run a full marathon to raise money for the brave local ambulance services, and we were talking about real, genuine heroes. The double attack technique was not only directed against the walls of buildings to gain entry, it was also used by Islamic extremists against civilians to create maximum casualties. They would attack with a first explosion that kills and triggers the rushing of help to the scene; then they would pitilessly return with a second attack that would kill many more people, among them the medical staff in the ambulances.

Given the insecure conditions, the marathon was to take place around the airport. The night before the race, the UN military stationed there asked for the race to be reduced to a half marathon to shorten the time and proposed starting at four in the morning instead of six. This was more than a request, it was an insistence, and so I got up at 2 am with the others, only to discover that the agreed breakfast was not there, and you certainly couldn't buy food outside in the middle of the night! On empty stomachs, we set off towards the road running alongside the airport with a few bottles of water, and then it was time for more security checks. Even though we were in shorts and without luggage, it still took us a couple of hours, so all nine of us turned up at the starting line very late. The UN staff and soldiers, the only other participants, had already left, but it didn't matter. It certainly wasn't a professional race, nor was there anything at stake.

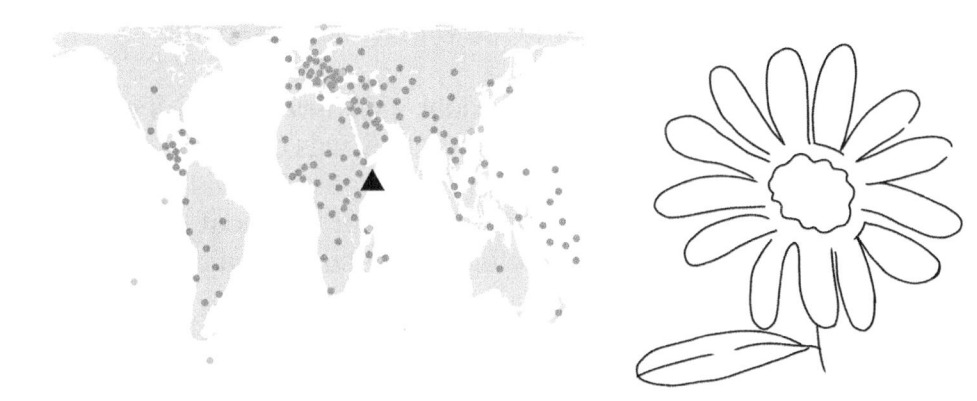

About a year earlier, an Italian girl who had left to volunteer in Kenya, a country bordering Somalia where Islamic extremists frequently raided, had been kidnapped. I was certain that they had taken the girl to Somalia precisely because it was a failed nation. So, well aware that Turkey and Qatar were among the few international intermediaries with these terrorists, I ran with a T-shirt asking the Emir for help. In recent years, Qatar had, on its own initiative, paid ransoms to free Americans and I had hoped it would do the same with the Italian girl. It was a small amount of money to him, and he would gain the favour of Western governments. The girl was actually freed a few months later, she had indeed been about 30 km from where I was running, and the liberators in the end were the Turks.

No one cared about my running in those days as the Covid in Italy had become a serious issue. Given the climate, I myself didn't even send photos to journalists, as I had planned. On the very day of the race, when I was still trying to recover from the 21 km tackled partly in the sand and on an empty stomach, there were rumours in the newspapers that the borders might suddenly be closed in some countries. The fears were justified and in fact, I received an email from Turkish Airlines forbidding Italians to board their planes. My sheet with the movements in Africa was useless, the ban was absolute for those with Italian passports.

The situation was paradoxical, my new Somali friends were urging me to stay saying that Italy was dangerous, and they were not wrong as the worst outbreak of Covid seemed to be there. But I was to stay in one of the most unstable places, spending a lot on hotels and security, in a part of the world where medical care is almost non-existent.

Fortunately, I didn't hesitate a single day but decided to return. I desperately searched for a flight while the airlines were making drastic decisions and found one with Ethiopian Airlines that would take me to Addis Ababa and then from there to Rome. The Ethiopians did not intend to cancel flights since their airport had already been connected to China for the entire previous month. If Italy had closed its borders I would have been stuck in Ethiopia, which would have been much better than in Somalia, so I went to the airport, arriving six hours before the flight as advised because of the endless checks, certainly not because of Covid.

The plane took off an hour early, because they were anxious to leave Mogadishu. Usually, once everyone was on board they would taxi, because the risk of attacks was high, so the staff want to minimise time on the ground, and I imagine the insurance companies are also happy with the rush.

On arrival on 8th March 2020, I found Rome Fiumicino airport in a ghostly condition with hardly anyone there. The next day Italy closed its borders, and the lockdown began. I watched the television in amazement, seeing the *Médecins Sans Frontières* (Doctors Without Borders) tents in Lombardy after having seen them on so many other occasions abroad. I'd gone from being a citizen of the world, to being as stuck as anyone, now finding myself in the little room I had slept in as a boy.

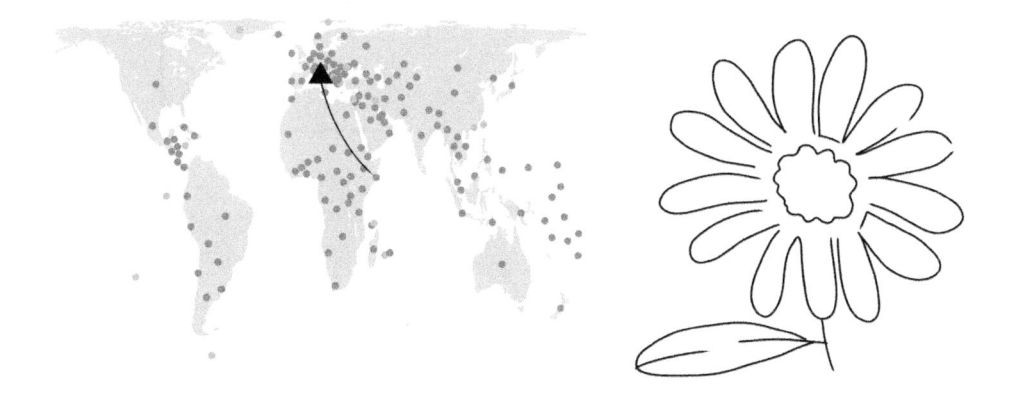

YEAR 7

QATAR	SOUTH SUDAN	CONGO
CAMEROON	CAR	CHAD
NIGERIA	IVORY COAST	SOMALIA

136/193

YEAR 8

During the lockdown I had tried to tidy up my travel notes and plan my next destinations. I was enjoying the total calm. I could use as many cotton buds as I wanted without rationing them, I no longer had to steal plastic teaspoons, I could buy paper books instead of just electronic ones, and I no longer had to take my clothes into the shower with me when I washed. I could use tap water freely for my teeth, and I no longer had to eat lunch off the top of my suitcase. In fact, eating took on a fundamental role in maintaining some semblance of routine.

Life was mainly marked by meals, and I ate together with my parents at set times, whereas during my travels, despite my best efforts, mealtimes had been chaotic. At home, however, I did miss the culinary experiments that I had now been initiated into. Insects and spiders or any other disgusting thing, had tasted more or less the same when fried, perhaps reaching the dizzying heights of a low-quality schnitzel when ketchup is added, yet this had been better than the sight of the worms that were visible in so many delicious European cheeses.

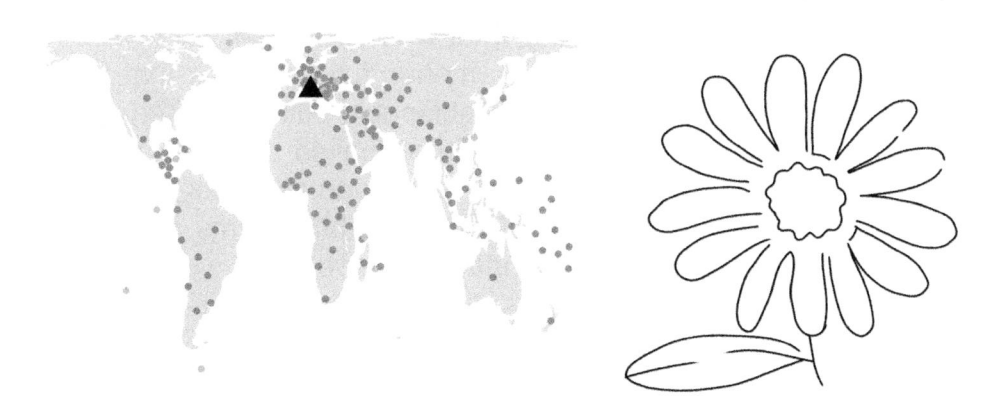

If you look beyond customary habits, there's not much difference between a scorpion and a shrimp once the tail is removed. And who decided that pepper and salt should be put on the table instead of guacamole or wasabi? Why should it seem strange to have everything together on one large plate instead of multiple courses? I think this is better, and certainly at one time it would have been so for the women who would have to serve only once. There is nothing absurd about eating rice and beans for breakfast, or raw fish instead of a croissant. On the contrary, it's quite logical to eat what's left over from the night before, just as we have invented pies with everything in them, omelettes with yesterday's vegetables, store cupboard soups and fridge-clearing salads that we eat for lunch or dinner. Drinking an alcoholic beverage in one mouthful and then taking half an hour to have a coffee is a choice, as is the Italian habit of drinking coffee in a few moments and leisurely sipping wine.

I was never convinced by the idea that eating with your hands gives more taste because you are in contact with the food, but I also never thought that silver cutlery adds flavour or makes the meal more enjoyable. I'd devoured a little of everything, because though we have the wonderful phrase 'I'd love to, but no, thanks all the same', translating it, and putting it into practice around the world had proved impossible. This greatly enhanced my experience, since it's in the kitchen where people become convivial, exchanging opinions, sometimes even becoming friends, and the visitor sitting at the locals' table is magically no longer a stranger.

I had learnt that it was best to eat on the street, avoiding fancy restaurants, not only to save money but also so that I didn't miss out on eating what was traditional. Otherwise, I would have ended up with menus full of dishes that belonged to distant and more fashionable cultures, often with just Western food. Of course, this entailed adapting somewhat, since, despite travellers' misguided requests for a 'local but clean' place, some of these establishments would be considered dirty by our standards. At one time I would have complained about finding a hair in my meal, whereas now, travel school had opened my mind about food to such an extent that I would just eat it. I'd also discovered that in some of the countries visited, it wasn't variety that was considered a privilege as everyone always ate the same things, rather it was the quantity that differentiated people.

Before leaving I would have considered a meal without bread or pasta incomplete, and then I discovered the magic of rice, corn, and bananas as dietary staples. In China and India, you could eat a new dish every day for years, however, after much experimenting, I voted Lebanese to be my favourite cuisine.

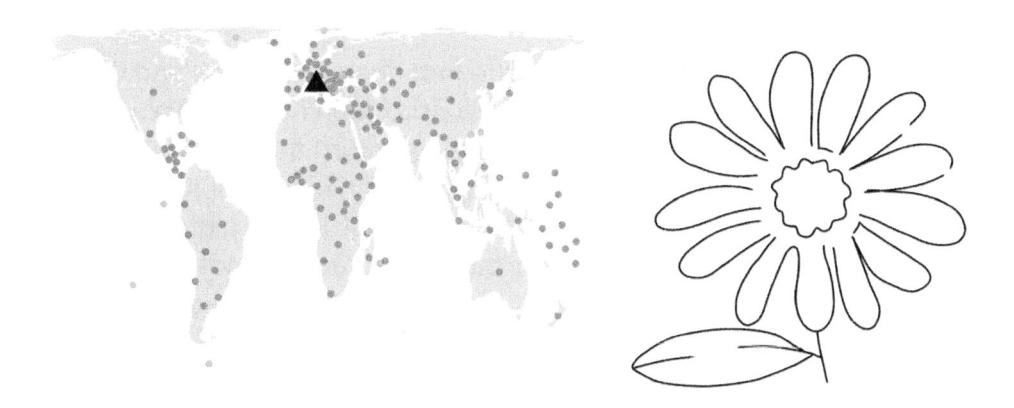

People who only eat Italian or their own national food cling to what they know and miss out on so many other things. They made an impression on me during the lockdown, as did the football fans, who were so desperate for some of their sport in those days that they avidly followed the Belarusian championship, it being the only one in Europe that was still playing. Surely that could have been an opportunity to discover other sports around the world. But even after so many travels, I too have to confess that I couldn't always keep my mind flexible. The cricket that drives India and Pakistan crazy, for example, I find deadly boring. In Eritrea one follows cycling which lasts even longer than a baseball game, a sport loved in many American countries. In Bhutan, it's archery that is the most popular. But perhaps my lack of openness lies in not realising that there can be other motivating forces at the heart of a sport's success besides competition, such as spending time with your family, feasting together, or dancing and singing in the stands.

My experience of the Covid restrictions was not filled with monetary fear as it was for some. I had not had an income for some time, so my worries about the future, quite simply, remained unchanged. My personal financial damage only involved a few flights and the cancelled tour of Syria that had already been paid for, which was insignificant compared to the dramas that people were experiencing. But for me, who had perhaps believed that I had been escaping from all the troubles and cares of life by keeping moving, this incarceration signified the destruction of all my dreams.

Once the lockdown was over, international travel remained forbidden and yet that was my whole life. Travel school had opened my mind, but now my area of action was reduced to a few km². It was precisely the way of life that had seemed to me to be the primary cause of the backwardness of some of the places I visited. The restrictions couldn't last forever, but the more time passed, the more the dream receded. A prolonged stop could have been a knockout blow even for a determined traveller like me. I had already put my life on hold for too long in pursuit of the goal of visiting all the countries.

In May it was my turn for the first dose of vaccine and with it came the chance to visit some European nations. About 15 months had passed since my hasty return from Somalia, so I told myself to get moving immediately. I did well to hold to that resolve as a few doubts had crept in the night before my departure. It wasn't so much a direct fear of catching

Covid whilst alone and far away, but more the sheer unaccustomedness to being away from home, a general malaise which almost amounted to laziness. Was I nervous about going to Andorra? I had never had second thoughts about travelling in the past.

A valuable lesson learnt during travel school came to my rescue on this occasion: you can do without comfort. Not that this is the goal in itself of course, but in the name of comfort we too often risk giving up adventures and encounters. We miss the discovery, the chance to learn something new, and ultimately even the fun, because we didn't realise beforehand that it would all turn out to have been worth it. That's the big problem with addictions and habits: if you think you have to sleep at a certain time you don't go out, if you want to see that TV show at 9 pm you pass up a dinner invitation, or if someone doesn't let you smoke in their car you don't join the group. Travelling whilst maintaining certain habits is difficult and not at all desirable. Far better to let yourself be captivated by what you encounter and forget the routines.

And so, as soon as I had fulfilled the conditions to enter Spain, I was on a plane to Barcelona and the first of a long series of Covid tests. After a few hours on a bus, I reached the tiny country of **Andorra (137)**, where I stayed for just two days. The little house I slept in had a name, which I found amusing, as normally only a villa or historic building would be entitled to a name.

Then I went back to Spain, took another test and from

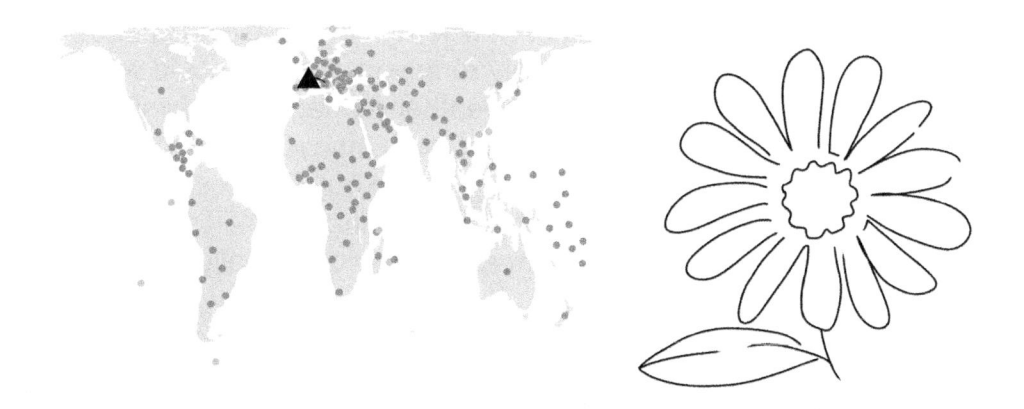

there I flew to Zurich in Switzerland where I rented a car. With cars it tends to be the other way around, and it's the old jalopy that is given an affectionate name chosen by the owner while a luxury vehicle has no nicknames, it's referred to by make or model. I couldn't even remember the last time I had driven.

The destination was **Liechtenstein (138)**. European borders have mainly been created by Europeans themselves, so no one else can be blamed for their positioning. Mountains and rivers were instrumental, and then the blood of the wars and the many treaties, but how did this tiny patch of land between Switzerland and Austria survive? Andorra is at least mountainous and therefore isolated, although the fact that to this day there are two co-princes in charge, namely the French president and a Spanish bishop is probably more bizarre than its actual existence.

Along with walks in the mountains, alone and without a mask, it actually felt good to have to wash my underwear and T-shirts again after such a long time. Although this procedure had become routine, I had calculated that I'd spent more on laundry whilst travelling than on buying the clothes I had taken with me on the trip.

I flew to Vilnius in **Lithuania (139)**, then to **Latvia (140)**, and finally to **Estonia (141)** where the anti-Covid measures had already been largely removed and you could walk around without a mask. The weather managed to be miserable even though it was summer, but I enjoyed having some freedom. In **Austria (142)** I looked up a guy I had met in Brazil. He had found difficulty there in getting people to identify correctly where he was from as they would usually assume he was Australian. He'd tried to say he was from a country close to Germany but in the end it all got very confused, and the Austrian had become known as the German without kangaroos. From Vienna I sailed along the Danube to Bratislava in **Slovakia (143)** and back to Austria. I'd already lost track of the number of tests I'd done but I was tallying up my expenditure instead. In Vienna, however, I had a pleasant surprise as the test was free, even for foreigners.

Once the UEFA European Football Championship was over, flights for the **United Kingdom (144)** became very cheap. I'd been there before as a teenager pretending to learn English; however, I was now more familiar with some of its ex-colonies than I was with the heart of this enormous but now defunct empire. The distances between the colonies are massive even by today's standards and I can't imagine how they managed to hold everything together long ago, yet they conquered very few lands closer to home. In comparison, Russia's eagerness to expand, engulfing huge but contiguous spaces, made less of an impression on me than these colonisers who had moved so far away.

Next, I visited **Sweden (145)** where there had been fewer Covid-19 restrictions, and it was here that I found the key to resuming full travel again. Italian regulations only allowed travel for tourism within Europe, with incomprehensible exceptions for a few islands. To go elsewhere you had to have a reason to work. Regardless of the Covid emergency, Libya didn't issue tourist visas, so I would have had to plan my visit 'for work' sooner or later as I had done with Saudi Arabia. I knew who to contact and so I posed as an oil consultant who urgently needed to travel to Tripoli. I applied at the embassy in Rome, which is the headquarters for Europe, and got the visa with no problem. I was also in time to get a visa for Mali. I could travel without transgressing any Italian rules because once in Libya I would be free to continue, only having to comply with the entry and exit requirements of the countries I intended to visit. The Italian rules, once I was out of the country, no longer concerned me, and my optimism was beginning to return.

My job as a 'consultant' would begin shortly, so in the meantime I took my second dose of vaccine and visited **San Marino (146)** where years earlier I had played tournaments along with two of my poker friends who had now joined me for a period. There was controversy between Italy and the small country at that time because its inhabitants had received the vaccine from Russia. This made me think about the incredible difference in size between Russia and San Marino and how this affects one's perception of home.

I myself still found it strange that a domestic flight could take many hours because to my 'Italian' mind, 'domestic flight' signified a short trip. In Sri Lanka, the long-distance train was the one that exceeded 100 km. In Bhutan, distances were not even measured because, due to the mountain roads being continually under construction or repair, the correct question was, 'How long does it take to get from here to there?'

Flights to Tripoli were only available from Turkey. They were few and costly because Libyan airlines are blacklisted and prohibited from flying over European airspace, which means that the route has to be longer than it would appear from looking at a map. You have to fly South from Istanbul, almost as far as Egypt and then fly due West to land at a military airport, so from Turkey to Tripoli takes almost five hours.

At Fiumicino, I boarded the plane for Istanbul, where I would stay for several hours before continuing on this peculiar early morning flight. To avoid trouble, as Turkey was not a country on the list of those authorised for tourism, I'd printed my ticket for the subsequent flight with the Libyan company and was ready to show the visa that I had obtained as an oil consultant. I hoped that I wouldn't laugh when confronted with questions about my work. But nobody asked me anything and I found myself in Istanbul with no trouble at all, where I slept in a hotel charged by the hour right in the terminal. It cost more than the hotels nearby, but I had chosen it so that I wouldn't need to go through Turkish immigration, being constantly fearful that I would get into trouble because of all the rules in place for Covid.

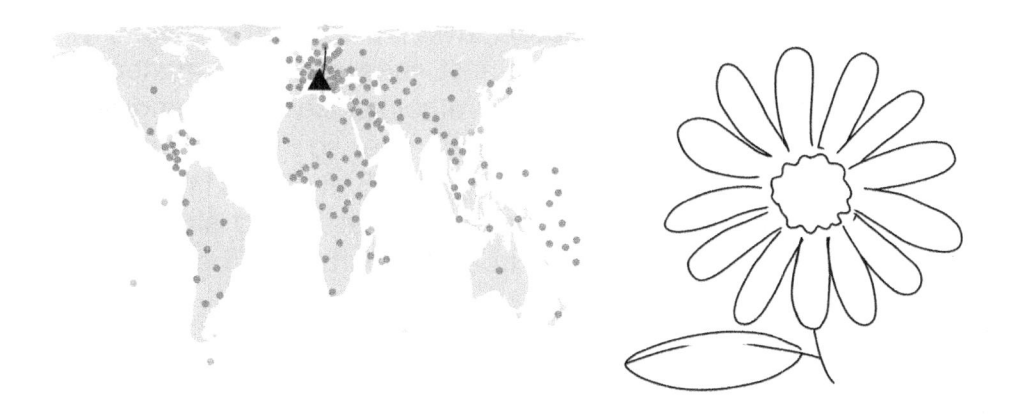

I got up at 3 am because the flight was supposed to leave at 7 am but soon discovered that it had been delayed, firstly until 10 am, then 1 pm, and finally 6 pm. I had enjoyed comfort at home for 15 months, so there was no point complaining now about the airport floor. Initially, I resisted the urge to swear until I received a message from the person who was supposed to pick me up from the airport saying that there was a curfew from 10 in the evening 'til 6 in the morning, so he would come the next day... I could finally complain! I'd left home more than 24 hours earlier, I was still in Istanbul, my Covid test would soon have expired, and I would have to wait another eight hours in the airport in Tripoli, but at least everything went smoothly at immigration.

I made it to **Libya (147)** and was finally back in action in earnest. I already no longer hankered after all the convenience and routine that I had created whilst staying at home.

The situation in Libya was not the best as the country was roughly divided into three parts, and I was only authorised by the central government. Many areas were off-limits to me, there was much tension, and at times the centre of Tripoli was subject to armed raids. One of the magical things about travelling is that you meet awesome, new and interesting people, but in such circumstances as these, you mainly have to be careful not to meet the few not-so-wonderful people.

As if that were not enough, disastrous news was coming from Afghanistan. The Taliban were advancing throughout the country and even Kabul seemed to be in trouble. Just as I had been there, I was now in a car with tinted windows, trying to avoid the constant roadblocks and busy times, because when you get stuck, the problem isn't the time you waste, but the impossibility of escape. If you take one route on the outward journey, it is good to take a different one for the return.

The person who was taking me around would laugh about the fact that there were 10,000 employees at the Ministry of Tourism, but the only tourist in the country was with him. And indeed, in *Leptis Magna*, a well-preserved Roman city, I found myself alone. In the past, those who had managed to get to such magnificent and remote places would engrave their initials, thinking perhaps that after so much effort they deserved to be part of the monument. Sometimes I think that 100,000 modern tourists behave better than a single one 100 years ago. I climbed up some marble, so I gave vent to my ego but without ruining anything. If you have this irresistible urge to make a place your own, at least nowadays a simple selfie allows your face to be in every landscape and work of art. I'm not a photo lover, I've never held up the Leaning Tower of Pisa or pretended to phone from a red London telephone box, but there are still more pictures of my face in existence than portraits of Napoleon.

To get out of the country you needed a Covid test, and a supposed doctor would come and take a sample at the hotel, take it to the lab and get the result in record time. I honestly don't believe anyone was analysing anything!

In Istanbul, on the other hand, the airport was highly organised. You could arrive just 90 minutes ahead of the usual time for your flight and have a freshly prepared test, with results in several languages provided via a QR code, genuinely complying with every possible requirement.

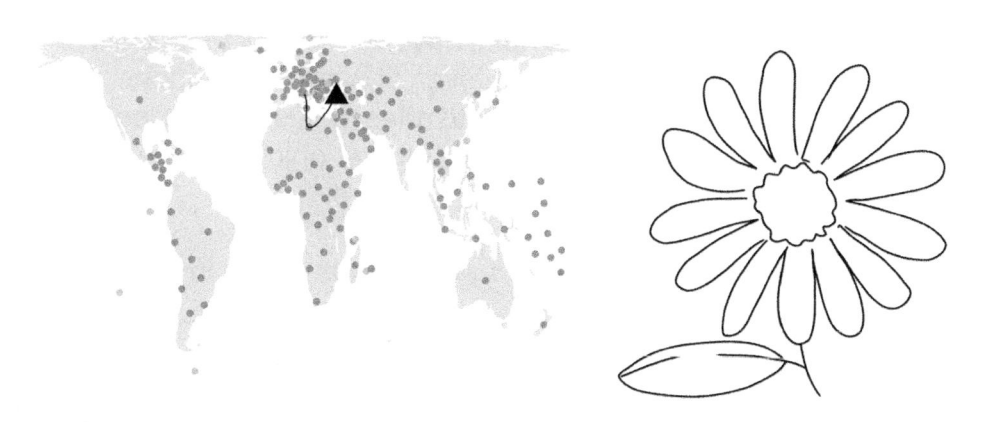

I enjoyed a few days in Istanbul, which is one of my favourite cities and I will never stop exploring it. At the beginning of the adventure, it had been nice to discover that my classical studies had familiarised me a little with ancient history, but I still didn't know much about what came after. I was uninformed about so many decisive events in human history and when I've bemoaned this state of affairs in public, people tell me that antiquity is important, a fact about which I myself have no doubt. But the point is that it shouldn't be seen to be more important than all that has been omitted. Is it possible that centuries of Indian and Chinese history did not deserve some coverage alongside the Assyrians?

I flew to Bamako in **Mali (148)** next, where I visited a few mosques that were largely built with mud. Every year when they are repaired there is a big party. The north of the country was completely inaccessible, including the famed Timbuktu, where there is very little to see. The name sounds magical, the gold was apparently never ending, despite the probability that it was never even there, and it was the place where Black Africa and Arab Africa met. The desert caravans would reach the river where it was possible to transport goods on water.

I caught a glimpse of a few famous *Tuaregs*, and one of them agreed to act as my guide. For me, these men are symbolic of the struggles between nomads and sedentary people, another great theme I had never really thought about.

Living in Europe, disputes of this kind barely exist, and yet some animosity does remain towards the few ethnic groups that are still perceived as nomads, despite them hardly being so any more in reality. Here I saw with my own eyes the meeting and clash of the two worlds. On the one hand, the nomad does not produce all the objects that he needs and therefore wants to trade, so the encounters are frequent, however, on the other he does have a mentality that conflicts with the rest of the world. A lover of war and weapons, his life is free, he does not submit to rules, he uses force, perpetrates raids, takes advantage of others, enjoys leisure time, and cultivates a relationship with nature.

Until recently, the settled person was a serf in the eyes

of the wanderer, tied to the land, and always working. In my love of travelling, I could begin to empathise with a modicum of their pride in the way they behave, but people like this are difficult to trust.

There is still suspicion today towards wanderers, vagabonds, and street vendors. I myself grew up hearing the phrase, 'You don't know them, what do you care...' many times, and it's true that even a non-nomadic person in a settled society tends to take on a bit of the same mentality of taking advantage the moment it's clear that they will never meet the other person again. Petty transgressions are among the few privileges left to those who are excluded from mainstream society because they have no fixed abode. Even in respectful Japan, the outcasts, traditionally wanderers, are the only ones who don't respect queues, never pay for a transport ticket, and cross the street when the light is red.

However, what is far more serious is that everywhere in the world, the few true nomads left are people who still don't send their children to school, don't pay taxes, and are violent with each other (in part because they don't have jails). They exploit resources for their own use and consumption, perhaps cutting down small trees, using farmland for grazing, and despising others because they are servants by nature.

In these parts of Africa, they used to enslave blacks and society remained organised by castes with them at the top.

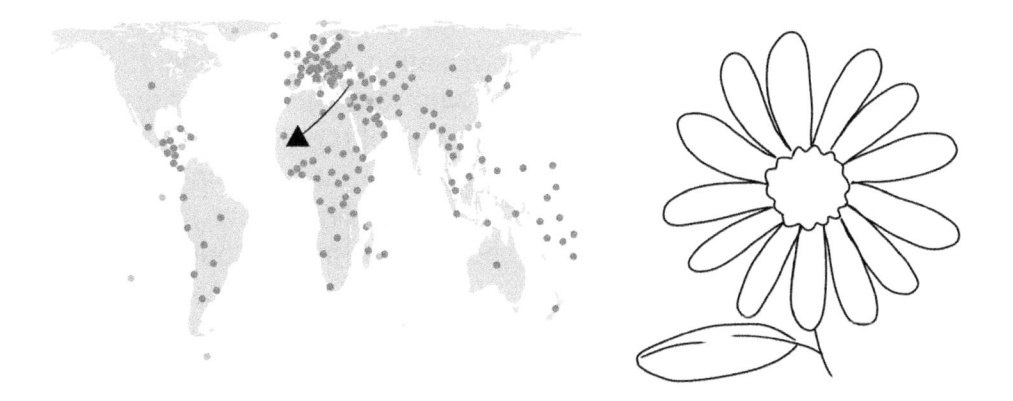

It's worth mentioning that in Mauritania, they are still openly enslaved, while the *Tuaregs* in Mali, that is, these men here dressed in blue, are in constant revolt against the government that pushes them to settle.

In the North they would like to have their own state governed by Islamic principles and their own culture, but some *Tuaregs* have instead surrendered and chosen to become resident. They've realised that they cannot accumulate because they are always on the move and can carry almost nothing with them. They are bound to be in dire need at the first sign of trouble and raiding is now no longer tolerated. Their sources of income are also disappearing, the caravans have been supplanted by roads and trucks, so truck driving has become the job of choice so that they can stay on the move, albeit with strict rules, and they are not living off the backs of others. For those who still want to rebel against authority, there is smuggling.

In Mongolia, a nomadic nation par excellence, many voluntarily settle around the capital, pitch their tent there and basically lead a normal life albeit in an environment that reminds them of freedom. The famous *Sherpa* porters in the Tibetan mountains, who once transported goods where there were no real roads, now work with tourists carrying their equipment and accompanying them on hikes.

Even the Bedouins, nomads of Arab origin (not Berber like the *Tuareg*), have found their own place. In Saudi Arabia, for instance, they have become the king's loyalists. As soon as the modern state was formed, they agreed to be incorporated into this new realm of civilisation, thanks mainly to the economic incentives for those who renounced nomadic life. The few water wells, the real wealth of the desert, were nationalised and access regulated to prevent in-fighting. Plenty of land was given to them but on a personal basis, not to the tribe. Then over time they became the main group making up the armed forces, the national guard and the religious police. All this loyalty is repaid with generous salaries, again thanks to wells, but this time of oil. Every Bedouin family has at least one member employed for huge fees by the state.

Something Bedouin certainly remains though, for example the love for the camel and thus the placing of the breeders high up in the hierarchies since they take care of the strongest and most functional animal, so they are the most powerful. On the other hand, living with camels really made a person an excellent soldier, just as it did with horsemen. A mount confers pride, strength, courage, and a habit of always marching onwards, of continuing through adversity.

To get out of Mali I took a Covid test at the hospital and was forced to pay a lavish and not at all spontaneous tip on collection of the report in order to avoid missing the plane to **Burkina Faso (149)**. I had an appointment there with a nun who had helped acquaintances in Italy adopt Burkinabe children. Reaching her was complicated because I'd got on the road very late as the airport provides visas on arrival, but only at certain times, so, I'd had to wait for the clerk to come back after an interminable lunch break and I was then finally able to get going. On arrival I found out that the orphanage no longer had any children, it was just a kind of convent, but at least it was interesting, though sad, to hear the horror stories about what was happening in the North of the country and how dangerous life was for the large Christian minority.

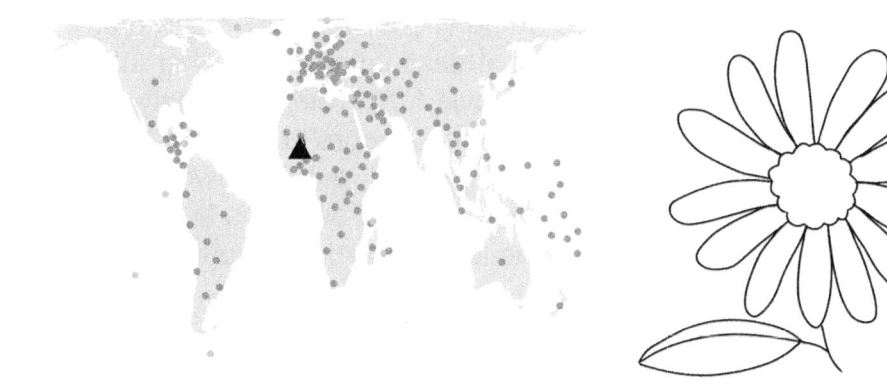

I couldn't visit or play with the children, but I did manage to do so with the crocodiles. In the village of Bazoulé there is a body of water where they are said to have been trapped a long time ago and have since been considered sacred animals and fed by the inhabitants. In this way, according to them, they were domesticated. Indeed, they were able to climb on top of a specimen weighing over 200 kg, pull its tail, and take photos that were as incredible as they were apparently careless.

The trick is in fact not in actually taming such a primitive animal, but in feeding them abundantly. The tourist can then climb on top of them, the weight of a man does not bother them. While they are being fed, they are voracious and dangerous, as you can easily imagine. They fight over the chickens that are given out and one won't hesitate to bite into the limbs of another and then twist, thus exerting maximum force and amputating the opponent. This double spirit, docile and ferocious, made me ponder how little I knew about animal behaviour. As a city boy I had observed how a fly endlessly bangs against a window when the opening is only a few centimetres away, but I'd had no idea that such a large animal could be so stupid and predictable. In this I had perhaps been carried away by social media where in every clip the animals seem intelligent and sensitive. When they play with each other they are adorable and seem to be able to communicate. But some animals are incredibly limited, like for instance when they are totally unable to understand the trajectory of a car on the road.

After two hectic days at the Niger embassy, I had managed to get a visa for my next destination and gather information on how to take the Covid test. There was only one authorised laboratory which took 72 hours to provide the result. Still, mindful of the time involved, the tests were valid for five days and not the usual three. Four days before the flight I queued up among the large crowds, obviously with a risk of contagion because people with suspected symptoms were sent there too.

To pay you had to go to a specific bank that was nowhere near the test centre, or you could do so via an app that required an additional registration that was only open to people from that country. The young man who had taken me there on his motorbike was smart and spoke a few words of English, which was why I had chosen him, and he offered to register on the app and pay online for me.

Now I had a second problem to solve: I only wanted to stay in Niger for four days. I would land on a Sunday, a day when the only authorised laboratory was closed. Even if I had gone early on Monday, I would have run the risk of not having the result in time to get out of the country and into the new one, because if it had taken 72 hours to get the result in Burkina, in Niger it was only going to be worse.

I had almost resigned myself to staying longer, giving up the low-priced flight I had found and growing bored at the fact that to leave Niamey, the capital, it was compulsory to organise an armed escort, which I did not want because it was too expensive. Instead, I woke up the next night with the solution: on Sunday morning, before embarking for Niger using the test I had taken four days earlier, I would take a further test! The result would arrive three days later but would be valid for leaving Niger.

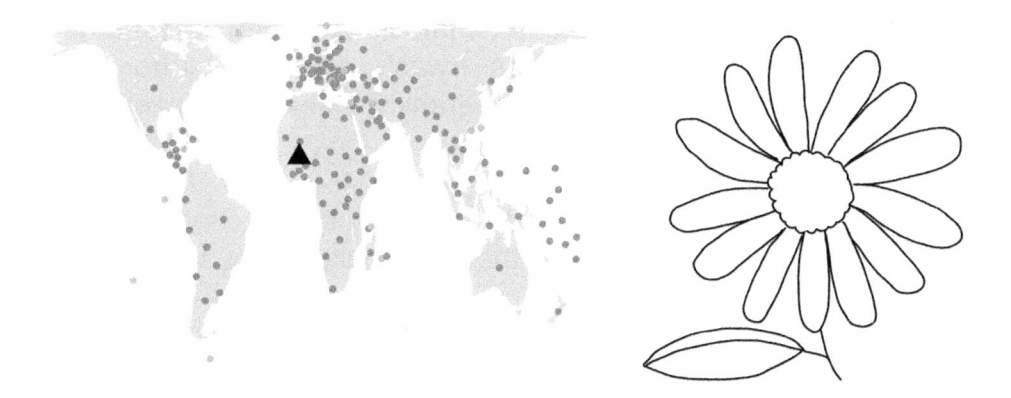

On the day of departure, my biker friend took me to the lab and paid again for me online. With the second test done, I was now dependent on him to come back three days later to collect my certificate, scan it, and send it online so that I could print it out to leave Niger and head for my next destination.

My travels were beginning to be heavily influenced not only by Covid itself but also by bureaucracy and inefficiencies. You had to be up to date with the laboratory schedules, stay in the capital the last few days to get access to the tests, be mindful of public holidays, and of course be prepared to fight with those who wanted money to issue certificates, to not 'lose' the test sample, or to not waste your time at the airport.

I landed very late in Niamey, **Niger (150)**. The Air Burkina plane was a jumble of pieces from other planes with inscriptions in different languages and formats between one seat and another, as well as in the toilets. Some of the suitcases were piled up in front of the emergency exit. In Niger the average age is very low and it's easy to find women who have ten children as the birth rate is the highest in the world. Imagine how your quiet town in Europe or the USA would be transformed if the average age dropped from 45 to 15. Chaos would descend immediately along with many small instances of unruliness. I was surrounded by hordes of shrieking children but, quite frankly, since I had plenty of time, I enjoyed myself.

Hundreds of children still seemed to be chasing me around once I was inside the huge national museum, but the spectacle there was very sad. It's basically a zoo where they leave the animals to starve. I had never seen such disregard. They also have a huge, valuable dinosaur skeleton inside which they let birds build their nests in. I was used to shabby and dilapidated museums. I'd been photographed instead of the works of art, a tourist there evidently being rarer than a beautiful statue. I'd smiled when the first room was completely dedicated to the director and his photos, but then had quickly become bored as the guides spent more time telling the day and month each room was opened than they did explaining its contents. I'd also been aware that the main focus was to steer me towards a little shop set up in the corner and run by the employees. But I have to admit, a skeletal lion and tiny bird cages overflowing with excrement was a first!

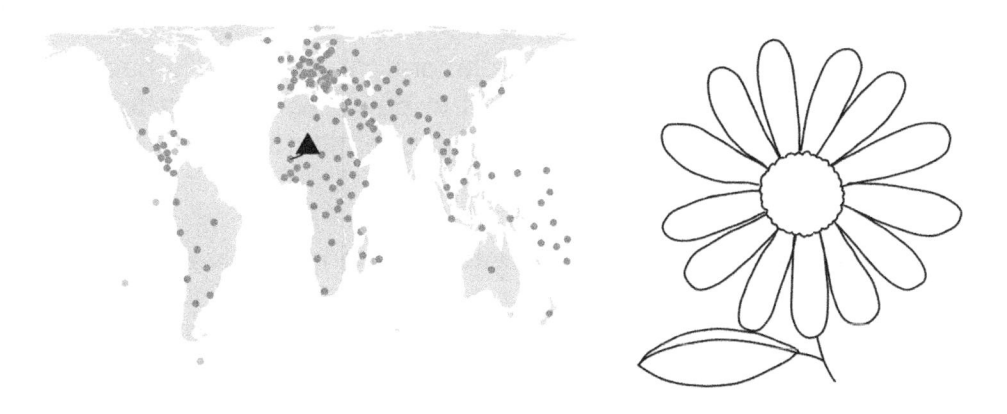

Unable to leave the capital without an escort, I headed for a village along the Niger River, which could be reached easily by boat. You can watch hippos along the way, keeping well away because they are aggressive and dangerous. Then you arrive at a place where, amidst the usual waves of children to welcome you, there was a woman possessed by a *jinn*, which is a creature that Muslims believe in. In agreement with my guide, we had brought a mountain of sweets and there was a big party atmosphere. I had found it bizarre, indeed wrong, to enter schools or slums in this way, but here it was exciting, and I didn't feel embarrassed. Who knows, maybe I had changed the way I thought about these things. Everyone was happy, children were jumping on me, competing to hold my hand, and the older men invited me to eat with them from a huge portion of rice that contained a few pieces of meat.

My guide was quick to advise me to be careful: the invitation was for rice, not meat. During the meal, I was asked whether Covid really existed or was an invention. For once, was a disease killing more of the rich people than the poor, and if so, did they have nothing to fear? As absurd as those assumptions were, in my mind the Covid worry had faded, or rather, became more of a bureaucratic nuisance than a terrible disease. In that village, swamped by children, I completely neglected to take any precautions for the first time. Even if I had wanted to, it would have been impossible. Everyone was eating with their hands and the children were constantly shouting at me just centimetres from my face.

My friend in Burkina Faso was thorough and since no one objected, I was able to leave the country using a Covid test done abroad. All African countries at that time required a molecular test to allow entry, but some, like Niger for example, also required it to leave, no matter where you were going. Maybe they did it for statistical purposes, maybe to give their laboratory which charged huge prices more work. However, I was better off than a friend of mine who visited South Sudan using the information I had passed on to him. He told me that it had taken five days to get the certificate there because there was no laboratory, the sample had to be sent abroad. You then had to pay a compulsory fee to have the certificate issued with a date after the sample was collected or you were trapped.

I arrived in **Guinea Bissau (151)** and received terrible

news from Afghanistan. The Taliban had now conquered the whole country, including the capital. The situation had become dangerous for the girls who had run with me. Anyone who had had dealings with foreigners was considered an enemy. Even if they were not singled out as 'rebels', they would soon no longer be able to study and would have to hide under the *burqa*. Some of them were in Kabul, the last place still in the hands of foreign forces and from where flights to safety departed. Fatima, the only female tour guide in the country, was trying desperately each night to reach the airport, along with the marathon organiser who had his wife and children, his elderly mother and three other girls with him.

One night Fatima lost her suitcase in the crush, and with it her memories and what little she still owned. I could not even begin to imagine the pain of seeing one's life disappear and losing everything. I could, however, understand the attachment to the suitcase and its contents. I had far more important things safe at home, yet I would have suffered if I had lost my luggage, I really felt that everything I owned was inside.

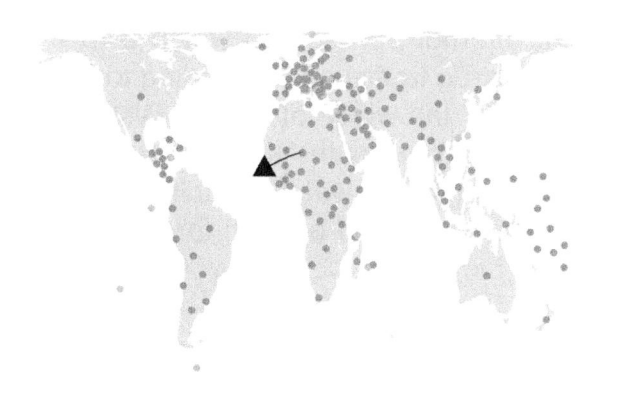

Aircraft safety announcements instruct people to leave their suitcases on board in the event of an evacuation, because, despite having plenty of replacement belongings back where they live, even in a moment of panic passengers instinctively make the mistake of wasting time with their travel bags while the flames rage. But I always wanted to take my suitcase with me. I would clean it, peel off every airport sticker, and open it gently. When I had to entrust it to someone, I would explain how much I cared about it. I always had the feeling that they would treat it badly anyway. I have seen people take similarly obsessive care of their cars, but for me, my suitcase was so much more, it was my home.

Flying into Guinea Bissau had been expensive, but it was easy to find accommodation for a few dollars a night and I was no longer used to spending so little. Back in the early days of my travels, when I would get all my budgets wrong, I would avidly read the headlines about how to feel like a king abroad on $10 a day and would wonder why it never worked out for me. By now, however, I knew it wasn't my fault. Even in countries like Guinea Bissau or the cheapest nations in Southeast Asia, the bill never seemed to add up to this famous $10 daily goal. Or rather, those who sell this scenario resort to tricks. Firstly, they exclude the plane flight from the average daily expense, then they assume that four people are travelling, so car transfers and rooms are optimised. It's only with these adjustments that you can actually live in Guinea Bissau or Laos for so little, and you certainly wouldn't feel like a king.

For the last few days of my stay, I decided to treat myself better, more like a 'prince' so to speak. I wanted to stay in the hotel to have decent Internet access and watch a few TV series about Colombian drug traffickers. According to reports, they had in fact 'bought' the whole of Guinea Bissau, first transporting cocaine here from South America and then dealing it in the West. I was unable to watch anything, however, because the Internet wasn't good enough for streaming.

Whereas at one time I would try to have most of my trip booked for my own convenience and to save money, now with Covid it was a case of living hand to mouth. I had to cope with constant changes in the rules on entry requirements, and of course with the risk of getting infected and having to stay put for a couple of weeks. This chaos didn't appeal to me as I preferred to be organised. I was spending my time on solving small problems instead of researching the country, had fallen behind on my reading and was anxious about being trapped somewhere in the middle of nowhere. It was not the time to enjoy travelling.

The only Covid lab in Bissau was a disaster, with no hygiene measures and everything written by hand in a most confusing manner, along with the usual demands for money for the result to be on time. I needed the test to visit neighbouring Senegal where I wanted to enter by land to explore the southern part of the country. The problem was that Guinea Bissau is rife with roadblocks, set both by police asking you for money and by locals repairing or claiming to repair roads and asking for a contribution. For an outsider, such unorthodox tolls become compulsory payments. And all this in Covid period, when traffic rules change all the time and every village you pass may have (or claim to have) its own very strict curfew, unless of course you pay an extra toll.

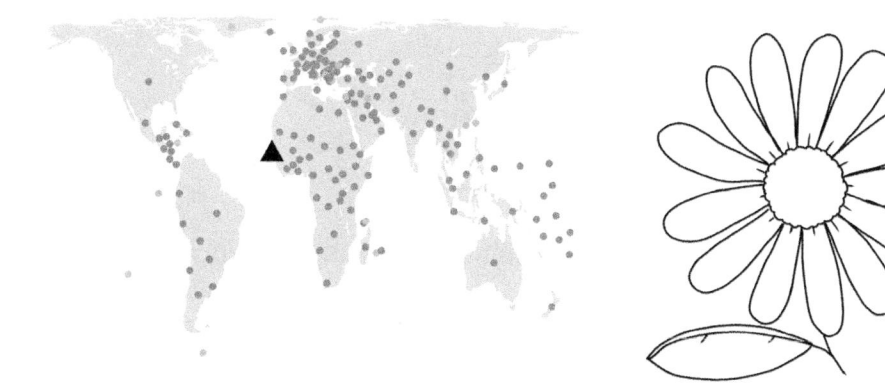

After putting together as many small denomination notes as I could, since receiving change was out of the question, I set off very early in the morning and as a weapon of defence for my wallet I opted for a big gun: I would show up at every checkpoint as a missionary. There are actually Christians in southern Senegal, which is why the area has been turbulent in the past and in my new guise, I could explain that I had urgent business and couldn't meet the purported curfew. More importantly, I hoped for some understanding, namely some discount on the 'toll'. A white man, alone on the road at that time, was very credible as a missionary, and between one instance of extortion and another, I did actually receive a gift of something to eat.

A few thousand potholes later, I reached the border where I crossed without any problems. I was now in **Senegal (152)** and seven-seater Jeeps would leave from there for various destinations. They would only start driving when all the seats were occupied and with Covid there were few people around.

I didn't want to be on those roads in the dark, so without batting an eyelid and not looking for any discounts, I bought seven tickets and felt myself becoming my own little version of Phileas Fogg who hadn't hesitated to spend for the goal of completing his round-the-world trip. For example, the English gentleman in the novel paid the then astronomical price of £2,000 for an elephant to travel along a stretch not covered by the railway, and then bought a steamboat that burnt its own wooden parts in order to continue sailing. The whole Jeep had only cost me €28, but as I impersonated a missionary and held seven tickets in my hand, I still felt like an intrepid traveller, brilliantly solving the problems he encountered!

On Sunday I went to watch the famous wrestling matches

involving entire villages. Since time immemorial, the current champion has become the most admired boy, the one with authority, the most respected warrior. Nowadays the fights are team matches where numerous wrestlers enter the field and as soon as a match is established between two of them, the others watch so that the scene is unique. The fans applaud their favourites, who join them if they win but are mocked by the opposing fans if they lose. It's traditionally a great way to settle scores and petty issues without bloodshed, just like cockfights in other cultures. Women and even children were also involved. It was truly entertaining, although some of the battles were so gentle that I thought the encounters were somewhat unrealistic. The guy from the hostel who was accompanying me explained that only some of the fights were soft, the bigger and stronger ones, in other words the champions, were definitely fighting for real.

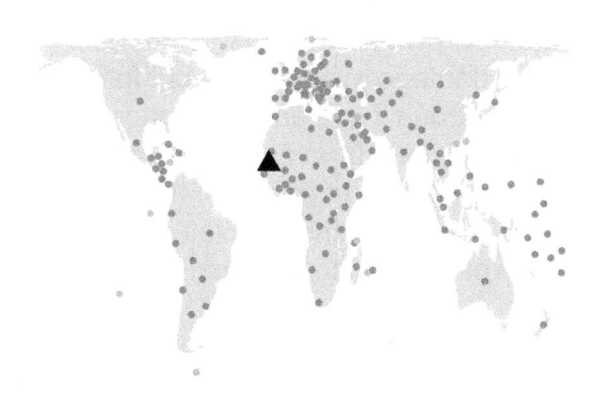

I chose to fly from the south to the north of Senegal because in between lies the whole nation of Gambia, which is perched around a river that penetrates into the interior of Senegal, essentially partitioning it. This thin nation was carved out by the British to penetrate French territory. Both countries became independent and tried to unite in the 1980s, but the union lasted only a short time before they reverted to colonial borders. Gambia embodies this role of 'barrier' within Senegal quite literally because to pass through one is subjected to great scrutiny and therefore corruption. Despite the small distances, therefore, my plan was to take a domestic flight to the north, and then from there fly to Gambia, partly because of the hassle surrounding the demands for money but mainly due to the Covid restrictions in place at the land borders being even more uncertain than those in the airports.

I was discovering that I had to deal with more requirements than just entering and leaving a country. There were the rules of the individual airport, which could require a test to enter the terminal, and even, in some cases, rules of the individual airline, which could require tests with different deadlines, or enforce a ban on having been in certain countries in the recent past, before authorising boarding. Rules and deadlines, once established, were not even uniformly applied. It was a Kafkaesque situation.

From Dakar, I was able to visit the island of Gorée from which ships loaded with slaves had once departed. Today there is a beautiful museum, with splendidly reconstructed buildings, and several rooms showing the horror of the wretches who were captured, mistreated and sometimes killed if they were in poor condition and therefore not worth transporting. The intense pain of the memory then fades between the beaches and pleasant restaurants – it's a successful mix.

I like these places because they manage to attract a wide audience by offering entertainment yet without disrespecting the enormous tragedy that had occurred. I had the place almost to myself, but this led to the usual annoyance that comes with being practically alone: I was stalked by the many guides who had been without clients for months. Covid has done incalculable damage everywhere, but for African tourism, it was truly disastrous. Here anyone working in the industry relies mainly on arrivals from Europe, America and Asia, domestic tourism is limited. In addition, there are no safety nets and so the guides found themselves, through no fault of their own, in truly miserable conditions.

Near my hostel, however, there were those who didn't have to fight to catch the customer. They were the geniuses at the crossroads, and were even more organised than the bricklayers in Sri Lanka, who had made money by selling. Here, too, it was always about coconuts. On one of the four roads was a cart full of the delicious drupes that were wonderful to drink. Opposite was a bank security guard, who had to stand there all day by himself. Thanks to his uniform he easily passed for a real policeman, and he only let cars park at the intersection if they were going to buy coconuts. On the corner of the fourth and final street, a boy in a wheelchair completed the teamwork. The guard authoritatively gestured for my taxi to pull up, I bought the coconut and as I drank, the wheelchair boy pushed by his friend joined me. I was trapped as it was impossible not to give him the change from the coconut purchase as charity. Then I imagine the four cronies would divide it up.

I flew to **Gambia (153)**, or rather The Gambia because the country wants the English article 'the' in front of the name so as not to be confused with Zambia. On landing, I had no problems, despite the sad reputation of customs which creates problems instead of solving them. I had very few things with me, in any case, nothing that could arouse attention. I had prepared a list of medicines in English with a prescription for each one. It seems to be accepted practice to ask for money from people who do not have a regular prescription, with the excuse that the drugs could be brought into the country to be sold.

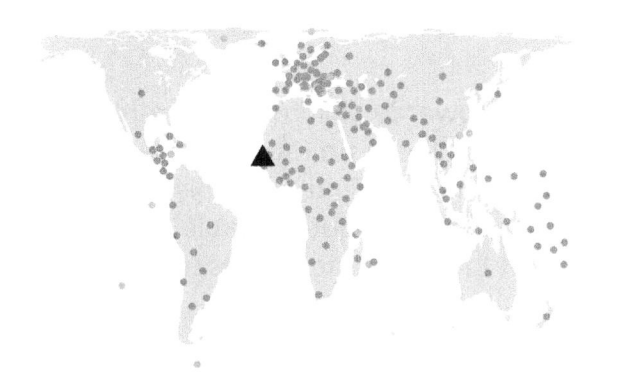

This could be a good thing considering that the former president, Yahya Jammeh, claimed to have discovered the cure for AIDS himself, forcing almost 10,000 people to be treated with a ridiculous concoction. Some patients were then forced to give thanks on live TV.

The Gambia may not have solved AIDS, but it has carved out a niche in sex tourism, specialising in women looking for a young escort. Traditionally it is the man who is accompanied by young girls, but here the opposite is true. There are entire resorts where the couples are unmistakably matched in this manner. Even the postcards for sale depict a plump, older white lady with a handsome young man.

I stayed only briefly and then headed for **Sierra Leone (154)**. Freetown, the capital, from a natural point of view is among the most beautiful cities. On arrival, besides having to show the usual Covid test, another one was taken. The wait was so long that I decided to stay overnight in Lungi, the village where the airport is located, and face the crossing of the large river delta to Freetown the next day. It is possible to move by land, but the transfer is longer since you have to follow the entire coastline. I would have been quicker on a boat, but it was pitch dark and the waters were a bit rough, so I would have arrived soaked. For years there has been talk of building a bridge but so far nothing has happened. If the nation's only international airport is so poorly connected to the capital, imagine the state of transport generally. I had never seen so many fights going on in the streets with scuffles and slaps between people queuing to get on any means of transport.

I also witnessed violence towards children in the streets. Policemen and vigilantes beat them up, sometimes using a kind of whip. However, this is not blind malevolence. On the contrary, while the method is very questionable, the aim is noble as they want to get the message across to parents that it is useless to put them out on the street to beg, steal or try to earn a living. They will come home sore, so send them to school.

In this nation, there is another unofficial school that shapes life. Secret societies that have existed since ancient times hold the 'classes'. In communities devoid of a police force, they kept order, took care of religious ceremonies, and managed the masks to be assigned to those who impersonated the spirits before a war, those to be invoked if the harvest went badly or if someone was to be intimidated. They would distribute the land to individuals since everything belonged to the tribe and those who did not adhere to society and its rules could be excluded, and marginalised, thus finding themselves with nothing to cultivate. Before the arrival of the Europeans, there was no real school, so the secret societies dispensed practical instruction in a kind of human and professional initiation. Today there is less need for this and in fact, the young people only spend a few weeks away from their parents in this pseudo-school, but it remains a key moment, especially for the girls, for it is here that one becomes a real woman.

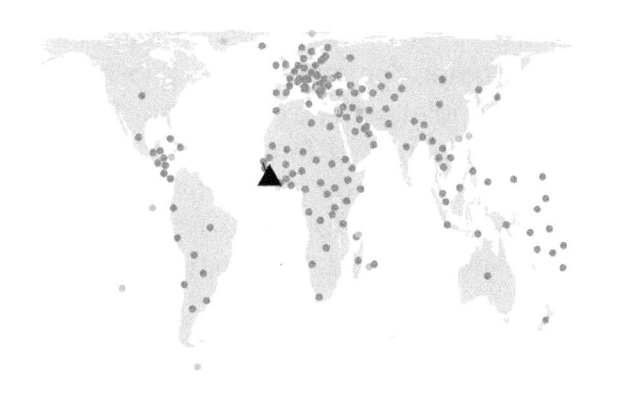

An initiation is needed, which unfortunately happens to be genital mutilation. This barbaric ritual is painful and dangerous. Even if all goes well, mutilated women remain more at risk of complications and death in childbirth, but the men would never agree to marry a woman who had not undergone genital mutilation, because that ritual is proof of being initiated. The young girl, after weeks alone in the countryside with the older women, has learned how to be a good wife, how to manage the house and the children, and how to submit. She discovers sexuality and is also taught how to give pleasure. A woman who still has an intact clitoris is despised because she hasn't learned the secrets of love and isn't submissive. She's selfish because she's still able to experience pleasure for herself and is at risk of being unfaithful because she enjoys sex.

There was a time when no one taught you anything about this, so some institutions may have made sense. After all, it is better to be prepared for life by the most respected elders in the village than just by your own parents. But mutilation is truly cruel, and the numbers of mothers who die in childbirth are very high, just as, albeit less severe, male circumcision offers no advantage.

Superstition and religion have damaged the lives of countless women. The only benefits left from these secret societies might perhaps be that they manage to create some camaraderie among women and most importantly can be a corruption free environment. The societies are inflexible, using tribal laws that everyone understands and deems to be fair. Essentially, measured revenge is always taken through their mediation, so there are no endless feuds between the wronged and the wrongdoer.

Virginity is an obsession in Christian and Islamic nations for both genders, though infinitely less for males. In some of the latter, genital mutilation is still widely practised and in Eritrea, Ethiopia and a few other communities, it also survives among the Christian population. A woman who does not bleed on her wedding day ruins her family's reputation and creates enormous financial damage as what was paid for her has to be returned by her father to her husband, who is also likely to disown her immediately. Sometimes this is one of the reasons for giving women away while they are still children, as they are definitely virgins.

I had managed to get the visa easily, but there was a hurdle for the test as the results would only be available three days later. For my destination that was fine, but for Brussels Airlines the test had to have taken place no more than 48 hours earlier. There could only be one explanation for this madness: Brussels Airlines had extended the parameters in use in Europe at that time to all its flights, but whoever had issued the directive had no idea of the reality in some countries. The solution was inevitable, and I had to pay the usual tip to get the test printed with the date the result was collected and not the date the sample was taken. When we boarded the plane, everyone was in the same position, and though nobody said anything, it was ridiculous to think that we'd had a molecular test reported in such record time.

The arrival at Monrovia airport in **Liberia (155)** is special because, in spite of its few flights, the runway is among the longest in the world. This is where NASA intended to land the shuttles in case of emergency due to the low population density and the distance from the city. Practically you are inside a huge rubber plantation, production that offers one of the few revenues for the country, together with the simplified registration of ships that sail the seas of the world flying the famous Liberian flag.

This nation has a fascinating history linked to the United

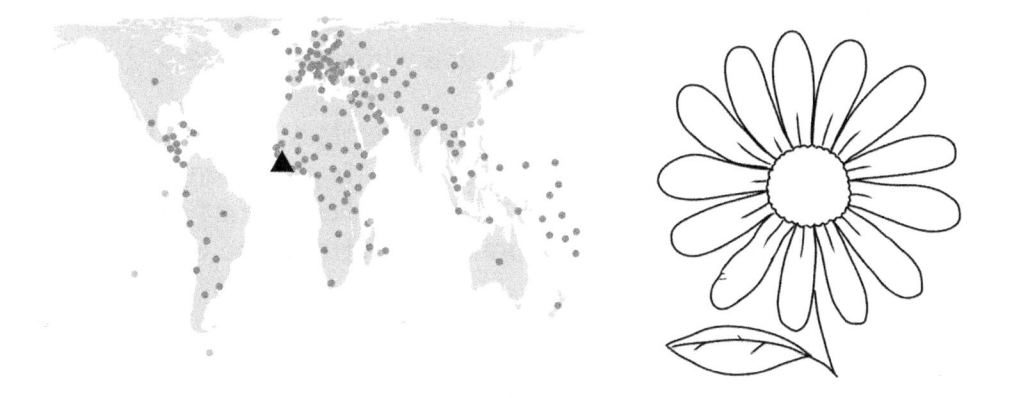

States. In the early 1800s, a philanthropic association, the American Colonisation Society (ACS) wanted to put into action what so many slaves had dreamed of and clamoured for, namely, to return to Africa. The terrible conditions they were subjected to, the distance from the homeland where they felt they belonged, and the belief that closeness with one's ancestors was essential all prompted them to idealise living conditions in Africa. So, the ACS bought land (it's not clear from whom) where the capital now stands. No one had colonised those places because of adverse winds that made it very difficult for ships to anchor there.

Over the course of a few decades, philanthropists helped more than 10,000 former slaves to settle there, creating a form of compensation for the evil that had been inflicted on them. The United Kingdom had also tried this in neighbouring Sierra Leone which is why the capital is called Freetown, but there were too many mosquitoes there and the mortality rate was very high. Here instead, with the help of the American churches, which financed the settlement in full on the condition that the already Christianised former slaves evangelised the locals, it was more successful.

What happened immediately afterwards though is extraordinary: the freed slaves became slave-owners. They immediately began to subdue the local Africans because they were not considered civilised. Although there were only a few of them, the seizure of power was very easy as they had real weapons brought from America. They became an elite that retained power for a long time and continued to dress in English clothing for decades, despite the tropical climate, to emphasise their diversity from the natives.

Just as some of the worst slave hunters had been born slaves, just as the mutilation of women was usually practised by women, here the freed slaves became the new masters. A similar dynamic happened in Sierra Leone where the freedmen behaved in an elitist manner, having support from the church. In fact, the members of the tribes who did not convert, the *Mandingoes* in particular, remained the most discriminated against.

The Liberian flag still resembles that of the United States. In the early days they mimicked many American rules and institutions until, in 1847, they declared independence, which was, however, only accepted by the USA about 15 years later. Despite having broken the link with Washington, the Firestone rubber company's influence on the country remained strong. The Americans participated in the Berlin Conference of 1884-1845, which started the so-called 'Race for Africa', a blossoming of European claims on other people's lands, but they did not have any colonies themselves. Liberia, as well as Ethiopia, remained the only free nations.

One evening I went to dinner with a German girl who lived there. She was accompanied by a Liberian descendant of the first freed slaves. For him, if Liberia had remained a colony, it might have now become the 51st state and in the end, even Alaska is detached from the continental bloc, so his idea was not so outlandish. Who knows what might have happened? Today, however, the country is still the victim of strong tensions, and some crazy rules persist, one of which stands out particularly: in order to have Liberian citizenship, you must be black-skinned!

The weariness of the difficulties associated with this kind

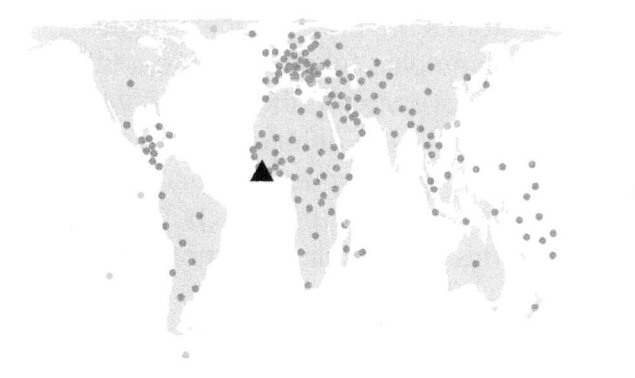

of journey was beginning to make itself felt. Several times I recalled the long downtimes, the transfers, the boredom, and the endless research and organisation work that always precedes these visits. But now the troubles were continuous, small perhaps, but truly uninterrupted. I had already travelled extensively in countries where living conditions were harsh, but at least I was left in peace. I had travelled to countries where I was the centre of attention, so everyone was pulling me from side to side, harassing me, but in doing so I suffered no prohibitions, I had the best seat, and everyone was ready to satisfy my desires. Basically, they would made me feel like a billionaire entering the Grand Hotel: he is forced to give lavish tips, but he is treated like a superstar. Here in West Africa, I had the worst of it from every point of view, always being pestered and receiving nothing in return. The whole thing was amplified by Covid, because the pandemic multiplied the rules and restricted the number of people available to be harassed. Basically, anyone could claim authority over me and there were no other potential victims, I was the only one.

Each test took a whole day to do and then hours to collect. I had learnt that as soon as I landed, I had to wander around the airport as much as possible to find out what would happen on the way out. Which laboratories were authorised? What was the certificate supposed to look like? Where was it to be collected? Every step was fragile. Some tests could give problems at the airport, the certificate had to be checked, the passport number could be wrong, and I have a double surname which is often taken for an American-style middle name. Some laboratories are only collection centres, so the forwarding of all the samples taken to the real laboratory only takes place in the evening. In this case, it was a mistake to go in the morning at 7 am as everyone did, better to go at 5 pm without even queuing, as the result would arrive on the morning of the third day anyway, but I would have gained about ten hours of eligibility for more flights.

Anything less than perfect would have encouraged a bribe that could not be opposed. That's why everyone wanted to inspect the Covid test. Airport staff going about their various duties, as soon as they saw the tourist, would come running with eager authority to ask to see the document. In Gambia my test had been requested at least ten times, by ten different people, each looking for some problem in order to get money to solve it. When they had finally opened the boarding gate and a small queue had formed, an attendant had run up to me, and had practically lifted me up so that I became the first in line, to my embarrassment. Of course, he then wanted money for this unsolicited and completely unnecessary service.

One day in Sierra Leone my mind had been stuck for hours on the failure to credit some air miles from a particular airline. They would have had a counter value of a few euros, but I was annoyed beyond logic by this detail. It is the pent-up frustration that drives one to focus on absolutely nothing. The person who was supposed to take me to a small island that day had arrived hours late again without batting an eyelid, my toilet had not flushed that night, mosquitoes were everywhere, queues of people followed you, the Internet didn't work, and every movement took hours. At the end of the day, I would reach my room and close the door, happy not to see anyone. My bad humour was partly to blame, but I had experienced few really good moments, although if I had had company, or spoken better French, perhaps everything would have been more pleasant.

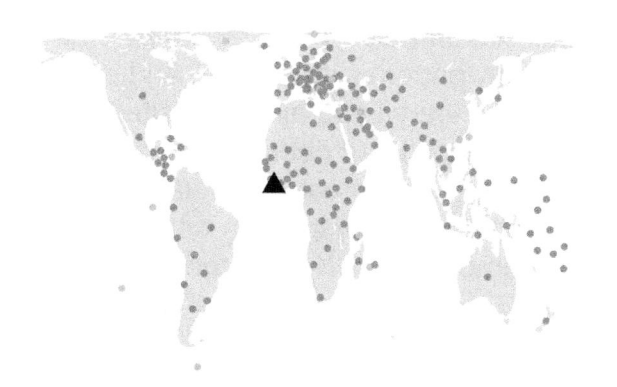

Had I reached my limit?

I made a wise decision. I was in the mood for travelling; it was being in West Africa at this time that I had had enough of. I was experiencing an African sickness of my own that was pushing me away instead of drawing me back. I needed to get away and recharge my batteries. Possibly the abundant year without travel school had made me soft. Returning home would have been the more normal choice, but we were living in 'abnormal' times. The ban on leaving Europe for those in Italy was still in force, so returning would have meant getting stuck again.

The cheapest flight out of Liberia was to Morocco and left late at night. I set off 12 hours early. The airport is a long way from the city and there is only one very expensive hotel opposite which I did not want to pay to sleep in for just a couple of hours. Facing the long transfer in the middle of the night was out of the question, one had to move with the light and those roads are a nightmare for potholes. I left in the afternoon and waited in the lobby for hours while enjoying a few drinks. Then I crossed the street in the midst of the ferocious chaos caused by the fact that almost all the flights leave at the same time, but the shouting and confusion suddenly seemed pleasant as I thought about leaving.

My stay in Morocco felt like paradise, I was so happy that I decided I would recharge my batteries right there. And so, I started wandering around a country I had already visited. At the beginning of the travel school, I had been too far behind in my reading to fully appreciate it, whereas now I had finally realised how unique it was. Never having been conquered by the Ottomans, unlike almost all of North Africa, it was influenced by Arabs, with a strong Berber presence, along with Andalusian, Jewish and then also French and a little Spanish.

Cyprus (156), my next destination, was an island effectively split into three. Part of it had been invaded by Turkey and now acts as a de facto nation, some British territory remains on one coast and in the middle where a military base is located, and the southern area is Greek Cypriot controlled. On my way to Northern Cyprus, or rather, the **Turkish Republic of Northern Cyprus (/)**, I crossed borders for the first time this year without the need for a Covid test. First, I 'entered' the UK, stopped at a typical English pub, then continued on to this nation that is only recognised by Turkey. I travelled along the long strip of land that juts out towards Syria all the way to the far end and thought about the tour I'd paid for before the pandemic as I fed cucumbers to the wild donkeys.

Syria still wasn't allowing tourists to enter, but I received some good news. It seemed I had finally found a way to go to Yemen, the most dangerous country left to visit. Apart from the personal discouragement in West Africa, which had not undermined my desire to travel, my enthusiasm was quickly returning. If I could actually manage to visit Yemen, my chances of succeeding in visiting all the countries of the world would have increased considerably.

For years, Yemen has been the scene of a civil war

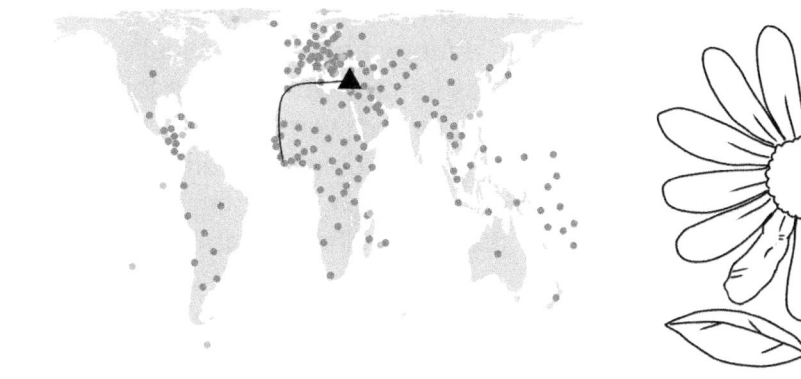

involving external actors, most notably Saudi Arabia and Iran on opposing sides. But apart from the dangers on the ground, I first had to deal with the difficulty of reaching the country. At that time, civil flights only operated from Cairo to Seiyun. There were actually also a few flights to the island of Socotra, which had formerly been Yemeni territory, but was now in the hands of the United Arab Emirates, which meant that there were connections by air between Socotra and Abu Dhabi. This island is considered to be a kind of Galapagos of the Indian Ocean, with famous 'dragon trees' that look like umbrellas and are able to withstand the strong sea winds. This was all the air transport offered for a nation of over 30 million people. And so, I would enter by land from Oman and then fly out to Cairo.

Doing it this way I would visit Hadhramaut and move inland to Seiyun where I would admire the first skyscrapers ever built. They were incredible, centuries-old buildings that had been constantly renovated, and were up to 11 storeys high, giving the city the nickname 'Manhattan of the desert'. The first step was to send money for the exit flight to my guide, as the Yemeni airline doesn't sell online. After paying, Western Union contacted me saying that my account was under inspection and I could hardly blame them since I'd set it up a few months earlier and had since sent money to Afghanistan, Pakistan and now it was Yemen's turn, with no other more normal transactions. But I argued hard and somehow managed to get it reactivated.

It was the only way to continue supporting the Afghan girls who were trying to escape and needed money to bribe the Taliban, because, even in a movement so fanatically religious, money still talks. Just as in Iraq, where some joined the Islamic State for glory, money and women, the Taliban were also approached by young boys looking for adventure, eager for trouble and seeking recognition, which in this case was fortunate. Fatima, the organiser of the marathon and the others, had managed to put together $300 to give to a Taliban who finally got them through an airport checkpoint and onto the first plane out. They were coming to Italy!

I had followed two sisters to whom I had sent money to bribe the Taliban at the land border where everything was easier, but then they were in Pakistan and not in Europe. I had asked Free to Run to issue papers to prove their participation in NGO activities because I hoped they would help to be accepted by some foreign nation. But those papers were a double-edged sword; if they had been found by the wrong people, they would have been conclusive proof that the girls were in contact with enemy forces. Their escape to Pakistan was hasty, but urgent action had been needed because the oldest had been the star of her school's presentation video, still visible on the home page, where she was demonstrating martial arts. Obviously not wearing a veil, she was basically the poster girl for a high school located in the area controlled by foreign forces. The Taliban were looking for girls like her to punish and make into a symbol of change in the country. Today she and her sister are happily in Canada.

My flight to Yemen was not for another two weeks and I had been planning to stay in Cyprus in the interim, when I found a better solution thanks to a new rule. It was now possible to be 'in transit' in Italy, avoiding both the obligation to isolate for ten days and the ban on leaving as long as you stayed for fewer than 120 hours.

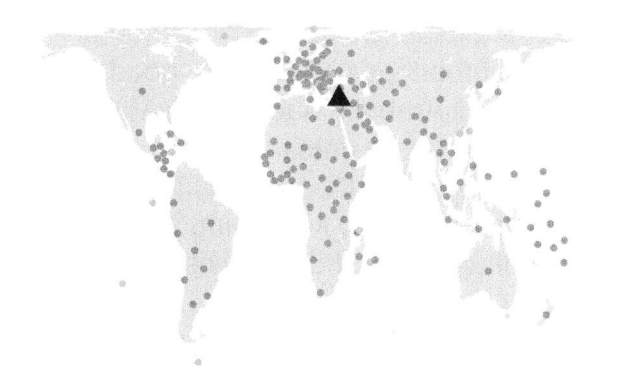

From Cyprus back to Rome would have cost me only €20, but I'd found something even better, and this time it was the destination rather than the price that was so appealing. I would fly to Bologna and from there would go and find Fatima and the other girls who were staying in a nearby charitable centre in Ferrara. The meeting was hugely meaningful for me. The marathon had been intended as a strong message against the Taliban, and yet due to the current state of affairs in the country, they were now seen as the big winners. Knowing that many girls had fled abroad consoled me a little.

I booked my flight to Oman on one of those sites that then tries to upsell you everything. I loathe the pressure to take out insurance against any minor inconvenience, because in my view it conveys a false message about the danger and problems that may be associated with the trip. Now of course medical insurance is essential, but for a delay of a few hours or a scratch on luggage it's quite a different matter. The most ridiculous suggestion was a charge of €7 to protect against the airline going bankrupt, which was so disproportionate that it was insulting. On a €300 ticket that was approximately 2% extra cost in order to receive a fraction of that money back months later, in the unlikely event that Qatar Airways, which had already weathered the pandemic, would go bankrupt in the next few days. Do such overly cautious people exist that they would take out absurd insurance like this? And were there people so reckless that they would go to Yemen?

I was ready to go, took the usual Covid test and soon arrived in Oman, a country that manages to cultivate good relations with both Iran and Saudi Arabia. I had already visited previously, so I spent the days lazily, catching up on some unfinished reading about Nizam al-Mulk, the Machiavelli of the area, and the sect of assassins who killed him, and then I finally had time for Ibn Battuta, one of the greatest travellers in history. The plan then was to take a domestic flight to Salalah from where I would drive to the border in a few hours. My visa was ready, a Yemeni armed with a Kalashnikov and a *Jambiya* dagger in his belt was waiting for me on the other side, and before I knew it, I was in **Yemen (157)**.

I would have to dress the same way as him while I was there. In Afghanistan, you wore local dress in an attempt to be inconspicuous, at least from a distance, whereas here it was a form of respect for the native culture because you were a visitor, not a tourist. However, I didn't have to overdo it, it was in no way meant to look like a disguise, and so when covering my head, I left my face visible. My dagger was cheap, and it didn't have the expensive handle made from the poor rhinoceros' horn. It was not at all beautiful, but it was necessary. Here you aren't a man without a weapon, and in fact, the punishment for misbehaving is sometimes the temporary confiscation of the dagger, which is regarded as a humiliation.

I would say that I was Turkish when asked, as that was one of the few well-known nations and implied that I was Muslim without saying so openly. Unfortunately, the first, and only question constantly asked was invariably, 'Are you a Muslim?'

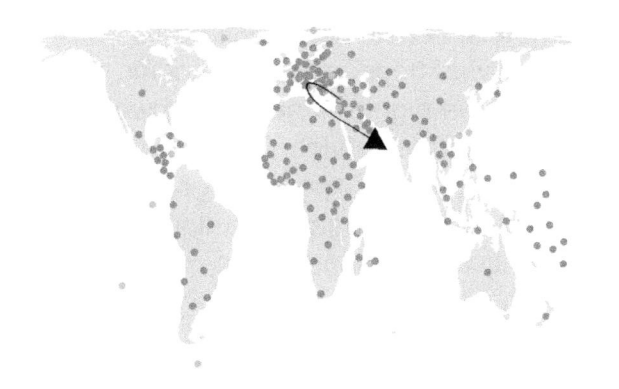

The person who was accompanying and protecting me was a tribal leader, so he knew how to get about, who to ask for help if there was trouble, and how to reach his territory or that of a friendly tribe. Yemen is notorious for kidnappings, especially of tourists, who are then used by the tribes to blackmail the central government, perhaps because a promise had been broken, some infrastructure had been neglected, or maybe simply because some of their members had been arrested. The foreigner is an excellent bargaining chip.

In my case this danger was minimal, but other threats remained. There were al-Qaeda members present within their respective tribes, who though they had formally renounced their previous actions, were still terrorists going about life as if nothing had happened. Mercenaries from the United Arab Emirates also constituted a risk, as often did Turks themselves, the central government forces, transitional government forces, rebels, sympathisers for the *Houthis*, the movement backed undercover by Iran, and finally, common criminals, driven by war, hunger and misery.

The country was full of government checkpoints, set up in an attempt to control the territory as much as possible, or at least cut off communication between terrorists. Restricting movement may get some results but it also means that people's lives become even more difficult. At every crossing, you had to roll down all the windows and show your documents. It was a time-consuming process, but more importantly in my case, meant that a lot of people would have become aware of my presence, not just the soldiers, but also any of the numerous loiterers who roamed around the blockade sites. A great number of people would have been able to work out where I was going since there were very few roads and even fewer working hotels. I could have declared a destination other than the one I was heading for but finding me would still have been easy. One night my guide was woken up by a phone call from their secret service saying that they had indeed gone to the hotel to check and hadn't found us. He replied, of course, that we had changed our minds at the last minute and received only a reprimand.

Almost the entire adult population was high from the afternoon onwards because they chewed the usual *qat* non-stop, just like in Somalia. Sometimes even teenagers do it which made me afraid of the young soldiers because they tend to overdo it. Imagine how frightening it was to see young boys who have had no training, chewing on stimulants and walking around armed. On the other hand, being around old people protected you. A photo with an elderly person was always a good idea, it was a tool to boast about your acceptance and acquaintance with respected local people.

At the checkpoints they don't need to search for weapons, as here they all have them on display. In restaurants, customers quietly leave their Kalashnikovs on the table while children play nearby. The daggers on their belts are capable of killing with ease. But the most disturbing thing that I noticed was quite subtle, it was the absence of Chinese businessmen. Usually, no matter where I went, even in the most remote and ill-advised places, there were always a few Chinese people doing business. Here, though, there was only me.

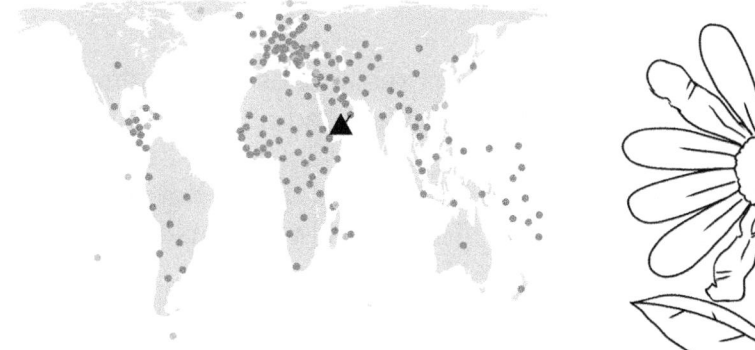

I experienced a horror movie episode firsthand when I went to visit the grave of a saint, a little outside Seiyun, where al-Qaeda had left a warning. They deliver the message by pouring black paint on any place that does not respect religious precepts. According to traditional Islam, the veneration of tombs is a forbidden practice. Saudi Arabia prides itself on being a nation without visible burial places, yet the prophet's is there although there has been debate as to whether even this one should be destroyed, because the graves are supposed to disappear beneath the earth.

My guide had a feeling that a car with Saudi plates was following us, so he changed places, and reached into the small reclining seat inside the boot for the Kalashnikov. Taking the safety off, he stood guard until the other car went on its way. After our visit, as we were getting back into the car, the guide clumsily tried to climb over the rear seats to get back into the small reclining seat and in doing so, let off a shot that pierced a hole in the door, struck the small wall behind me and bounced off.

This was more than just a little frightening. My guide had fallen suddenly into the car, bleeding profusely, and the driver had received a small wound on his back from the ricocheting shrapnel and was now in a state of shock. I was unharmed, but I couldn't hear anything out of one ear and felt like my head was about to explode. I hadn't understood where the shot had come from, although I had seen the guide's face contort in pain and so I cowered instinctively under the car, and it took me a few seconds to realise that there was no enemy shooting at us.

Fortunately, the damage was minimal, and we just had to bandage the wound. He had shot himself, losing his little finger, but the hand had stopped bleeding so heavily on its own after only a few moments. The driver was beginning to recover from the shock, so we picked up the finger and gloomily set off.

In Yemen a gunshot doesn't really cause any alarm. At weddings they are constant anyway, and at least as far as we could see, there wasn't a living soul around us. Very cautiously, we put the safety catch back on the Kalashnikov and discussed what to do. The guide was conscious and able to speak, so I felt reassured. The objective now was to locate a hospital and get there without running into any checkpoints, where we would have to explain ourselves, something that none of us had any intention of doing. I had an outbound plane booked for the next day and didn't want to be detained, and since 'I shot myself' isn't very plausible, despite being the truth, they would also be in a lot of trouble. Any checkpoint would have stopped us and taken us who knows where to find out who we'd had a firefight with and who we were.

Getting to the hospital took about an hour. Upon arrival, the driver carried the wounded man inside and I stayed hidden in the car, not wanting to be recorded as being anywhere, not even at the hospital. The medical staff rushed to the door, and he babbled some ridiculous explanation, unnecessarily as they saw plenty of people who had shot themselves there.

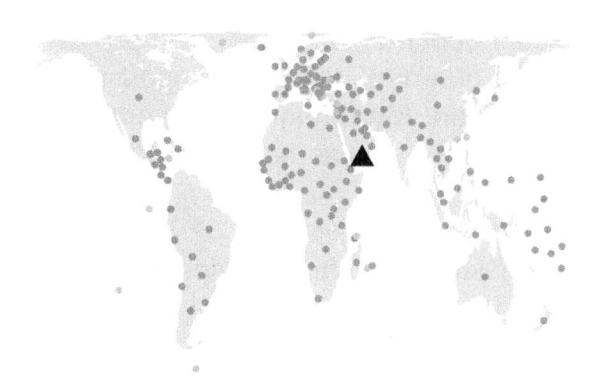

Health care in Yemen is minimal, so it's usually not worth having small things attended to because you run the risk of coming home sicker than when you went in. But he was lucky to be seen by an Italian volunteer doctor, whom I greatly admire. Italy and Yemen have had good relations since 1926 when Italy, having been present in neighbouring Eritrea, signed a friendship treaty with Yemen excluding any colonial initiative. It may not seem like much, but at the time most European nations were colonialists, including of course fascist Italy, so talk of 'friendship' was remembered as a progressive relationship that put a European nation and Yemen on an equal footing.

I tried to keep myself busy with something useful during the two hours that I spent in the car full of blood so I thought about what would I have said and done if they had called me from inside the hospital, particularly if, in the worst-case scenario, someone else wanted to ask me questions? Luckily, the driver returned, saying he would take me to the hotel. Having parked the car in the inner courtyard, I really felt like *Mr Wolf* from Tarantino's film *Pulp Fiction*. He's the one who solves problems and gives directions on how to clean up a car in which a man has been shot.

In the movie, there is a similar accidental shooting, although with far worse results. I had to be both *Mr Wolf* and the one he asked to do the cleaning in the end, but for the first time in my life, a film was actually useful in real life. We used my Yemeni-style skirt cloth as a seat cover because it was dark in colour and covered the stains. We cleaned the surroundings a little and threw away all the bloody handkerchiefs. The stock of the Kalashnikov was red with congealed blood. The guys working in the hotel looked at us, but no one offered to help, and no one dared ask any questions.

The guide was relatively okay, he had been medicated and put on strong painkillers. The hand has so many nerve endings that the pain is excruciating even though the damage is not very serious. My hope was that he would recover in time to accompany me to the airport in the morning because he had the necessary documents for the checkpoints and the airport was heavily guarded, so it was impossible to get there without being seen. My thought was perhaps somewhat selfish, but to be frank, it was he who had shot himself, or rather shot at me!

As I went up to my room, still dazed from having to clean

the blood, I noticed that my faithful backpack also needed a wash. As I prepared myself for this second cleaning job, I had a sudden flash of memory – I needed to take the Covid test in a hurry! I sprinted to the driver's room to find that he had understandably taken to his bed for a moment.

His wound was worse than it had appeared to me before. In addition to the pain, I imagine that he thought he'd lost his job since it depended on the guide who had now screwed things up. He had three wives to support but no children, which caused him great despair. Of course, in such a society the 'blame' always falls on the women, but it was more likely that the problem was his own and he admitted it. His remedy, however, was a bad one as he tried to chew more *qat* for extra energy, when in actual fact, *qat* itself can cause infertility.

We went to the only authorised laboratory. The car was less conspicuous than before, but still soiled, covered and of course it had a hole in the door. We still needed the driver to find a way to avoid all the checkpoints. If they rolled down all the windows, there was a risk that something fresh would be seen on the seat. At the lab they promised that the result would arrive soon, which it did. Again, I doubt that anyone tested anything, but in this case all the better. In the film *Mr Wolf* has no experience of being confronted with a positive or missing test, so he would have been no help and I would have had to come up with a solution of my own.

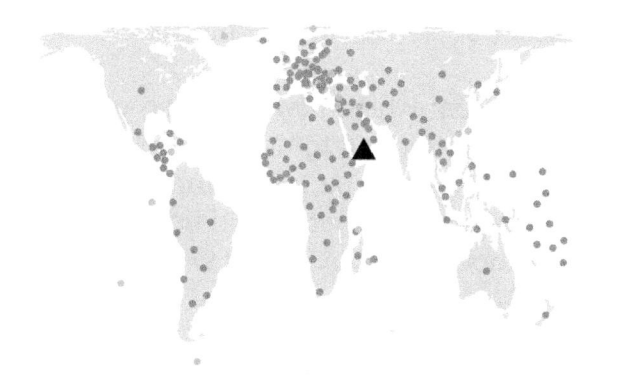

In the evening I slept for a few hours relatively calmly considering what had happened. The hypothesis that if I'd been 20 cm further over, I would now be dead wasn't really appealing to me, and the idea of finding myself seriously wounded and detained for a long time in Yemen scared me so much that I didn't want to think about it. Would someone have run in support of me in a T-shirt asking the Sultan of Oman to help me? Would I have deserved it?

My guide appeared unexpectedly early the next morning. With the enormity of his earlier inattention to live down, he had then done everything necessary to keep me safe. As an extra security measure, however, the driver had also collected the necessary documents, and printed out the usual ten copies of everything so that we could leave one at each roadblock, so in actual fact we were independent and could have managed without him. On the way to the airport, we had a good laugh about his bandaged hand, and I promised to send him the last photo in which he'd had ten fingers. Fortunately, no one investigated the bandage too much at the checkpoints. I told him about Tarantino's film, but he didn't know it.

At the hospital they had suggested he fly to Cairo immediately to pursue the small chance of reattaching his finger, but he refused. My rickety plane was actually full of sick people on board who were going to Egypt for treatment. My ear was slowly regaining the ability to hear, and was torture on the flight, but I was incredibly calm. As usual I felt privileged to be able to leave, I didn't have to take any of the problems with me, whereas the other people had to stay there.

The Hadhramaut region from which I was leaving is so conservative that women are forbidden to undress, even in front of the doctor. They don't want to be photographed because for a woman to risk being identified would bring serious trouble. No one must know who they are or where they go. Just like in Afghanistan, not even your best friend should ask how your wife is doing or, for that matter, have seen her face as an adult. Al-Qaeda sought out and punished boys who exchanged pictures with faces on their mobile phones, as if a smile were a pornographic film.

Yet there are some unveiled women. They are part of the ethnic group of outcasts known as the *Al-Akhdam*, and are abused, hated, and often used as prostitutes and slaves. Pasolini's famous erotic film, *Arabian Nights*, was shot in Yemen, and had brought the country into the spotlight, which led to the preservation of its monuments. On the set, it had been possible to have naked Yemenite women as actresses only because they had belonged to this caste.

It's evident that society is divided into castes, with sheikhs (elders) at the top, religious clerics, influential members of tribes, those who practise noble work, camel breeders, peasant farmers according to what they cultivate, and then descending as usual to blacksmiths, tailors, butchers, fishermen and barbers. Anyone who has contact with death, body hair, or impure materials such as skins, along with those like blacksmiths who practise 'magic' by modifying materials, and fishermen who work with dead fish and search for sea scraps, all these are marginalised. Then, lower still are the *Al-Akhdam*, the true outcasts.

On arrival in Egypt, I was able to obtain a visa for $30 but my next flight was only ten hours later, and with the traffic in Cairo it wasn't worth going anywhere. I headed for the transit area, intending to stay at the airport, when instead, I and all the people on the flight were stopped and isolated, transferred into a room where they then brought our luggage. After they had established each person's identity, you could go to an attendant and state which connecting flight you were on. I went first because I had no luggage to wait for. When he had taken note of my flight, the officer put the paper inside my passport and kept it with him. I had to stay there until three hours before my connecting flight, which in my case meant I had to wait seven hours in a corridor full of people, unable to sit down, and with no food or drink.

When I realised what was happening, I asked for my passport back so that I could go to immigration and get my visa to enter the country, but I was denied. I said that I had changed my mind and wanted to stay in Egypt for a few days, but it didn't work. They didn't even give me a drink, there was no way to buy anything, and the water from the bathroom would have been too risky to drink. It was a very different welcome from last time when two chauffeur driven cars had been waiting for me!

I suspect that the deliberately rough treatment was reserved for the flight from Yemen, I can find no other explanation. In fact, the others seemed quite relaxed and calm, they obviously knew what was in store for them. But the seven thirsty hours passed quickly, and considering the unpleasant adventure I'd been through, I had been glad just to get out of the country unscathed, so there was little to complain about. Especially when I remembered that I had pictures on my mobile phone of a car door with a bullet hole in it, a bloody Kalashnikov, and a wounded driver, not to mention the fact that my backpack had a nice blood stain on it. It was definitely not wise to argue with the people who had taken custody of my passport – much better to keep quiet and aloof.

Had it been a mistake to go to Yemen? I would say objectively yes. But not due to the bad experience in itself, indeed that was the wrong way to consider the matter. It had been an error of judgement because I hadn't paid attention to the absence of the Chinese entrepreneurs, which should have told me in no uncertain terms that others had judged the level of danger differently. I used to criticise Italian and sometimes foreign government sites for exaggerating, but this time it was me who had not successfully gathered all the information.

Another valid factor demonstrating that it had been too risky a trip was the fact that small crowds had formed around me continually to see the foreigner. It would only have taken one person shouting '*Allahu Akbar*' for fun, or 'Death to Israel' as happened several times, and tempers would have risen. Crowds in general are dangerous, especially if you are the one attracting attention. Excitement plays tricks, and people who gather to demonstrate are often already angry. The foreigner runs the risk of getting in the way, even if he is on their side. Misunderstandings exist, and as with a game of Chinese whispers, a sentence spoken on one side can be totally distorted and misinterpreted before it reaches the other. It's best not to approach groups of people and to avoid being seen around at all if it's election day or there's a protest. Just as to ask for help you have to isolate one person, an angry party only needs to select one target, and that could be you, the one in the limelight.

So, in reality, I had underestimated the risk, and there's one further reason to consider my decision foolish. The island of Socotra could have been reached with less danger. By going to Yemen, I had placed a losing bet, just like those who insure themselves against the failure of Qatar Airways.

From Egypt I went to **Malawi (158)** and was once again confronted with problems that I was more familiar with in the form of the entry visa. It could be obtained on arrival, but like a good planner I had applied and paid about a month before, as advised by the government website. Since then, my visa had remained 'pending', in other words, in the process of being approved. No one had ever responded to my reminders and on arrival immigration wanted me to pay again, even though I had the receipt in my hand. In the end they told me to come back the next day and it would be approved.

So, I did. I got to the airport and had a long wait for permission to go to immigration without a departure ticket, all in vain. Of course, they told me once again to come back the next day, but I wanted to move on, and it was becoming clear that returning another day would be pointless, it was just a ploy to pass the problem onto another colleague. After lengthy discussions, they issued me with a provisional paper that authorised me to stay in the country without a visa but required me to complete the procedure within ten days. My plan was to resolve it on the very day of my departure, since I had to be at the airport anyway, and of course, then no one would be able to tell me, 'Come back tomorrow'.

My guide back in Yemen was doing better, but he was desperate because he knew he would not be able to see his family in Sana'a, the capital, for a long time. To reach them he would have to pass through areas where there was still fighting and with a recent wound it was impossible to think that he wouldn't get into some sort of trouble.

For me though, that incident was over, and I wanted to distract myself by going to Lake Malawi. I found a wonderful hostel where I finally relaxed. My bungalow neighbour was an Englishman who was travelling by motorbike from South Africa to Saudi Arabia with his girlfriend. A lovely couple.

The hostel owner and his wife were much less so. Both South Africans, and she a passionate Italian speaker, they invited me to dinner to try a 'real' chicken. They were right, I had no idea what kind of chicken it was. It was so tough that it took all my strength to cut the meat, despite it being well cooked, to the point that my index finger with which I was pushing the knife hurt, and the taste was completely different.

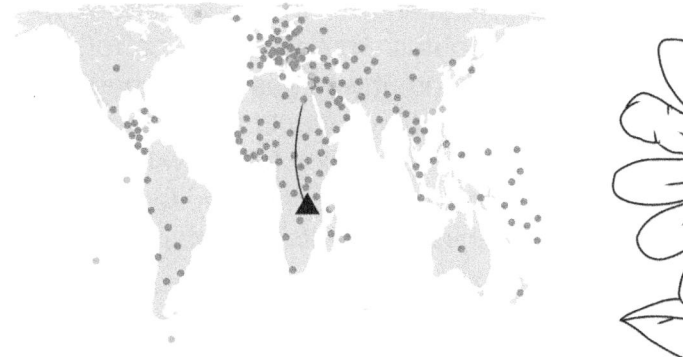

The problem, however, wasn't the toughness of the chicken, but the conversation, since they were clearly racist and very angry about their condition. They had sold everything to move to Malawi and get away from the violence at home. The drama of whites being driven out of South Africa does not make the news much, but many of them were born there, having burnt all bridges with Europe centuries ago, and their family has now been African for perhaps 300 years. The violence was revenge for what had happened, for Apartheid, but it also served to leave a ravaged and useless land.

People in Malawi commonly believe in vampires, who in some of the stories become blood-sucking white men who ride around in their ambulances and kidnap people. This is a ridiculous form of conspiracy theory, but to have a shred of credibility, they link it to something real, in this case, the stretchers that carry people on board, and the fact that the doctors and nurses take blood for testing.

Albinos also fare badly. Having such white skin under that sun is a torment in itself, but also, they are believed to be spirits of white people who have become lost and now enter tribes where they do not belong. They are hunted down to be dismembered and their limbs are used for magic rituals. In neighbouring Tanzania there is an island in the middle of a large lake where a safe village has been created for albinos.

Fortunately, such criminal acts don't exist anymore in Europe, there are no longer any lost ghosts, but the idea that a person can bring bad luck still lingers. Who knows how many lives have been ruined by a joke that then became more frequent, until it was an everyday thought. And the person who, though he was born in Italy and has all the tools at his disposal to understand yet crosses the street if a certain person passes by, would probably have been hunting vampires and albinos had he been born in Malawi.

In those tired days of beaches and strolls, I was able to add another pearl to my collection of the most brilliant ways to earn money. A group of youths were waiting for a tourist car to pass by on a stretch where it was easy to get bogged down in the sand, at which point they would appear, and offer to help push, displaying great exertion for a few minutes. Then one of them would show up with some wooden planks to put under the wheels, which made it quite easy then to get the car out and the tourist felt obliged to pay for the rescue service. There were very few tourists now, but I'm told that previously a constant stream of cars had been getting stuck and then promptly rescued. According to the racist, they were the ones who had put the sand there.

On my way back to Lilongwe, the capital, I went for the usual Covid test and observed this sprawling city with its many still deserted areas. You go straight from the central streets to being in the middle of nowhere. The city had been a village until the 1950s, and it was only developed when Kamuzu Banda, the nation's father dictator, wanted it as his capital so that he could relocate power to areas where none of the tribes that had been hostile to him lived. He had studied in the West and had become a doctor, speaking perfect English yet very poorly in the local languages. He would dress smartly, he supported the Apartheid regime and became a real dictator, or president for life with the support of the West who considered him a fervent anti-communist. To make himself more 'African', along with his impeccable waistcoated suits, he walked around with a kind of sceptre in his hand that had a lion's tail and an ivory handle. But after seeing the photos of the former slaves in Liberia dressed in bowler hats and white gloves under the blazing sun, nothing surprised me anymore.

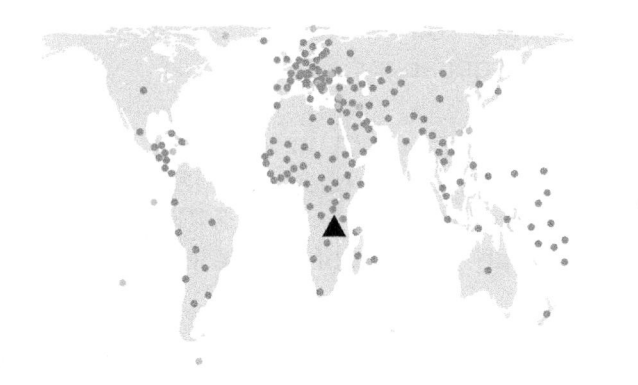

At the mausoleum of Banda, I couldn't believe my eyes when I went to sign the guest book. There was the name of someone I knew through Facebook, and as I flipped back through the pages, I found still others. They were serial travellers like me, and I was in touch with them via social media. One had suggested the name of the hostel on the lake. Sometimes I felt special on these travels, but was I too, in some ways, following a predetermined circuit? Visiting all the countries in the world restricted some of the choices, but lately, had laziness perhaps pushed me to lean too much on other people's suggestions instead of exploring and discovering on my own?

Armed with the usual test, I went to the airport well in advance. I needed to get out of the country but first still had to do the entry paperwork. I spoke to numerous people at immigration, until the person in charge arrived and told me that $10 would solve the situation for me. I paid and lost another hour as well as the money but received nothing. Another immigration officer came and told me to pay for the entry visa all over again, get the entry stamp, go and check in and then finally get the exit stamp, which I did. The Malawi government had done well out of me as I'd tried to comply with their governmental advice. I'd paid for the visa twice, plus a useless $10 bribe, and then a triple meet and greet at the airport. At the check-in I happened upon an incredibly slow clerk. When the boarding pass was finally ready, she kept hold of it, writing on it for a few minutes. What was she up to? Finally, she gave it to me with a smile, and on the back, she had written 'Jesus loves you' and drawn a silhouette resembling Christ. I couldn't get angry.

In **Zimbabwe (159)**, the last country in alphabetical order, nobody relies on the local currency, so US dollars are used. In one of the shops there was a $100 trillion Zimbabwean dollar note with pictures of people protesting next to it, shouting ironically that they were the only starving billionaires in the world. In my own small way, fortunately on another level, I also felt that I looked like a rich man as I continued to travel, but I would soon find myself penniless. But my decision was now irrevocable. In the poker terminology so dear to me one would say that the player is all-in. He has gambled it all.

The whole country had experienced economic ups and downs, but the highs had all been reserved for a racist elite and the lows for the rest. The white community in Zimbabwe was strong and in charge, so much so that Britain, the colonising nation, sought to dilute their power by creating a federation to unite them with Zambia and Malawi. It was short-lived, and independence from the United Kingdom, as expected, turned into a transfer of power from the distant colonialists to the local ones.

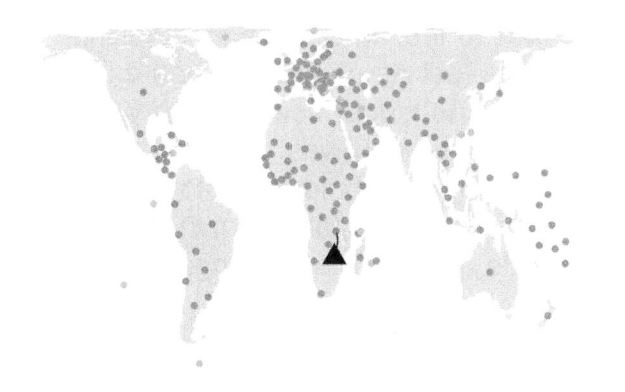

It wasn't exactly a historic novelty, after all, similar things had happened with the United States, Canada and Australia, but there was one fundamental difference here. In the other cases the whites had become the majority because they had arrived en masse, and with their diseases and misdeeds they had already decimated the small local populations. Here, by contrast, they were a tiny minority. Their leader, Ian Smith, refused numerous agreements that would have allowed them to retain great privileges whilst granting more rights to the blacks, and it was this greed that was his downfall. When the neighbouring Portuguese colonies, which had offered support to the whites of Zimbabwe, collapsed, they were overwhelmed, and Mugabe took power. A few years later he requisitioned their land and reassigned it to his veterans. The symbolism of this act was strong and spoke of justice, and the images of burning tractors, and of exploited people now sleeping in the elegant master bedroom were striking. Also brilliant was the idea of telling the dispossessed to ask the British to reimburse them.

But few of the new owners knew how to cultivate or manage a large farm and the country began to collapse. Production shrank enormously and people went hungry, including the holders of the ridiculous high denomination banknotes, which were basically just so much wastepaper.

However, I was here to explore a more remote past, namely the ruins of a civilisation called 'Great Zimbabwe'. What remains is located about 250 km from the capital and I found a very knowledgeable guide, who showed up with his wife dressed as the driver. Women do in fact drive even in male-dominated countries, but very few would drive with a man present in the car. To some extent, this is still true in Italy, so I was delighted with the novelty. The walls and structures of Great Zimbabwe are stunning, works of such sophisticated engineering that archaeologists could hardly believe they had been built by ancient Africans. The most outlandish theories were concocted, from the usual lost tribe of Israel scenario to Arabs or perh extraterrestrials, a little like what happened with the Mayans.

I was finally getting back to feeling real joy in travelling, having fully recovered from West Africa and the bad experience in Yemen. Even Covid no longer seemed scary. But perhaps what put me in a good mood was the widespread use of the English language since I could get in touch with the locals. These chats are a fundamental part of the school of travel and in Africa people are open to meeting, perhaps more so than anywhere else in the world. Encountering different people opens the mind, the world expands and unveils far more than just visiting a monument would. Other people's thoughts can astonish you, alternating between naivety, amazement and curiosity. I wanted to get to know as many people as possible everywhere, but unfortunately, when you don't speak English, you have to go through someone's translation. Or, even worse, you have to rely too much on a guide's thoughts when they are just one single person, and probably not representative because speaking English in a non-English speaking country puts a person above the average.

During this period of serenity and rediscovered enjoyment of travelling, I reflected more calmly on the constant discomfort I had experienced in West Africa. With a clear mind, I now saw the world differently because of that experience. I had grown up thinking that cultures were all equally valid and that one could, and indeed should, judge individuals by their behaviour since in every society there are both wonderful people and rotten apples, geniuses and imbeciles. I had been taught that excessive comparison between cultures leads to dangerous suppositions and justifications for being overbearing.

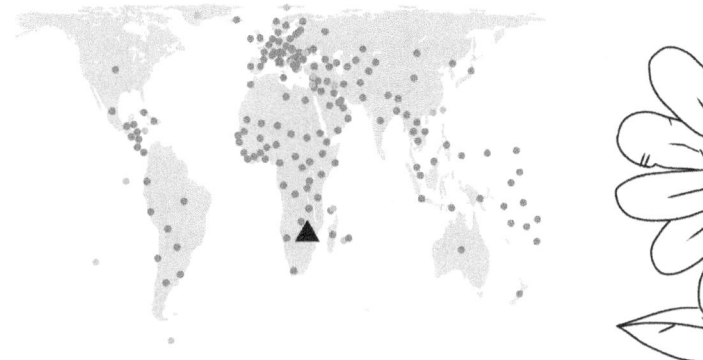

We had started along this route once and had ended up justifying the invasion of other lands in the name of a supposed civilising mission. But now that I was having such profound experiences of my own, with new clarity of mind, and drawing from experience of a considerable number of different realities, I found it unhelpful to think of everyone as good. There is something good in every culture, but they are not all equal. Having schnitzel, paella or sushi can all alike be considered wonderful traditions, just as children's drawings in kindergarten all deserve praise. But when you go to university, grades have to be awarded differently, and then you have to assess, for example, how cultures treat women, or children, or foreigners.

Some cultures are clearly behind with respect to others. A combination of varied factors contributes to the different ways in which a culture is moulded. The past, real or mythical, has an effect, as does religion, geography and even luck. It's good for each person to be able to be proud of what is good in their lives and to see themselves reflected in their culture so that they can both enjoy it and feel a sense of belonging there. I understand too that hymns and parades may remain necessary to arouse patriotism, as we still live in a world where one might be called upon to die for a flag.

But improvement comes through respectful confrontation and reasoned assessments. The greatness of the West lies precisely in a constant evaluation of our past. We alone fiercely judge our ancestors, apologising for the mistakes that were made, laughing at the follies of the past, and criticising religion so deeply that we have built statues for those who were once considered heretics. And we do all this with increasing vigour. These days, however, we are not so keen on applying the exercise of making judgments about others. In my opinion, it would be wrong for me to continue travelling and talking about the diversity I see, but to refuse to evaluate whether each thing is better or worse. Rather than an act of humility, that would seem to me to be a deliberate switching off of the brain, afraid of where it might wander off to.

On the other hand, I was developing much more tolerance when it came to assessing the individual. In West Africa, the people who kept harassing me, and trying to cheat me, were desperate. What was I going to do? In their culture, what I call harassment is acceptable because there is no personal space, and so the feeling of intrusion is different. And conning the foreigner, or inflating prices for him, is downplayed in a way that must be understood. For example, think of us: back in the day, it was acceptable for Europe to exploit Africa and Africans. So, in my opinion a poor motorbike driver in Sierra Leone is right to sleep peacefully if he asked three times the actual price. We continue to do this after all, albeit selectively, and usually with those we perceive to be stronger. For example, if our president came to the country today saying that he had wrung favourable terms out of a contract with Mozambique he would be frowned upon; whereas if he did so with Germany he would be applauded. When I'm walking around looking for a ride on a motorbike, I'm Germany to the drivers.

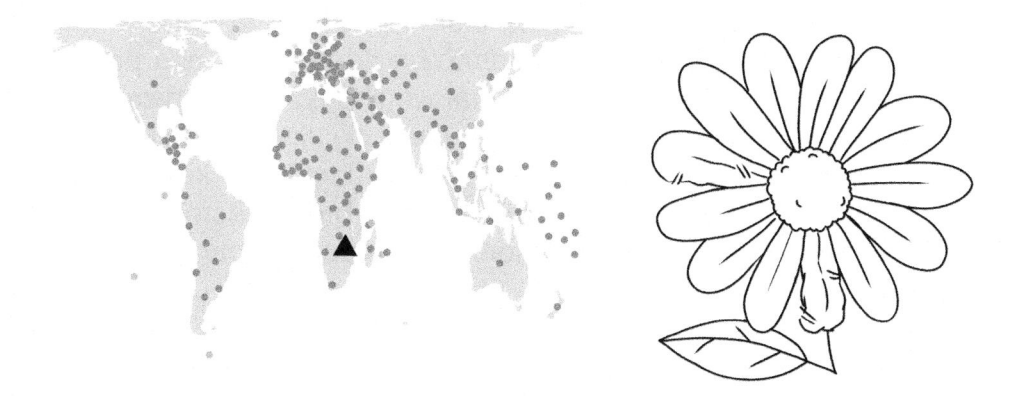

When you meet people who seem to be lazy and parasitic, you have to evaluate them in the knowledge that if one person in the family is successful, it's normal for others to live off him. It is permissible to take advantage of the only one with a good salary. I met a Senegalese man in a hotel who worked in France and didn't have the courage to go directly to his house because he would have been mobbed by dozens of people. He preferred to stay in the hotel and face relatives and friends one by one. You can empathise with such a situation at home by thinking that those who win the lottery prefer to remain anonymous, otherwise, everyone demands a share and takes offence if they don't receive anything. The lucky person's relationships become so complicated.

And then of course the people who pester you on the street probably have nothing to eat at home and need to sell something. Typically, they grow up without a father because it's a world where there are huge numbers of single mothers, and again, a culture that exalts masculinity is to blame. The real man, the alpha, has children by different women. In the most extreme cases he thinks he has 'bought' the woman by paying the bride price and can now treat her as he likes. So many of the Africans we met never had someone to teach them how to critically approach a problem, how to plan for the long term, or the importance of not living hand-to-mouth.

We have no idea what it means to live with nothing in your pocket. If you order fish at a restaurant and it takes two hours to arrive, in Europe you'd make a joke to the waiter asking if they'd gone out to catch it, whereas here it's likely they've actually gone to buy it. Is there no toilet paper in the bathroom? It can't be left in there as it would get stolen immediately. Was the hole supposed to be repaired? They just put some soil on it, and yes, the problem will return soon, but there is no money to do it right and fix it. So many structures are partially built, and since there is no way to get a loan from the bank, everything has to be done in bits and pieces. To be productive we feel that we should have a nice big desk, a monitor, a comfortable chair, lighting, and silence. Try to put yourself in their shoes and imagine working while standing up, on a small laptop with a broken screen, with no arrows to move the cursor to one side, as your software constantly crashes, the power goes out regularly and people are shouting all around you.

It is the poverty trap. Solving each problem individually is possible, sometimes even easy when it is only a matter of putting up a mosquito net but tackling the causes all at once is very difficult and the solution remains far away.

Despite the harshness of some of my thoughts, I was becoming more tolerant than I used to be. Yet perhaps I was becoming more intolerant in the West, because knowing what you are entitled to can leave you disappointed. Every now and then I would go further, and would ask myself if someone who was violent with their wife in Italy would have agreed with stoning as a just punishment for some behaviours had they been born in Afghanistan? Or I would think of Fatima, born a shepherdess in Afghanistan and yet willing to study hard and learn so much with minimal help from outside, and able to learn English on her own. If she had been born in Italy would she be Dante, Leonardo or Fermi?

Travel school is about judging with an open mind, going to a place, and letting it get inside your head. I was beginning to convince myself that I had taken part in the most intense and informative master's course in the world. And just like in a master's degree, you have to be prepared to learn from everyone, often more from the other participants than from the professors.

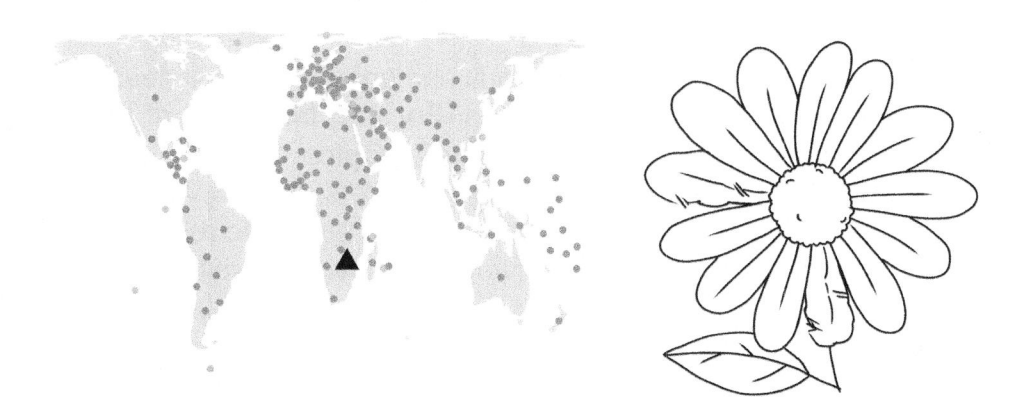

My obsession with planning life down to the last second could cause me to lose the joy found in the moment, and tiny deviations from what is usual can enable you to live life to the full. When travelling, try to feel like a child who hasn't had to tidy the toys today, or a teenager who is allowed to stay out late at night for the first time. And don't shy away from giving something to strangers either. Happiness is really a result of 'social connection' and this concept applies to relatives and friends as well as people you briefly cross paths with.

I support tourism that leaves its mark in both directions. In fact, the goal of leaving no trace of one's passage may be fine if it refers to the environment, but not if it refers to people. I am quite happy to suggest that child labour should be banned in certain contexts or that a woman should not be beaten, which in essence means pushing to break traditions. Indeed, for so many cultures and beliefs I am glad that they are lost forever. This applies to horrific things like genital mutilation, as well as fairy tales about parents abandoning children in the woods. We perpetuate mistakes, even horrors, under the guise of tradition, without question, thinking that if my parents did it to me, it's alright for me to do it to my children, without taking any burden of responsibility. That's why for me the arrival of schooling in a place is always welcome. I'm well aware of how it disrupts the community, and how those who have studied then often want to live elsewhere, putting an end to the community itself. I am happy that it's the children of those who do not believe in education who study because they are the ones who need it most.

Every human life is precious and unique, but that doesn't mean that every culture is too. For me, the rights of individuals come before the rights of peoples. I regret having lazily leaned on certain ideas and beliefs where everything is equal. And the one thing that no one seems to regret, especially not some time afterwards, is having travelled.

From Zimbabwe, I flew to **Botswana (160)**, a nation of just over two million people. If there is one country in the world that's successful at not maintaining traditions, it's Botswana. At the time of independence in 1966, it was arguably the poorest nation, with an estimated 20 graduates in total, a couple of schools run by missionaries, about ten km of paved road, and no hospitals. The then leader, Seretse Khama, is one of the people I most admire among those who are not world famous. As if the country's troubles were not enough, he had dared to marry an English woman, drawing the wrath of neighbouring South Africa where mixed marriages were forbidden. But despite this resentment from the whites towards him, he was rational and decided to take advantage of their skills instead of kicking them out. Botswana under his leadership broke tribal traditions, became a democracy, fought corruption and when he was lucky enough to find diamonds, he used this wealth intelligently. Today, the nation continues to prosper, and moreover has a phenomenal nature that it diligently preserves.

Once I arrived, I did not leave the airport because I had booked a scenic flight a few hours later over the Okavango Delta, the great river that does not run into the sea but finishes its course in the desert, transforming the landscape. Predators have changed their habits, and in fact, some of the big cats have learnt to fish! I was in paradise, I had never seen anything like it, as my travel school continued to allow me to discover nature and come into contact with an incredible number of animals. The next day, using a small boat, I was able to get right amongst the elephants. I could observe hippos so well that I realised for the first time why they are called sea horses since they don't actually swim but propel themselves upwards using the seabed. My small boat relied on the same technique: the oarsman used a kind of long, flexible stick, and rather than moving the water, he pushed hard against the riverbed below and drove us forward. Hippos, though, despite not being very good swimmers, are agile, dangerous, territorial and will attack anyone who gets too close.

I was immersed in a unique and well-kept natural environment, yet Botswana is sometimes criticised for allowing some elephants to be hunted for money. When you say it like that, it actually sounds like a reckless action, especially for a country that relies on tourism. The reality is that they have too many and some must necessarily be culled to preserve the habitat. This being the case, why not offer hunters the opportunity to do it and, what is more, pay for it? What scandalises well-meaning people are the photos on Facebook of the hunters with the shot animal on their side. The image is disturbing, but I think it is quite natural to post what one is proud of, so for those who have just spent €30,000 for the right to shoot an elephant, it seems normal to brag about it on social media. The problem is being proud of the kill, not the photo.

One night in Botswana I myself went 'big game hunting' but to no avail! Despite having opened the mosquito net hours before and wrapped the whole bed, on going to lay down, I found a huge spider inside the covers. I chased it with mosquito spray but without success and I slept badly that night. This is one of the problems with staying at an eco-lodge. They are sustainable lodgings, which offer the tourist close to the comfort of a hotel whilst being completely surrounded by nature, but precisely because they are comfortable and spacious, it is impossible to guarantee that there are no unwelcome guests. In contrast, in my tiny tent that had been with me for so many uncomfortable nights, I could check the entire area in a minute and then sleep peacefully knowing that I was alone. That mega spider did not just disturb a single night, it ruined forever the only sadistic pleasure in my life, hearing a mosquito buzzing around me while I was protected by the net. That 'Zzz' had made my wakefulness a pleasure as I enjoyed the thought of the mosquitoes' futile effort to sting me. But if somehow a spider had passed through…

It was time to go through Johannesburg once again and travel to **Lesotho (161)**, a small nation completely surrounded by South Africa. The other two similarly situated states are both in Italy as San Marino and the Vatican have only one neighbouring country and no access to the sea.

Lesotho exists because a king opened its doors to missionaries who, in order to thank him, legitimised it. Then during the Anglo-Boer wars they sided with the victors and so the British didn't incorporate the kingdom. Finally, part of the credit goes to its geography, because the country is completely mountainous, the only one with an elevation above 1,000 m everywhere. More recently, Lesotho has served

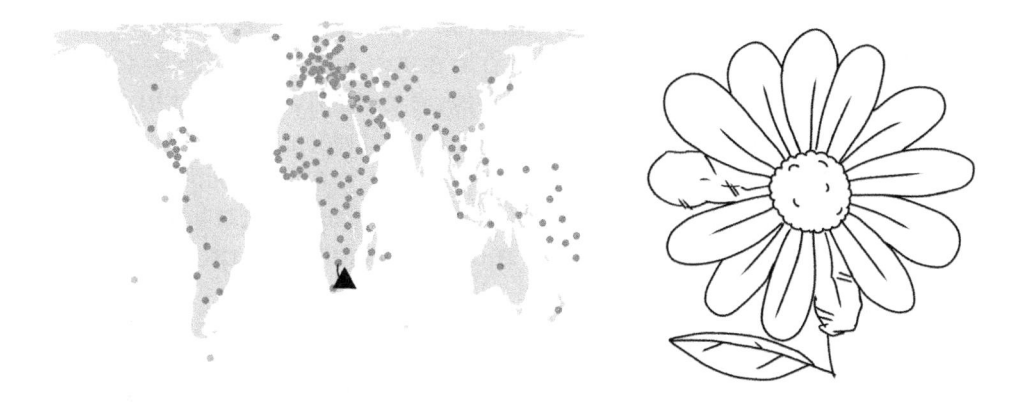

South Africans well in circumventing some of the sanctions imposed because of Apartheid, and a bit like Saudi Arabia with Bahrain, the puritanism of some South Africans stopped at the border. Unfortunately, it is also the country with the highest rate of HIV and rape. Almost one in four adults is HIV positive and about two in three women have experienced sexual violence in their lifetime.

My hotel had a casino on the ground floor and was basically a brothel. This virus has caused the life expectancy of the population to plummet, pushing it close to 50 years. Even the more developed and educated South Africa suffered from the HIV epidemic, and their response had been slow and sometimes absurd. Superstition had suggested that it was the work of witches, and even President Mbeki had cried conspiracy, denying that HIV was the cause of AIDS. Some thought that raping a virgin woman cured it, because just as the 'bad' blood of a sick woman passed on the infection, the 'healthy' blood of a pure woman eliminated it. And conspiracy theorists went so far as to say it was an invention of white people to keep blacks from having children.

Living in Lesotho had meant being saved from Apartheid. But now that the segregation regime no longer exists, many would like to be integrated. Here people starve, poverty is rife, and combined with the cold it becomes even more painful. You walk around wrapped in these heavy blankets that get dirty from the dust dragged in by the strong wind that blows morning and evening. Having a balaclava is essential if you have to be outside for hours. The inhabitants seemed to me to be a mixture of Maasai, also wrapped in blankets because morning and evening in some of their territories are cold, and *Tuareg* with their faces perpetually covered to protect themselves from the sand. Incomprehensibly, we only use blankets in bed, while they have great qualities compared to a jacket. More than one can be used at a time, they have no size and so can fit a child as well as a grown man, they can be used as a rug and even as a saddle.

And the saddle in particular was giving rise to bizarre discussions in Lesotho, the question with no definitive answer being whether it was better to ride with or without. Everyone had their own theory and the discourse reminded me a little of the debate surrounding the use of a manual or automatic gearbox for our cars. I also had my say, and discussing similar topics with passion gave me enthusiasm. My interests and experiences had grown by leaps and bounds without making me lose track of what I had learned in the past. That evening I was as at ease as I used to be in the casino/brothel, but I was also not surprised that a ten-year-old child was parking cars in the hotel courtyard.

At the airport I found myself absorbed in a long chat, very easy in this case, with the check-in steward who was considering his favourite things about Italy, namely Totti and Buffon the footballers and champion skier, Alberto Tomba! He was a big sports fan, so I had to listen to how Lesotho is improving even though they have never won an Olympic medal. I certainly didn't tell him that I was more excited about the opening ceremony with the flags at the Olympics than the competitions, but I was sympathetic, so he eventually gave me seat 1A as a courtesy, since they were all the same.

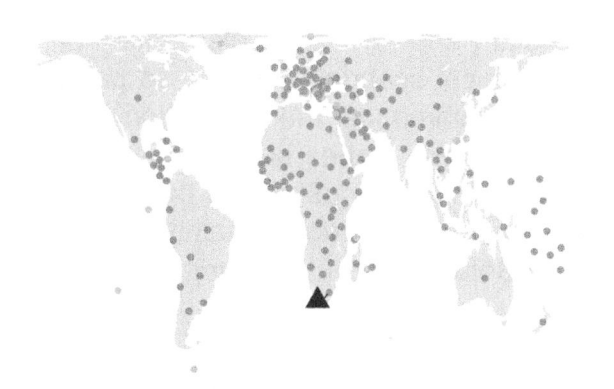

Once past security, which was a door, I noticed great excitement in the boarding hall. The only plane arriving, the same one that would take me back to Johannesburg, had the Prime Minister on board, I guessed sitting in the seat I would soon be occupying. A guard of honour was on the tarmac practising to welcome him, with fine uniforms and musical instruments. But in front of the windows were two journalists who attracted my attention because they looked like the reporters from my school had done when we used to play at impersonating different jobs. Armed with the classic notebook and pen, they were very young, enthusiastic, with a huge, shabby microphone to put under the prime minister's nose. They were the only ones there to ask him questions about his visit to South Africa. My astonishment, however, was unjustified, after all, the entire nation is comparable to a portion of a large South African city and its economy is less than 1/50 of that of the Johannesburg region alone.

After the plane flight, the weather remained chilly because Johannesburg is also high, rising to 1,800 m. Rich mines have been discovered in these mountains and the long, modern roads, made from the scraps of what was mined, are probably full of gold. This is why the town sprang up and attracted such a large population. Pretoria, the administrative capital of the country, is 50 km away and the two now 'touch', unlike the two halves of Old and New Lilongwe, the capital of Malawi, which are only a few kilometres apart, yet have bush (complete with hyenas) in between.

I had been to the great Congo, a country so rich in copper, cobalt, diamonds, coltan and rare earth elements that it has been called a 'geological scandal', yet it is so poor. In Sierra Leone, despite the diamonds, the population was starving, and indeed the precious stones had been one of the causes of the civil war. Here in South Africa the mines had made some people very rich, although certainly not the population as a whole. In Botswana, on the other hand, an entire nation had made a remarkable leap forward.

The same process can be observed with oil: in some nations very few have become rich, in Venezuela they even manage to become poor, while in Norway it is for the good of all, including future generations. Whether resources are a blessing, or a curse depends on many factors, but in general, you can't expect them to turn into wealth automatically. Extracting oil requires technology, there are risks associated with prospecting the land and it is possible to fail. Before the 'profiteers' from abroad came along, oil was simply waste that ruined the environment and smelled bad. Huge investments in machinery are necessary for a successful mine, and they are usually located a long way from the sea, therefore transport can be a logistical challenge. Also, some metals have only gained a usage with the invention of chips and iPhones. So, the idea of fair distribution of this wealth has to be explored on a case-by-case basis.

But of course, the mines in particular were and are the symbol of man's greed triumphing over his fellow man and nature. Miners are mistreated and pushed into risky situations with no laws to protect them, and children are used with very few scruples. Mining takes priority over respect for the environment, with enormous consequences for those living in the area.

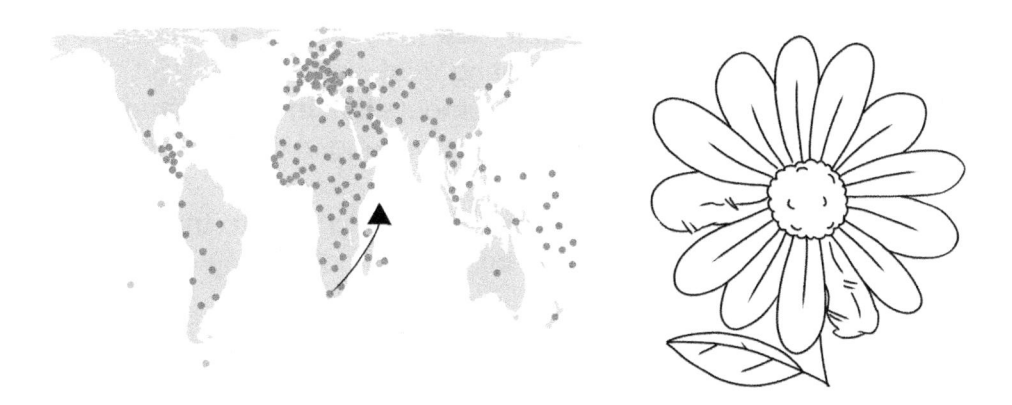

South Africa, especially Johannesburg, is for me a hotbed of such conduct. The wealth was generated by those who lived in the country and the profits stayed in place, yet the injustice is blatant, and the cruelty there for all to see. Miners lived in appalling shacks, and during Apartheid were alone, without their families because women who didn't work were not allowed a pass to enter certain areas. The skyscrapers and living areas for the white people tower above the slums, which is a disturbing contrast.

I left the problems and dangers of South Africa and headed for a paradise, the **Seychelles (162)**. Alone and without wanting to spend too much money I experienced the islands differently from those who rely on the classic tourist circuit because I slept in a normal flat away from the beach. I was hosted by a guy, who was a typical surfer who just smoked marijuana all day. In this supposed tourist paradise about 10% of the population are heroin addicts, which shows how going on holiday to a wonderful place is quite different from living there.

As I was leaving the country, heading towards Addis Ababa, there were rumours of a new variant of the virus that had been discovered in South Africa where I'd been recently. I was in Ethiopia for the umpteenth time for a very specific reason, a special mission of sorts. According to the person from Equatorial Guinea I had been in contact with, there was a chance of getting a visa in Addis Ababa. I was so focused on the end goal that flying to a country just to chase a visa seemed normal to me. Especially in this case, because Equatorial Guinea is an isolated country with no interest in tourism, its political class is corrupt to the core, it is sanctioned in Europe and they, in retaliation, have closed their embassies, only cultivating relations with the USA and China. My hope relied on the rumours that this guy managed to succeed by tipping the people working in the embassies.

So, I presented myself with a smiling face to the secretary who had provided this information, obviously equipped with all the required documents. After a few hours, the first person arrived and openly asked me for $100 to get my documentation onto the ambassador's desk. Before paying, I wanted to find out how many levels there were until the visa was obtained, otherwise the procession of every person working there asking for money would begin. In a lengthy back-and-forth, with the intervention of the secretary, eventually the highest-ranking person came and asked for $500, which he would then distribute.

Officially I had to pay because I had no authorisation from the Foreign Ministry. According to him, an insignificant tourist had to first get an official invitation, then go to the embassy to get a visa. I'd had no doubt that it was among the most corrupt countries in the world, and now I had first-hand experience of it. These people were wearing clothes that I could not afford, yet they were asking for money to get me in to visit their country. While in the Uzbek embassy it was perhaps a single, low-level person who made deals with the agencies dispensing visas, here it was all of them and some of them high-level. This was a really annoying type of corruption, paying rich people to get something you are entitled to, but at least I was now talking directly to the person issuing the visas.

The bargaining closed at $200, which I would pay the next day when I collected my passport. Although at the beginning of the day I had tiptoed into the embassy and been called into a shadowy room by the secretary where we whispered and she predictably asked for money for herself, eventually the bargaining over the bribe had become public and I think even the people tidying the embassy garden knew that I was being asked for extra money. I left exhausted but happy because my dream of visiting all the countries of the world was getting ever closer.

As I stepped outside elatedly, I was assaulted. On one side a man pretending to sell masks grabbed me by the arm, while on the other his accomplice took my mobile phone out of my pocket. At the same time, a group of children started to circle me. I remained clear-headed because I had prepared myself for this kind of eventuality. I didn't shout, I didn't resist, and I certainly didn't run after the person who had robbed me. It wasn't worth it because you never know who is in front of you, how desperate they are, or if they have a knife. I calmly explained to those children, I guess forced to be accomplices, that I would give $100 to the one who would bring my mobile phone back and that I would be back there in two hours.

The thieves had stolen my phone on the assumption that a white guy coming out of an embassy had something valuable, while mine had a broken screen, and was a Chinese sub-brand that was years old. It was hardly worth anything, so I hoped they would accept the $100, since a kid going back there can easily say he found it on the ground a few metres from where it was stolen.

I try to use the same technique with my suitcase: in the inner lining there is a note with my contact details and a sentence in which I suggest to anyone who finds it 'by chance' to bring it back. In return, I'll pay a $250 reward. And about my underwear and T-shirts, what would you do with them? They're actually of some value to me, but hardly to you. Theft aside, suitcases do get lost in good faith, by airlines, by porters, or in hotel storerooms. I've heard all kinds of things, but what impresses me most are the tourists, always ready to take pictures of every insignificant bowl of cereal at breakfast, yet not having a picture of their suitcase to show!

I calmly walked to a nearby coffee shop, asked to use the wi-fi, triggered deletion of the contents of the phone via my laptop, and waited the two hours without too much anger on my part. I didn't even think of going to the police as I knew it was useless.

No one returned my phone, so I went to the shops with the taxi-driver to buy a replacement. I needed a cheap mobile phone with a good battery and little else. With my kind of travelling, the less you draw attention to yourself, the better. An iPhone attracts a whole lot of trouble because the urge to steal it is enormous. Once I had found something cheap, the problem was how to get the Italian number back, especially as I needed it to authorise online purchases and transfers. In Italy I could have had the SIM back quickly if I'd notified the police and obtained a theft report, but this was out of the question, I would have had to go to the Ethiopian police with an interpreter, and then have the report officially translated into Italian, which would have been madness as it would have cost me more than the new mobile phone.

The next day when I returned to the embassy, the secretary was agitated saying that she had called me several times without managing to reach me to say that the passport had been ready since the afternoon of the day before.

I explained what had happened and inadvertently discovered the only advantage of having been robbed as she had certainly wanted to ask me for more money in those phone calls, saying that it was her job to speed up the process and supervise, or solve some imaginary obstacle. I collected my passport, locked everything in my backpack, then, after having carefully scanned the street where the incident had taken place, I went out and cautiously headed for the hotel. I just wanted to go back to my room and ponder having obtained this tricky visa, one of the last bureaucratic hurdles of this long adventure.

From Addis my ticket was the usual one to Johannesburg. Due to the discovery of the new Covid variant, Italy had banned anyone from entering the country who had been in South Africa in the previous fortnight, but I had no intention of returning anyway. From there my destination was **Eswatini (163)**. This small country on the border with Mozambique used to be called Swaziland but the king, fed up with the confusion with Switzerland, changed the name. Assonance aside, it really is impossible to mix up the two countries.

There was an absolute king here who seemed to have come out of the Middle Ages; when he passed by you had to throw yourself on the ground. He decided on the life and death of his subjects, the only limit to his power being the strange stipulation that he must rule together with his mother. The king was Christian but polygamous; and every year he would add a wife to his already rich collection after the virgin maidens of the right age had danced for him. He probably had HIV or some other sexually transmitted disease, not only because of his numerous wives and concubines, but because traditions dictated strange couplings, he even had to have sex with a bull.

Women in Eswatini, and in Southern Africa in general, still run the risk of *Ukuthwalwa*, which is being kidnapped in order to be married. It's more or less the same story as is seen in Kyrgyzstan, demonstrating that humanity, at different latitudes, has conceived similar horrors. It's always women who pay the price, sacrificed to prevent strife for a single individual. Men were given the green light to kidnap them for personal choice or to settle a marriage negotiation with overly exorbitant demands, and the matter would end there. Interestingly similar abominations also existed in Italy until recently. A raped woman in southern Italy, even a few decades ago, could be asked to marry her rapist, to avoid scandal and eliminate the crime.

I spent the days in the company of a very knowledgeable guide, a British woman who had lived there for 50 years. She told me about secret societies that function the same way as they do in West Africa or Papua New Guinea, showing again how widespread some forms of human organisation are. What is unique, however, is the uproar that Eswatini women have made in the Western media because they have managed to accuse Google and other big companies of mistreating their culture because they censor bare-breasted dances. Apparently, Google has adapted and now allows exceptions to their prudish censorship. But a bare breast is certainly not the problem in this society.

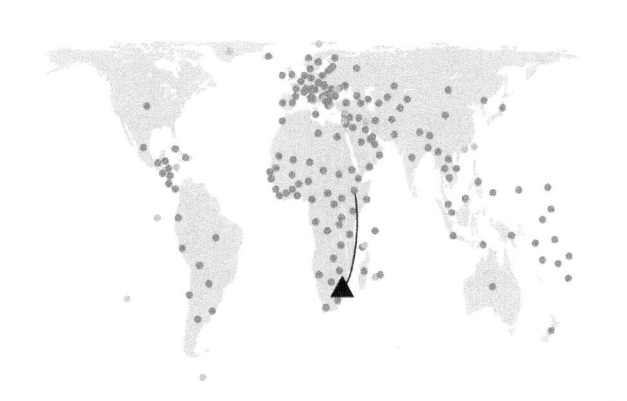

Strange sexual customs aside, this nation is one of the last places on earth where a single man, the king, has everything while the rest starve. He owns dozens of Rolls Royces, some painted pink for his wives, and he built a new airport for his private plane that needed a longer runway. The king of Eswatini doesn't hide his wealth, he has his shopping trips televised with a parade of spendthrift wives in tow, and his hungry subjects applauding as they return. In the village there are also huge inequalities, but you need to look much harder to identify them.

To consider how difficult it is to see differences, let us change our perspective. Imagine how an uneducated woman from Eswatini would see Milanese Italians. They would all appear equal because everyone has a house, hot water and electricity. Returning to cars, in her eyes even a VW Golf and a Ferrari would appear identical since both transport you wherever you want, and probably at the same speed within Milan. We look at the people of the village with the same uneducated eyes and for us every hut, meal and dress appear the same. We don't spot what signifies wealth and status, not even things that in different cultures are as flashy as a pink Rolls Royce.

My Eswatini guide's car however was in a class quite of its own! As he was driving me to the airport, it lost power, went very slowly, kept going for a few minutes, and finally left us stranded. There were no taxis on those roads, but luckily, when it came to it, good old hitchhiking worked like a charm, one of the passing cars was going right to the airport and I arrived in time.

At this point I was ready to dive into formerly Portuguese Africa. The first stop was **Mozambique (164)**, a country so immersed in the Anglo-Saxon world that it is part of the Commonwealth despite not speaking English. To get there, as usual, you had to pass through Johannesburg, where this time I found the airport practically deserted. The new 'South African variant' had drastically reduced the number of travellers.

Mozambique grants visas on arrival, but recommends obtaining them in advance, which I'd had no intention of doing after my experience in Malawi, so I presented myself in Maputo, the capital, without a visa. Those who did not have it were penalised with a long wait, so it took a few hours before I could finally get into the car in the company of my guide. We were then stopped by two policemen on foot who wanted a ride into the city centre and so we had to accompany them.

Before undertaking my travel school, I had mistakenly thought that African colonisation had lasted for centuries, when in fact it was the explorations that went way back in time, and hardly anyone had stayed to live there. Colonisation had lasted about 80 years, that is, from the famous 1885 Berlin Conference until the 1960s.

There were exceptions though, for example in countries like Algeria and South Africa colonialism had really lasted centuries, because they are in the North and South of the continent, so the climate was good, almost European.

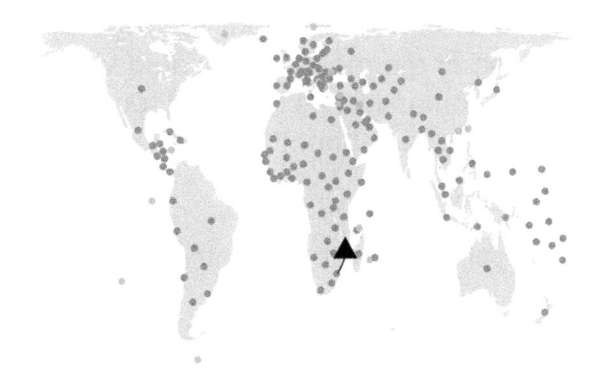

And again, my misconception had been that once colonisation had begun, only a few people had moved in, whereas here in Mozambique I was discovering how Portuguese peasants had arrived en masse, hundreds of thousands, only to be expelled after independence. This was one of the reasons that there was a much bloodier liberation struggle here than elsewhere, just like in Algeria. The Europeans had been living in the country for years, and then after independence from Portugal, many of them were only given one day to leave and were allowed to take a maximum 20 kg of belongings.

I had assumed that Apartheid had been unique, which was also incorrect. When I was exploring Mozambique, I saw traces of how marked segregation was. In the capital there is a district symbolic of the division that I was able to visit, accompanied by a local as it would have been unwise to go alone. The masonry buildings had been reserved for whites, so that you could quickly pull down a black man's house and easily chase him away.

Some blacks in Maputo were allowed to enter the areas reserved for whites, provided they passed 'civilisation' examinations. Those who wanted to come into contact with whites had to be baptised, have studied something, and be able to eat with cutlery. These pass-holders, the 'assimilated', could receive surprise visits to their homes to check that good manners were maintained at all times. Each child had to have a single bed, but above all they checked on how the women were being treated. To be an 'assimilate' you had to let your wife eat at the table with the men and not keep her segregated in the kitchen.

From Mozambique there was a direct flight to **Angola (165)**, a country that had one of the most complicated visa procedures. But finally, I had some luck, as they had recently simplified it. I'd found a Portuguese born there who would get it for me for $100.

His father had been expelled from the country in 1975

under the very same rules as had been imposed in Mozambique after independence when many of them had had little time to leave and had lost their properties. He had only been one year old at the time. The assimilated had also fled to Portugal for fear of retaliation and perhaps because they wanted to live like Europeans.

He had returned in the 1990s and so had lived most of his life in Angola but had not yet obtained citizenship. The first thing he told me was that the hotel I had chosen was dangerous, 'They will rob you, but trust me, I will take you elsewhere'. He was right, but I knew this too. When I asked for cost estimates from the guides, I would provide details of a cheap hotel as my accommodation because in my experience, they calibrate all the other costs on the basis of that. This time I had forgotten to communicate the change. Since we were immediately on good terms, I confessed this little ploy of mine to him. We had a good laugh and he declared that he had a nice little trick to show me too, so we started our Angolan adventure from the best hotel in town, because it was free. We didn't sleep there, but we did have everything else. We could walk in the large garden, use the spotlessly clean toilets, ask the reception desk for advice on activities and restaurants, and the wi-fi password was shared right away because everyone took it for granted that the two white people were staying there.

But privileges can quickly turn into disadvantages and on the long drive we had a small accident with the car, and usually, the foreigner was at fault. While overtaking a sort of cart in the middle of the road, we had hit something protruding from the edge with our wing mirror and overturned some bottles. Nobody was hurt, so the situation was relatively calm, but we were still surrounded by people.

It was a bit like what happens to the football referee when the players all stand in front of him, chest out, hoping to intimidate him, a sorry spectacle in sport, but quite dangerous on the road. Luckily my guide had experienced many similar situations, he lived in the country and spoke the language, so he handled the situation perfectly. With his chest out as well to show that he was not intimidated at all, he isolated the owner of the broken bottles from his supporters and began to talk to him about money. With a hand on his shoulder, he accompanied him as far away as possible from the small crowd and without the victim, the crowd was already less threatening. After a few minutes of conciliation, the deal was done, inside the car, so the owner could now lie about how much he had received from the foreigners. The higher the compensation, the more he ran the risk of finding himself surrounded by demands from people who felt they deserved a share.

I can understand the discomfort felt when you live on the street and are continually passed by large, flashy, expensive vehicles, and no one misses an opportunity to let off steam. The hatred against the Portuguese has diminished, partly because almost 50 years have passed since the independence struggles, but also due to the Angolans having realised that their new elites have already stolen more than the Portuguese did over centuries. Africa as a whole was poorer in the 1980s than before the Second World War.

Luanda, the capital, has become one of the most expensive cities in the world thanks to the oil boom, and the daughter of the long-time dictator, now no longer in power, is considered the richest woman in Africa. She steals from her country and then transfers the money to Europe so that it doesn't even benefit local business. In Angola, you can visit entire cities commissioned from Chinese firms that stopped work halfway through because they were no longer being paid, the money allocated magically having vanished over time.

Outside the cities, people come to hunt illegally to survive and some of the small buildings along the roads, like the one we had bumped into, display all kinds of suspended animals. There are monkeys, mice, and scraps that are still edible, everything is for sale. Even in the city there are those who have it really bad, and some markets cater to the poorer clientele who cannot go to a supermarket or modern shop, or those who simply don't have a refrigerator at home. You can still buy in very small quantities because people only have tiny amounts of money, someone gives credit on bad days, sometimes trades are accepted, and the market is always open. In the West there is talk of making packages smaller because families now consist of one or two people and there is waste. Here you buy the single portion for lack of cash, then it is divided among a large family. In these markets there is more poverty than merchandise on display.

The Covid exit test in the only authorised laboratory cost $200 which was daylight robbery of course, but there was no alternative. My destination was the islands of **São Tomé and Príncipe (166)**, another former Portuguese colony.

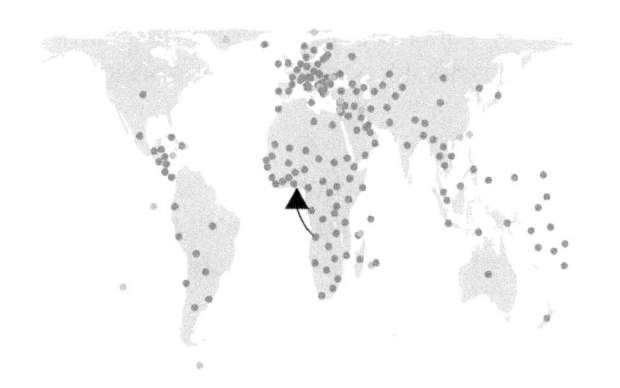

They had been uninhabited and were then populated by slaves brought from Angola. Portuguese slave ships had left from here, and, more generally, from the Gulf of Guinea. This human traffic was not managed directly by any one nation, but all the great powers had at least some small access to the sea. Even Spain, the great outcast from Africa, had land, namely present-day Equatorial Guinea, so that it could transport slaves to South America. The United Kingdom also deployed its fleet here after 1833, the year of the abolition of slavery, to impose an end to the trade on other nations. After so many British misdeeds, this is unprecedented in human history and deserves mention: no nation had ever before fought for the others to stop the human trade.

From 1885 onwards, because of the great changes in the world economy, all the aims of the Europeans focused on Africa's raw materials, not on men.

I had arranged to meet a Polish friend of mine whom I had got to know in Sudan, a great expert, and a writer of travel guides by profession. He now lived in Denmark and had been following me at a distance since I had started travelling again, to the point that I called him 'coach'. His knowledge helped me to organise myself, and he enjoyed having a player in the field to bring him up to date on the Covid rules, theoretical and real, of so many countries. His research trip at the time was to São Tomé and Príncipe, so I juggled the dates in order to spend a few days with this man who is such a mine of information. He did me another favour too and brought me the Italian SIM card with my number. My sister had managed to get it for me a few weeks after the theft and then it had been easier to post it to Copenhagen than anywhere else.

We were staying in a central hostel where the Portuguese lady proprietress entertained us. She told us about the marvels of nature on the island of Príncipe and described to us the small, very close-knit community that existed there. It's a story we have heard a thousand times before about other islands, you can leave your front door open, there are practically no police. The reality is that certain goods can't be stolen on small islands, you certainly wouldn't be able to drive a car you'd taken right under the owner's nose for instance. A small, close community protects itself. To steal would be to risk being ousted and losing everything. When you have no alternative to that community, the rules are respected more. And you don't have to lock your door, because no-one is escaping easily from this tiny island that forms such a large prison.

I didn't visit Príncipe because that would have required an additional Covid test. Instead, I went to **Gabon (167)**. The country had allowed entry to anyone with a passport from a G20 member nation, that is from any one of the world's largest economies, but with Covid it seemed that the rule had been suspended. I had applied online to avoid any risk and they had asked me to provide an invitation, which I had forwarded but then not received a reply. In São Tomé and Príncipe, I had physically gone to the Gabonese embassy, applied for a visa and got it in two days. It was not the first time I had paid double, so I was not even angry.

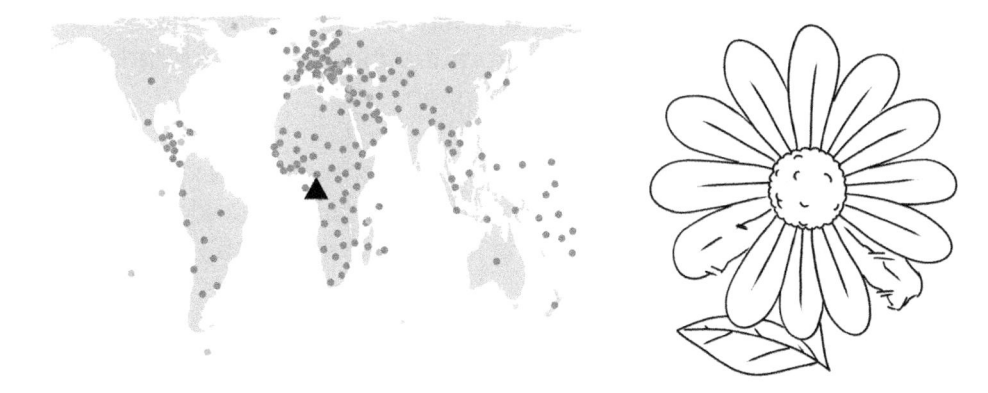

On arrival another farce played out as I was detained because I was entering with the visa I had in my passport, but in their immigration area there was another visa in my name! It was the one I had applied for online, which they had approved without telling me. Having two visas (both for a single entry) came in handy, however. I was using one now, and then I had the option of returning to Gabon using the second one after visiting my next destination, Equatorial Guinea.

In Gabon, for the first time, I realised that I did not feel like doing anything. I hardly cared about the entire country, and whatever a guidebook or website offered was of little interest to me. I'd already seen every animal and had every tourist experience. I'd only come to Gabon to complete a tour of the world; it had nothing more to offer me. Did travelling like this make sense?

I had waited for the weekend to approach and then had set off in the direction of Malabo, a city that sits on an island and is the capital of **Equatorial Guinea (168)** for six months of the year. In spite of its name, the country isn't exactly on the equator. It has most of its surface area on the mainland where the other capital (Ciudad de la Paz) is located, but it has some small islands a few steps away from Cameroon encircled by former Portuguese lands. There are just over a million inhabitants, and they are quite unique. They use the Central African franc, a currency anchored to the euro and linked to France, they speak Spanish but also French, and on some islands Portuguese is prevalent.

In addition to the usual Covid test to be presented on arrival, plus having to take one on site, there was a mandatory five-day quarantine awaiting me. Then to be free, yet another test had to be taken on day three, four or five, it wasn't clear. This was why I had chosen to arrive on a Friday, so that the week would begin from the third day of quarantine and the laboratories would be open.

Visiting this country was really laborious and expensive. Previously I had had to fly to Addis Ababa to obtain a visa, pay $200 in bribes, now the test on arrival €153, another

€153 for the exit test, and the quarantine forced me to spend €110 a day in a hotel. It was a madness that only those who are chasing all the countries of the world can conceive. I was obviously the only tourist as the other people on the flight were oil rig personnel.

The passports were requisitioned by a woman who threw them into a rubbish bin, fortunately empty, which she was holding. In the absence of a better container, she'd had the ridiculous idea of using this, and for me, seeing my trusty passport buried under a pile of other documents inside a dustbin was a stab in the heart worse than any quarantine.

The first post-independence dictator had truly lost his mind once he had taken power. His crazy communist ideas of moving everyone back to the countryside had turned Malabo into a ghost town where only a few concentration camps remained. The president had banned religion because he feared that priests and missionaries were Francoist agents and had proclaimed himself a kind of God. He had cultivated relations with North Korea where he'd had his children raised. He also sought out anyone who had previously had sex with his women in the past and had them killed.

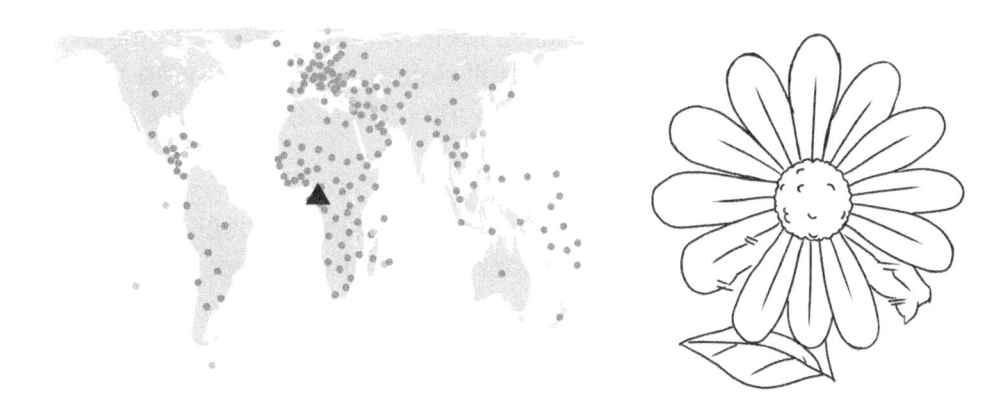

It would be almost impossible to do worse than this, but the current dictator and his clique are also on a bad path. They are corrupt and paranoid, for example it is forbidden to carry binoculars, or cameras with powerful telephoto lenses, and everything is under control by a government that leaves the population in poverty. Yet the GDP per capita is the highest in Africa thanks to the discovery of oil. For me, the family that rules in Equatorial Guinea is the symbol of every evil in Africa: it never abandons power, and its greed knows no bounds. My money was going into their already swollen pockets since even the quarantine hotel was theirs, apparently belonging to the first lady or the president's son, a famous Instagram playboy who loved luxury and crazy amusements that he would then show off.

During the five days of enforced rest, I could move freely around the hotel, and in the lobby the Spanish poetry book *De Cuarantena* (About Quarantine) was wittily displayed. On the third day, I asked my guardians to take me for the Covid test but when I arrived at the lab, they sent me back, and instead picked me up on their own initiative on the fourth day. When the response came back the next day, I was free to go.

The island is small, and apart from a bit of nature and a few animals there is not much to see. At the checkpoints they ask for money to let people through and threaten all kinds of fines. Not having a clear Highway Code makes everyone fineable, so for the first time I supported the behaviour of 'flashing headlights' between motorists to warn them that there is a blockade nearby. In Italy, this is criminal behaviour, but here it was self-defence. The guy who had invited me joked that in this country it is only the police who steal your wallet.

To maintain power, the dictator assigned useless public jobs to those who support him, with salaries that are not always enough to live on. This system is even more deleterious than giving away public money because the plethora of clerks, tasks, and petty powers hinder life. Each of them wants to be involved, to have a slice of the corruption, and to have their say. They would be better off at home doing nothing. Even at the airport, there is so much chaos and duplication of roles that check-in has to be done the day before departure! I was exempted because I had no luggage. Thanks to the double visa I could now go back to Gabon.

For weeks I had been trying to get a visa for Guinea (Conakry), that is the French one. Guinea means 'land of the blacks', which is why it was a frequently used name. Bissau was Portuguese, Equatorial was Spanish, and then there is Papua New Guinea in Oceania, also named by a Portuguese. It was impossible to pay online, the system did not accept any credit cards, and I had tried numerous ones, from different people, in various countries. I had tried going to the embassies in person, most recently to Malabo, but the answer was the same: you have to apply online. And they denied that the system didn't work, saying that according to them it was fine. But when I proposed that they pay for me with one of their credit cards and I would immediately reimburse them, nobody wanted to do it.

For the first time, it was me who offered money in an embassy instead of receiving the request. I proposed payment for the service because for me to leave this part of Africa with only one country missing would have been a waste of money. Airline flights were very expensive because of the huge distances involved, plus the countries in question charge higher than normal fees to the companies for the use of their airspace. And lastly, there had recently been a coup d'état in Guinea and there were very few flights left.

Consequently, I flew to **Cape Verde (169)**, which in comparison, is touristy and well-organised. The contrast with the poorer countries was huge and I perceived it in some of the more subtle behaviours such as the amount of meat I found on the plate prepared by the lady who cooked for me.

Elsewhere in West Africa, even if you're paying, they go and buy what you would consider very little, which is indicative of what a normal portion size is among those who have money and add a little something to their rice. They haven't cheated you; they just manage on very little.

However, many people from Cape Verde also seek a better life and part of the population has emigrated, curiously enough, to Luxembourg where I had lived and remembered them well. These islands have no indigenous population, and you can see this in the variety of somatic features, the result of the different ethnic groups brought together by the Portuguese.

Portugal had sailed the seas so much because a king, Henry the 'Navigator', had created a kind of Silicon Valley for exploration at the time. He had put together engineers, sailors, builders, and cartographers. In 1445 the Portuguese arrived in Cape Verde and by 1475 they had already crossed the equator. Diaz arrived at the southernmost tip of Africa in 1488, then the great Vasco de Gama used that route to reach India. The king gave privileges to some traders who had settled in Africa on condition that they explored at least 100 leagues of coastline every year. I had visited the geographical places that symbolised the advancement trying to understand its importance. If you go to Lisbon today, be sure to visit the Monument to the Discoveries erected 500 years after the death of Henry the Navigator.

My exit flight was to Morocco, but that country had just suddenly closed its borders, so I went to Istanbul. The plan was to try again with the visa for Guinea Conakry at the embassy in Turkey. Every day I attempted to request it online, but two weeks later that visa remained a mirage, so I went home. There was the third vaccination dose to be administered and then my passport needed to be changed for the fourth time. Also, to leave Italy again, I would have had to make something up as the ban on tourism outside Europe was still in place.

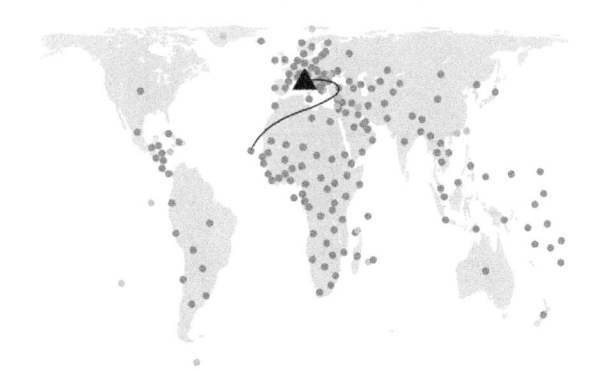

YEAR 8

ANDORRA	LIECHTENSTEIN	LITHUANIA
LATVIA	ESTONIA	AUSTRIA
SLOVAKIA	UNITED KINGDOM	SWEDEN
SAN MARINO	LIBYA	MALI
BURKINA FASO	NIGER	GUINEA BISSAU
SENEGAL	GAMBIA	SIERRA LEONE
LIBERIA	CYPRUS	YEMEN
MALAWI	ZIMBABWE	BOTSWANA
LESOTHO	SEYCHELLES	ESWATINI
MOZAMBIQUE	ANGOLA	SAO TOME AND PRINCIPE
GABON	EQUATORIAL GUINEA	CAPE VERDE

169/193

YEAR 9

I had recently posted a picture of myself on Facebook and a friend had commented, 'Do you always wear the same grey T-shirt?' It certainly wasn't meant to be an insult, but it made me think – yes, it does feel like I've had that shirt forever. Nine years earlier I would always have been impeccably attired, yet now I didn't notice anymore just how badly I dressed. When I returned home, I would find the sensation of changing shoes after months very strange as the only pair I usually had with me felt just like my feet.

In Rome, I had finally managed to pay for and receive the online visa for Guinea, and I'd also applied for the one for Algeria. For once everything had seemed to go smoothly, but when I collected it, I discovered that they had only given me a fortnight, which had already started. I'd wanted to catch my breath a little, but I had to hurry. Rome has a direct flight, so I arrived in **Algeria (170)** quickly and no one at Fiumicino asked me anything about the reason for the trip.

The army, which still has descendants of the Ottomans in its high ranks, is in control of the nation. Who knows what it must have looked like in the early 1900s when over 10% of the population was French? In Algiers, you can find European-style balconies, an underground system and a *casbah*, which is a fortified citadel and contains a *medina*, the term by which the heart of the city is now generically identified. Inside is the usual market selling precious objects, which is so important for women because with high inflation, gold is the traditional investment to avoid seeing your savings evaporate day after day.

In this market crowded with traders, there's no risk of being scammed, as everyone keeps an eye on the others to protect their good name. Their unity is also effective against ill-intentioned outsiders. Some of the little streets are so narrow that they have to use donkeys to empty the bins.

The country is the largest in Africa and you have to fly to get around, but the domestic flights are the cheapest I have ever seen. To go south into the desert, however, the government requires you to have an escort, which is only provided at weekends. The Roman remains are impressive, while in Oran you could almost be in Spain as religious prohibitions are relaxed and you even see single women sitting at cafes. In my experience of Islamic lands, the café is a man's place, while tea houses, sometimes called 'gardens', are more feminine.

I took the Covid test inside a taxi parked on the street and went to **Tunisia (171)** despite the curfew imposed because of the virus. There were few tourists due to all the rules, but I joined a Belgian girl who was a guest in the same place as me and had hired a guide. This girl's grandfather was an Italian who had died tragically in a mine in Belgium. She talked to me about the ordeal, adding that at least as a result of that loss, the victim's six children had studied at the state's expense, which meant that she too now had a better life.

Together we visited Carthage and Kairouan, the latter being considered the highest in importance of the holy places of Islam after Mecca, Medina and Jerusalem. In my experience, every Muslim country claims to have a city that has played a key role in the formation or expansion of the religion within its borders, which of course is possible, but then they all claim their own as the 'fourth' holiest…

In addition to the Romans and Islam, there are also traces of modern Italy because over 100,000 Italians lived in Tunisia towards the end of the 19th century. Despite this, in 1881 it was seized by France, who wanted to fortify the Algerian borders, and Italy, in that perverse logic of conquest, had no choice but to wrest Libya from the Ottomans as compensation a few decades later.

The relationship with religion is mixed as its presence is constant, but the nation is secular. In an image that summarises the contrast, two women entered the gym in my hotel completely veiled and then ran alongside me on the treadmill in leggings. The guide who had shown me around was very unhappy with the situation and wanted to emigrate. Tunisia is indeed a country in trouble, but I didn't understand the constant comparison between this country and France, despite there being other neighbouring countries. If you only ever compare yourself to the top of the class, it is difficult to be satisfied.

As for me, when I got out of the capital, I had found a room for a few euros, which was well-lit, and from which I could hear the sound of the waves. In those conditions I could bear any thought, in fact, it was not even tolerance,

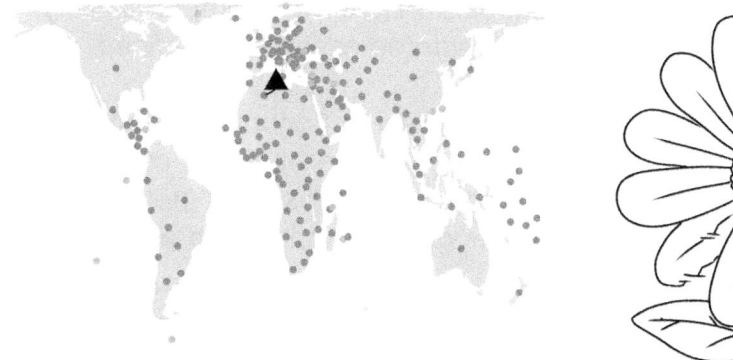

I could simply be done with any worry. It was the perfect preparation for travelling alone to Guinea in West Africa, where they spoke French and there had recently been a coup d'état. I wanted to arrive in optimal mental condition to be ready for anything.

One of the few flights to Conakry in **Guinea (172)** departed from Tunis. Coups in Africa are frequent and easier to pull off than one might imagine. The armies consist of a few thousand people, but there are only a few generals who matter. As soon as a few of these agree, they promise advantages to their soldiers, who are usually ethnically selected and very loyal to their leader, and that's it. To avoid being ousted, some dictators rely on mercenaries from neighbouring countries or surround themselves primarily with generals and soldiers of their own ethnicity.

On arrival, I was immediately impacted by the chaotic crowds and tried to enjoy it. I was eager to find the particular type of market that springs up as soon as there is a hump in the road, with vendors holding goods over their heads and banging on your window, also useful for alerting you to the bump ahead. I enjoyed listening to so many different languages again, confirming in person for the umpteenth and final time, that every African is at least bilingual, and sometimes even speaks four or five languages fluently. There were always a lot of children around as the schools worked double shifts, so some went in the afternoon. The clothes were very colourful and flamboyant, and what the men wore looked comfortable, as in all of West Africa, dressing in baggy tunics is an elegant look. In Europe, incomprehensibly, comfortable clothes are considered casual or unrefined.

Getting into the taxi, as a guest of honour I was allowed to control the window knob. This piece of plastic comes off on purpose and is guarded by the driver so that the passengers do not keep pulling the glass up and down or arguing about how to regulate the window opening.

After a few days, it finally sank in that Africa was the continent with the most nations and I had visited all 54 of them – quite an achievement, not least because most states require a visa, and few are ready for tourism. Africa is huge, three times the size of the United States or China, and it's 8,000 km from Algiers to Cape Town, which is the same as from Rome to Beijing. Not counting the islands, it's 7,000 km from Dakar to Somalia on the other side. But something that is beginning to be common to each nation is the presence of the Chinese. Reading articles and watching videos describing this phenomenon is not enough, you have to go in person to realise the extent of it.

China has a larger population than the whole of Africa. About a million Chinese live on the continent and many Africans are convinced that they are convicts constrained to carry out forced labour. They may still seem few, but they occupy key positions and have a supportive government behind them. As a visitor to tourist areas, restaurants and hotels, I can testify that their presence is constant. At Addis Ababa airport, the real hub for Africa, there is an Ethiopian Airlines desk with Chinese-speaking staff.

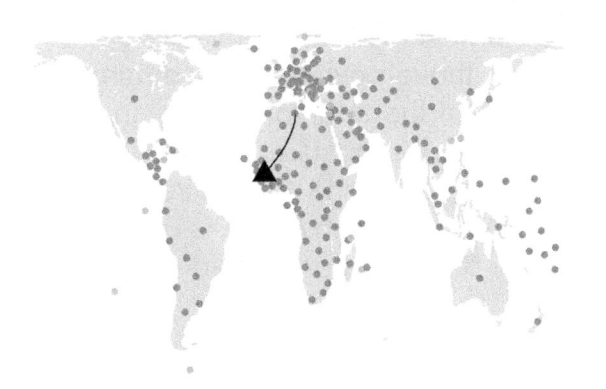

It all started because Mao was looking for support from the United Nations against Taiwan, the island where the losers of the civil war had taken refuge. Africa, with so many nations already free or on the way to independence, was the perfect field in which to garner votes. China had what it took to make a good impression there – it wasn't the usual white people coming to impose their rules, in fact, quite the opposite as they too had been colonised. They had emphasised the suffering that they themselves had been subjected to in order to make it clear that China would never do to others what they had endured. It was a far-sighted policy that came to fruition with the construction of a railway between Tanzania and Zambia (the *Great Uhuru Railway*, meaning the great freedom railway).

The world is astonished today at how China's economic expansion has lasted for decades, but what's even more surprising is how poor it was until 1979 and yet despite the hunger at home, it managed to supply labour and money abroad. Since then, the construction of major projects has continued. The Europeans were mainly building them to export and import products that interested them. China is also uniting Africa through and for Africans. Major works give a long-term perspective, showing that China will still be there many years from now. The constructions may be made with shoddy materials and certainly without respecting environmental or workplace safety rules, but it is all actually completed, and quickly. They also know how to make themselves popular because, in addition to dams and motorways, they are committed to bringing fast Internet, television channels, stadiums, and entertainment.

In order to finance the works, money needs to be lent to Africa, and China also offers this service as it has a huge surplus. The Asian nation is now the largest investor in the world and projects in Africa, though expensive and numerous, constitute less than 5% of the total for Beijing. In this way, even more 'Made in China' products enter Africa, new favourable markets are opened up and the entire supply chain is managed. The product arrives in Africa, is unloaded in a port also managed by them, is transported on roads built by the Chinese and, to top it all off, ends up in Chinese shops that then complete the retail transaction.

Notoriously with Africa, the risk of money not being returned is high, so Beijing sometimes guarantees reimbursement through the right to exploit the land, fishing permissions, or the use of a port. However, all this is done without colonising, and without seeking to impose any of their models, certainly not Communism, nor Confucianism. China doesn't dictate policy to any African government, doesn't care about human rights, doesn't want exclusivity and does business with any dictator. Consequently, it's undermining countries that had historically had influence in the region.

The only area where the Asian nation loses to the West is in appeal. Many Africans go to study in China but dream of America.

The days in Guinea were not nearly as demanding as I had feared, but the penultimate one was tense because I had to take the Covid test to leave. The agreement had been for the doctor to come to my hotel early in the morning, so I waited a couple of hours, after which my telephone chase began since the vague messages announcing his arrival just weren't convincing.

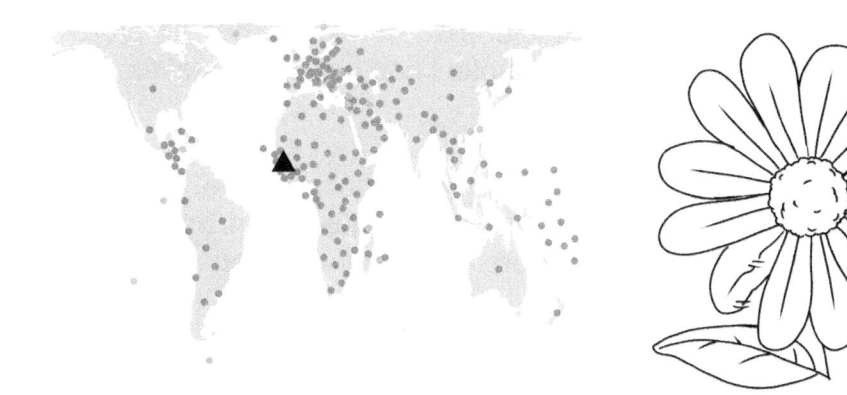

After another two hours, I asked him where he was so that I could get to him and set off. Nothing. He finally gave me another appointment at a booth in the middle of the street where for a fee they help people fill out forms on paper or online. The doctor appeared and took a sample from my nose on top of a filthy rubbish bin with chickens strutting around it. I paid and he left without even apologising. I told him I would be at his laboratory the next morning to wait and wouldn't move without the result. I turned up at the agreed time and after four hours of waiting I received my piece of paper. I had held out well until those last moments, and now I was happy to leave again.

That night on my flight to Tunis I was squeezed between a large man and a portly lady whom I asked to get up several times in order to go to the toilet, much to her bewilderment. As I tried to climb over her one more time, she looked at me in confusion, whereupon I had an inspiration. I told her clearly in French that I was going to the toilet and her face lit up with joy at the discovery: she was bursting!

In Tunis, I was among the unfortunate ones selected to be tested again on arrival, even though I was in transit to France, and they were so slow that I almost missed my connection. I arrived in Paris completely exhausted, without having slept, and when they asked me where I had come from at immigration, I honestly couldn't remember. I was so tired that I couldn't even say the first thing that came into my head. Any answer would have been fine, rather than my extremely long hesitation, and they stopped me, wanting to see my various documents. I probably looked like I was under the influence of some substance when I had actually just gone gaga all on my own! With my Italian passport, three vaccinations and a molecular test, however, I had no problem and finally reached the hotel I had booked to rest for the night.

In Guinea, they still hate France because she left in a rage, taking with her even the last desk, pen and office painting. All relations were abruptly severed because

Conakry, unique among the French colonies, courageously and recklessly refused to join a 'Community' that would unite the French-speaking and French-cultured peoples. They had wanted immediate independence, which had sounded like ingratitude to France, while for Conakry it had seemed cowardly of them to cut off all support.

France had dreamed of uniting its territories with a railway from Dakar, the capital of Senegal, to Djibouti. It wanted to assimilate these populations, introduce them to 'civilisation,' and turn them into true French citizens. A very different model from the English, who had never aspired to this. For them, it had been enough to rule and so they left the local elites in power, acting as their representatives. However, the British also had ambitions to unite their vast territories with a railway from Cairo to Cape Town. It was a project comparable in length and difficulty to the construction of the Trans-Siberian Railway in Russia, or to the huge network developed in India by the British themselves. But here in Africa, the project remained unstarted.

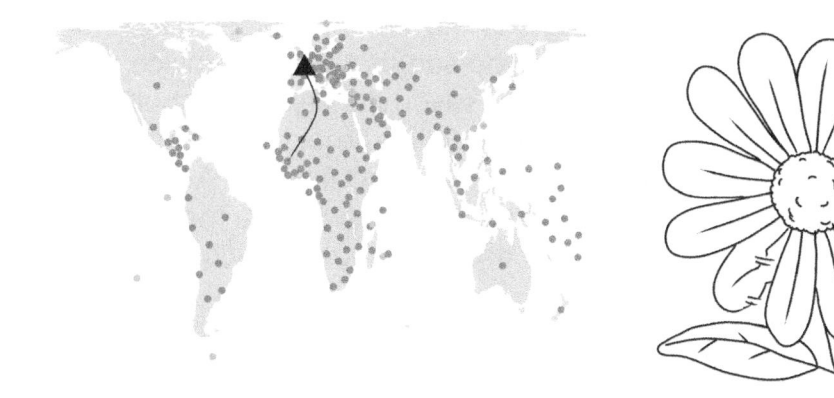

Since the 1960s, on the other hand, two countries theoretically opposed to colonisation have intervened heavily in African affairs, the Soviet Union by supporting the various communist groups, and the United States with the intention of bringing democracy but in reality, supporting the worst dictators, as long as they were anti-communist. The future will show what impact will be made on the continent by China, a dictatorial country in its own right, and Turkey, which obviously has historical and colonial contacts with North Africa as well as having the Islamic card to play and being very present in Somalia. Then finally, there is India throughout East Africa and in South Africa.

My travel school in this part of the world was over. It is the most difficult continent to explore but it is the one that can offer the greatest culture shock. Once in a lifetime, if you have the chance, it is good to go and take a punch in the stomach to see and understand with your own eyes. So many say they can imagine suffering and despair, but their understanding is limited by remaining so distant. These same people despise the rich world for not helping enough, they accuse the media of not reporting sufficient news from Africa. I, on the other hand, accuse those who could visit, yet choose never to travel. Nothing is in the shadows, nothing is swept under the carpet, and everything is in view if you go in person. You have access almost everywhere; this is not North Korea.

Just as from the sofa at home, watching TV, you can't properly comprehend the desert or the savannah, even if someone passionately tells you about them, you have to spend a few days without electricity and walk a distance to collect water to understand how pleasant it is to have both immediately available in your house. That way, the abstract talk about defeating hunger in the world becomes concrete and your anger mounts as you see that $2 can provide the mosquito net that would have saved the child's life, but you realise that not even a trillion dollars in aid over time has been enough to make a decisive leap forward. A hospital in the middle of nowhere is useless, you need a road to get there, a school to train new doctors, a power station nearby, and so on. If you pause a little longer, you realise that even with the $2 mosquito net, things get complicated because by donating them, you put the African companies that were producing them out of business. Nothing is as simple and automatic as the average Westerner thinks from their couch, not even the direct distribution of food, because hungry people do not line up neatly.

On the other hand, in the Central African Republic, in the middle of nowhere, I had the pleasant surprise of seeing children going to school with UNICEF backpacks. Fatima was attending a class organised by the Red Cross in the Afghan mountains. I too had cynically thought 'Who knows where the money ends up', but as I travelled, I was delighted to discover that sometimes it reaches just the right place.

Regardless of aid, you will only realise by going in person that you can be very happy even in extreme poverty, though of course, you are not happy because you are poor, you are happy despite being poor because when you have all the truly important things, the rest count for little. This triviality becomes a concrete lesson when you observe it with your own eyes and are prompted to focus your efforts on the essentials.

Another of the experiences of Africa is that of enjoying certain privileges and feeling like minor guest stars. You amusedly accept invitations from people who want to strut their stuff in front of their neighbours because they 'hang out' with foreigners. But be prepared for the consequences of these honours. If they treat you like a human ATM, that's because you are one, you are incredibly rich compared to those who ask. Give cheerfully though, because you will certainly see the effects of your generosity and you'll appreciate why everyone who has ever been to Africa changes their profile picture on Facebook for one from that trip.

You'll feel embarrassed when someone mistreats other people and pushes them away from you to please you. Laugh at being taken for a ride, especially if you have an African as your guide. Take him out of the ambiguous situation of seeming to take your side if there is a minor dispute or bad service, give him carte blanche to say that you are demanding and a pain in the ass, and that he too is fed up with you.

Do your homework, and don't arrive without knowing the history of the country, the religion, and the customs, rather than just asking your guide 20 questions. Even on safari, it's good to have done your homework and tried to get to know about the animals and vegetation, both to be respectful and for personal convenience. If all you have to go on is your cousin's opinion that the park was splendid, you might end up in a place where the animals have migrated. Find out how many other parks he has visited to determine that this was the best.

Form your own idea about colonialism which certainly was a dark page in history that so deeply affects relationships. Personally, I doubt it was the main cause of Africa's troubles. Ethiopia and Liberia remained free, yet they are among the worst in some respects. African borders are sometimes ridiculous, for example, the great Congo has a strip of land that creeps into Zambia partly because the Europeans wanted to get to a hunting ground. In general, though, they are more logical than they may appear. If you look at the straight-lined borders of the United States, they will seem absurd, just as, for the opposite reason, the jagged borders of Europe itself do when they follow no geography at all. Italy has a region where more German is spoken than Italian, Belgium is an invention, there are ridiculous micronations, in Switzerland four languages are spoken, and so on. The absurdity lies in the borders having been made for others (not a single African was present at the Berlin conference) but not in the way they were made.

You will see with your own eyes that Africa is racist, and its society has castes. In some countries, women use bleach to look lighter with great health risks. I didn't expect this, I thought it was a bad Western attitude, but then on reflection, if there is still so much racism in Europe and the US, how could I expect it not to be there elsewhere? To discover all this, however, you need to visit in person. And rest assured, going there is easier than you think. Phileas Fogg was the archetypical methodical man accustomed to comfort, who had once fired his butler because the water for shaving was a degree too cold. Yet, once he set off on his journey, he adapted.

From Paris I travelled to the **Dominican Republic (173),** landing in Punta Cana, a tourist spot with luxury resorts and beautiful beaches. As usual, I was alone, didn't want to spend too much and wasn't on holiday, so I stayed for a day and then decided to explore other parts of the island.

They boast here that they were the first colony in America, Christopher Columbus is still a hero to be celebrated, the bringer of the true God and civilisation, while elsewhere he is known as the one who started the trouble and extermination of the natives. Whichever way you look at it, I find it absurd that everyone knows the name of his three ships by heart, while few have a clear understanding of the history of the explorers' encounters with the local people.

In this country, the enemies are not the Spaniards but their neighbours, the Haitians with whom they share this most populated island in the Americas. Racism towards them is fierce. The Dominicans pride themselves on being white and Christian, while the Haitians are black and believe in witchcraft. In the past, there have actually been massacres, most notably that of 1937 when at least 20,000 Haitians were slaughtered in a few days. They singled them out (proving that the difference in skin colour is not as clear-cut as the Dominicans say) by asking suspicious people to pronounce the word *perejil* (parsley), which is difficult for those who are French speaking like Haitians and not for those whose mother tongue is Spanish.

More recently, the constitution was retroactively amended causing Dominicans with Haitian blood to lose their nationality, and tens of thousands were deported to Haiti where they had perhaps never before set foot in their lives. The real independence celebration here is the liberation from Haiti, not from Spain.

The person who hosted me in Santo Domingo was Italian, his only requirement was that no chicken or eggs be eaten in the house because he had grown up on a farm where they had eaten every dying chicken, along with lots of eggs. Now that he was grown and independent, he had sworn he would never eat one again.

A cart selling sugarcane juice stood in front of the house and I would drink one every evening with some Italian pensioners who had been enjoying the cheap life and pleasant climate there for years. The chatter was largely humdrum, the most interesting topic revolving around the strange businesses that the guy who had rented me the room would suggest, which then led us to reflect on what hard work it was to be a street-seller.

There is an Italian expression, 'pulling the cart' which means that someone is living a harsh and difficult life, but I had now changed my mind about the application of this saying. The problem isn't the hard work of pulling the cart and selling outside in the sun, because there are hard jobs even in rich and developed countries. The issue is everything that comes after work. In Europe, at least, when the hard shift is over, you return to a comfortable home, there's a social security system and you have a pension. Those who 'pull the cart' in the Dominican Republic live in an uncomfortable house, have no health protection, and are forced to continue this backbreaking work even when they are old. Their only hope of any sort of pension comes from their children's appreciation.

As I was saying goodbye to my landlord, he actually suggested that we open a brewery together, which made me laugh as I had to admit that the pensioners had been right. I headed for the airport and my next flight, which was to Caracas in **Venezuela (174)**, one of the last dangerous destinations I had left, though the situation had improved recently.

Italians are not required to obtain visas in advance for entry here, but at immigration they insisted that I show a return flight to Italy rather than just a flight out of the country. All I had was a return flight to the Dominican Republic and I couldn't understand why they were so interested in where I was going after I had left their soil. I was rescued by the person behind me in the queue, who also had a return flight to a destination other than their home country, and spoke Spanish so was able to respond to the absurd requests.

I underwent the compulsory Covid test on arrival, then for the next two days in Caracas I wandered around without too many problems and returned to the hotel before dark. I only stayed in neighbourhoods that were considered safe, though in fact, most prostitution took place in those areas, usually close to churches, because the sex workers felt free from danger there! By now I was used to looking at things from another's perspective, just like I had learned concerning the taxi drivers. Venezuelan money no longer had any value and you had to pay in US dollars. In the metro, the turnstiles were open, and no one would buy a ticket.

This nation, prosperous until recently but now completely devastated by insane policies, was another lesson for me. In Italy I had been tempted every now and then to say, 'Everything's terrible, it can't get worse than this', yet I think Venezuela is the perfect example of how there's always something to lose. Once Italians had emigrated here in search of a better life, yet today millions of Venezuelans have flocked to neighbouring Colombia and dream of reaching the United States or Europe.

A guy I met online through a mutual acquaintance came to see me on the afternoon of the first day and played down the situation by saying 'Every country has its troubles', a convenient phrase that allows you to gloss over certain issues, but decidedly out of place in this circumstance since here it is the police themselves who organise the kidnappings as they are desperate for money, and fathers steal to buy medicine for their children on the black market. When you receive your salary in 'wastepaper' and are hungry, or when you see that there are doctors in the hospital but there is a shortage of medicine, the concept of just and unjust changes.

My tactic for getting around without too much danger was to have my mobile phone in one pocket, then a $100 note and a $20 note in the other. If someone had pointed a gun at me, I would have given everything to them straight away, and the $100 note would make someone happy. If I had felt I was in danger, I would have played it by ear, going to the person I thought was threatening me, and saying that I was aware of the difficult time in Venezuela and that maybe I could help by giving what I had in my pocket, which was $20. There was a strong possibility that he would then forego any bad intentions. However, someone like me doesn't stand out, and as long as I kept quiet and didn't take photos, I might as well have been local.

My goal after Caracas was to fly to Canaima, visit the national park and reach the mythical Angel Falls waterfall, the highest in the world, at almost a kilometre, with over 800 m of uninterrupted waterfall. The domestic flight terminal was quite dangerous, as the internal passages from one area to another were closed, so you had to go outside into what had become the perfect places for organising robberies and kidnappings. At the destination, however, you were immersed in a quiet community that still lived well thanks to Russian tourists in search of a better climate and adventure.

It took me a whole day to reach the waterfall, because the river water was low, and it was necessary to dismount from the small boat and push to get over the sandbanks or other obstacles. I felt a little guilty slathering myself with sunscreen while the poor boatman struggled, but I had soon realised that pushing was dangerous due to the strong current below and there were rocks you could get your feet stuck in and easily break a leg. Nevertheless, halfway down we were all in the water as we had to lighten the boat and push. My socks were holed from friction with the stones in the river. Pushing with shoes was impossible and bare feet were even more slippery, so the socks offered the best performance.

I slept the night in a hammock with immense pleasure and the next morning we began the ascent to the observatory on the waterfall. It was a magnificent spectacle: in front of me a unique spectacle of nature, behind me a Venezuelan guy who was proposing marriage to his girlfriend.

The next day I decided to spend $400 to get one of the four seats on the helicopter that flies over the top of the waterfall. What had taken two days of effort to get to the base could now be covered in a few minutes and from the top one could appreciate the many waterfalls that cascade down from these very special rock formations. It was the ninth year of my trip, and yet, on this plateau immersed in the forest, the wonder reached one of its peaks. Such a panorama cannot be had anywhere else.

I went back to the Dominican Republic for a few days and from there I flew to Cartagena in **Colombia (175)**, a wonderful city. By the second day my nose was running a bit, so I went for a test and, as feared, I had Covid. The law required you to self-isolate and that was all, so once I realised that I was doing okay, I had two options in front of me: call my insurance company and let them take care of everything, including financially, or do it myself. I was afraid that the insurance company would send me to hospital or some government sanatorium, so I took a room in a central hotel.

It was an international chain hotel, where they spoke English and were open 24/7 with room service. This way I would have any assistance I needed. I told the hostel owner that I was positive and went away to isolate myself, fortunately I had slept alone. It was a long ten days, and my room was a mess because I wouldn't let the cleaning lady in. I could see people going to the beach from the window while I was bored to death. However, I wasn't suffering at all from the Covid itself, so there was no point in complaining.

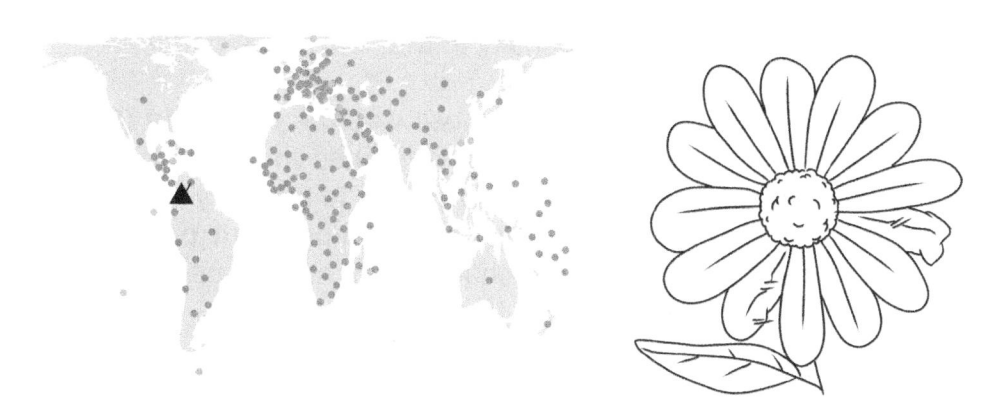

Once negative, I flew to Medellin, the city of the famous drug trafficker Pablo Escobar, where you can take a themed tour. It would be like being in Sicily and taking a tour of the mafia sites, where the various attacks took place, the prisons, and the streets where the bosses lived. Controversial, but after seeing a museum dedicated to Stalin in Georgia, Mao's mummy, tours of communism in Warsaw complete with a badge, I was no longer surprised.

Escobar has killed and tortured a huge number of people, perpetrated a terrorist attack on an airliner, and tarnished Colombia's reputation around the world, yet in some quarters he is considered a hero, a sort of Robin Hood, albeit still an outlaw, who helped the poor and loved his fellow citizens. Particularly in working-class neighbourhoods it was his criminal organisation that imposed law, order and support, as is often the case in slums around the world.

I'd had the same feeling of disbelief in Somalia, where the notorious modern-day pirates are supported by part of the population. These criminals, who are certainly not as likeable as in the Disney films, bring order to the territorial waters of a nation that fails to exercise its sovereignty. The pirates sustain this very dubious narrative, saying they attack ships that pollute or fish illegally, taking advantage of the power vacuum. They set themselves up as the heroes of Somalia.

The last few days in Colombia I was again able to organise my next trip well in advance. Having contracted Covid, the risk of testing positive again in the following months would be minimal, so I optimistically booked a cruise, the activity considered most risky at the start of the pandemic.

The first stage after the illness was the **Bahamas (176)** where I had already been several times for poker tournaments. On those occasions, in addition to the entry fees having been covered, I had also enjoyed a beautiful, paid hotel room. But now my life had changed, as had my needs and I chose a six-bed dormitory in the cheapest part of the capital. The taxi from the airport wouldn't even take me there, the driver claiming that I had probably fallen for some woman's trap, and once lured there I would be robbed. But the dormitory existed, I was the only customer, and the room was horrible but very cheap.

My going from hero to zero was not limited to the comparison with past accommodation. A Swiss friend, who I had met on a trip to Armenia, had moved here a few years ago and become the manager of a bank. I only realised exactly what that meant when I arrived at his office and was ushered by deferential staff into a large, luxurious office to meet with my impeccably dressed friend whose whole demeanour oozed success, all this whilst I was wearing a T-shirt and shorts after having travelled half the island by bus and walked the last kilometre. I was treated like a real king during the day that I was with him. He took me to the gym and to a restaurant at a resort where the membership cost an insane amount of money, then to a party at a multi-million-dollar house, and to a restaurant where the appetiser cost more than my entire budget for all the days in the Bahamas.

The travel school had opened my eyes to poverty, a banal concept but one that needs to be investigated on its various levels. A person is considered poor if they don't have the money to go on holiday, but the same description is also used for someone who doesn't have a pair of shoes for when the road is hot, or who is actually hungry.

Now, on the other hand, I was discovering levels of wealth that I had not even imagined, for example, owning a house that allows you to accommodate 50 people in luxury, dining every night served by a personal chef who brings a dedicated menu to your terrace. First class on an aeroplane pampers you, but in the end, you leave and arrive with the others, but these were people who could afford to leave as they pleased by private plane and on their return, immigration would go to their house to register them.

I was a kind of Cinderella and once the evening in luxury was over, I would go back to the dormitory where only the landlord was waiting for me, very kind but always drunk and high. On the last evening I returned on foot and was wandering around in the vicinity of the house when I began to doubt Google maps and realised, I was lost. A rough looking face appeared at a window and said in a gloomy voice, 'Hey, you're in the next street on the right'. My host was a drunk but very popular in the vicinity, and the neighbours knew who I was and where I slept. On arriving home, he took me to the only drugstore that was open at night, we bought a bottle of rum, and he told me he had been a diplomat in Switzerland but had been fired for wrongdoing.

The next day, his father accompanied me to the airport, an austere big man who spoke ill of his son during the entire journey, calling him a hopeless drunkard. I did my best to defend him, partly out of principle, partly because I liked him. At the end of the ride, despite such sharp words, he told me that the ride was free for me. Of course, I insisted on paying, but he left without offering any explanation. Here was a father who, despite everything, still loved his son deep down.

When I arrived in **Jamaica (177)**, my sleeping quarters were even worse: I slept with a lady who had rented me the sofa in the entrance hallway, the only privacy being a kind of curtain behind which I could change. A metre from my bed was the television which a small child watched continuously. I had chosen such accommodation because it was run by an Austrian lady with good references. She had fallen in love with a Jamaican man who had abandoned her as soon as she had the baby, so my evenings were spent listening to the same sob story over and over. The frustration must have been strong since she had sold what she owned in Austria, bought a house, changed her life completely for a man and now found herself alone in Jamaica.

In the face of such situations, so frequent in some cultures, I wondered whether patriarchy, in its oppression of women, at least had the value of empowering men. Once the bride was bought and removed from her clan, it was difficult to abandon her. The woman would be absorbed into the male's family circle which is why the advocates of these 'arrangements' deemed it right that the family should be involved, and that marriage could not be the free choice of the two protagonists. In some traditions, then, to make the abandonment of one's family less of a traumatic and drastic change for the woman, she would end up marrying a first cousin. The damage to the health of the children was, however, enormous, just look at Pakistan today where the custom is still widely practised and genetic disorders are prevalent. In some African traditions, and therefore to some extent also Jamaican, the man is instead freer to run away and back out, because the woman remains with her birth family who will help her raise the child.

There is one constant I have found at every latitude: the husband is older than the wife. Of course, there is biology involved, but I suspect it is so as not to circumvent the two 'rules', namely, man in charge of woman, and older rules younger.

The Bob Marley Museum is the most fun one I have ever seen. They would sometimes make you sing and dance, and they treat you like a child, but you leave having learned about the history and impact of his songs in the country. Marijuana is very much present, here called *ganja* using the Hindi term because it arrived with the Indians who had been brought by the British. For some Jamaicans, it is part of a religious ritual, marijuana supposedly bestowing wisdom since it grew on the tomb of Solomon, the wise king par excellence. No stigma is associated with smoking, so any time is the right time. The result is a lot of idleness and slow-motion movements.

In Iceland, until 1989, it was forbidden to drink beer, while any other alcoholic beverage was allowed. This seems counter-intuitive, but they feared that beer, with its low alcohol content, was not in fact perceived as a real drink and was therefore being consumed continually starting in the morning. Previously this had seemed a crazy and anti-liberal rule to me, but after seeing Jamaica and its marijuana, the rule no longer appeared so wild, just constraining.

But the real protagonists of this island are the freemen par excellence: the pirates. These characters are historically different from how they have been portrayed. Perhaps they really did have numerous wooden limbs because there was a carpenter on board and not a surgeon. Perhaps the parrot kept them company, but otherwise, they were just sailors who were fed up with the hard life on board and chose a shortcut to riches. Sometimes all it took was one assault to change a life. After all, even for soldiers – regulars and mercenaries – plunder has always been one of the great incentives to participate in war. On board a pirate ship, the distribution of booty was strictly regulated by a code of ethics that even provided assistance for widows.

Jamaica was a perfect hideout, like all the Caribbean in some ways. The seas were calm and easy to navigate for most of the year, and the seabed was shallow, so it was hard for warships to chase them. Finding pirates amongst those islands would have been like looking for a needle in a haystack. Morgan, a famous pirate born a slave, lured sailors by wearing gold and jewellery and showing how rich one could become by joining him. He ended up becoming governor of Jamaica! My only disappointment was discovering that gambling on board was banned...

My hostess's young son seemed very sad to see me leave. I'd played with him every day and who knows how many other father figures had come into his life only to suddenly disappear.

On arrival in **Trinidad and Tobago (178)**, I discovered that the famous carnival had been cancelled because of Covid. The custom dates back to the time of the French, who had in turn learned it from the slaves, who had used this event as a way to make fun of their masters. The islands had then become British after having also been Spanish. This mixture of peoples was completed by the arrival of Indians who had been driven by poverty to land here. They had falsely given the surnames of higher caste brahmins and warriors on arrival, and since no one in this new land knew any better, they enjoyed this new status freely. Actually, both originally and to this day, they were farmers who soon managed to take ownership of much of the arable land. This is the main reason why there's always been bad blood between Indians and the other peoples.

My host, on the other hand, was of Italian origin and did his best not to let me miss out on Carnival. In the hostel on the evening of Shrove Tuesday, all the bottles that had already been opened were taken from the small bar and the alcohol was poured into a huge pot, creating a mega cocktail without following any recipe. People drank to get drunk, but the taste was not bad. The music came from a mobile phone to which big plastic cups were attached to act as amplifiers and the sound was so loud that it reached neighbouring houses. Apart from at parties, music has become a private affair for us as we use headphones more and more often. In the Caribbean, on the other hand, it is always something to be shared. Listening to music alone is for losers, and it probably also seems quite lame to travel alone.

As you may have guessed, personally, I consider a 'solo' trip to be a learning experience. As I reached the end of my adventure, I felt I could confirm, or rather reinforce every statement I have made in previous years: it's really a little proving of yourself, you experience the pleasure of being in your own company, you don't care about other people's stares when you eat in a restaurant, but most importantly you enjoy doing as you please. You can choose everything, there are no compromises, you eat at the time you prefer, and you take part in the activities you genuinely want. As a kid, you were dragged by the group, perhaps to a disco where you didn't want to go. As an adult, this occurs a little less frequently, but on a solo trip it never happens. You also experience the impact of a new place without another person's filter, without your partner, or friends who start by saying that a place is not that nice and so condition your thinking a little. Finally, without anyone who knows you, you can leave that version of yourself at home and show up with the face you prefer to wear that day. Starting from nothing, you can try things out and perhaps discover how you can be better than you are used to.

Trinidad and Tobago offer one of the few air links with **Guyana (179)**, a nation of six distinct ethnic groups: Portuguese, Europeans (excepting Portuguese), Africans, the indigenous population, Indians and Chinese. There are multiple Guianas that make up what we know today simply as Guyana. One has been encompassed by Venezuela and speaks Spanish, another is within Brazil, so the language is Portuguese; and then there's French Guiana, which is the last large colony on the mainland. Finally, there are two that are independent nations and add another two languages – Suriname, which is Dutch Guiana, and finally English Guyana, which I was just visiting.

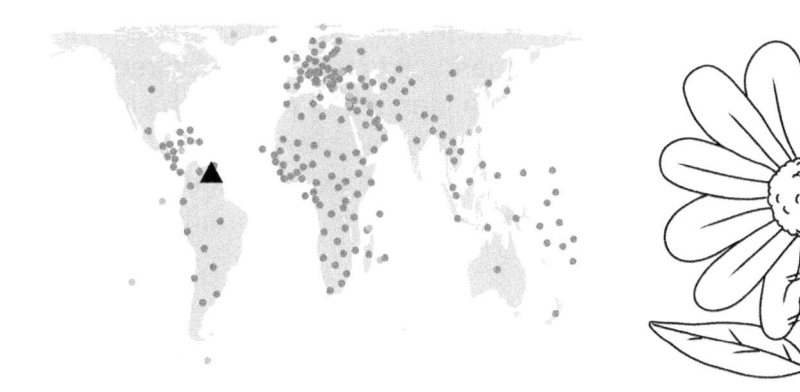

This coastline was colonised very late, and apart from the strip of land near the sea, nothing is very hospitable. Behind it lies an impenetrable forest where the rivers running into it are difficult to navigate. Tourists can only visit some of the places by plane because even today there are hardly any roads. The forest is impressive seen from above, you can only see rare breaks in the vegetation where mines are being dug.

In 1978, in the secrecy of those places, a US religious cult ordered its followers to commit suicide and there were almost 1,000 deaths. Only 9/11 had a more serious death toll among American civilians.

I'd had a bad night in my hostel because an American guy had spiralled out of control. In flashes of lucidity, he said he had run out of his medication and therefore had not been able to sleep for two days. The way of handling this situation in places like this is usually a mixture of fright and magic. Mental illness is treated with medication in a few countries, while elsewhere it comes down to isolation and beatings. In the past, exorcism was used to terrorise the sick person to such an extent that they would stay quiet for a while.

The next day, I took a small plane to the Kaieteur Falls, which dropped 200 m and carried an enormous amount of water. An Indian girl at lunch told the group that her brother had recently committed suicide by throwing himself off a bridge; she told me that this water was magnetic. Now, it may have been because of the difficult night, but I was left with a strong feeling of dread. In Georgetown, the capital, the person who was taking me back to the hotel stopped by the roadside to show me some plants that had black stems which I had to watch out for because they were used for black magic. I felt surrounded by strange situations in this other-worldly place that perhaps is more affecting than you might expect.

From Guyana I went to **Suriname (180)**. In 1975, at the time of independence, anyone who wanted could become a citizen of the Netherlands. The boy I was walking around with had scolded his grandfather for choosing the new country. Here too I found a mixture of peoples and religions, indeed there was even a mosque attached to a synagogue. Jews had come directly from Holland, as had Muslim Indonesians who were under Dutch rule at the time. I got to know a girl who had never met her grandparents, which really made an impression on me. Here I was, flying all over the world, and she hadn't had the chance to go to Indonesia even once in her life.

In the forest, I was able to visit a community of *Maroons*. They were slaves who had escaped from their masters and had managed to find refuge in the impenetrable vegetation. They had formed communities there, joining the natives and had started new lives in freedom. Sadly, even today the *Maroons* are discriminated against because they are considered less civilised. Just like the Aborigines in Australia, they don't fit into a normal labour market. All it takes is one of the frequent bereavements in the village and they disappear to mourn for weeks without a word. They follow tribal law, and the violence against children and women is still brutal.

In **Barbados (181)** I slept in a house that had a huge 'Not for Sale' sign on the wall, apparently because there were con men going around pretending to be the owners. Houses here fetch astronomical prices because the islands are less prone to adverse weather phenomena due to their geographical location. There are no cyclones and no volcanoes, so there is no risk of the house being destroyed.

The guy who managed the beds spoke a form of English that I understood with difficulty. He insisted on communicating in the local creole language. The slaves, coming from distant areas, had found it hard to communicate with each other, and so over time, a new language had been born for practical purposes. Initially, this dialect, full of terms from different languages, abounding in simplifications, and with minimal grammar, was called a pidgin. It then became a creole when the pidgin had been adopted as their mother tongue by a generation. In Jamaica there is a creole made famous by Bob Marley's songs, in Haiti, there is a French-based creole, and in the Solomon Islands, it's called One Tok (one talk, 'one language'), with an English base, Melanesian grammar and so on. Especially in Melanesia, where it's still common not to understand those just a few kilometres away, it is very useful.

English is the official language, or at least one of them, in a quarter of the world's nations. The Chinese elite study English, and in India the 400 million people who already speak English will soon be joined by the other billion. If there is one certainty that this trip around the world has given me, it is the importance of studying English. Italy is incredibly behind in this respect.

On the last day, I was joined by a group of people I had connected with on Facebook without ever having met in person. They were serial travellers, admirers of little-travelled countries, flag lovers and 'bag collectors' just like me! We were all there for a cruise that was ultra commercial and touristy but had been tempting for us because it would stop in each of the six small independent nations of the Caribbean. I went to embarkation calmly, as I had recently had Covid, so a double test to get on board was not a concern for me. The current very low price had also played a part in us being here – less than $300 for a week, with excursions and drinks costing extra. In essence, it was seven days in the Caribbean for less than $700.

The first stopover was **Grenada (182)**, a small island that had been invaded by the United States in 1983 after a communist coup. The pretext was the protection of a few hundred American students who were taking courses here because their grades had been too low to be admitted to the Stars and Stripes' universities.

It was my first time on a cruise and travelling became simple with no more Covid rules or cancelled airline flights. Once on board, I sailed at night with all the comforts of home and in the morning, I was where I wanted to be. The only problem was that staying only a few hours in a country feels awkward. For the past two years I had already accelerated by my standards because I was driven by the desire to complete, but was cruising too much of a rush? I think everyone would tend towards 'Yes'. This way you see the world too quickly.

But on reflection, in the end it was more than fine with me. The islands are really small and sparsely populated, and also quite similar to each other. Using population as a parameter, spending six hours on an island that has 100,000 inhabitants (and they actually have even fewer) is equivalent to spending 14,000 times the six hours in China, which has over 1.4 billion inhabitants. So, six hours in Antigua and Barbuda is equal to ten years in China. And if we use the extent of territory as a parameter, well, Russia is on average over 30,000 times larger. The six hours on each small island becomes proportionally a good 20 years. To summarise, when you want to travel around the entire world, some compromises are necessary and these are the right places to hurry, both out of necessity and because, on balance, it does make sense. The truth is, if any of these islands were not an independent nation, I wouldn't even go there.

There were 15 of us on the boat chasing the EVERYCOUNTRY goal and in **Antigua and Barbuda (183)** we celebrated the milestone of 100 countries visited by a member of this group. As I stepped off the ship to visit the driest of islands (even home to cacti), I received the news that Syria was reopening its borders and slowly resuming the authorisation of tourists. As my thoughts focused on rushing to the Middle East, it was curious to discover that the shops in the capital's main streets were run by Syrians and Lebanese, often Christians, who had emigrated to South America and the Caribbean to avoid persecution.

On the third day we visited **St Kitts and Nevis (184)**, the smallest country in all the Americas. The landing of a 1,000 people on a handkerchief of land has an impact. I've read all kinds of things under the definition of 'sustainable tourism', but the cruise certainly has a strong impact on the land, nature and people. These islands see the negative effect but prefer to carry on because they earn a lot from the big ships, despite the fact that this form of tourism is run by Western companies that take most of the revenue.

Cruises are a package deal where everything is included or provided by them. When I join group tours there is probably a balance in profit between the tour provider – often a large Western company – and the people in the places visited. And when I travel alone my money goes straight into the pockets of those who run the hostel, drive the cars, or sell food on the road. But I have no clear opinion on what is right or wrong. Each community has to assess for themselves the disadvantages and benefits of having these giant monsters coming into port laden with hordes of tourists who take pictures of any nonsense.

I don't despise mass tourism, on the contrary, the more people travel, the happier I am. Even on board a ship, where you never leave your comfort zone and only seek relaxation by the sea, some small thing still remains afterwards, and those who set off just once a year attracted by the Christmas markets perhaps also learn something.

In the past, some travelled for business, others for pilgrimage. The school of travel was a very rare commodity, and the children of rich Europeans sometimes came to Italy for culture. It was elitist tourism. In the 19th century there were the first cruises on the Nile, Thomas Cook offered the possibility of visiting some of Europe by train, the carriages created by Mr Pullman allowed people to sleep on board, there was the famous Orient Express, but they were always luxuries. Today, tourism lowers prices and makes travel affordable. I get the impression that those who hate mass tourism (which is almost everyone if you believe what they say), consider themselves to be part of an elite, the only ones allowed to enjoy the beauties of the world. Essentially, their own trips are fine, while those made by others ruin nature, landscapes and places.

In **Saint Vincent and the Grenadines (185)** an Italian American I had become friendly with on the cruise bought a piece of jewellery that had cost $6,000. Here was a huge expenditure made locally that I would never have thought of. I was in the worst cabin with no porthole, I was alone, and I was trimming down my expenses, thanks to the advice of other serial travellers. I discovered that by using someone's American address you could save even more, then I joined a mailing list that gave further discounts and so on. But there were those on board who were bringing wealth to the places they visited.

Besides precious stones, the locals would try to sell tourists all kinds of trinkets, including cheap beads. For me, it seemed a wonderful reciprocation since the Europeans had been allowed to explore some of the coasts of Africa and America by gifting glittering beads to the locals who wanted to stand out in the tribe. Now it was they who were exploiting this human instinct to feel beautiful and special by showering Westerners with beads.

Dominica (186), the penultimate stop, is unique in the Caribbean because this island is still rich in wildlife. Colonised long after the others, a sort of reserve survives here where a few thousand Caribs live. This ethnic group arrived in Dominica about 1,000 years ago, subjugated and exterminated the indigenous *Arawak* people, and took over the island until the arrival of the Europeans. Today there is deep racism against them, and they are mistreated.

Unfortunately, even on cruise ships some people are

treated worse than others. Different rules apply on board depending on the nationality of the worker with wages, rest shifts, and number of hours per day varying. This seems, and indeed is, profoundly unfair, but if it were not so, some nationalities would not find work as they are hired because they cost less or have less protection.

The last stop was **Saint Lucia (187)**, the only country in the world named after a woman, and once again, the name of a saint. Even the subdivision of the island was into 'parishes'. The cruise was coming to an end, and I was sad to leave that holiday atmosphere, the group, and the wonder of the rapid dawn and dusk at the equator.

The only pleasure was getting away from so many people always taking pictures. There were endless snaps, and continuous duplications of photos already taken. I understand that they are precious memories, and the holiday is a moment of joy that it is a pleasure to relive over time, but I recommend taking 90% fewer photos and then, once home, eliminating a further 50%. At that point, the remaining photos will be important, they will stimulate the memory and you will really look at them again. And if you have fewer to show, you won't get so many fake smiles from friends who are too polite to tell you they're bored. If it doesn't come naturally to you, do what I do and ask yourself before you shoot if you would be willing to spend a euro for that click. Only press the button on your phone or camera if it has value.

Now Syria awaited me, but there was one last hurdle before leaving the ship: the Covid swab. Those who tested positive would have to stay on board locked in their cabin for ten days, which was almost certainly another of the reasons my cruise had been so cheap.

I disembarked in Barbados and after a long series of flights, arrived in Lebanon from where one of my final adventures would begin. The 193-nation goal had been ambitious and had prompted, even 'forced' me to travel more and more despite the pandemic. Now the approaching finish line was sending me the opposite message as once I had achieved the objective, I would be obliged to stop!

In Beirut I stayed in a small hotel where I met the owner who was preparing for a political career which meant that having a foothold in the hospitality industry was a big advantage to him. A great man, the sort that takes care of others, must have a place to gather, where he can be the centre of attention at any event. The proprietor is in a position to host a wedding, a birthday, or a party, but more importantly he can organise private meetings for others. He is the one who seats people at the restaurant table so that they can have a discussion, and he can act as a peacemaker.

Numerous buses crossed the border from Beirut to bring home Syrians who had been working in Lebanon during the war. The border was a dangerous place for them because everyone knew they had their hard-earned money on them. I thought back to those who claimed to have seen immigrants in Italy with thousands of euros in cash. Maybe they were telling the truth, but the impression that they are not poor is false: they simply had everything they owned with them.

Syria (188) was a tourist country before the war, but nowadays it's destroyed. The damage had already been evident in the vicinity of Damascus, but walking around the country was a continuum of rubble, gutted houses, and piles of asphalt. At first there was the mesmerising 'waterfall effect', where you couldn't take your eyes off that spectacle, those poor women emerging from those places, and the clothes hanging from what was left of the balconies. Then the 'zebra effect' I'd experienced on the safaris took over, the destruction blended into the landscape, and I no longer cared, just as a child asking for money no longer upset me after months. It is probably normal to become so cynical, it is a form of self-defence, like a doctor who goes home peacefully despite having lost a patient.

The Islamic State has destroyed some of the monuments and treasures because in their narrow-mindedness many works are considered blasphemous, for example, the temples of Palmyra dedicated to other Gods. In general, images and statues are forbidden in Islam, as is playing musical instruments.

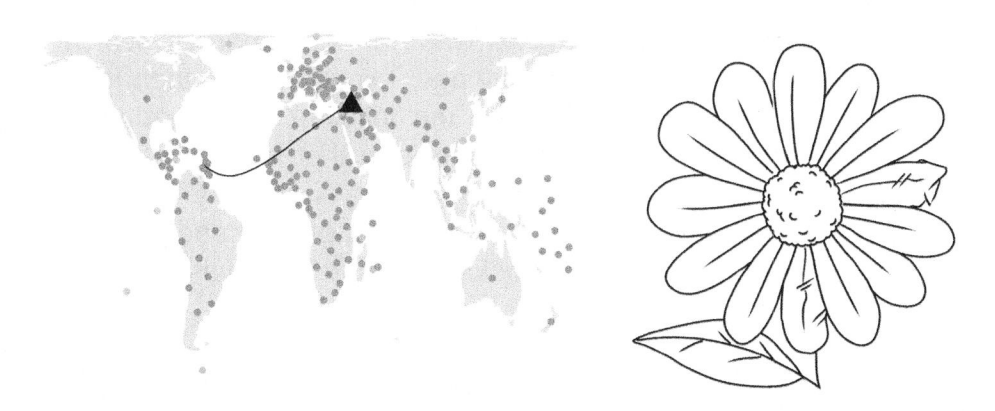

It was an immense pleasure for me to see a little girl playing her violin in what remained of a Roman amphitheatre. The site of that little performance had been carefully chosen because it was there that the Islamic State had staged one of the most brutal and macabre acts of that dark period when the terrorists had forced children to kill 25 captured soldiers. On the day of my visit, I was also interviewed by a television network, as a foreigner present at this tiny show. I was free in my answers but could not mention the Islamic State.

To travel to what was once an oasis in the middle of the desert, a place known as Palmyra, the Ministry of Tourism required you to have armed protection. Once I arrived, I realised that in reality my safety also depended on Russian tanks, all with the mysterious letter 'Z' drawn on them, as the invasion of Ukraine had already begun. Russia has had a close relationship with Syria for many years because they desperately need the access to the sea that this country provides.

During my lunch in a side street, there was a *Hazara* battalion guarding the perimeter. They were the Afghan Shia ethnic group to which Fatima belongs, and it was in their territory in the centre of Afghanistan, that I had run the marathon where the Taliban had destroyed the two large statues of Buddha that had resisted even Genghis Khan.

I had seen many disasters caused by religious extremists in the world, and in general, they want to go back to the origins of their respective divine revelations, believing that this will magically fix the world. Inevitably they turn the world into a worse place.

Talking to local people was easy since a good number of them knew foreign languages. I found an elderly gentleman who spoke good Italian and introduced myself as a tourist, but I know that I am not always believed. What he reproached me about however was not being married, which for him was unheard of at my age. I knew well by then how the thinking goes. Apart from the religious commandment to get married, and besides the idea that not having children is selfish, in these societies there is also the fear that you are dirty and unkempt. If the roles of man and woman are so segregated, who cooks for you? Who washes your underwear? A real man cannot do it himself...

Syria is officially a secular country, and near the hotel, there was a shop selling alcohol. The agent from the Ministry of Tourism, who was always with me and the members of my group, had given us permission to go out alone within 200 m of the hotel as long as we stayed away from a nightclub right next door. So, we went out together into this designated space. He met us angrily on our return, saying that the secret service had followed us because we had gone beyond the permitted boundaries. In fact, some people had taken a look at the nightclub, just from the outside out of mere curiosity.

Was his anger because of the disobedience, because the nightclub was dangerous or because of the alcohol? It certainly made an impression on me to discover that I had been followed without realising it. Should I have been pleased or worried?

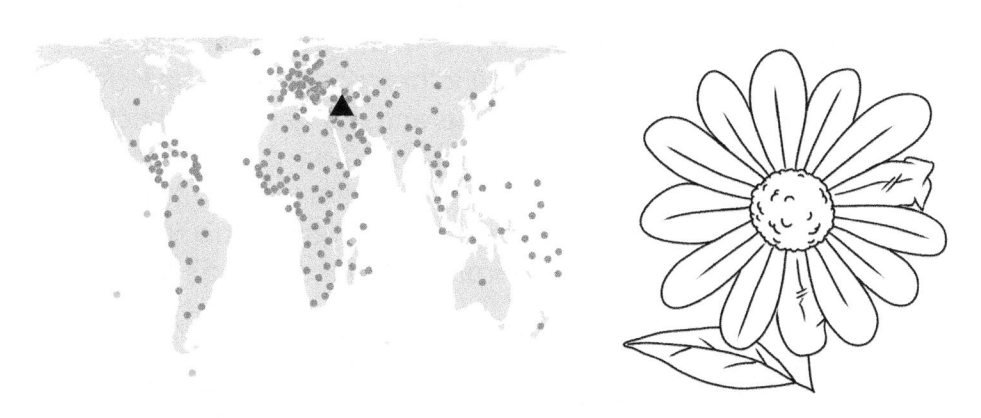

I did, however, cultivate a good relationship with this ministry agent, who then acted as a tour guide. He had a son who was desperately trying to emigrate to Europe, but by this time no one trusted the local ground staff at airport check-ins, and they would send one of their men to clear Syrians to board. So, you could no longer bribe the people working at the desks to let you through. I understood his worries, but he still did not comprehend how I could be so crazy as to want to visit Syria now, or how I could be so careless about the future that I had not yet built a family or cultivated a profession. For him, any risk was foolish and without purpose. And in an old-fashioned existence, designed like this, where you have only one woman, one house, and one job, you only ever have something to lose, never to gain in trying something new.

After returning to Lebanon, I made my way to Istanbul because the few remaining flights to **Belarus (189)**, Russia's strong ally, were leaving from there. Europe had closed their airspace to planes bound for opposing countries, and obviously no scheduled flights passed over Ukraine because of the war, so you had to fly the entire length of Turkey, over the Caucasus, into Kazakhstan, make an arc over Russia and then turn back to reach Minsk, making a seven-hour flight which was about three times the normal duration.

In free countries, you get to see almost everything, while in dictatorships very little. Belarus certainly falls into the dictatorship category, but I was surprised by how freely the young men I met spoke to me. On the street, albeit in English, they would say the worst things about Lukashenka without fear. In the end, the only prohibition that applied to me was not being allowed to take photos of government buildings, military personnel and policemen, but this applies almost everywhere in the world. Even where the rule is not explicit, it is better to abstain because it can turn into an excuse to come and ask for money.

A contact of mine was in Belarus, and we met up briefly. He'd been living here for a few months because he didn't want to get vaccinated! The other possibilities had been Ecuador and Mexico, but in the end, he had fallen back on this country with the worst climate because it was cheap. He lived in a tiny flat in the city centre, but for weekends he had a *dacha*, which is a small house in the countryside surrounded by greenery, which he ironically described as the best way to carry on working over the weekend while distracting himself from the week's work.

When I returned to Istanbul from Minsk, I had some peculiar feelings because for the first time, I had no future arrangements to organise. On my previous passage through Turkey en route to Belarus, I'd managed to book every flight and all the accommodation, right down to the last country. It was liberating because since the advent of Covid, organising travel had become a burden rather than a pleasure. Nevertheless, every now and then I was nostalgic for that routine: it was fun to obsessively open flight sites to see if prices had fallen, to buy books about the country to read up on it, to research where to go. My successful trip to Belarus had also induced a sensation of euphoria. When not at war it would have been a very easy country to visit, but actually, it had made me nervous.

It was all downhill from now on, and I was slowly beginning to get a foretaste of the final finish line. The objective still required travelling many thousands of kilometres, but from my perspective it was just around the corner!

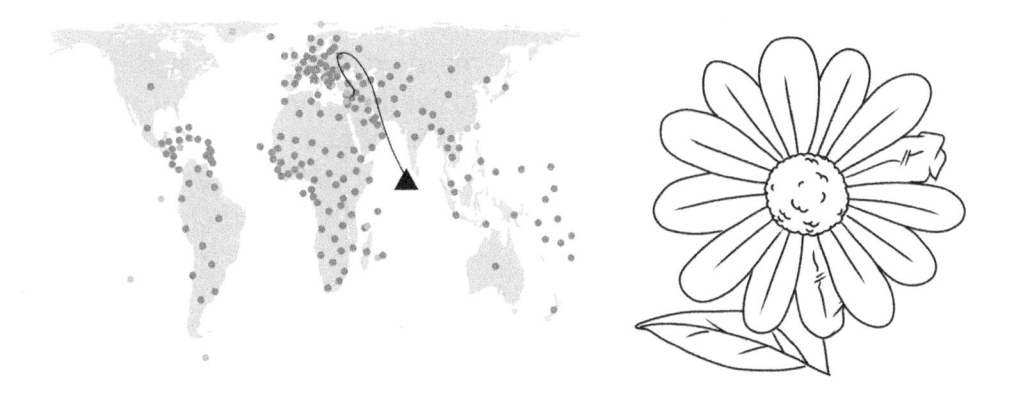

With these pleasant sentiments, I embarked for the **Maldives (190)**, a country where people usually go on honeymoon. In my head, however, it was the last of the 47 Asian countries. I was not going to luxury resorts, I was heading for some of the cheaper little islands, for non-Western tourists, where Islamic law, the *sharia*, is in force.

The Maldives, in fact, have a split personality that sometimes escapes the tourist who hasn't done his homework. Granted, there are atolls, sun and a magnificent sea, but this archipelago does not allow freedom of worship meaning that those who renounce Islam lose their citizenship and can be sentenced to death for apostasy. Women suffer as they are squeezed by rigid rules that unfortunately I was already familiar with from the stories of Afghan girls. For example, if you are raped and report the crime, you risk finding yourself in jail or whipped, because to prove rape it is difficult to provide evidence and have witnesses, and without these you are effectively admitting to the crime of adultery. It's a situation as paradoxical as it is sad.

On the island where I was staying, you couldn't drink alcohol, you had to be married to share a room, and many Pakistanis were there on holiday. Even dogs were not much appreciated because they were considered unclean animals by the religion, so they were driven away. We had an interesting discussion with the Sri Lankan person who managed the rooms, because he found the behaviour of Westerners towards dogs absurd. According to his accusation, we keep them prisoners in 5-star hotels, namely our small houses, castrate them, feed them kibble and force them into a life of solitude.

Back in familiar Istanbul, my next destination was tiny **Luxembourg (191)** where I had lived as a young man working in a company's marketing department. I had been invited back to the headquarters and met my old boss and a few colleagues again after about 20 years. Little had changed it seemed!

What had most definitely changed was me. While I had worked there, I had been the archetypal structured person who had worn a jacket and tie and had two university degrees – all the so-called healthy values of a former time. Then poker had come along, and I had made it into a proper profession, complete with bow tie and scientific methodology. Now, very content with these earlier choices that had allowed me to accumulate some savings, I had become a nomad, open to the world, but also without a career or income. It was a partly deliberate, partly accidental transition.

So how would I be as I went about my business in the future? Would I have a smart hat and casino tie, or continue to wear my old shabby boots? Would I carry a briefcase or a hobo's bundle? The past nine years had shown me that life is more interesting when you know how to wear all kinds of clothes, to continually add to your character, without taking anything away. It's good to travel, even if only briefly, to discover something new and beautiful, to change clothes, for the pleasure of variety, rather than to remove those parts of life we do not like.

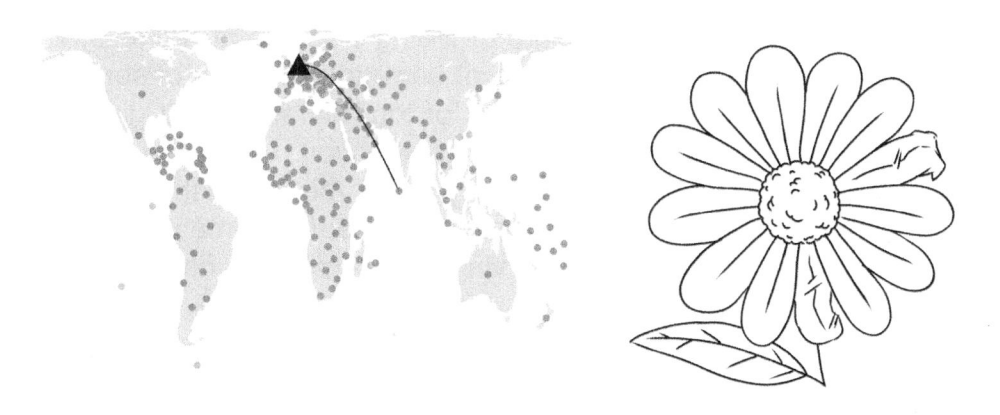

I could fully visualise the benefit of a long journey with great clarity. To judge and compare different cultures, I no longer needed the mediation of my own, in other words, my thoughts didn't triangulate with 'home' every time. I could move directly between distant territories, both in a physical sense and more importantly mentally. I used to judge everything by relating it to my family, my friends, my neighbourhood. My key ring now opened many doors that communicated directly with each other.

Twenty years ago, I had not met a single African in Luxembourg; this time I stopped for a couple of hours in the early afternoon in a bar run by Cape Verdeans. The owner told me that as a child, who had just emigrated here with his father, his job had been to run to the armchairs where people relaxed to read the newspaper and pick up the coins that slid from their pockets. A child's hands were perfect for slipping between the padding and making a decent haul at the end of the day.

The real explorers, in the broadest sense of the word, even more so than extreme travellers, are the people who emigrate. Some are desperate, coerced, cornered, but many cultivate the worthy ambition to discover something new, to be able to have and give something better to the world. Some cultures and places are traps from which it is difficult to escape. Closed, isolated environments, without any exchange with others, inevitably lead to amplification of mistakes. In Afghanistan, for example, the local people boast that they have not been conquered by anyone in the past centuries. In my opinion, this is one of the reasons why everything is taken to excess, because there has been no encounter with anything different. The arrival of 'others' brings ideas, novelties, offers original views, and changes judgement. Even tourists can bring some benefit.

Some Cape Verdeans in Africa, on small islands, had that attitude of passive waiting, of willing displays of laziness. I witnessed traders assume that unmistakable face of someone who had earned enough for the day and didn't give a damn about you, didn't even answer you. I watched them set a table for ten people only when the hot dishes were ready, when there would have been plenty of time in the 30 minutes of preparation. Arriving in Luxembourg, however, in a different environment, the Cape Verdeans ran the bar with rhythm and passion.

As soon as you give yourself better rules, stimuli arise, there is pleasure in dealing with so many people in this situation in the centre of Europe. You perfect yourself in meeting others. I had sought out the best aspects of cultures, the most beautiful rules and customs in all the nations. I had left thinking that the world had much more to offer than what I had at home, and I'd had full confirmation of this with my own eyes. Italy, so important in history and art books, today represents less than 1% of the world's population and its economy seems to be slipping towards that same small percentage. Our culture is loved and certainly a good place to begin. But the best way forward lies in the Luxembourg model. They say that their motto is 'We want to remain what we are', but in practice they are open to the world, full of immigration from all over, ready to embrace the best. This is how I closed my visits to the 43 countries of Europe, by going to its small heart, to this country where people speak French but almost everyone also knows German, attached to Belgium, with around 20% of the population of Lusitanian origin, and also full of Italians.

From Luxembourg I had found a very cheap flight to Washington and stayed in America, a nation that symbolises immigration and the meeting of different backgrounds. Too many Europeans, including those who have travelled there, make the mistake of presuming things about this country, thinking that it is a place full of people with little culture and little concern for others.

In actual fact, Europe should strive for better understanding. This is a place where ideas and dreams flourish, composed of foreigners who quickly manage to fit in and become true Americans. They've failed in bringing democracy to the world but have succeeded in importing democratic people. It's a journey that began over two centuries ago but is still in full swing, because compared to Europe, the US is sparsely populated and there is still plenty of room. Their social system is not very generous towards their citizens and even less so towards those who come to the country. The bottom line is that the immigrant must contribute to the country rather than receive from their new community. It may sound selfish, but in this way large migration flows can be sustained, because those who enter are not a burden, but a resource.

From the American capital I travelled to Toronto, **Canada (192)**. This city is as expensive as it is lively, full of Indians and Chinese who have lost some of their typical traditions, so much so that in this part of the world Indians are quite free to marry whoever they want. Finally, the husband and wife no longer have to be of the same caste, are not chosen by the family, and do not have to live within a few kilometres of each other. You can marry the person you love rather than having to learn to love the person you married.

The Chinese also have great freedom in love; however, it made me smile to see that their shops were no different to the usual. They are deliberately shabby, with few lights, and as spartan as anywhere else in the world. Their message to the customer is clear: we are cheap. It's the opposite of an Italian fashion shop, full of lights and colours, trying to convey the idea that beauty and status are for sale alongside a T-shirt.

The Niagara Falls are beautiful, but a large part of their success lies in having turned nature into a playground. I met a childhood friend there whom I had not seen for decades and together we took the photo that immortalised me in front of the falls with a huge map showing the last leg of my journey. But first I wanted to explore this nation of huge lakes, that boasts a territory, Nunavut, which alone is as big as Western Europe but almost uninhabited, and a very long straight border with the United States.

In the hostel where I had slept, the last night was particularly restless. The guy in the bed above mine tossed and turned, making strange noises, seemingly finding no peace until the police came to pick him up. I'm pretty sure it wasn't because he was disturbing the other guests, so who knows what he had been up to. We were all forced to get up, turn the lights on, and search the room to make sure we could work out what belonged to him.

I was taking it very philosophically as it was the last time I would book a dormitory in this long adventure. There had been so many messy nights, but the fun had outweighed any annoyances, and besides, these are places to hang out, because this is where travellers find each other and exchange information. It is in hostels that you meet people walking around with big key rings, lots of experiences to tell and a desire to share.

Being constantly in noisy dorms in the company of young

people I understood why 'budget travel' allows you to get closer to others. The barrier isn't having money itself, taking off that precious tie and expensive top hat, nor the renunciation of comfort or luxury. The distance comes from the mental fear of having something to lose, the fear that there is a threat around you, that someone wants to take advantage. When you own almost nothing and the message you convey to the outside world is clearly that there is no money to be made in being close to you, on the one hand you attract sincere people, and on the other, you yourself become open to experience and adventure. Suddenly it completely sinks in that you have more to gain than to lose. At home, it's impossible to have this mentality beyond a certain age, whereas on the road you can find it or regain it at will.

I celebrated the completion of the 35 nations in America with sour cherries, a fruit I had encountered for the first time outside Italy. I returned home briefly and invited the Afghan refugee girls in Italy to meet my family.

There was a phenomenal surprise, for Fatima in particular. My sister had submitted her CV to Bocconi (one of the most prestigious universities in Italy), which had granted her a scholarship. A shepherdess born in the only country that forbids higher education for women, destined to be illiterate, now had access to one of the best universities in Europe. She was learning Italian in record time, but classes would be in English, so she was ready. The nights before the marathon in Afghanistan I had told the girls that I had no idea how to help with a scholarship in the US, but it had been possible for one of them in Italy!

Sadly, tragic places do exist in the world, and my travels

hadn't allowed me to overturn certain prejudices. However, I consoled myself somewhat by noticing the humanity that comes out even when it is forced by events to confront trouble and despair. It's in those circumstances that you discover the strength of some men and women. I have personally appreciated the brilliance of minds and hearts that are able to understand certain concepts and apply them without anyone ever explaining anything to them. As a traveller in those desolate places, you're privileged to observe more than just petals as magnificent flowers sprout from the mud.

I've been witness to objective improvements around the world, and maybe the easiest piece of evidence for this is precisely that I have visited all the countries. I truly believe that wherever a tourist manages to get in, a microscopic opening is formed that sooner or later widens, helping those who want to get out. Foreigners are a constant stimulus for the locals and the best example was provided by the very country where I started, Nepal. Eventually it was Nepalese mountaineers who were shattering all records, they had climbed three difficult mountains in just two days and reached all 14 peaks over 8,000 m in about six months. Until recently, the Nepalese had been secondary characters, sometimes even extras, in the service of Westerners who received all the accolades for climbing, even though it was clear that they had only succeeded with their help. This meeting of the tourists with the locals stimulated some Nepalese to show off their incredible skills, made those places richer, provided jobs, and also realised the big dreams of wealthy Westerners of making the ascent to the top.

But in the newspapers, this incredible success was portrayed as a disgrace. The many Nepalese mountaineers who climbed for profession or passion were joining the Westerners. The rhetoric of overcrowding on the mountains was born, the problem became the rubbish left in the base camps, which altogether is less than what I have seen on some forgotten African waterfront. So even at the top of the world 'mass tourism' has become the enemy, and the modern world is destroying what was thought to be one of the last untouched paradises, namely the peaks above 8,000 m.

After having toured all the nations, my conviction that there is no such thing as a 'heavenly place' is a certainty. Every tourist is free to search all they want, but at best they will find what appears to be a paradise for them for a couple of weeks a year. No place remains wonderful if you live there for longer. Pure happiness lasts an afternoon, the pleasure of a holiday wanes after a few weeks at most, whereas travelling is a school that gives us moments of enlightenment that will remain for a lifetime. It is a flower that never fades. The journey is therapeutic, it eases pain, and marks a turning point. It is a tattoo that needs no ink, it punctuates time, it brings out the best in each of us, and helps us to face the problem, to focus on it from afar, to adjust our perspective. But it doesn't work miracles, you don't escape from real life with a journey.

There were two months to go before the last leg, so I went back to Uganda where I had started writing this book. I found a nice room with a view of Lake Victoria. Downstairs a lady cooked for me and with this arrangement I had a further 'life experience', I wore no shoes at all on my feet and was very comfortable. In Italian, if you want to insult an author, you would say, 'You wrote this with your feet!' But if you enjoyed it, feel free in your review to attribute part of the credit to also having walked barefoot and carefree.

I had everything at hand in a country where getting around is frustrating, and transport is chaotic. When there is no public transport, you rely on the initiative of the people who have a bus and start a business. They try to sell tourists the one seat next to the driver at a higher price than the other seats. Thousands of motorbikes are on the move, and they honk at people requesting a paid ride. Some are so unprepared that they don't even have proper shoes for driving and braking, and in fact wear flip-flops, which is dangerous, have broken mirrors, and don't have the waterproof jacket that is essential in any temperature for those who live in traffic.

Then there are the *tuk-tuks*, the sort of mechanical rickshaws that invade the streets. Some drivers own the vehicle, others are very young people who rent it by the day and turn into taxi drivers, creating anxiety, creeping in everywhere without any respect for the rules. Payment for the rental is made at the end of the day, so there is no need to have money in your pocket in the morning. In fact, it can be the case that you get on board and stop straightaway at the petrol station because the penniless driver was waiting for the first customer before they could refuel. And because the human mind is always busy, this is also why in Uganda young girls are working at the petrol pumps, so as to attract these transport personnel who are all male. As you travel, you catch a glimpse of the mesh of a society where you least expect it.

While I was busy writing the book, and therefore reliving and sharing my long adventure, I woke up one night shaking and with joint pains. I had a high fever and was very cold, yet it was 25°C, so it was the easiest medical self-diagnosis in the world: I had malaria. I hadn't taken prophylactics for years because I had reached my consumption limit. *Malarone*, for example, which is considered the best drug, should be taken for a maximum of 28 continuous days. I'd been using it for months and the side effects had manifested themselves. It was an unpleasant three days, but I was able to stay on my feet, wandering restlessly around the garden of the house and talking to the boy at the guardhouse who'd had malaria 20 times, according to him. What surprised me about him though wasn't the astounding number of episodes, but his ability to spend his days in front of the gate, alone, with nothing to entertain himself with. He had no telephone, and not even a newspaper, radio or television. Nothing.

A month later I was on my way to Seoul and looking at the board of flights departing from Addis Ababa I realised that I had been to every single destination offered at Africa's most important international airport. This small discovery gave me great pleasure. However, it was the map on the screen in the plane that relaxed me. During long flights I like to visualise how much time is left until arrival and how far I have come. In this case it was the final countdown as the famous song says, South Korea was the last destination, the last petal.

I had taken about 500 planes and travelled a million kilometres. Adding the distances travelled by train, bus, car, motorbike, foot and the ever-present hot air balloon so beloved of Phileas Fogg, it all added up to the distance that light travels in a few seconds.

I was in my 80th month of actual travel, I had spent a little over €300,000 in total, averaging about €125 per day for the 2,400 days. The Covid tests had increased the cost by €5,000, all of which was over and above the 'Contingencies' fund, which, in turn, had gone way over budget. The visas accumulated in five passports had cost €10,000 euro, and another €5,000 had been spent on tips. Medicines, mainly for the prevention of the malaria that I had just contracted, accounted for €2,000 along with another €2,000 for insurance, which fortunately I had never used. Transport had been the biggest cost, for planes alone I had exceeded €100,000, a third of the total. I had spent it all with no regrets. You don't have to be rich to travel, but visiting EVERYCOUNTRY does require money.

I have been beaten, robbed and even shot at, but to travel that far you don't need any special qualities or a strong physique. It's probably enough to have no specific problems, a little spirit of adventure and a lot of adaptability. My best quality has been my ability to read and study in all conditions, on winding roads full of potholes, or in the midst of a rough sea, which has allowed me to entertain myself and made the constant travelling worthwhile. The long waits make the destinations magical, but you have to learn to hang in there. And you have to have the capacity to love solitude. I've told you about numerous encounters in the book, but in reality, I ate alone many more times than with others.

The secret to travelling peacefully lies in making the people who are helping you feel good, complimenting them, encouraging them, and appreciating what they are doing for you.

In the end, I just visited 193 countries, at my own pace, choosing the optimal window for the dangerous ones, trying to limit the risks once I arrived. I played a nine-year long poker tournament, thanks to which, despite losing €300,000, I won a great prize.

On arrival in **South Korea (193)** there was one last Covid test to pass, then I would set foot in the country and officially finish. As a child I used to get excited about foreign number plates, especially an alien one in Italy, and now I had seen them all. I had saved this country for last because it was so exotic and far away, yet so straightforward to visit. And it was ideal for if someone had wanted to come with me to celebrate the achievement. My sister's family and my friend's family joined me, along with two other friends who work in the film industry, and they proposed turning the celebration into a documentary. As far as they knew, such a celebration had never been done before.

But first we had to discover a country 9,000 km from Italy, split in two, mountainous, and with few natural resources, which in the 1960s had been among the poorest in the world. No one would have bet on Korea, as they did on Botswana, and yet it is now prosperous, civilised and progressive.

We were among the very few tourists, we slept in a UNESCO heritage temple and made preparations for the party. We would celebrate it right on the border with North Korea. I personally had had the privilege of crossing so many borders and my hope was that this division that keeps over 20 million North Koreans isolated would eventually disappear.

We bought a replica of every flag in the world to decorate a patio, five inflatable globes, and giant balloons with the numbers 1, 9 and 3. I had 193 embroidered on a scarf, but most importantly we invited one person from the North and one from the South to represent a people who are united despite war and politics. I brought my five passports to be put on display in front of a themed cake and on a map that we scratched with pennies we had fun discovering all the countries and finally just had little South Korea to complete. We made a toast, and so this adventure came to an end amid champagne and soap bubbles.

In almost everything measurable, the West and the few other rich countries are the best. But each of us has personal priorities, desires and aspirations, so cultures affect and fascinate us differently. I have learnt a lot, almost everywhere, but for a top-class travel school you don't need 80 months or even EVERYCOUNTRY, indeed, a dozen or so countries done right, with an open mind, and a hunger to be amazed and to study, that's enough.

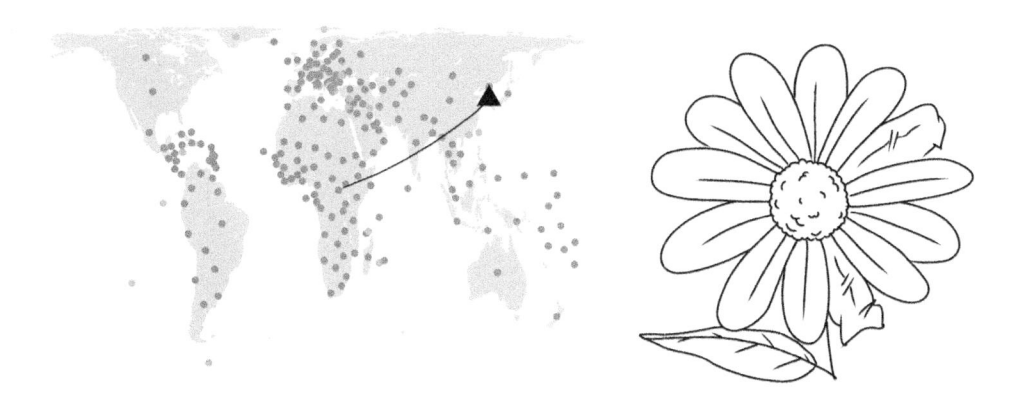

The first step towards exploration requires 'adopting' a country, or rather one of the world's many petals. Choose a country that you like, that has something that fascinates you, be it a monument, a city, an animal, a flower, or even a football team, anything goes. Then start to delve deeper, learn 100 words in the language, follow the current affairs, hum one of their songs, invite your relatives for a typical dinner on the day of the national holiday, become virtual friends with a local person, and try to find out what they think of your own country. Even one different perspective doubles your horizons and allows you to question your convictions. If you can, once in your life, visit your adopted country. And then the entry on your CV where you say you love travelling will be genuine.

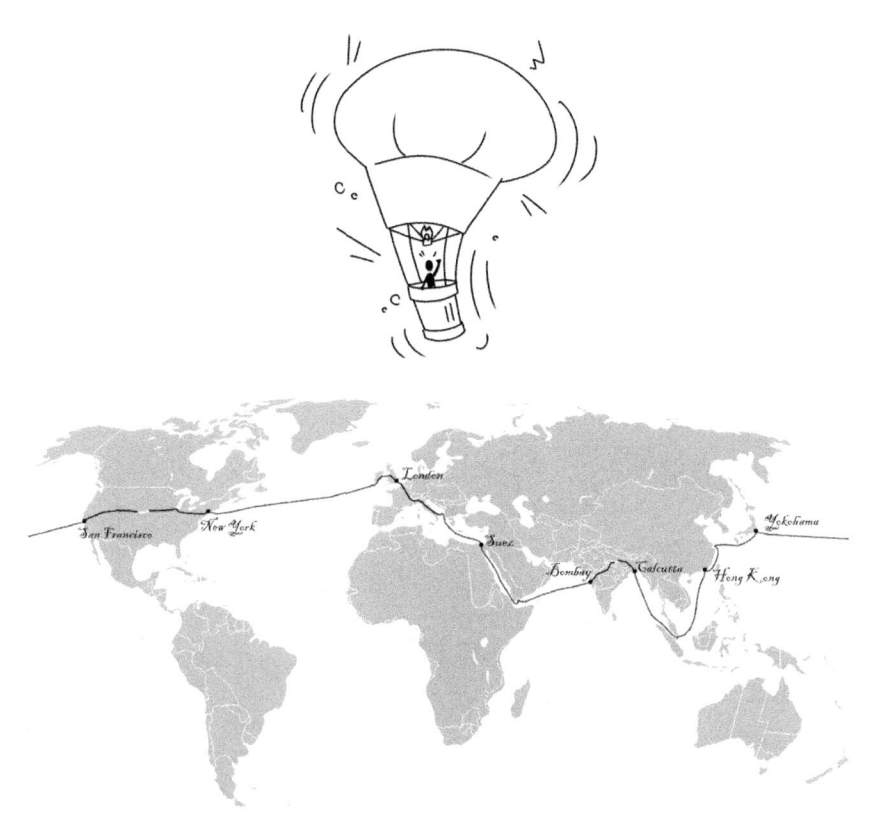

Phileas Fogg's journey in *Around the World in 80 Days*

The dark grey dots mark the 193 sovereign nations of the world. The light grey dots mark some of the unrecognised nations, along with islands of particular importance that were visited.

YEAR 9

ALGERIA	TUNISIA	GUINEA
DOMINICAN REPUBLIC	VENEZUELA	COLOMBIA
BAHAMAS	JAMAICA	TRINIDAD AND TOBAGO
GUYANA	SURINAME	BARBADOS
GRENADA	ANTIGUA AND BARBUDA	SAINT KITTS AND NEVIS
SAINT VINCENT AND THE GRENADINES	DOMINICA	SAINT LUCIA
SYRIA	BELARUS	MALDIVES
LUXEMBOURG	CANADA	SOUTH KOREA

193/193

Would you like to travel with me?
Find me at www.everycountry.travel

or on any of the main social media platforms

Fatima Haidari - The first female tour guide in Afghanistan during the Taliban regime

> *The book transforms you from reader to traveller. It took me back to Afghanistan in my mind, to the beauty of Bamyian, but also to the terrible moments I experienced at the Kabul airport when I was trying to escape from the Taliban. Thank you for talking about the suffering of women. I have treasured the travel tips in the text and dream of visiting some of the places I discovered whilst reading!*

David Langan - Record-breaking traveller, one of the very few to have visited all 330 places selected by the historic Travelers' Century Club

> *This book is at its best when Flavio is in a reflective mood. I love the observations and attention to detail. As a fellow traveller, it brought back memories of my own experiences, enabling me to relive past moments, feeling those emotions once again. It's impressive how much research the author did before setting off for some of the lesser-known nations.*

Ric Gazarian - Voice of the 'Counting Countries' Podcast, Organiser of 'Extraordinary Travel Festival'

> *Flavio has covered it all from A to Z, literally having travelled to every country in the world. Yes, even that one! Along the way, he has had malaria, been attacked, robbed, and even shot at while taking over 500 flights. Yet, it is all worth it, as he shares lessons and experiences from his journey which are singular.*

Randy Williams - The Sultan of the 'Republic of Slowjamastan', the world's youngest nation!

> *From dream vacation spots to hostile territories, to countries you didn't even know existed, Flavio grabs you by the hand and doesn't let go as he takes you on an exciting adventure to every country in the world. And you don't even need to pay for the airfare!...*

Renee Bruns - Guinness World Record Holder, on her way (118/193) to visit every country in the world in a wheelchair

> *Flavio's journey to every country in the world is full of excitement, adventure, and knowledge. And I do agree that pure happiness lasts an afternoon, the pleasure of a holiday wanes after a few weeks at most, whereas travelling is a school that gives us moments of enlightenment that will remain for a lifetime.*

Printed in Great Britain
by Amazon